Nation Building in South Korea

THE NEW COLD WAR HISTORY
John Lewis Gaddis, editor

Nation Building in South Korea

Koreans, Americans, and the Making of a Democracy

GREGG BRAZINSKY

The University of
North Carolina Press
Chapel Hill

© 2007 The University of North Carolina Press
All rights reserved
Designed by Kimberly Bryant
Set in Adobe Jenson by Keystone Typesetting, Inc.
Manufactured in the United States of America

This book was published with the generous
assistance of the Korea Foundation.

Korea Foundation
한국국제교류재단

Library of Congress Cataloging-in-Publication Data
Brazinsky, Gregg.
Nation building in South Korea : Koreans, Americans,
and the making of a democracy / Gregg Brazinsky.
p. cm. — (New cold war history)
Includes bibliographical references and index.
ISBN 978-0-8078-3120-5 (cloth : alk. paper)
ISBN 978-0-8078-6181-3 (pbk. : alk. paper)
1. United States—Foreign relations—Korea. 2. Korea—
Foreign relations—United States. 3. Democracy—
Korea—History—20th century. 4. Korea (South)—
Politics and government. 5. Korea (South)—Economic
conditions. I. Title.
E183.8.K6B72   2007
327.7305195—dc22   2007000414

cloth 11 10 09 08 07 5 4 3 2 1
paper 14 13 12 11 10 5 4 3 2 1

for my mother, Carol Weiner

Contents

Illustrations

Acknowledgments

In the years that I have spent working on this book I have acquired a great number of intellectual, economic, and personal debts. I first became interested in American diplomatic history as an undergraduate at Amherst College, where I had the good fortune to study with Gordy Levin, who set an example as a teacher and scholar that I have long sought to emulate. At Cornell University, where I earned my Ph.D., my interests in American foreign policy in general and U.S.-Asian relations in particular were further nourished by Tim Borstelmann, Sherman Cochran, and J. Victor Koschmann. Professor Borstelmann helped me develop a more expansive view of U.S. foreign relations and see the significance of my own work. Professor Cochran taught me to approach the question of how Asians have responded to American and European influences with greater nuance and sophistication. Professor Koschmann stimulated my interest in intellectual and cultural history and helped me understand the connections between these areas and America's relations with Asia.

As I completed this book, my colleagues in the History Department and the Elliott School of International Affairs at the George Washington University provided me with a stimulating environment in which to work. Kirk Larsen and Ron Spector, in particular, read parts of this manuscript and pointed me toward some useful sources. My codirectors of the George Washington University Cold War Group, Hope M. Harrison, Jim Hershberg, and Jim Goldgeier, have not only been a source of scholarly inspiration but also, by including me in their numerous conferences, seminars, and meetings, have continuously prompted me to think about many of the issues addressed in this book.

At the University of North Carolina Press, Chuck Grench and Katy O'Brien have helped shepherd the book through the various acquisitions and editing processes; Paul Betz and Stevie Champion have assisted greatly with copyediting the manuscript. I was very fortunate that the Press chose William Stueck at the University of Georgia as one of my readers. Professor Stueck went far beyond his role as a reader in helping me improve this manuscript and has become a valued friend. It is an honor to have this book included in John Lewis Gaddis's New Cold War History series. Professor

Gaddis's comments on drafts of this manuscript induced me to make a bolder and, I hope, more persuasive argument.

I could not have completed this book without the generous financial support of several organizations. A grant from the Eisenhower World Affairs Institute enabled me to spend several months doing research in the Washington, D.C., area in 1999. A grant from the Lyndon B. Johnson Library made possible a two-week trip in 1999 to Austin, where I discovered many valuable materials. In 1999–2000 I received a Fulbright Scholarship from the U.S. Institute for International Education, which allowed me to spend a year in South Korea. While conducting research in Seoul I was affiliated with Korea University's Asiatic Research Center, whose director, Choi Jang-Jip, and other faculty members and fellows offered a stimulating intellectual environment. During the summer of 2003, I was able to return to South Korea for additional research through funds provided by the Association for Asian Studies, the Sigur Center for Asian Studies, and the George Washington University Cold War Group. As a Kluge Fellow at the Library of Congress for the 2003–2004 academic year, I benefited from the opportunity not only to do research in the library's collections but also to interact with the other fellows at the Kluge Center.

Finally, I would like to thank my mother, stepfather, and sister for being constant sources of comfort and support. My mother, Carol Weiner, in particular, has always had faith that I would complete this project and her encouragement has been indispensable.

Nation Building in South Korea

Introduction

Nation building has been a ubiquitous component of American foreign policy during the last century. The United States has attempted to create and sustain nation-states that advance its interests and embody its ideals in places ranging from the Philippines to Vietnam to Iraq.[1] At no time did Washington engage in nation building more intensively than during the Cold War. The United States deemed capturing the loyalties of the vast regions of the globe emerging from colonialism as crucial to the struggle against Communism. To achieve this end it launched vast efforts to carve diverse parts of Asia, Africa, and Latin America into reliable "Free World" allies.[2] U.S. officials believed that, by providing the right kinds of resources, they could stimulate economic development and democratization in regions where neither of these phenomena had made significant inroads. This book examines one of the most extensive, costly, and arguably successful of these efforts—South Korea. Of the numerous places where nation building was attempted, South Korea was one of the few to emerge as a wealthy democracy at the end of the twentieth century.

Yet when Americans first occupied the southern half of Korea in 1945, the prospects for establishing stable, democratic institutions did not look bright. In previous centuries Korea had been governed by emperors who remained formally subordinate to China as part of a tributary system. The system endured until the country was colonized by Japan in 1910. The subsequent thirty-five years of Japanese imperialism had left the country's population polarized into extreme right and extreme left factions that drowned out the voices of the few moderate democrats. Moreover, the demise of Japan's Pacific empire shattered the Korean economy, which had been tightly integrated with Japan's during the colonial period. The decision made jointly by the United States and the Soviet Union in 1945 to divide the peninsula into northern and southern occupation zones exacerbated both the economic hardships and the political divisions. It cut off the South's agricultural economy from the industries of the North while enabling political extremists on both sides to gain support from Great Power patrons.

Between 1945 and 1953 American policymakers made a series of decisions that would commit them to the task of nation building in this deeply troubled country. Unable to compromise with the Soviet Union on the creation of a unified Korean government, the United States supported the division of the peninsula into separate states in 1948. By doing so, it invested a substantial amount of its own credibility in the survival and success of anti-Communist South Korea. Even before the Korean War broke out, Americans recognized that divided Korea might play a role in the developing world that was akin to the role that divided Germany played in Europe.[3] The splitting of what both sides acknowledged to be a single national people into spheres of Free World and Communist influence made the Korean peninsula a natural showcase in which the relative merits of these two systems could be demonstrated to the other postcolonial nations. In 1949 one high-ranking U.S. State Department official explained that it was vital that the Republic of Korea (ROK) survive and flourish in order to "create continuing resistance in the minds of hundreds of millions of people in the area to the acceptance of communism." The official argued:

> Korea is the only area in the world in which democratic and communist principles are being put to the test side by side and in which the U.S. and the U.S.S.R. have been, and no doubt in the estimation of the world, will continue to be, the sole contenders for the way of life of 30,000,000 people. The entire world and especially Asia is watching this contest. To the degree that the Republic succeeds, the people in the still free nations of Southeast Asia and Southern Asia and Oceania will be persuaded of the practical superiority of democratic principles. To the degree the United States continues to support the efforts of the South Korean people to develop a self-supporting economy and a stable democratic government the people of this area will be persuaded of the firmness of U.S. determination to support Democracy and oppose Communism.[4]

The Korean War added to America's perceived stake in South Korea. The fact that American lives had been expended in the defense of the country ensured that the United States would suffer a tremendous loss of prestige if it abandoned its commitment there.[5] Indeed, Washington continued to regard South Korea's significance as pivotal for the duration of the Cold War. Throughout the 1960s strategy papers of the U.S. Agency for International Development (USAID) regularly claimed that the ROK had "become a symbol of the determination of the United States to assist the nations of free Asia to defend themselves against communist aggression" and that if South Korea turned to Communism it would jeopardize "the entire strategic and psychological position of the U.S. in the Pacific area."[6]

Perceiving Korea as a vital Cold War battleground, U.S. officials prioritized military and financial assistance to the country. During the fifteen years after the Korean War, South Korea frequently topped the list of U.S. aid recipients. Kennedy-era policy documents referred to South Korea as one of the "big five" countries—along with Pakistan, Vietnam, Taiwan, and Turkey—that received both military and economic support. In 1960 alone the United States dispensed to South Korea $380 million—more than it provided any of the other big five and 7.6 percent of the total U.S. foreign aid budget.[7] Private philanthropic groups, such as the Asia Foundation and the American-Korean Foundation, that were active in the country supplemented official largesse with millions of dollars to support social and cultural programs.

Despite the scale of America's nation building in South Korea and its undeniable impact, virtually no scholars in either country have studied the topic systematically. The failure of American historians to do so is the result of neglect: most of the handful of American scholars fluent in the Korean language have not focused on the Cold War, especially the period after the Korean War.[8] The reasons for the absence of archival research on U.S.-ROK relations are more complicated. Some of them are political. Until the early 1990s South Korean historians faced official limitations on what they could say or write about their country's relationship with the United States. Moreover, many of the issues they need to confront in considering American-Korean relations remain extremely divisive, and Korean scholars have understandably been hesitant to address them. The uneven nature of South Korea's economic expansion, the suppression of civil liberties by successive ROK governments, the prolonged torment of Korean families divided by Cold War politics, and the sacrifices made by countless Koreans seeking both to challenge and defend Cold War orthodoxies has made writing critically about modern Korean history difficult for many South Koreans. Only recently have several excellent younger scholars begun exploring various dimensions of this topic in Ph.D. dissertations and journal articles.[9] Despite their contributions, however, there are still virtually no archival-based studies of the subject in either English or Korean. The questions of how Americans approached the task of nation building in South Korea and how they contributed to the dramatic transformation that occurred there have been left largely unanswered.

The most relevant work for understanding the evolution of American influence in South Korea is Bruce Cumings's landmark two-volume study, *The Origins of the Korean War*. To show the civil origins of the Korean War, *Origins* analyzes the processes of state formation in North and South Korea. It explains in great detail how the United States sided with Korean conservatives, many of whom had collaborated with Japanese imperialists, at the expense of an indigenous mass-based movement with leftist leanings in the south. The result was a strongly anti-Communist but highly autocratic South Korean state that was destined for war with its northern rival.[10] Cumings's work remains an essential backdrop against which the subsequent history of American nation building in South Korea must be viewed. The decisions made in Washington during the years before the Korean War had an undeniable impact on the evolution of South Korea's political economy. But Cumings's study ends with China's entry into the war in November 1950. At the time South Korea was still impoverished, autocratic, and involved in a conflict that exacerbated both of those conditions. Few could have predicted that within a generation the ROK would garner international recognition for the dynamism of its economy and the vibrancy of its democracy. This dramatic reversal of fortunes begs the questions of how South Korea was transformed from the indigent, despotic nation that existed at the time of the Korean War to the wealthy democratic one that emerged by the early 1990s and of what role the United States played in its transformation.

South Korea's road to prosperity and democracy was a tortuous and ironic one. The conservative Syngman Rhee regime supported by the United States in 1948 remained in place until 1960. During these twelve years it managed to stabilize the country but remained highly autocratic and failed miserably at the task of economic development. A student revolution toppled Rhee's government in 1960 and quickly set up a fully democratic political system. But democracy in South Korea lasted only thirteen months before a military junta seized power. For the next three decades the country's military dictatorships proved remarkably efficient in maintaining stability, developing the economy, and controlling dissent before finally allowing free elections in 1987. Despite the fact that South Korea had been governed by some of the harshest conservative autocracies in the world through much of the Cold War, it somehow became one of the most dynamic democracies in Asia by the 1990s.

Noted scholar and political commentator Fareed Zakaria has argued that, since World War II, nation-states like South Korea have established durable democratic institutions only because they did not become democratic right away. Instead, they underwent an evolution from autocracy, to "liberalizing autocracy," to democracy. Liberalizing autocracies, according to Zakaria, were regimes that developed the economy, preserved order, and liberalized the rights of worship and travel *before* surrendering power. By doing so, they inadvertently created an environment in which democracy could thrive.[11]

Zakaria's concept of liberalizing autocracy is a reasonable characterization of the military regimes that governed South Korea during the sixties, seventies, and eighties. Much of the scholarship on the ROK's political economy has shown clear connections between the country's rapid industrialization and the ability of its governments to intervene in the economy without popular input.[12] It was only after South Korea had emerged as one of the "Asian Tiger" economies that democracy firmly took hold. Its military governments did not, of course, move consistently in the direction of liberalization, as Zakaria's term seems to imply, so I have used the phrase "developmental autocracy" to describe them in most places. Nevertheless, like the other autocracies that Zakaria mentions, they did promote economic development, build institutions, and finally surrender power albeit reluctantly. South Korean military dictators were far from benevolent despots. They carried out inexcusable transgressions against the basic human rights of their citizens, which may never be forgiven despite their record on economic issues. But their relentless pursuit of industrial development and their determination to integrate South Korea into the global economy helped to satisfy some of the preconditions for democratization.

While Zakaria provides a good description of *what* happened in South Korea, he does not fully explain *why* it happened. Dozens of autocratic governments emerged in both the Free and Communist worlds during the Cold War, but only a few of them transitioned to developmental autocracies and democracies. Moreover, although developmental autocracies may create some of the preconditions for democracy, there is no guarantee that they will eventually be supplanted by democratic governments. Malaysia and Singapore experienced rapid development steered by single-party states, but today they are still not fully democratic. Zakaria's analytic framework leaves unanswered the question of why South Korea was different from the numerous other postcolonial nations where dictatorships supported by the United States either remained in power or fell to Communism. This failure to account for how developmental autocracies emerge has left him open to criticism (which I believe is somewhat unjustified) for seeming to offer open-ended support for authoritarian governments.[13] Given the infrequency with which developmental autocracies arise, understanding how one evolved in South Korea is vitally important.

This book argues that American nation building and Korean agency worked in tandem to produce this distinctive pattern of political evolution.

Americans did not originally set out to create a developmental autocracy, and when one emerged they did not have an immediate plan for converting it into a democracy. Nevertheless, the policies that they adopted enabled, and in some ways encouraged, this metamorphosis. On the one hand, through much of the Cold War, the United States was willing to support dictatorial regimes in South Korea that could develop the economy, ensure security, and serve American interests. On the other hand, even while the United States supported these governments, Americans working on the ground in South Korea created new institutions ranging from the military, to schools, to academic organizations through which they attempted to strengthen the indigenous demand for development and democracy. They saw this kind of institution building as a way of fostering a sense of progressive nationalism and giving the Korean people the ability and the will to participate in a democratic society. These efforts to reshape the very thinking of South Koreans were at times based on disturbing assumptions of cultural superiority, but they facilitated the emergence of elite groups that were determined to develop the economy and democratize the country.

Analyzing the American approach to nation building in South Korea offers at best a partial explanation for what occurred there, however. U.S. policies toward Vietnam, Iran, and numerous other postcolonial nations featured similar support for rightist autocrats and developmentalism yet failed miserably.[14] Indeed, Odd Arne Westad has recently noted that, of the more than thirty postcolonial nations where the United States intervened, South Korea and Taiwan were the only ones that achieved the combination of stable growth and stable democracy that Washington ostensibly sought to promote.[15] So what made South Korea different? Part of this might be explained by the magnitude and duration of U.S. assistance there. But I argue that Korean agency was the most crucial factor in shaping the country's transformation. The ways that South Koreans adapted to American influence were ultimately as, if not more, important than anything the Americans did.

Long before U.S. forces occupied South Korea in 1945, Koreans had acquired hundreds if not—as many Koreans would claim—thousands of years of experience adapting foreign philosophies to their own needs and values. Smaller and militarily weaker than most of its neighbors, Korea had little choice but to accept hegemonic systems that were not of its own making. For many centuries the peninsula had been part of the Chinese tributary system. Over this long period Korea's intellectual and cultural life frequently came under the influence of its "middle kingdom" neighbor. The introduction of foreign religions and philosophies such as Buddhism and Confucianism into the country was not entirely a product of the Koreans' own choosing, but Koreans nevertheless chose the ways they made these belief systems their own. An old Korean proverb—"When the whales fight the shrimp gets crushed"—has long been used as an expression of Korea's precarious geographic position between Great Power rivals. But when it came to negotiating the different social and cultural orders imposed by stronger powers, Korea just as often proved to be the dolphin that outsmarted the whales. Or, to borrow Michel de Certeau's phrase, Koreans' "use of the dominant social order deflected its power, which they lacked the means to challenge; they escaped it without leaving it."[16] South Koreans adapted to American influence with the same flexibility and creativity that had long marked their dealings with other stronger powers. During the Cold War, the legacy of Japanese imperialism and the trauma of the Korean War amplified and gave direction to this long-standing tendency.

Japanese colonialism had exposed millions of Koreans to a highly authoritarian model of development that continued to influence their thinking when they encountered American nation builders. By locating modern heavy industries on the peninsula, conscripting Koreans into the Japanese military, and allowing limited indigenous participation in the vast colonial bureaucracy, the Japanese had given thousands of Koreans experience in new modes of governance and production.[17] In some instances, Koreans' capacity to draw on their colonial experience meshed well with U.S. tolerance for autocracy. It facilitated key components of anti-Communist nation building, such as creating a military establishment and finding a model of development that could be implemented by a strong capitalist state. At the same time, the colonial legacy left many Koreans with an ideal of modernity that was very different from the one America strove to introduce. The state, the armed forces, and many institutions that emerged in South Korea embraced a degree of centralization that went far beyond the measure of autocracy that Washington endorsed as a necessary evil.

Korea's colonial past also impacted U.S. efforts to transform its culture. In contrast to the Middle East and much of Southeast Asia, Korea had been colonized by an Asian power but never by a Western one. As a result, postcolonial nationalism in Korea was not inherently anti-Western as it was in other parts of the world. Korean nationalists could reconcile American cultural influences with their own aspirations in ways that nationalists in other developing nations could not. Many Koreans responded enthusiastically to U.S. attempts to democratize the country's educational system, improve its media, and promote new ideals among the younger generation. At the same time, having had their sovereignty annulled for thirty-five years, Koreans were extremely wary about the possibility of falling victim to new modes of foreign domination and were determined to avoid the sort of cultural subordination that had been foisted upon them by the Japanese. They proved highly selective in appropriating American ideals of democracy and modernity, rejecting elements that did not match their own objectives.

The tragedy of national division and war that befell Korea after World War II added to popular ambivalence about the United States. The invasion by the Democratic People's Republic of Korea (DPRK) and the tremendous costs of fighting against Communist forces during the Korean War convinced many South Koreans of the virtues of capitalism and of the need to contain Communism. The heroic sacrifices that Americans had made to defend the ROK during this conflict did not fail to elicit gratitude. Unabashedly pro-American Koreans could be found in nearly all regions and social classes by the time the war ended. Nevertheless, the division of the peninsula and the destructiveness of the war that followed greatly intensified Koreans' sense of victimization at the hands of the Great Powers, including the United States. These events made Koreans keenly aware that U.S. involvement in their affairs was born at least partially of self-interest. South Koreans anxiously strove to ensure that their own priorities as well as those of the United States were represented in the shaping of new national institutions and ideals.

This book examines how the actions of both Americans and Koreans shaped South Korea's transition from autocracy to developmental autocracy to democracy over the Cold War era. It devotes the most attention to the period between 1945 and 1972. These were the years of the deepest U.S. involvement in South Korea and the most active American nation-building efforts there. During these years Americans helped to encourage the emergence of a powerful developmental autocracy on the one hand and a set of institutions and ideals that would prove vital for the country's eventual democratization on the other. Although full-blown democracy only came to South Korea in 1987 after a protracted struggle between the state and dissidents, I would argue that neither the demand for democracy that existed in South Korea by the 1980s nor the state whose power the democratic movement contested can be understood without looking at the prior four decades of U.S.–South Korean relations.

The first chapter begins in 1945, when the United States occupied southern Korea and sought to secure it against Communism and social revolution. It explores the process of anti-Communist state building in South Korea. Establishing an anti-Communist bulwark on the peninsula required the United States to support the creation of a separate South Korean state in 1948, defend it in a three-year war between 1950 and 1953, and prop up its shattered economy when the war ended. Throughout this period, U.S. officials provided crucial political support for the conservative nationalist Syngman Rhee despite his indifference to development and democracy. They did so primarily because they regarded him as the only figure capable of blocking the influence of the Korean left. The United States inadvertently helped deepen Rhee's authoritarianism by providing his regime with massive military and economic aid that he could manipulate to reward allies and punish adversaries.

But even while the United States provided formal support for a dictator, other dimensions of American nation building gave rise to institutions and groups that were frustrated by Rhee's ineffective governance. In particular, Chapter 2 argues, U.S. civilian assistance programs sought to build up the education system, improve the media, and train new bureaucrats. By the late 1950s, through a combination of U.S. assistance and Korean initiative, South Korea was brimming with students, journalists, and civil servants who demanded better economic policies and more political participation. Although these groups possessed a sincere commitment to social change, in the end they were unable to act on their ambitions. The key reason was that none of these new groups of civilian elites could compete with the South Korean military in terms of political power and organization.

Chapter 3 describes how Americans assistance and training programs built the South Korean military into a powerful political force that was destined to govern the country. Over the course of the Korean War, given South Korea's need for a formidable military to preserve its security, the United States helped build the ROK army into one of the largest in the world. In doing so, it cultivated a nucleus of nationalistic officers who were highly trained in technical areas and confident of their superiority to other groups in Korean society. The reformist zeal, ability, and power of these officers had, by the late fifties, paved the way for military government.

Developmental autocracy took hold in South Korea in 1961 after a turbulent period of successive student and military revolutions. Chapter 4, which covers the period during 1960–61, shows how a student-led revolution produced the country's first democratic government in April 1960. But this regime struggled with the challenges of maintaining order and jump-starting economic development. Impatient with its civilian leaders, a military junta led by Park Chung Hee seized power in May 1961. Washington decided to back the junta because its leaders were fiercely determined to promote economic development, which, as the security situation on the peninsula stabilized, had become a top priority.

Once the military was in power, the United States sought to simultaneously grease the engines of economic growth and pave the way for South Korea's eventual democratization. Chapter 5 examines how American officials and Korean military officers created and sustained a developmental autocracy between 1961 and 1972. Unease that Park was not strong enough to pass crucial economic reforms during the mid-sixties led the United States to assist him in implementing unpopular policies and weakening his opposition. But rifts between Washington and the Park regime appeared because the two had different visions of how a developmental autocracy should function. U.S. officials insisted that while Park centralized control over economic decision making he must tolerate a certain degree of dissent. By the late 1960s, however, Park had grown increasingly wary of the opposition and looked for ways to shut it down. American concerns about the government's weaknesses gave way to fears that Park had become too autocratic in the late sixties and early seventies. U.S. officials stationed in South Korea tried to limit the state's growing control over the economy and society without undermining its successful development programs. But as the regime grew stronger, American influence diminished. When in 1972 Park abandoned all pretenses of democracy and announced the introduction of Yusin, a harsh authoritarian system, Washington believed that it had little choice but to go along.

Even as the Americans encouraged the formation of a strong, developmental state, they sought to increase citizen participation in national politics by creating a community of interests between the state and potential dissident groups on economic and political issues. U.S. officials hoped that if students, intellectuals, and other critical elites embraced the idea of capitalist modernization, they would eventually be able to participate in the country's politics without threatening stability or growth. Chapters 6 and 7 explore how Americans managed their relationship with the two groups they considered most vital to the future of South Korean democracy—students and intellectuals. Intellectuals and students welcomed American ideas on modernization and democratization but also transformed them, making them more suitable for their own aspirations and eliminating their assumption of Western superiority. In the 1960s modernization became an important basis for dialogue between the state and democratic elites about the nation's future. But many students and intellectuals had been attracted to these ideals because they offered the promise of a freer, more democratic society. As the state grew more autocratic, however, they were forced to either abandon their ambitions for democratic modernization or side with the state. The civilian elites cultivated by the United States in some instances became the vanguard of resistance to Yusin.

By 1972 American nation building had helped create both a powerful South Korean state intent on maximizing its control over society and a formidable opposition committed to bringing democracy to the country. The fifteen years between 1972 and 1987 were marked by a continuous struggle between the two sides. Economic growth increased the size of the working and middle classes, both of which favored democratization. But the regime responded to pressures for political change with repression. After Park Chung Hee's assassination in 1979, a new military dictatorship—far more brutal than Park's—assumed power, causing the battle between democratic forces and the state to escalate to a new level. Chapter 8 covers this struggle. It contends that American influence declined during this period as a result of both increased South Korean autonomy and a reduced U.S. commitment to Asia generally. The United States nevertheless attempted to manage this conflict between state and society by encouraging restraint on both sides and placing a premium on stability. But as Cold War frictions eased and the inherent weaknesses of Communist models of development became apparent during the mid-eighties, a subtle shift occurred in U.S. calculations about how stability could best be preserved. The Americans were less convinced of the need to support anti-Communist dictatorships and more willing to trust Korea's democratic leaders. The chapter ends in 1987, when the military regime agreed to surrender power in the face of massive protests and American pressure. Full-blown democracy would emerge in South Korea within a decade.

Throughout these chapters, I have sought to demonstrate the agency of South Koreans in determining the ultimate impact of the United States on their society. To the extent that the U.S. influence could be called hegemonic, American hegemony was a dialectical process that Koreans played a significant role in shaping. To emphasize this point, I have approached the process of nation building from both sides through the use of American and Korean sources. This analysis makes it clear that the evolution of the South Korea we know today did not entirely reflect the will of Americans or Koreans. It was achieved only through constant negotiation between the two.

The South Korean state would never have come into existence in 1948 without American intervention. Nor would it have survived the hardships brought on by national division and the horrific war that followed without vast U.S. military and economic assistance. For the United States, building and stabilizing South Korea came at an enormous cost in terms of both material resources and human lives. But the state that Americans made such great sacrifices to support was a highly autocratic one that frustrated their ambitions to spread democracy. Washington was only willing to make massive investments to sustain a highly questionable regime because it believed that the security of the United States and of its Asian allies would be jeopardized if southern Korea did not become a bulwark against the expansion of Communism. For U.S. officials, the preservation of democracy at home often meant support for anti-Communist autocrats abroad even if the costs were exorbitant.

State building in South Korea proved to be particularly expensive. The problems usually faced by new states, such as eliminating domestic rivals and establishing territorial integrity, were more difficult in the Republic of Korea (ROK) because of how the country was created. The inability of the United States and the Soviet Union, which occupied the southern and northern halves of the Korean peninsula respectively, to agree on a framework for national elections led to the formation of mutually antagonistic nations. Efforts to destroy the ROK from both within and without would soon follow. National division left the southern economy, which had been tightly integrated with that of the industrial North, in shambles. The dire economic situation that prevailed in South Korea remained a source of potential instability for a decade after the Korean War ended. Only U.S. assistance enabled the ROK to weather the storms of social division, insurgency, military invasion, and economic turmoil.

American largesse fostered a process of state building in South Korea that was very different from the one that had occurred in Europe. The chief beneficiary of U.S. assistance was the fiercely anti-Communist nationalist Syngman Rhee, who Washington reluctantly backed because it doubted that more moderate leaders would combat leftist influence with sufficient intensity. Unlike most European heads of state, who had to bargain and compromise with the citizenry to acquire the necessary resources for bureaucratic, disciplinary, and military institutions, Rhee wheedled funding for institution building from the United States. In Europe, according to sociologist Charles Tilly, bargaining between the government and the governed helped create and confirm individual rights vis-à-vis the state; when authorities "sought to draw resources and acquiescence" from different groups, these groups could demand new privileges or force the state to limit its own power.[1] With the United States covering the costs of war and economic reconstruction in South Korea, such negotiation was unnecessary. The Rhee regime could afford to ignore the will of the governed and to be indifferent to national development. While U.S. assistance enabled the ROK to survive, before 1960 Syngman Rhee's heavy-handed methods of state building ensured that it would not thrive.

Creating a Government

The most basic component of state building is establishing and consolidating governing institutions. When American forces occupied the southern half of the Korean peninsula in 1945, two distinct possibilities for creating such institutions existed. One possibility was aligning with the Korean left, which had formed a provisional government with strong popular support in the brief interim after Japan surrendered to the Allies at the end of World War II and relinquished its empire. The provisional government established local branches, or "People's Committees," that helped maintain order and assumed local administrative functions in provinces throughout Korea. Originally called the Committee for the Preparation of Korean Independence, the interim government's leaders met in Seoul on 6 September 1945 and rechristened it the Korean People's Republic (KPR). The KPR committed itself to destroying the vestiges of Japanese imperialism through land reforms and other social changes.[2] The second possibility was to reconstitute the vast centralized bureaucratic structure that the Japanese had used to govern Korea—one that had organized, mobilized, and exploited the Korean population to serve Japan's interests.[3] The American military, which occupied the southern half of Korea on the basis of an agreement reached with the Soviet Union in August 1945, was in a position to determine which of these two political structures would govern the southern half of Korea.

Bruce Cumings's *Origins of the Korean War* demonstrates in great detail how the U.S. occupation of southern Korea resurrected the preexisting colonial bureaucracy at the expense of the KPR.[4] American officials doubted the capacity of Koreans to govern themselves and suspected that the KPR was connected to international Communism. John R. Hodge, the commander of the U.S. occupying forces, called Korea "a decadent nation without the slightest concept of political life as the free nations of the world know it" and argued that the KPR was a "Communist regime set up before our arrival."[5] With suspicions of the KPR prevalent among the highest officers in the military government—the U.S. Military Government in Korea (USAMGIK)—Washington unsurprisingly opted to govern through the colonial power structure rather than back the KPR. During its three-year occupation, the United States more or less rebuilt the colonial bureaucracy. The occupation forces established a formal military government that, according to one official source, used the "existing administrative machinery of the Government General."[6] Only superficial changes in the organization of the bureaucracy, such as renaming the "bureaus" of the colonial era "departments," were made. The Americans filled most of the highest bureaucratic posts with Koreans who had been affiliated with the KPR's rival organization, the Korean Democratic Party (KDP), a group of Korean conservatives —some with unquestionable nationalist credentials but others tainted by collaboration with Japanese colonialism.[7]

The American occupation went beyond merely resurrecting the bureaucracy. It also played a key role in eliminating rival political organizations. Usually when confronted with determined opposition, centralizing states must consolidate their rule through a lengthy process of coercion and co-optation. But despite the opposition's popular appeal, the military government had little need for co-optation because it was backed by overwhelming American power. USAMGIK not only stripped the KPR of its authority but also eradicated a vast majority of the People's Committees that had continued to function in some provinces. Some committees collapsed swiftly, whereas others mounted more determined resistance. But by the fall of 1946, these organizations no longer posed a significant challenge to USAMGIK's authority.[8]

By routing out the People's Committees and reestablishing the colonial bureaucracy, the United States created a powerful political tool. But the question of who would control this tool still remained. During the U.S. occupation American commanders directed the bureaucracy at the top while staffing it with Korean conservatives, many of whom had been affiliated with the KDP.[9] The Americans realized, however, that the occupation could not be indefinite and that control of the bureaucracy and of South Korea itself would have to be surrendered to indigenous leaders. But Washington was reluctant to turn the government over to the KDP. Occupation officials worried that too many Koreans associated the KDP leadership with Japanese colonialism. They also wanted to ensure the legitimacy of this political structure by making at least a nominal effort to see that a variety of factions were represented, even if the right dominated.

In 1946 and 1947 the United States repeatedly attempted to establish a coalition of conservatives and moderates to whom it could entrust the South Korean government. The Americans hoped to identify political leaders who would govern in a liberal, democratic mode. But moderate democrats were scarce in Korea, and Americans undermined their own efforts at coalition building by constantly stacking key institutions with conservatives. Recognizing that they had an upper hand in the South, Korean conservatives also obstructed U.S. efforts to promote moderation by lashing out against both the left and the occupation forces.[10] As mounting tensions between the United States and the Soviet Union made a unified Korean state increasingly unlikely, a clear opportunity arose for Koreans who had sufficient nationalist credentials to govern with some semblance of popular legitimacy and sufficient conservative credentials to garner American support.

Among the Korean leaders who possessed these characteristics, Dr. Syngman Rhee was the most well known and the most ambitious. The seventy-year-old Korean nationalist had spent much of the previous two decades in the United States. After attending the George Washington University and Princeton, where he earned a Ph.D., Rhee had wasted years vainly lobbying the U.S. government on behalf of Korea's independence. The American occupation forces had pressed for Rhee's return to Korea and welcomed him back in October 1945. At the time, Americans hoped that Rhee would use his prestige as a nationalist to rally Korea's population against Communism and for democracy. Having encountered years of ambivalence if not hostility from the U.S. government, however, Rhee was far more concerned with pursuing his own ambitions than with advancing the goals of the occupation. Although he shared with the Americans a determination not to let Korea fall to leftist revolutionaries, Rhee had little interest in joining or promoting a coalition of moderate democrats. He realized that his own interests would best be served if Korean politics remained polarized. On returning to Korea, Rhee aligned himself with the conservative bankers and landlords who constituted the base of the KDP while denouncing the KPR and the left.[11]

Rhee cemented his control over politics in southern Korea by sabotaging negotiations between the United States and the Soviet Union over the creation of a unified Korean government in 1946 and 1947. These negotiations took place within a body known as the "Joint Commission," to which Rhee announced his opposition while encouraging other Korean conservatives to do likewise. He guessed correctly that if the United States was faced with the choice of either abandoning the commission or risking the unification of the peninsula under a leftist regime, it would opt for the former. In part because Rhee opposed the Joint Commission, the United States could not reach an agreement with the Soviet Union on the fate of the peninsula, and in September 1947 it decided to turn the issue over to the United Nations (UN) General Assembly.[12] This decision guaranteed that Korea would remain divided and that the South would fall into the hands of Rhee, who had become the most powerful conservative figure in the country. After UN-sponsored elections for a legislative assembly were held in May 1948, Rhee got his wish. When the country's independence was formally announced on 15 August 1948, he became the first president of the ROK.

Americans had recognized that if a separate South Korean government was created, Rhee would gain control of it. This prospect did not elicit universal enthusiasm. By 1948 U.S. officials were already critical of Rhee for his autocratic tendencies and intractable nature. An "intimate report on Syngman Rhee" prepared for the U.S. State Department contended that it was "difficult to imagine how a political leader with such a small quantity of actual ability and substance to offer his following has been able to attain such great popularity."[13] Nevertheless, Washington understood that Rhee's age, education, and nationalist credentials gave him a prestige among his compatriots that many other Korean conservatives lacked. He was the best-known Korean political leader who was untainted by affiliation with Japanese colonialism and willing to resist leftist subversion at any cost. For the United States, these were ample grounds to offer him support.

Once in power, Rhee continued to consolidate his control over the South Korean state. In particular, he struggled to gain dominance over his erstwhile allies in the KDP who, after August 1948, competed with him for the upper hand in national politics. Rhee realized that consolidating his own grip on power and keeping his rivals in check would require the strategic manipulation of both allies and adversaries. The new South Korean president proved to be a master at this task and made full use of the resources provided by his office to build a base of support. He especially used his authority to reward those who had demonstrated their unswerving political loyalty with bureaucratic posts and to eliminate potential rivals. Soon after assuming the presidency, Rhee began purging from the bureaucracy KDP members who had served in the military government and replacing them with individuals who were deemed more loyal and reliable. In March 1949 the American embassy reported that none of the ministers and vice ministers in the new regime had held significant positions in the military government. It noted that the "chief motive for the appointment of Cabinet Ministers seems to be their personal relationship and loyalty to Rhee" and that there had been "a lack of any attempt to include in the present Government varying opinions or political groups."[14] The use of the bureaucracy to reward allies and exclude dissenting opinions rapidly became a hallmark of South Korean politics during the Rhee era.

By the beginning of 1949 the basic political system that would govern South Korea until 1960 was already in place. Under this system, Rhee exercised strict control over a powerful bureaucracy that the American occupation had built from the preexisting Japanese power structure. Although some KDP members retained a post in the new order, the defining characteristic of individuals occupying the upper echelons of government was not their affiliation with the KDP, Japanese colonialism, or the U.S. military government. Rather, it was their personal loyalty to the South Korean president. Rhee had rapidly emerged as the most significant locus of political power in South Korea, yet the potential challenges to his position were substantial. During the next eleven years he would shrewdly use American assistance to manage nearly every crisis and opportunity that arose in a way that strengthened his grip over South Korean society.

Agriculture and Land Reforms

Among the issues confronting the new South Korean government, none was more urgent than deciding how to distribute land and extract resources from it. Although some industrialization had occurred during the colonial period, the South had remained primarily agricultural. Meeting the rising demands for land ownership of the country's large population of tenant farmers was a potentially explosive political problem. Forming alliances with powerful landed elites, as many state-building regimes had done in Europe, was not an option for the Rhee government. In Europe, large agricultural producers, with the assistance of the state, forced peasants from the land and created a land-poor labor force. The consolidation of landholdings, in turn, facilitated more efficient cultivation and enabled the government to extract more tax revenue from agriculture. But this process had occurred over three centuries.[15] The peculiarities of Japanese colonialism had produced a politically conscious peasantry that demanded immediate reforms and would not wait for opportunities to arise through urbanization and industrialization.

The Japanese colonial government had sought to initiate in Korea an accelerated version of the European pattern. It had enabled some landlords to engage in commercial enterprises that could elevate production while forcing peasants to leave the land and work in industry. But when Japan surrendered its empire at the end of World War II, peasants who had been coerced into industrial labor often had no choice but to return to their villages. Although a few Korean landlords had engaged in different forms of entrepreneurship without Japanese backing, most of them seemed likely to resume traditional methods of governing their land. These circumstances were bound to limit agricultural productivity, slow economic development, and leave peasants unwilling to wait for new opportunities to arise.[16] In the absence of commercially oriented landlords or an industrial base to absorb landless labor, consolidating acreage in the hands of a few landed elites would have only exacerbated the already seething social discontent.

Land reform seemed to be the most viable option for managing the contentious issue of land distribution. Although the potential effects of such changes on agricultural production were uncertain, their political benefits for the new ROK government were readily apparent. The conservative landlords who comprised the bulk of the KDP were now Rhee's most serious political rivals. Taking land away from them and redistributing it to peasants would destroy the basis of their political strength. Moreover, by giving the peasantry a material incentive to support the Rhee regime, land reform would alleviate a major source of social discontent.

Between 1945 and 1948 the U.S. military government had taken significant steps to settle this thorny problem, although it had left the most fiercely contested issue unresolved. Early in the occupation USAMGIK set the maximum rent that landowners could charge their tenants at one-third of the annual crop. For tenants, this was a substantial improvement over previous rates, which had averaged 50 percent of the crop. More importantly, the military government sold large tracts of former Japanese holdings to Korean farmers. The American occupation had assumed responsibility for 686,965 acres owned by Japanese landlords during the colonial period. Through the sale of this property beginning in the spring of 1948, 587,974 tenant families, or 24.1 percent of southern Korea's agricultural population, acquired new land.[17] But while these measures improved conditions for some Korean farmers, they represented only a partial solution to the country's land problems.

The U.S. occupation was unable to resolve the most contentious issue pertaining to land reform in Korea—how and if the property of Korean landlords would be redistributed. Although USAMGIK was eager to see land reforms carried out, it was far more tentative in handling this question than it was in selling former Japanese holdings. In 1946 the U.S. military government prepared an ordinance that it hoped would become a Korean version of the Homestead Act that had distributed 270 million acres to the American public during the late nineteenth century. Like the Homestead Act, the ordinance was based on the principle of turning over land to the tiller. It stipulated that tenants could acquire title to the acreage that they farmed after paying 25 percent of their crop for fifteen years. The U.S. occupation never implemented this ordinance, however, because Koreans surveyed by USAMGIK preferred that this issue be handled by a Korean provisional government rather than the United States. The interim legislature that finally convened in December 1946 consisted primarily of landlords and conservatives who were unwilling to sacrifice the source of their political power. Americans pressured the legislature to create a National Land Reform Administration, but the assembly refused to act.[18] As a result, virtually no land owned by Korean landlords had been distributed in the South when the occupation ended.

Nevertheless, land reform remained at the top of the agenda when the new South Korean government was inaugurated in 1948. After a year of debate between the Department of Agriculture and the National Assembly, the ROK government in June 1949 drafted a law providing for the redistribution of all land not cultivated by the owner and all holdings of more than 7.5 acres. The measure stipulated that the government would calculate the land's average annual production and then compensate landlords at 150 percent of this sum. Farmers who bought the land were to repay the government 125 percent of their average annual production over a ten-year period. Strapped with financial difficulties, the ROK passed a revised version of the law in March 1950 raising the percentage paid by purchasers to 150.[19] Naturally, the KDP-dominated assembly resisted the legislation because it would deprive landlords of the very source of their social dominance. But Rhee strong-armed the lawmakers into passing the law by holding a series of meetings in the provinces that mobilized peasant associations and left landlords politically isolated.[20]

Although the statute was clearly on the books after June 1949, scholars disagree about how seriously the Rhee regime took its implementation. Some historians have argued that while the ROK eventually carried out the reforms as stipulated, it did so only with great reluctance during the Korean War to counter North Korean propaganda or appease the United States.[21] These arguments are supported by reports of American officials during the months prior to the conflict that generally describe land reforms as partially complete at best.[22] In his highly regarded history of the Korean War, South Korean scholar Pak Myŏngnim disputes this claim. Drawing on ROK documents and reports on land reforms in various provinces, Pak contends that the South Korean government did not wait for the Korean War to implement reforms. According to Pak, the Rhee government made a serious effort to carry out land reforms well before June 1950, and by the time the war broke out his government had already redistributed a significant portion of the land.[23]

While American and South Korean sources do not offer a consistent picture of precisely when the land reforms were implemented, substantial land redistribution did eventually occur in the ROK and both the Rhee regime and U.S. officials supported it. Whereas the wealthiest 3 percent of farming households owned 64 percent of the land in 1944, the wealthiest 6 percent owned only 18 percent by 1955. During the same period tenancy dropped from 49 percent to 7 percent of farm households.[24] Ultimately these reforms satisfied the objectives of both the Rhee regime and the United States.

Rhee probably promoted land reform so vigorously because it enabled the state to control the process of social change in South Korea and eventually strengthen itself. The reforms weakened but did not destroy the regime's rivals within the country's landholding class. The tenancy system had been the basis of the landlords' political power, and without it they were dependent on the state to preserve their status.[25] At the same time, South Korean landlords were not subject to public trials or self-criticism meetings as were their counterparts in North Korea and Communist China. Instead, the state provided modest opportunities for these former property holders to recoup some of their wealth and influence by encouraging them to invest in industries and offering them priority in the public sale of formerly Japanese-owned industrial plants. Government efforts on this front were not very successful, but they did ease the transition to a new social order for a few landlords.[26] When the reforms were completed landlords were a much less potent political force, but opportunities still existed for those who would demonstrate their loyalty to the regime.

Land reform also strengthened the Rhee government by bolstering its popularity among farmers. When the Soviets allowed land redistribution in northern Korea in 1946, they fueled the aspirations of peasants living in the South for their own land. If Rhee had ignored the demands of tenant farmers, he undoubtedly would have created an enduring and potentially powerful source of opposition to his regime. Recognizing the dangers inherent in that approach, the chief American economic adviser in South Korea, Arthur C. Bunce, recommended in late 1949 that the Land Reform Act be "put into operation immediately so that much of the land can be sold to farm operators this fall and winter." If such action were taken, he argued, "farmers would be more contented because they would own the land that they till."[27] By the spring of 1950 land redistribution had already eased American concerns. U.S. officials noted that the discontent of the ROK's agricultural population was beginning to dissipate. Indeed, John Muccio, the American ambassador to South Korea, wrote in April 1950 that the country's farmers were no longer a source of potential dissent but rather a "strong element of stability."[28] Land reform had thus swiftly created an important new base of support for the regime.

American aid was really what enabled land reform in South Korea to take a relatively moderate form. In contrast to the North Korean regime, which simply seized land from its owners without compensation, the South Korean government paid landlords up front for their property.[29] Land reforms in South Korea were thus more costly to the state than those implemented by Kim Il-Sung in the North. Official ROK documents showing where the money used to compensate landowners came from are unavailable. But even if the United States did not provide it directly, American aid funds applied in other areas would have helped compensate for the deficit created by buying rather than seizing property.

Although land reform in South Korea was less radical than that in the Democratic People's Republic of Korea (DPRK) and the People's Republic of China (PRC), its consequences proved enduring. Politically, it created a new social structure that helped preserve the regime for years to come. During the course of the Korean War, the vast majority of the rural population remained loyal despite North Korean attempts to foster subversion. After the war, agricultural villages were one of Rhee's few reliable sources of political support. The economic consequences of land reform were more controversial. Although it reduced agricultural poverty, it also limited the size of landholdings, thereby restraining agricultural production for at least two decades.[30] Americans hoped that when landlords sold their land, the profits would become a source of capital formation to stimulate the growth of industries. But the failure of government efforts to promote this kind of investment would make the ROK even more dependent on U.S. aid for its economic recovery. At the time that land reform was debated and implemented, however, economic growth was not the government's primary concern. A much higher priority was to ensure the loyalty of the country's population as the regime faced almost overwhelming threats to its security.

War Making and Internal Security

In South Korea war making was an integral part of state making, much as it was in other parts of the world. Historically, wars have often been crucibles in which modern states were either consolidated or destroyed. On the one hand, wars promote territorial consolidation, centralization, and monopolization of the means of coercion, giving states a motive to fight in them. On the other hand, war sometimes places excessive strains on the national economy that can foment opposition to the government. Wars can also exhaust or destroy the forces needed for domestic control, facilitating revolution or emboldening opponents of the state.[31] The fact that the former rather than the latter set of tendencies prevailed in South Korea between 1948 and 1953 was due in a large part to the United States. Although the violence that persisted during this period was a complete disaster for South Koreans, American assistance helped turn it into a boon for the South Korean state.

The years between 1948 and 1953 were ones of almost perpetual armed conflict in South Korea. Guerrilla warfare and leftist insurgency plagued the new ROK government during the two years after its creation. These two years of internal conflicts were, of course, followed by three years of a massively destructive war against adversaries that would have destroyed the South Korean state altogether in the absence of American intervention. But this was a period not only of fierce military struggle but also of aggressive state building. The ROK's troubled security situation enabled it to constantly prevail upon the United States to provide funding for the expansion of its military and security forces. Unlike European states that relied on taxation and resource extraction to support their militaries, South Korea acquired armed forces that were far in excess of what it could have afforded with its fairly limited capacity to raise revenue. These forces could be used not only to defend the security of the state but also to eliminate its opponents and suppress dissent from within.

Violent threats to the South Korean government appeared soon after its creation. In April 1948 leftist supporters of the People's Committees had initiated a major insurrection against American authority in Cheju, an offshore island located near Korea's southwestern coast, that had still not been suppressed when the new ROK government was formed in August. For months, rebels in Cheju engaged in combat with South Korean police and constabulary forces, both of which had been assembled and trained by the United States. In December 1948 President Rhee decided to make a concerted effort to end the insurrection by dispatching units of the newly formed South Korean Army. This decision only elicited further chaos and violence. One army regiment refused to embark on the mission and seized the city of Yŏsu before the state could take action against it. After killing local police, the regiment moved on to capture the city of Sunch'ŏn twenty miles north of Yŏsu. More than five thousand people died before loyal army units finally put down the mutiny one week later.[32] But guerrilla activity persisted for months afterward, especially in Cheju and the southwestern province of Chŏlla. According to official U.S. reports, in the spring of 1949 guerrilla forces had "most of the rural areas" in South Chŏlla Province "under their control or in perpetual ferment" while Cheju remained "virtually overrun" by rebels.[33]

Given the turbulent conditions that prevailed in South Korea in 1948 and 1949, Washington recognized that building up indigenous security forces was a sine qua non for the country's survival. The American occupation had already created a constabulary of roughly 40,000 men in 1946 that had been used to combat guerrilla activity. In the fall of 1948 the United States dispatched a military advisory group that reshaped this constabulary into a formal army. As U.S. occupation troops withdrew from South Korea, they left their weapons and equipment for the state's armed forces. But as rebellions flared throughout the countryside during the winter and spring of 1949, Americans realized that the ROK Army was woefully inadequate for the pressing security needs of the new republic. In March 1949 the Truman administration made a more explicit commitment to South Korea's security through the adoption of National Security Council (NSC) 8/2. The document concluded that the United States should continue supporting a 65,000-man army "suitable for maintaining internal order under conditions of political strife and inspired disorder and for maintaining border security." NSC 8/2 also called for the maintenance of a 35,000-man police force capable of "performing normal police functions." By June 1949 Washington had spent $56 million to implement this program.[34] Security forces funded and equipped by the United States ultimately played a key role in wiping out the guerrillas who remained in Cheju and South Chŏlla. In the fall of 1949 the ROK Army launched a major counterguerrilla offensive in the countryside, and by the spring of 1950 American observers noted a significant decline in subversive activity.[35]

Despite the initial success of its armed forces, the Rhee regime was not satisfied with American military assistance. Alarmed by the spectacle of violence that had unfolded in the months after he gained power, President Rhee was intent on augmenting his troops to levels well beyond those considered necessary by the United States. In November 1948 his government passed the National Defense Act calling for a 100,000-man army and a 10,000-man navy. By 2 September 1949, the South Korean army had almost reached its target while the South Korean National Police had grown to 50,000, more than twice the size of the force that the Japanese imperial government had relied on to control all of Korea.[36]

The Americans worried that a military establishment of this size exceeded what South Korea's economy could support and were reluctant to yield to Rhee's constant pleas for more funds. Between November 1948 and September 1949 his multiple requests for additional military assistance totaled $200 million. When the United States denied these seemingly exorbitant appeals, the ROK government usually covered its defense spending by borrowing from the Bank of Korea and printing more currency, much to the chagrin of American economic advisers. The Rhee regime then used other forms of U.S. aid, especially the Commodity Assistance Program, to keep the inflationary effects of such actions under control. The Commodity Assistance Program countered inflation by increasing the supply of fertilizer, rubber, raw cotton, and other desperately needed goods.[37] Washington had hoped that this program would promote economic stability in South Korea, but as the ROK government spent sums on defense that greatly exceeded its revenues, the program's main accomplishment became preventing inflation from spiraling completely out of control.

By accepting and manipulating American assistance, South Korea acquired armed forces that defeated violent threats to the state's authority and enabled the state to monopolize the means of coercion. As its power increased, the regime used its muscle against not only armed challengers but also political opponents. The National Security Law (NSL), which was passed in December 1948 ostensibly as a response to the Yŏsu rebellion, officially empowered the state to deploy the army and police for these purposes. Through vaguely worded language the statute made any citizen who criticized the government or its policies subject to draconian punishment. By 1950, 80 percent of the 60,000 South Koreans serving prison sentences had been charged with violating the NSL.[38] The state ceded to the

Korean National Police almost unlimited power to enforce this law and monitor the citizenry for infringements. According to Gregory Henderson, who had worked as a diplomat in the ROK, the South Korean courts did not once refuse the police a warrant for an arrest between 1948 and 1950.[39] By the spring of 1949, U.S. reports frequently condemned the application of the NSL to critics of the government. The American embassy was especially dismayed by the closing of the ROK's largest newspaper, *Seoul Sinmun*, for reasons that "appeared inadequate and arbitrary on their face" and the arrest of assemblymen who were rumored to be Communists.[40]

Although ROK security forces enabled the Rhee regime to control its own territory, external threats continued to trouble the fledgling state. North Korea constantly challenged South Korea's legitimacy, and the two sides engaged in border clashes along the 38th parallel with increasing regularity. On 25 June 1950 the DPRK finally launched a full-scale invasion that threatened to destroy the South Korean government. This action quickly led to a greatly expanded American commitment to South Korea's security and transformed the relationship between state and society in the ROK. The United States sent hundreds of thousands of American troops to the peninsula and spent hundreds of millions of dollars to expand South Korea's armed forces. As a result of U.S. assistance, the ROK would emerge from the war with its territory more secure, a military establishment that could not have been imagined prior to the conflict, and far greater control over society. As the Korean War raged across the peninsula, American human and material resources helped consolidate the South Korean state.

The role of U.S. forces in defending the basic sovereignty of South Korea has been well chronicled. The 1.3 million Americans who served in the war constituted the bulk of UN forces in Korea and saved the ROK from nearly certain annihilation at the hands of its adversaries. On two occasions—once in September 1950, when General Douglas MacArthur made his famous Inch'ŏn landing, and again in early 1951, when General Matthew B. Ridgway's Operation Killer pushed back a Sino–North Korean offensive that had captured Seoul—UN troops were indispensable to the recapture of lost territory. Finally, the United States played a pivotal role in negotiating the armistice that left ROK territory more secure than it had been before the conflict erupted.[41]

Whereas the role of American forces in the Korean War has been well covered in the literature, far less attention has been paid to the impact of U.S. assistance on indigenous security forces.[42] For the purposes of state building in South Korea, the growth of these indigenous forces was, if anything, more significant than the arrival of U.S. troops. Whereas most governments must bargain with key elites or the general population to acquire the resources necessary for waging wars, Syngman Rhee wheedled support for the expansion of ROK forces from the United States. The ROK president recognized that the war had turned his country into a test of American credibility and that the United States could not let it disappear. When the PRC's entry into the war in November 1950 turned it into a protracted conflict, Rhee shrewdly made use of the fact that the American public supported expanding the South Korean military as a cost-effective alternative to the commitment of additional U.S. forces.[43] He skillfully played on both American thinking about the conflict and South Korea's poverty to wrest more military aid from the United States. Over the course of the war the South Korean military grew from roughly 100,000 to almost 700,000 men. This expansion was all the more remarkable considering the country's inability to support a 100,000-man force before the war.

Rhee bluntly used South Korea's economic travails to obtain U.S. military assistance during a series of pivotal conferences held in July 1952. At these meetings, the two governments decided to increase the size of the ROK Army to 437,240 troops. The ROK government constantly reminded American officials of the desperate condition of its finances and its reliance on U.S. military support. During one conference the South Korean minister of finance said that his government was "in acute financial distress and on the verge of bankruptcy" and that "the Republic of Korea does not have the money to support sizeable strength increases of ROKA[rmy]." According to Mark W. Clark, the U.S. commanding officer, the Rhee regime was unwilling to take action on the planned expansion of the military until it received "a firm and positive statement . . . as to the exact ROKA[rmy] strength that will be supported by the United States and as to what new and additional types of military aid would be forthcoming."[44] These circumstances presented American officials with a bleak choice. They could offer South Korea extensive military assistance, or they could send more U.S. troops to the Korean theater.

The decision was an easy one. Supporting the expansion of the ROK military would not only save American lives; it would also afford the United States a much cheaper means of fighting the Korean War and, eventually, containing Communism. On the basis of this logic, leading U.S. military officers continuously advanced the case for funding the expansion of the ROK Army. James Van Fleet, the commanding general of the Eighth U.S. Army in Korea, was particularly assertive in lobbying the Pentagon on this issue. He argued that the "cost of organizing and maintaining an expanded ROK army is so small in comparison to maintaining a similar US force that in the end the US would realize a great saving in money by such an expansion, in addition to the saving of American manpower."[45] Mark Clark, who became commander in chief of UN forces in Korea in April 1952, agreed with Van Fleet. In a letter to the chairman of the Joint Chiefs of Staff, he maintained that the cost of an ROK division was "fractional in comparison with similar US forces" and that "strong, well-trained and adequately equipped Asiatic forces should be developed to carry the burden of combating Communism in Asia."[46] Recommendations from high-ranking officers like Van Fleet and Clark were vital in persuading American civilian leaders to approve funding for a twenty-division South Korean army by 1953.

With the United States assuming much of the financial burden for South Korea's security during the war, the Rhee regime could focus on cementing its grasp over domestic politics. The constant state of emergency created by the military conflict often furnished a convenient excuse for the regime to crack down on its domestic opposition. Although most of the ROK military remained preoccupied with the combat situation, the regime could still use some of its security forces for political purposes. Frictions regularly flared between Rhee and the United States because his government was flagrantly ignoring the democratic principles for which the war was supposedly being fought. But Rhee could always use the Korean National Police or special military units under his control regardless of American criticisms of his actions.

Military and police units were especially brutal in exacting revenge on South Koreans who had cooperated with the North Korean military during the early months of the war. In the summer of 1950, when the Korean People's Army (KPA) occupied the majority of ROK territory, a significant number of South Koreans had assisted DPRK forces in reestablishing People's Committees, seizing and redistributing Japanese property, and maintaining order. South Koreans who sided with North Korea included liberated political prisoners and labor leaders whom the ROK government had stripped of any real power. When U.S. and ROK troops recaptured territory south of the 38th parallel in September 1950, many Koreans who had helped the DPRK fled the South along with the KPA. The South Korean police and army mercilessly punished and sometimes slaughtered remaining dissidents. The National Assembly attempted to curtail such brutality by passing a measure over Rhee's objection that required the government to exercise greater prudence in punishing citizens for traitorous acts. But Rhee ignored the assembly's resolution and continued to use a joint army-police inquiry commission to try and punish those who had committed acts of treason.[47] Meting out death sentences to its opponents or forcing them to flee further consolidated the regime's political dominance.

Rhee adopted similar coercive tactics to force his opponents in the National Assembly to revise the constitution during the war so that he could remain in power. The South Korean constitution had originally stipulated that the assembly could elect the president every four years, which meant there would be a presidential election in August 1952. The assembly seemed likely to replace Rhee despite the fact that the country was then in the midst of a war for its survival. Desperate to prevent such a move, Rhee proposed a constitutional amendment calling for the president to be chosen by direct election instead of by the assembly. When the assembly refused to pass the amendment, Rhee declared martial law and ordered military police units to hold the lawmakers hostage until they finally agreed to his proposal in July 1952. Rhee's triumph over the legislature during this crisis set the precedent for extending his tenure in office in 1956, when he again coerced the assembly to accept changes in the constitution.[48]

Rhee had modified the constitution in the face of resistance not only from the National Assembly but also from ROK military leaders and the United States. He had been forced to rely on military police rather than regular army units to impose martial law because Yi Chongch'an, the army chief of staff, had refused to divert combat divisions from the front lines for this purpose. Rhee eventually dismissed Yi for his response but not before Yi personally met with E. Allan Lightner, the chargé at the American embassy, and promised that "with a handful of soldiers and a few Marines his people could put the President, his Minister of the Interior and the martial law commander under house arrest."[49] Lightner, like many other U.S. diplomats stationed in South Korea, had come to despise Rhee; he advised the State Department that "serious consideration should be given at least to exploring the practicability of letting the ROK's through their Chiefs of Staff take the situation into their own hands."[50]

Ultimately, however, Washington opted against Rhee's removal. The U.S. assessment of South Korea's internal politics had not changed very much since 1948, when America had enabled Rhee to gain power in the first place. U.S. policymakers doubted the capacity of any South Korean leader to fashion a liberal democratic government and, in the absence of such leadership, preferred to support Rhee, who could at least be counted on to guarantee internal security. Secretary of State Dean Acheson argued that there had to be "some leadership in the ROK Govt.," and this leadership could "best be provided by Rhee under some controls and in a more chastened mood."[51] The tolerance of high-level U.S. officials for Rhee's despotic style eased the president's efforts to strengthen his political position during the Korean War.

When the war ended Rhee's control over South Korean politics was virtually unchallenged. American assistance both in combat and in building the ROK military had enabled his regime to reap all of the benefits that states typically accrue during wars while avoiding the destabilizing effects that frequently occur. As importantly, the conflict had forged a long-term American commitment to maintain South Korea's armed forces. New agreements extended large-scale U.S. funding for ROK security forces into the postwar period. In October 1953 the United States and the South Korean government signed a Mutual Defense Treaty, which they followed up with an "Agreed Minute" in September 1954. In the latter document the United States agreed to assist the ROK in supporting a military of up to 720,000 troops.[52] Until the 1960s U.S. military aid to South Korea generally totaled at least $300 million a year and constituted as much as 87 percent of the country's annual defense budget.[53]

For the Rhee regime, these security forces continued to serve not only as guardians of the state's territory and sovereignty but also as a political tool. During the mid- and late 1950s the State Department received a steady stream of communications from American diplomats detailing the ways that Rhee was using the national police and army units to intimidate and control his opponents. One embassy dispatch in 1957 explained that the "Executive will is enforced by a centralized national police," which was "deeply involved in political affairs, especially the surveillance of opposition groups."[54] Although most of the military remained focused on protecting the ROK against another Communist invasion, a small number of units continued to monitor and suppress political opponents of the regime. According to one U.S. report from 1955, Rhee used both the ROK Army Counter Intelligence Corps and the Joint Provost Marshal Command "for security as well as political actions."[55] Throughout the Rhee era these two secret units continually employed extralegal and violent tactics, including the outright murder of some of the regime's opponents.[56] With the Korean War having already done much to weaken the opposition, these special units proved sufficient not only to prevent insurgency but also control most sources of political dissent until the late 1950s.

While U.S. military aid generally advanced the cause of state building in South Korea, it did place one important limitation on Rhee. The ROK's reliance on American assistance for its security forced it to cede to the United States much of its ability to control the military. During the Korean War the United States had demanded that Rhee place his armed forces under the UN Command.[57] The United States could and sometimes did thwart Rhee's efforts to use the military for objectives that it opposed. Rhee had vehemently contested the armistice ending the Korean War, and during the postwar years he frequently threatened to initiate new hostilities against North Korea unilaterally.[58] U.S. control over the ROK military was one of the major factors that prevented him from doing so. American policymakers were confident that the South Korean military would obey the UN Command rather than Rhee if a crisis emerged. One State Department official noted in 1955 that "the present leaders of the [ROK] Army are friendly to us and it is our belief that they will not act against our interests even under orders from Rhee."[59]

While the Americans could limit Rhee's use of the military for political purposes, they could never hope to eliminate it. Washington was unwilling to run the risk of jeopardizing the security of a country that had, by the end of the war, become an important symbol of Free World solidarity. President Dwight D. Eisenhower made this point explicitly during one high-level discussion of military assistance to South Korea when he argued that the country was "psychologically and politically of such importance that to lose it would run the risk of the loss of our entire position in the Far East."[60] Although the cost-conscious Eisenhower administration wished it could consider reductions in military aid to South Korea, it feared that a decrease in funding would lead to the country's collapse and absorption by the Communist North. And as long as U.S. aid supported a massive South Korean military establishment, it was virtually impossible to ensure that the regime would use no portion of it for political purposes. The United States thus had no choice but to foot the bill for country's security even if doing so actually hindered the cause of democracy. American policymakers hoped that they could at least persuade South Korea to contribute more to the cost of its own defense by stimulating economic development after the Korean War ended. But here too, the Rhee regime limited the effectiveness of U.S. efforts.

Economic Rehabilitation and Development

The need for rehabilitation and development programs in South Korea was desperate throughout the decade and a half after World War II. Even before the Korean War erupted, the country was plagued by crippling economic problems. The sudden dissolution of the ROK's close economic relationships with North Korea and Japan produced a myriad of hardships. Throughout the colonial period northern Korea, southern Korea, and Japan had functioned as a tightly knit economic unit. The more industrialized northern half of Korea supplied minerals and fertilizer to the agricultural southern half, whose surpluses were sent elsewhere in the Japanese empire. Moreover, Korean industry had become dependent on its links with imperial Japan for capital goods and certain stages in the production of consumer goods. Agricultural and industrial production declined precipitously in both halves of the Korean peninsula after World War II.[61]

Even the wrenching economic dislocation that plagued South Korea after World War II, however, paled in comparison to the poverty and desperation that prevailed there immediately after the Korean War. Total property damage from the war in the ROK was estimated at more than $3 billion. Three years of fighting had annihilated 900 industrial plants, reduced the textile industry by one-third, and wiped out more than half of the country's freight cars, trucks, and locomotives. Its sawmills, papermills, metal plants, and small industries had almost disappeared. The war had destroyed 600,000 homes and rendered thousands of others uninhabitable. In all, five million South Koreans—roughly a quarter of the country's population—had been forced to leave their homes.[62] Finally, the country's weakened industrial base and shattered agricultural economy produced severe shortages of both jobs and food for an expanding population.

Washington worried about the threat that such economic devastation posed to stability. Seeking to ameliorate these conditions, the United States funded extensive economic assistance programs for South Korea. These programs supplied hundreds of millions of dollars, as well as prominent development planners to manage the money. The task of these experts was to restructure the South Korean economy so that it could achieve long-term self sufficiency. Rhee, however, saw American aid as a political tool that could reward his allies and strengthen his regime rather than as a means for stimulating economic growth. Despite bitter American protests Rhee used the U.S. funds to fashion a political economy that served his own purposes rather than those of the United States or, for that matter, the South Korean people.

Before the Korean War, American economic assistance to South Korea was substantial but it generally attempted to plug holes in a sinking economic ship rather than chart the course for economic development. Between 1945 and 1948 USAMGIK administered $301 million from the Government Aid and Relief in Occupied Areas (GARIOA) program. But the money went toward relieving shortages in food, clothing, and other basic goods rather than toward long-term capital investments that could stimulate growth.[63] After South Korea attained statehood in 1948, some American officials wanted to create more comprehensive development plans for the country. In the same year the United States sent an Economic Cooperation Administration (ECA) mission to the ROK. This organization oversaw the large-scale economic reconstruction programs that were being carried out in Europe under the Marshall Plan and in other parts of the world after World War II. Arthur Bunce, who had served as an adviser to the American occupation, led the ECA mission. But the Truman administration had difficulty convincing an increasingly parsimonious Congress to support Bunce's plan. Although the ECA initially proposed an ambitious, multiyear program totaling $410 million, South Korea saw little of this money. Congress approved only $50 million of the $180 million the ECA requested for fiscal year 1950.[64]

Congress loosened its purse strings in the wake of the Korean War. The plight of the Korean people during the conflict had received a great deal of attention from the media and spurred the Eisenhower administration to make South Korea one of its top priorities for foreign aid. Appropriations for South Korea generally ranged between $200 and $300 million annually during Eisenhower's presidency. The United States initially vested responsibility for administering this aid in the commander in chief of the UN Command. The UN Command created a new Office of the Economic Coordinator (OEC) and appointed C. Tyler Wood, an ECA official, as its chief. Wood presided over what was the largest American economic mission in the world at the time. The OEC consisted of seven program offices that employed as many as 377 Americans and covered fields such as "Economic and Financial Policy" and "Program Planning."[65] The office included numerous technical experts who not only decided how to administer U.S. aid but also advised the South Korean government on how to use that assistance more effectively.

American development experts who worked in South Korea during the late 1940s and 1950s grounded their programs loosely in theories of "balanced growth" that had gained prominence after World War II. At the time, prominent economists argued that the "vicious circles" of poverty that prevailed in underdeveloped countries could be broken by planned, synchronized investment across several sectors of the economy.[66] Two widely circulated economic recovery plans for South Korea published at the end of the war called for the use of this strategy. In 1952 the Eisenhower administration appointed Henry Tasca as special representative for Korean economic affairs, and one year later Tasca issued a report on "Strengthening the Korean Economy." Tasca proposed "an integrated plan" for simultaneous investment in agriculture, mining, industry transportation, and power.[67] In 1954 Robert R. Nathan Associates, an American consulting firm, submitted a program for Korean economic reconstruction to the United Nations Korean Reconstruction Agency (UNKRA) with similar recommendations. The Nathan Report argued that "all sectors of the economy—including over-all levels of production, consumption and investment—should move ahead in orderly balance."[68]

Central to both the Tasca and Nathan reports, as well as to the U.S. aid policy toward South Korea in general, was increasing the country's agricultural production and mining output. American policymakers wanted the Koreans to restrain domestic consumption of these commodities and export the surplus abroad, especially to Japan. They argued that export earnings could then finance imports of machines, equipment, and other goods that would in turn help expand production. The Tasca Report concluded that South Korea would have to "root out irrational, emotional reactions which now hamper the reestablishment of . . . trade with Japan" and reintroduce "the prewar pattern of export of fine grains and import for consumption of coarse grains."[69] Along similar lines, the Nathan Report asserted that "an agricultural production policy must be combined with a shift in consumption habits to yield an export surplus of rice."[70] The OEC attempted to act on these recommendations by importing fertilizer to boost agricultural production, encouraging the ROK government to modify its exchange rate to create a climate more favorable to exports and designing stabilization programs to promote investment.

But while this strategy looked good on paper, putting it into effect would be almost impossible. Rhee vehemently opposed America's "balanced" growth approach, which he viewed as an effort to benefit Japan at South Korea's expense. Throughout his presidency, he obstructed its implementation by undermining U.S. assistance programs and diverting aid funds to his own purposes.

The agricultural relief programs were among the first to fall victim to Rhee's obstinate scheming. His regime deliberately subverted U.S. fertilizer distribution programs, keeping agricultural productivity below the levels it had reached during the Japanese colonial period. In the 1950s the United

Security over Democracy

States supplied South Korea with as much as $45 million worth of fertilizer annually to make its nutrient-poor soil more productive. But, according to reports received by the American embassy, the government and private merchants covertly manipulated this supply at the farmers' expense. The regime allowed fertilizer provided by the United States to be moved from government warehouses to merchants' stores, where it could be sold at a higher price. The government then restricted its own sale of fertilizer, forcing farmers to purchase it from merchants. Farmers who waited to buy government supplies at lower prices often received the fertilizer too late for use on intended crops.[71]

Americans suspected that South Korean officials obtained illicit rewards from merchants who benefited from their policies. Edwin Cronk, the economic counselor to the U.S. embassy in South Korea between 1956 and 1960, recalled that the Agency for International Development was unable to ensure that fertilizer and other goods supplied to the ROK were used properly because "the whole system was pretty rotten." According to Cronk, "the politicians and bureaucrats had their hand in the till" while "the poor people like the farmers didn't have political clout and they probably continued to end up being short-changed."[72] Ultimately, Rhee's agricultural policies led to food deficits rather than surpluses. South Korea could not export grains to Japan but instead needed as much as one million metric tons of grain annually from the United States.[73]

Even if more surplus grains had been available for export, Rhee's monetary policies would have made doing so difficult and unprofitable. Between 1953 and 1960 he resisted constant American pressure to devalue the South Korean currency, the won. He pegged the exchange rate at 500 won to the dollar despite American claims that the real value of the dollar was as much as twice that.[74] According to Edwin Cronk, this exchange rate made "impossible exporting anything without a loss" because exporters "wouldn't end up with enough to pay for raw materials or labor." On the other hand, Cronk explained, if "you were one of the lucky ones to get an export permit which was of course issued by the government you were an instant millionaire!"[75] Under this system, the government could issue import licenses to political allies who would repay the regime with gifts and other favors. Rhee's policies completely frustrated American plans to promote exports. During the three years after the war exports stagnated, totaling only $25 million in 1956, or one-third of the amount projected by the Tasca Report. In the same period, imports increased from $199.7 million to $389 million, creating an enormous trade deficit.[76]

Rhee further hampered export growth by petulantly refusing to establish official diplomatic relations with Japan, the country that Washington considered the ROK's most likely trade partner. The Americans pressed hard for a restoration of commerce between the two countries not only to boost South Korea's exports but also to find markets for Japan's expanding industries. But reestablishing relations with Japan was an explosive issue in Korea, where Japanese colonialism had left a legacy of deep animosity. It was also an issue where Rhee's policies were a fairly accurate reflection of popular sentiment. Whenever U.S. officials urged his government to seek a reconciliation with Japan, Rhee always had an abundance of excuses for why it would be impossible—ranging from fears of renewed Japanese domination to Japan's disloyalty to the Free World. On several occasions Rhee personally wrote to President Eisenhower to explain his position. In one letter, he complained that American efforts to revive Japan's economy by aiding South Korea would have the "immediate effect of once more placing our economy at the mercy of the Japanese."[77] In another, Rhee wondered how "any thinking person" could believe that "Japan will be a reliable friend" since it was "already lining up with the Soviets, Red China and North Korea."[78] Partially by turning the United States's own Cold War logic against it, Rhee managed to resist American pressure on this issue throughout his presidency.

With few export earnings or other sources of revenue to support investment in development projects, South Korea was forced to rely almost entirely on the United States to furnish the resources for them. But the regime undercut American efforts to promote such projects by rejecting suggestions that it curb inflation and stabilize the economy. In the postwar period the Rhee government's expenditures constantly exceeded its revenues, partially because of the amount of money poured into security forces such as the Korean National Police. When the government printed more currency to cover its expenditures, the cost of basic commodities often skyrocketed. Before 1957, when the Eisenhower administration finally compelled South Korea to agree to a stabilization program, the United States was forced to concentrate two-thirds of its aid resources on "non-project" assistance, meaning commodities that could lower inflation. Fewer funds were available for what the OEC called "project assistance," which included the construction of power plants, bridges, roads, and other infrastructure improvements that could stimulate long-term development.[79]

American aid to South Korea during the fifties was ample enough that, despite the limitations created by Rhee's policies, some development projects could still be completed. Many of these projects did improve living conditions in South Korea for both the short and long term. During the five years after the Korean War, the OEC funded the construction of three new power plants and paid for the rehabilitation of several older ones. Power generation grew by nearly 80 percent as a result. The OEC also implemented transportation and public works programs that built hundreds of bridges and contributed to improvements in the country's system of railroads and public highways.[80]

Not all of the OEC's development projects were sterling successes, however. Rhee's demands sometimes had to be taken into account in decision making for specific ventures, and the president was far more political than practical when it came to South Korean development. Rhee first and foremost sought funds for projects that provided symbols of his regime's progress. This meant support for expensive industrial sites and highways that employed the newest technologies even if they would not have an immediate impact on living standards. Only months after the Korean War, members of the U.S. House of Representatives who visited Seoul worried that Rhee's "insistence on building memorials to his administration," rather than attending to basic needs, would impede the process of economic reconstruction. According to one American lawmaker, Rhee wanted to span the country with a four-lane superhighway and had requested that the world's largest radio transmitter be built in Seoul. Members of Congress feared that some of Rhee's demands would have to be accommodated because South Korea was "a sovereign state and an ally."[81]

In at least some instances, American aid officials did acquiesce to Rhee's plans even though it went against their better judgment. They made one of their worst decisions in 1954, when they agreed to his request for the construction of a urea fertilizer plant in Ch'ungju. Dennis Fitzgerald, who served as deputy director of the International Cooperation Administration (ICA), recalled that urea was a new kind of fertilizer involving a complicated manufacturing process that South Koreans had virtually no experience with. He recommended that, because Korean farmers had been "using ammonium sulfate since they started using fertilizer," an ammonium sulfate plant be built instead. But his advice went unheeded. According to Fitzgerald, "We built them a urea plant which was a mess, just terrible. It cost I don't know how much more, several times more to build than the estimates, and it wasn't built right. . . . There weren't any Koreans who knew how to run it. . . . We finally hired an American company that had built and run an urea plant in the United States to go over there, I believe it was for two years. That cost another pretty penny."[82]

The Ch'ungju plant did not begin to operate at full capacity until 1963, long after Rhee had been overthrown. Ironically, some officials in Park Chung Hee's government blamed the United States for the debacle. O Wŏnch'ŏl who, as chairman of the Commerce Ministry's Chemicals Department, took charge of plant operations on the South Korean side, wrote that Koreans had believed the promises made by the American firm appointed to build the plant "like a kindergarten child believes absolutely everything that his mother says." Rather than hope, O contended, the delays and failures that occurred during construction had given "the entire Korean people an unbearable sense of frustration."[83]

By the mid-1950s, the harmful effects of Rhee's approach to economic development were obvious to U.S. officials. A 1955 assessment of the South Korean economy excoriated the regime's policies. It charged that "inadequate fiscal and credit policies—combined with unwise and politically motivated controls on foreign trade, domestic business and foreign investment have produced disastrous inflation, stifled initiative, disrupted normal price relationships, prevented capital formation and so paralyzed the productive process in general that massive U.S. aid is producing little net progress in the economy."[84]

Rhee continued to pursue such policies because, although they stunted economic development, they strengthened the power of his regime. The economic system fashioned by Rhee kept South Korea dependent on American aid, but it also kept South Korean entrepreneurs dependent on the state. In a relatively closed economic system, he could essentially buy the loyalty of capitalists by dispensing import licenses, U.S. aid goods, and other resources that the state monopolized. Many now world renowned South Korean economic conglomerates (chaebŏl) owe their origins to Rhee's patronage policies. Perhaps the most prominent of these is Samsung, whose founder, Yi Pyŏngch'ŏl, got his start refining sugar that the state acquired for him through American aid programs. The Rhee regime also revived the business career of Pak Hŭngsik, who had amassed a fortune through collaboration with the Japanese colonial government. Rhee's government helped Pak acquire a Japanese spinning factory and a UN loan of $850,000 for the purchase of equipment. In return for the state's largesse, these entrepreneurs made sizable donations to Rhee's Liberal Party, enabling the regime to continue to dominate its opponents.[85]

U.S. officials were by no means unaware of the way that Rhee was blatantly misusing the support of American taxpayers. They were often appalled by the corruption and inefficiency that they witnessed. At the same time, the United States was initially hesitant about forcing Rhee to adopt sounder policies. State Department officials believed that American interests and credibility were so intertwined with the fate of the Rhee regime that taking action to discipline Rhee would jeopardize America's strategic position in Northeast Asia. Although U.S. officials working in South Korea often advocated making assistance to Rhee less unconditional, their superiors in Washington seldom listened to them. When the American ambassador to South Korea, William Lacy, wrote to the State Department proposing that the United States administer a sort of "shock treatment" to the Rhee regime that would make it more amenable to the OEC's advice, he was rebuffed. The Eisenhower State Department doubted the effectiveness of such a course of action, explaining:

> We understand and appreciate frustrations which arise from dealing with complexities of the Korean situation with added difficulty of President Rhee's fixed ideas about exchange rate but there is no simple way [to] cut through all the problems which arise in dealing with another sovereign country. This is especially true of ROK which is on [the] frontline in [the] Far East and where our position is vital to our general strategic and security interests. . . . There is no way in which we can punish ROK without also injuring larger U.S. and Free World objectives in the area.[86]

The administration's unwillingness to pressure Rhee to modify his behavior only added to the frustration of U.S. economic advisers in South Korea. Edwin Cronk complained: "We faced a hopeless situation; the misallocated exchange rate became a given; we got so we didn't dwell on it because we were just beating our heads against the wall." The issue was "never forcefully presented" because Rhee himself "was viewed in Washington in a sense as a symbol of a democratic South Korea even though he wasn't very democratic."[87]

However Rhee was viewed in Washington, within five or six years after the Korean War ended, it was clear to Americans that economic and political progress would be difficult if not impossible under his regime. Although South Korea was eking out modest 3 or 4 percent economic growth rates by the late fifties, this was slower than the rate being obtained in the Communist North and far below the expectations of U.S. officials who had poured hundreds of millions of dollars of aid into the country. By 1960, though the threat of Communist aggression had subsided somewhat, most South Koreans were neither significantly more prosperous nor freer than when their state was first created.

America's alliance of convenience with Syngman Rhee helped build and sustain an anti-Communist state on the southern half of the Korean peninsula. But it did so at an enormous cost. Americans sacrificed not only their lives and resources but also their ideals to launch the process of nation building in South Korea. The U.S. alliance with Rhee enabled a type of state building that mocked U.S. claims of promoting democracy and preserving the Free World. American tolerance for the regime's excesses was not irrevocable, however. By the late 1950s U.S. policymakers were becoming increasingly insistent that Rhee modify his policies. Yet before they could be fully comfortable with the idea of replacing Rhee, credible alternatives to his regime had to be developed. Even while supporting Rhee's government, they were building new institutions that could provide such alternatives.

By the end of the Korean War, Syngman Rhee had trapped the United States into supporting his government despite its blatant disregard for U.S. economic and political objectives. But American policymakers did not intend that South Korea be governed by such a regime perpetually. They sought to use their vast influence over South Korean society to make its future more democratic. In the years after the war, U.S. officials working on the ground in South Korea attempted to develop groups and institutions that would eventually bring about political change. They focused on rebuilding the country's educational system, professionalizing its media, and improving its civilian bureaucracy. The Americans sought not only to reconstruct or improve these institutions but also to make sure that the Koreans who managed them embraced U.S. ideals.

South Koreans eagerly seized the opportunities provided by the United States to develop indigenous institutions. By the late 1950s they had a new school system that accommodated an increasing proportion of youth even at the highest level, a mass media that published a remarkable variety of journals and newspapers, and a corps of highly trained government servants. The students, journalists, and bureaucrats who populated these civil institutions—far from subservient to their American patrons—exhibited a nationalistic determination to forge their own vision of South Korea's future. U.S. assistance also offered them access to global currents of political, economic, and social thought. As new elites gained a greater understanding of foreign economic and political models, they came to harbor ambitions for a wealthier and freer nation. American efforts to reinvigorate South Korean society were intended to deepen U.S. hegemony to be sure, but they fostered a demand for change that would eventually shake the country out of its economic and political inertia.

Rebuilding the Educational System

Americans believed that reforming South Korea's system of education was critical to democratization. No other institution so directly influenced future generations. By providing greater educational opportunities and revising the school curriculum, U.S. officials aimed to instill in young South Koreans a sense of national responsibility and prepare them for life in a democratic society. Ambitious programs supported by extensive funding were designed to rapidly increase the number of schools at all levels while introducing new teaching methods.

American efforts to transform Korea's educational system began modestly during the U.S. occupation. Schooling had expanded under Japanese colonialism but not quickly enough to keep pace with the surging demand, especially at the higher levels.[1] Americans were particularly concerned about the cultural and psychological impact of colonialism on Korean instructors. Horace H. Underwood, an American missionary who had lived on the peninsula for several decades and advised the U.S. Military Government in Korea (USAMGIK), reported that Korean teachers had been "taught and drilled in Japanese methods of authoritarian education." As a result, he observed, they had "no conception of modern education as we know it and few ideas beyond the lecture system."[2] Americans and Koreans agreed on the urgency of increasing educational opportunities for all South Koreans and expunging Japanese influence over their schools.

Working together, American educational advisers and Korean administrators looked for ways to achieve these objectives. Experts in the USAMGIK met regularly with the Korean Committee on Education, an advisory group composed of prominent Koreans in the field, to draw up a blueprint for reforming the school system. The committee included Koreans who had received training in the United States through the assistance of American missionaries and were well-versed in American teaching techniques.[3] The U.S. Military Government also appointed a special adviser to take charge of the Bureau of Education and set up new departments that would be responsible for revising the general curriculum.[4] In 1948 formal control of South Korean schools was turned over to the ROK government, but a contingent of American advisers remained, enabling the United States to continue to make its influence felt on education.

The USAMGIK helped to initiate a dramatic expansion of the South Korean school system. During the three-year occupation, the proportion of students attending primary schools increased from under 40 percent to more than 70 percent. The number of secondary schools climbed from 52 to over 250, while institutions of higher education grew from 19 to 29.[5] In January 1946 American advisers launched the first of many teacher training programs, establishing a training center where Korean educators could observe American instructional methods firsthand. Although this program was modest compared to those introduced after 1953, it did produce a coterie of enthusiastic participants. According to one report, 340 Koreans graduated in the center's first class.[6]

The massive destruction of schools and classrooms wrought by the Korean War necessitated much more extensive educational assistance programs. The United Nations Korean Reconstruction Agency (UNKRA), created in 1951 to rebuild war-torn South Korea, played a major role in furnishing and directing this assistance. Recognizing that schools lacked even the most basic necessities such as classrooms and books, UNKRA began by funding classroom reconstruction. Between 1952 and 1956 it purchased enormous quantities of cement, lumber, and other materials to restore damaged schools. Through the combined efforts of UNKRA and the United Nations (UN) Command in Korea, almost 9,000 classrooms were built or repaired in 1952 and roughly 3,000 more were reconstructed annually between 1953 and 1955.[7] The American-Korean Foundation (AKF), a private U.S. organization headed by Milton Eisenhower, the president's brother, supplemented this work by donating money to particularly needy schools.[8]

American assistance agencies did not stop at the construction of new facilities. Some programs literally put supplies into the hands of needy children. In 1953 the AKF sponsored a "Korea Train" that toured cities throughout the United States. In each city, thousands of American students loaded the train with boxes of school supplies for Korean youngsters. The foundation planned to have six hundred carloads of goods filled by millions of students across America.[9] Another urgent need of South Korean schools was new textbooks. To remedy shortages, the UNKRA funded the construction of a new printing plant in Seoul that was capable of printing 30 million books per year, an amount judged sufficient to meet the requirements of all South Korean elementary schools.[10]

Other American agencies supported the reconstruction of South Korea's colleges and universities. Elite universities such as Seoul National University (SNU), Yonsei University, and Ewha Women's University were especially successful in appealing to the United States for aid. SNU, the nation's most prestigious public university, signed a three-way agreement with the International Cooperation Administration (ICA) and the University of Minnesota. The contract not only provided SNU with desperately needed funds for the reconstruction of its Colleges of Agriculture, Engineering, and Medicine but also dispatched technical experts from the University of Minnesota to assist in setting up new facilities.[11] Leading private universities, like Yonsei and Ewha, which had been founded by American missionaries in the late nineteenth century, used their long-standing ties to Christian denominations to acquire financial support after the war. Both Yonsei and Ewha sent representatives to the United States to collect funds for rebuilding from American churches. Ewha received additional support from the Asia Foundation and the AKF.[12]

These diverse forms of assistance produced a dramatic expansion of educational opportunities within a remarkably short time. By 1960, the number of students attending school at all levels had increased well beyond even prewar levels. Primary school attendance surged from 2.4 million pupils in 1948 to nearly 3.7 million by 1961. Between 1948 and 1958 the number of middle-school students jumped from 280,000 to 440,000, while the population at liberal arts high schools swelled from 59,421 to 275,612. During the same period the number of college and university students grew from under 35,000 to 140,000.[13] These increases were partially a result of the demographic boom after the Korean War, but they would have been impossible without the thousands of new schools and classrooms constructed through UN and U.S. support.

As the number of students at all levels ballooned, the UNKRA and other relief agencies focused on what the schools should teach. By 1952—when the war was still raging—the reconstruction agency was already devising far-reaching strategies for revising South Korea's educational curriculum. In the summer of 1952 the UNKRA dispatched an international team of experts to survey conditions in the country and formulate a five-year program to rebuild and reorganize its school system. Its findings appeared in a lengthy report entitled "Rebuilding Education in the Republic of Korea," which laid out in unsparing detail the perceived problems of the Korean system and the changes that needed to be made.

The UNKRA report attributed the weaknesses of the "method and content of education" to the country's legacy of colonialism and its traditional culture. It argued that the "Japanese regime in Korea both taught the Koreans undemocratic ways of education and cut them off from opportunities to learn of the progress of education in other countries." By imposing their harsh system of military discipline on administrators, teachers, and children, the Japanese had implanted in the Korean culture "a whole system of human relations antithetical to mutual respect and regard." But the Japanese alone could not be blamed for all of the problems plaguing educational development in South Korea. Indeed, the report asserted, the system imposed by the Japanese had represented "little change from the old traditional Korean way of Chinese origin, in which education was confined to classical learning."[14] The UNKRA team hoped to convince South Korea's schools and teachers to break free from the inhibiting grip of the past so they could offer a modern democratic education—an ambitious task.

According to the UNKRA team, South Korea's educational curriculum in particular needed drastic change. For instance, elementary schoolchildren were acquiring only "isolated items of knowledge without coherence and devoid of implication in their lives." Instead, it argued, students needed to gain "knowledges, skills, competencies and attitudes" and use them "in the pursuit of individual and group goals and in the solution of problems that are real to the learners."[15] Such improvements in the curriculum had to be accompanied by changes in existing teaching methods, which did "not show understanding of the learning process." Korean teachers were using rote memorization and "concert repetition of correct answers" rather than making use of "procedures involving understanding, reflective thinking, application and creative expression."[16]

The UNKRA team was convinced that the very future of South Korean democracy hinged on correcting the defects of the country's educational system. It argued that schools must become laboratories where students learned the obligations of participatory democracy, for "the success of a democratic society depends to a large extent upon the harmonious and cooperative participation of the individuals composing it." Its citizens had to acquire traits such as tolerance, open-mindedness, and a sense of responsibility. "In order to prepare pupils for this kind of democratic participation," the report emphasized, "experience of that type must be provided in school."[17]

Seeking to ensure that schools provided the right kind of experience, the UNKRA resumed the teacher training initiated by the USAMGIK with a new vigor. UNKRA specialists visited "normal schools," which prepared future teachers. They incorporated workshops, conferences, and short courses into an ambitious in-service training program whose primary objective was to familiarize students "with the necessities of the primary school curriculum, from the point of view of life needs."[18] By requiring all participants to engage in "one or more aspects of organized community life, such as literacy work with adults, programs of health improvement, recreation, institutional rehabilitation and the like," the UNKRA team aimed to fashion teachers who embodied the ideal of communal responsibility and would transmit it to their students.[19]

When the UNKRA began phasing out its activities in 1956, the ICA, the United States's central foreign assistance agency, took over and expanded

the teacher training programs. The ICA negotiated a contract with Vander-
bilt University's George Peabody College for Teachers under which college
faculty traveled to South Korea to assist the Ministry of Education. Members of the Peabody mission often shared the UNKRA team's views of the
country's needs and problems. The program's director reported that Korean
teachers lacked "an understanding of the important aspects of community
life, a clear concept of the emerging ideals of Korean democracy, and an
understanding of the social changes which are being brought about as the
society moves from a largely agrarian society toward a modern industrially
oriented society."[20]

To correct these perceived deficiencies, the Peabody mission set up demonstration programs at normal schools in every province. The "lecture,
assign, recite, test procedure," which American specialists regarded as lega-
cies of Korea's stagnant Confucian past, were to be exchanged for "a more
modern pattern of techniques" that encompassed "principles of learning
based on research, pupil involvement," and "problem solving."[21] The Peabody team worked with the Ministry of Education to design a five-year
program of workshops and conferences for South Korean teachers. Through
translators, professors from Peabody explained the newest teaching techniques and methods for using local resources in the classroom to several
thousand participants.[22] Educators who showed the most promise were
rewarded with the opportunity to take year-long courses at Peabody College
in Nashville, Tennessee. Between 1957 and 1962 roughly twenty South Koreans, including normal school teachers and professors of education, studied at
Peabody each year.[23]

Although the objectives of these assistance programs were clear, their
impact on South Korean educators was somewhat ambiguous. A significant
number of teachers appreciated the opportunity to receive instruction from
Americans and took what they learned seriously. Korean education specialists explained the need to embrace or adapt new teaching philosophies with
great conviction in periodicals such as *Sae Kyoyuk* (The New Education) and
Kyoyuk Munhwa (Educational Culture). Articles demanding reform regularly appeared in these journals. A typical article in *Kyoyuk Munhwa*, entitled
"My Reflections on the Purpose of Education," by Hŏ Hyŏn, a middle-
school teacher, dismissed the Confucian philosophy of education that had
prevailed in Korea during previous centuries for "taking no account of
individual experience." Instead, Hŏ called for an educational system that
could spur national development. "The center of our national reconstruction movement," he contended, "is education." The country would have to

open itself to scientific information that had been "discovered and experienced throughout the world." To introduce these scientific principles to their society, the people would need freedom. Like members of American educational teams, Hŏ concluded that, to ensure such liberty, South Korea's "educational institutions would have to become social laboratories."[24]

But others were not as certain that American concepts could be applied to indigenous circumstances. Sŏng Naeun, who served as a translator for American educational teams, claimed that U.S. programs failed to create a national dialogue about "the impoverished realities of our nation and our education system." To the contrary, South Korean educators had attended lectures that emphasized only "capitalism and social utilitarianism." Sŏng likened this to the way that "White Americans had refused to coexist with Native Americans and forced them to adjust to the capitalist system."[25] Americans also encountered resistance to their agenda from the conservative Korean educators whom Rhee appointed to key posts in the Department of Education. These conservatives argued that the rapid influx of American liberal values was undermining discipline and called for a system that would give teachers greater authority.[26]

Americans were sometimes disappointed with the degree of change they observed in South Korean schools. When Marion Edman, a professor of education at Wayne State University, traveled to Korea on a Fulbright grant in 1961 to study the attitudes of South Korean educators, she reached somewhat sobering conclusions. Teachers in South Korea, she argued, gave "low priority" to "the teaching of the skills of individual and group thinking." Edman also found that they continued to lean "heavily on the textbook and the curriculum guides that the Ministry of Education provides" and doubted their "own ability to construct the curriculum."[27] It is possible that South Korean teachers made a genuine effort to change, which Americans, who were accustomed to a very different educational culture, simply could not recognize. At the same time, given the Rhee regime's resistance to reform and the limited experience of American educational teams in working with Koreans, it is also likely that U.S. reports noting continuity rather than change in teaching methods had grains of truth to them.

Whereas Americans had difficulty convincing South Korean educators to change their teaching methods, they found it much easier to influence the ideological content of what was taught. UNKRA teams worked with the Ministry of Education to revise textbooks so they emphasized anti-Communism and democracy.[28] Many new texts, especially those in social studies and the humanities, encouraged students to emulate American

Hundreds of schools, like the one pictured here, were constructed or rebuilt in South Korea as part of America's postwar reconstruction efforts. (U.S. Army Collections, Dwight D. Eisenhower Library)

models of patriotism and self-sacrifice. History books regularly introduced revered figures in the development of American democracy such as George Washington, Patrick Henry, and Abraham Lincoln. They also highlighted American generosity toward Korea and the rest of the world. One new social studies textbook at the elementary school level explained that "the United States takes money from its own tax payers and spends huge sums on foreign assistance. This is to improve the lives of peoples of other countries and to block the spread of Communism." It even included a picture of Uncle Sam dumping bags of money on prospering South Korean farmers and workers.[29] Even if South Korean students were not educated by means of the most cutting-edge techniques, they certainly read about democracy in their textbooks.

The ultimate impact of the United States on South Korean education was far broader than what could be learned from textbooks and in classrooms. American assistance worked in tandem with the high priority that Koreans had long assigned to formal learning to enable a generation of young people to attend school, become literate, and gain a better understanding of the political and economic possibilities available to their nation. Education fostered a new outlook that was most evident among the growing ranks of university students. By the late 1950s this elite tier of youth, more than almost any other group in South Korean society, understood political liberty and was willing to challenge authority. Its increasingly defiant attitude toward the government was a product of the new opportunities that had been opened to students, the liberated atmosphere that prevailed at institutions of higher learning, and a more enduring ideal in Korean culture that placed the responsibility for advising and criticizing the government on intellectual elites.

South Koreans who attended universities during the mid- and late 1950s have remembered that a degree of freedom—in contrast to the oppressive atmosphere that hung over the rest of society—could be found in academia. Kim Chŏnggang, who enrolled at SNU in 1958, recalled that the ambience was "open" and "liberal." He observed that "whether in private conversations or public speeches, worldly strains of thought were abundant." Kim, who majored in political science, was exposed to the existentialist and in many ways radical philosophies of figures like Sartre and Heidegger.[30] As students immersed themselves in global crosscurrents of political and economic thought, they gained new avenues for evaluating and critiquing the conditions that prevailed in their own country.

While students tended not to criticize the government in public forums for fear of state-sanctioned reprisals, they formed secret societies or "circles" that discussed and espoused ideas that in the context of 1950s Korea were heretical. One of the most influential circles was the Sinjinhoe, formed by humanities and social science students at SNU during the mid-1950s. According to one of its former leaders, the Sinjinhoe "criticized both the model of Western capitalism centered on the United States and the model of Communism espoused by the Communist camp." Members advocated "social democracy" (sahoe minjujuŭi), which had many similarities to Western European socialism, as a guiding ideology.[31] Although groups like the Sinjinhoe promoted versions of democracy that differed from the American one, they nevertheless shared with the United States an interest in ensuring the long-term democratic development of South Korea and, as their ideas brought them into increasing conflict with the Rhee regime, looked to America for support.

The halting nature of the postwar economic recovery spurred student cynicism toward the South Korean government. The ROK's universities were producing more graduates than its sputtering economy could absorb. In the late 1950s some newspapers estimated that only 10 percent of college graduates found satisfactory employment.[32] As students recognized that the Rhee regime was exacerbating the country's economic travails, they monitored and protested its actions with increasing determination.

Within a decade, South Korea's educational system had metamorphosed from a war-shattered, almost desperate operation into one of the most vibrant sources of opposition to the Rhee government. Awakened to the possibility of change and frustrated with their political leadership, many student organizations had begun seeking support for their views in the society at large. One of their most potent supporters was the ROK news media, which was also blossoming in part because of American aid.

The Media and Print Culture

An educated citizenry was pivotal to American plans for the democratization of South Korea, but it was not in and of itself a guarantee of social change. Literate citizens needed outlets to express and engage new ideas. Americans were well aware of this and tried to ensure that the press would serve as one such outlet. U.S. assistance agencies provided financial support for the growth of newspaper and journal publishing and cultivated selected reporters, essayists, and writers. At the same time, they strove to inculcate South Korean journalists with an understanding of the responsibilities of the media in a free society. They hoped to promote a print culture that advocated change in a direction conducive to U.S. interests and ideals.

Journalists and writers had stood at the forefront of Korean society before. Indeed, historian Andre Schmid has argued that newspapers were the primary location for discussions of national identity at the beginning of the twentieth century.[33] Although the Japanese colonial government limited the growth of publishing in Korea in the 1920s and 1930s, it did award licenses to select newspapers and journals, some of which became increasingly sophisticated.[34] After liberation, a host of new publications rushed to join those that had been active during the colonial period. But the Korean War leveled printing presses and other crucial facilities, decimating the country's capacity to circulate newspapers and magazines. Once the war ended, U.S. and international relief agencies worked on restoring these facilities and providing some South Korean publishers with needed tools and finances.

Americans started by alleviating the most basic problem confronted by indigenous publishers—the severe shortage of paper. The commodity was scarce because the war had devastated production facilities all over the country. During the years immediately after the war U.S. assistance agencies supplied currency for paper imports to struggling publishers.[35] At the same time, the UNKRA attacked the root of the problem by restoring the war-damaged Korea Paper Manufacturing Company in Kunsan. When the plant finally reopened in 1957, it could produce one thousand metric tons of newsprint a month and satisfy one-third of the country's requirements.[36]

But simply supplying paper was not sufficient to help many magazine publishers get off the ground and thrive. Both the U.S. government and private American foundations often provided direct subsidies to South Korean publications so they could continue their operations. In the 1950s Korean periodicals such as *Yŏksa hakpo* (Historical Bulletin), *Chindan hakpo* (Journal of Korean Studies), and *Tongbang hakchi* (Journal of Oriental Studies) received support from the United States Information Service (USIS), the Rockefeller Foundation, and the Harvard-Yenching Institute.[37]

Boosted by American aid and a growing demand for information from an increasingly well-educated population, South Korea's print industry boomed during the years after the Korean War. Existing newspapers drastically increased their circulations. The circulation of the country's leading newspaper, the *Tonga ilbo*, soared from 17,000 in 1953 to 400,000 by 1964. In May 1960 the South Korean government reported that six hundred newspapers and journals were registered for publication.[38] For a state that was still struggling to overcome the ravages of war, South Korea could boast an astonishingly rich and diverse print culture.

Washington wanted the South Korean media not only to flourish, but also to project ideas that would contribute to development and democracy. Almost as soon as it launched its first assistance programs, the United States began looking for ways to shape the content and tone of South Korean journals. Funds from private and public U.S. sources were critical to this task because they could make or break cash-strapped Korean publishers. Throughout the 1950s Americans backed journals and newspapers whose message and objectives seemed consistent with their own.

The USIS began using publication subsidies for such purposes in 1952. The cultural affairs attaché at the U.S. embassy in Seoul determined that the information service should support magazines that "specialized in the academic treatment of current problems in ways which followed the interests of the USIS in Korea." The magazine *Sinsaeng Kongnon* (New Life Public Criticism), which the attaché noted "had been running a series on Korean Rehabilitation and the Role of the UN, discussing the status of the Korean situation in world opinion," was among the first to receive funding from the U.S. government. American officials hoped that coverage of these issues would spread optimism about economic development and the impact of U.S. aid on South Korea. The USIS supported another journal, *Chayu P'yŏngnon* (Free Criticism), as early as 1952 because it had produced a series of articles "showing the relationship between the Korean constitution and the constitutions of other democracies."[39] Although these articles were hardly an indictment of the Rhee regime, they found favor in Washington, which wanted to sponsor some discussion of democracy but not risk destabilizing a delicate wartime situation.

Once the war ended, the United States was much less hesitant about supporting publishers who openly criticized Rhee. Chang Chunha, the founder of the highly regarded intellectual journal *Sasanggye* (World of Thought), was among the best-known publishers receiving American funding. During the colonial period, Chang had aligned himself with conservative Korean nationalists who opposed Japanese imperialism. Although Chang initially refused to participate in Rhee's government, he joined some pro-U.S. organizations during the American occupation and built good relations with U.S. officials. Ideologically, Chang embraced a rare combination of nationalism, opposition to authoritarianism, and admiration for the United States that enabled him to benefit significantly from American generosity. He received USIS funding to cover the operating expenses of *Sasanggye* and was awarded licenses to publish the Korean versions of *Time* and *Life* magazines.[40] By the mid-1950s *Sasanggye* had become the country's leading intellectual journal and an indispensable venue for South Korea's most eminent scholars and fiction writers. Although essays appearing in the journal were not uniformly positive in their evaluations of the United States, they tended to be strongly anti-Communist and supportive of democratization. Ultimately, its publisher exemplified how, in the desperate circumstances that prevailed in postwar South Korea, opportunistic Koreans could benefit from American influence, even while helping to spread it.

Although supporting moderate, pro-democratic journals such as *Sasanggye* provided an avenue for influencing the South Korean media, the strategy had its limits. Newspapers and journals were growing exponentially, and Americans could fund only a fraction of them. In the mid-1950s the United States began cultivating elite journalists whom U.S. officials hoped would broaden American influence over the media at large. A U.S. report on cultural exchange programs argued that "able newspapermen who understand something of America and are friendly to the United States can be exceedingly influential in a country where the printed word carries great weight."[41]

Seeking to influence elite journalists, the State Department in 1955 launched an exchange program that brought leading Korean reporters to the United States. U.S. officials hoped that participants would gain a professional admiration for the American media and a deeper appreciation for the American way of life. The selection process was highly competitive. The USIS chose twelve to fifteen journalists annually from hundreds of applicants. They were generally ambitious young reporters who worked for South Korea's most prestigious newspapers or for foreign press agencies. The Americans reasoned that such a group would be most capable of influencing wider journalistic circles over the long term. Many of the journalists selected either had experience working with American agencies or exhibited an interest in topics whose coverage U.S. officials believed would contribute to economic development or democratization. In 1958 participants included Kim Sanghyŏn, an economic editor at the *Tonghwa sinbo* who covered American economic aid programs and was interested in visiting the Tennessee Valley Authority, and Pak Myŏngjan, a feature writer for the *Segye ilbo* (World News) who had worked as an editor and translator for the USIS during the Korean War.[42] The Americans were confident that young reporters like Kim and Pak could improve the quality of South Korean journalism, help to foster an indigenous demand for development, and encourage pro-American sentiment among their colleagues.

State Department officials realized that some participants had views that were deeply at odds with the politics of the Rhee regime. At times they deliberately chose reporters who seemed likely to challenge government authority. In each of the exchange program's first two years, the United States supported reporters from the *Kyŏnghyang sinmun*, a Catholic newspaper that was often highly critical of the regime. But the USIS considered the paper's dissident reputation a virtue rather than a fault. A U.S. report cited the selection of one *Kyŏnghyang sinmun* reporter, Chŏng Chongsik, for the program as "an excellent one" because he worked for "one of the leading opposition papers."[43] By cultivating journalists critical of the Rhee regime, the United States sought to associate itself with democracy in South Korea even while continuing to aid the country's autocratic government.

The exchange program itself was tailored to immerse South Korean journalists in the culture of the American media. Grantees received a brief orientation at Northwestern University in Evanston, Illinois, before they were assigned to various newspapers for two months to take part in the editing and printing processes. They were then allowed to travel freely around the United States for several weeks. Often they received special opportunities during these tours. Park Sangjin, the chief news editor at the Korean Broadcasting System, was able to broadcast the flight of American astronaut Gordon Cooper live from Cape Kennedy.[44] U.S. officials believed that permitting Korean protégés to not merely observe but actively participate in producing newspapers and radio broadcasts would instill in them a lasting admiration for the principles that purportedly guided American journalists.

As South Korea's print culture became more diversified in the late 1950s, USIS exchange programs included South Koreans from a broader range of publications. A USIS plan in 1959 worried that despite the "strong development of Korean magazines" and the "increase in their influence on social, political, economic and international questions," only a few South Koreans associated with this expanding media had traveled to the United States. The plan established "media leader" grants that sent a small number of magazine publishers to U.S. venues every year with the expectation that the impressions of America that these publishers brought back to South Korea "would find thoughtful expression which would be transmitted to a very wide audience."[45]

The media leader program continued into the sixties, and many of its graduates gained prominence in their field. According to a 1963 State Department report, the "percentage of the most influential Korean journalists who have been sent to the United States under Embassy sponsorship is high, perhaps one-fifth." Many program participants returned to their country "with much zeal for the principles of responsible journalism" and "freedom of the press."[46] A similar report noted that these graduates were "introducing more and more American viewpoints and techniques into Korean newspapers."[47]

Korean writers and publishers, exuberant after their USIS-sponsored travel in the United States, often insisted that American journalistic techniques and standards should be adopted in South Korea. When Kim Chang-chip, the president of the Korean Publishers Association, returned from his tour in 1955, he lavished praise on the American publishing system and urged his colleagues to use it as a model for their own industry. Kim told a group of Korean publishers that the United States was "the most civilized nation on this earth" and that this was a result of "the industry and energy of all of the American people." He later presented to the ROK National Library a collection of two hundred books that he had received as a gift from the Macmillan Company, citing the books as an example of the sophistication of publishing in America.[48]

For some journalists who participated in the USIS program, American influence proved even more enduring. The first group of six South Koreans who attended the exchange program at Northwestern became particularly committed to emulating American journalistic standards. On returning to Seoul, they began holding regular meetings and invited a few other eminent Korean journalists and writers to join them.[49] Im Panghyŏn, an editor for the *Han'guk ilbo* (Korea Daily), was among those invited. Im remembered that "after seeing the advanced state of American journalism and experiencing the training process at an American university, they could not but reach the conclusion that Korean journalism was lagging too far behind." According to Im, this was almost always the main subject of discussion.[50] These meetings served as a springboard for the creation of the Kwanhun Club, named after the district in Seoul where several of its founding members shared a boardinghouse. The club's official goals were to promote a better understanding of the principle of freedom of the press and to encourage the adoption of responsible journalistic principles. Its members planned to achieve these goals first and foremost by educating their colleagues.[51]

The Kwanhun Club swiftly grew in numbers and influence. It aggressively recruited leading journalists and by December 1959 had forty-seven members, nearly all of whom represented South Korea's most respected newspapers and publishers. The club held regular meetings to discuss the role of the media in society and began publishing *Sinmun yŏn'gu* (Newspaper Research), which featured articles on the journalistic profession. American officials and journalists often received invitations to speak at club meetings and typically expounded on a well-known set of themes. John McKnight, the chief of the USIS in Seoul, appeared on several occasions to talk about journalism in the United States, the importance of objective reporting, the meaning of freedom of the press, and other topics. U.S. officials realized the growing importance of the club and attempted to cultivate its members. When important foreign journalists whose reporting defended American foreign policy visited Seoul, USIS officers sometimes held receptions at their homes and invited members of the Kwanhun Club.[52]

American influence was also readily apparent in the pages of the Kwanhun Club's research journal, *Sinmun yŏn'gu*. The first few issues contained articles on familiar subjects like "The Responsibility of Newspapers" and "Freedom of the Press." *Sinmun yŏn'gu* blatantly put forward the American media as a model for South Koreans. Articles praising the American media and training in the field by practitioners who had studied in the United States regularly appeared in the journal. Indeed, its first issue contained a piece on "The Situation of the American Newspaper" that lauded American newspapers for respecting civil liberties and personal privacy.[53]

By the late 1950s, the American-educated journalists who populated the Kwanhun Club had become the ideal practitioners whom South Korean newspapers sought out, hired, and promoted. Knowledge of the English language became an important credential for journalists at leading South Korean newspapers, in part because it was one of the key criteria that the United States used in selecting candidates for its exchange programs. Many Korean newspapers began to recruit reporters through competitive examinations that included an English proficiency test. In 1958 American diplomats were already noting with admiration the English-language proficiency of applicants for the U.S. exchange program.[54] The increasing English-language fluency of South Korea's press corps accelerated and deepened the exchange of ideas between Americans and Korean journalists.

Within a short time, a new generation of South Korean writers and publishers made the ideal of a free press a widely sought-after goal within their country's journalistic community. In 1957 the Korean Publishers Association, which represented a broad cross section of the country's media, explained in its official bulletin that "it is now common sense that without freedom of the press there can be no democracy."[55] But just as many journalists were devoting themselves to the pursuit of a free press, the Rhee regime was starting to worry that it had been too lenient in dealing with its critics in the media. Friction between the government and the press flared over a wide range of issues.

The expansion of the media and the educational system in South Korea produced a liberal intelligentsia that congregated around prominent intellectual journals and by the late 1950s criticized the government with particular ferocity. In *Sasanggye*, these writers regularly vented popular frustrations against both the country's leadership and its dire poverty. An article by Kim P'albong subtitled "What Is to Be Done?," published in the December 1957 issue, captured the widespread dissatisfaction spawned by the regime's corruption and brutality. The author excoriated the political leadership for allowing South Korea to fall into a state of economic poverty and moral turmoil. He charged that "during the last seven or eight years when we have received not only commodities but also money from the United States, nobody has even devised a plan for the needed power output, the required amount of fertilizer or for anything necessary for the national housekeeping." At the same time, "ruthless taxation policies" had made it "impossible for the peasant to live in the village and then forced dealers out of business in the city." The article proceeded to lambaste the political transgressions of the Rhee government. It scathingly criticized "the fraudulent constitutional amendments" that had been passed in 1952 and 1954, "election irregularities," and "the frequent cases of embezzlement in the Public Safety Bureau, Metropolitan Police, and tax offices."[56]

Opposition newspapers in South Korea were, at roughly the same time, becoming even more aggressive in their criticism of Rhee's authoritarianism. The two Catholic newspapers, the *Kyŏnghyang sinmun* and the *Maeil sinbo* (Daily News), were especially attuned to instances of administrative malfeasance. They zealously sought to expose the regime's wrongdoings partially out of a genuine desire for democracy and partially because of sectarian animosity against the Methodist Rhee. These newspapers intensified their attacks after the regime forced the National Assembly to pass a revised National Security Law in December 1958 and ordered the police to suppress subsequent protests. The *Kyŏnghyang sinmun*—by that time the nation's second largest newspaper—published a series of stinging editorials in early 1959. An editorial on 11 January characterized the "inconsistency of the government and the Liberal Party" in responding to the protests as "ridiculous," adding that "one can only sigh for the future of the nation."[57] Worried about the ramifications of allowing such blunt criticism, the Rhee regime ordered the paper to cease publication in April 1959.

The decision to shut down the *Kyŏnghyang sinmun* was only part of a larger campaign of intimidation against an increasingly assertive media. The government claimed that its opponents in the press were aligned with Communists intent on carrying out subversive activities. This served as Rhee's justification for blatantly disregarding the constitution and waging an all-out war against opposition newspapers. The regime allowed the sacking of the *Maeil sinbo* by rightist youth groups associated with the Liberal Party and closed the ROK's largest newspaper, the *Tonga ilbo*, for several months for a typographical error in the name of the South Korean president.[58] Ultimately, however, these efforts at suppression did little to quiet the media.

Rhee's assault on the press put U.S. officials in an awkward position. They were forced to choose between supporting the South Korean government, a key partner in the global struggle against Communism, and adhering to the principle of freedom of the press, which they had worked hard to teach South Korean journalists to appreciate. Although the Americans generally continued to back the regime publicly, they privately attempted to dissuade Rhee from bullying his opponents in the media.

Washington initially hoped that straightforward diplomatic pressure would convince Rhee to reconsider his hard-line stance. In their meetings with the South Koreans, American diplomats often voiced their displeasure about the closing of the *Kyŏnghyang sinmun* as part of a broader effort to discourage the ROK government from violating freedom of the press. When Assistant Secretary of State Walter Robertson met with the South Korean ambassador and minister of foreign affairs in June 1959, he criticized the government's move and urged that it take a more conciliatory approach in responding to its critics. Robertson told the ROK ambassador that closing the paper "embarrasses us" and that the United States "could neither explain nor defend this action." When Korean officials protested that the paper had printed falsehoods designed to subvert the regime, Robertson rebutted that "distortions and false information appear . . . in the press of every democracy" but that "closure of a newspaper is not a way to deal with press abuses."[59] Although U.S. pressure did not persuade the regime to revoke the *Kyŏnghyang sinmun*'s suspension, it did make Rhee aware that his dictatorial tactics were weakening American support for his regime.

Meanwhile, the USIS continued to encourage journalists to defy the regime. In its plan for 1960, the information agency called for the continuation of its exchange programs, which were necessary to "keep at a strong level the fostering of a free democratic and informed Korean press." In addition, it requested funding for a full-time American press specialist to work with the Kwanhun Club and other American-trained reporters in South Korea.[60] Much to the regime's vexation, the USIS also subtly encouraged indigenous newspapers and magazines to make known American distaste for Rhee's campaign against opposition journalists. The agency provided *Sasanggye* with editorials from U.S. newspapers censuring the regime for forcing the National Assembly to revise the National Security Law in December 1958 and for shutting down the *Kyŏnghyang sinmun*.[61]

Such efforts to safeguard the integrity of South Korea's media were at some level self-serving and geared at deepening U.S. influence. But they were more than mere propaganda. In fact, they were instrumental in assisting the media to become one of the most powerful pro-democracy forces in South Korea during the postwar years. As the Rhee regime became increasingly autocratic and inefficient in the late 1950s, the media, with tacit American support, helped galvanize public opinion against it. But while encouraging support for democratic media strengthened dissent against the government, it did not offer an alternative source of political leadership that could govern the country effectively. U.S. policymakers recognized that seeking out and cultivating such leadership needed to be a key priority.

They attempted to do so through programs geared at training, improving, and influencing promising bureaucrats and public officials.

The Bureaucracy and Public Administration

Americans regarded the development of a capable group of bureaucrats as a prerequisite for political and economic progress in South Korea. Stuart MacCorkle, who in 1959 was appointed principal adviser on public administration to the ROK, explained that U.S. "efforts to assist other countries" such as South Korea "to raise their living standards" had continuously faced serious difficulties because their governments were "inadequate" and their leadership was "untrained in the management of modern, large and complicated public enterprises."[62] In South Korea under Syngman Rhee these problems were particularly severe. Many high-level posts in the bureaucracy were filled either by Rhee's political allies or by Koreans who had been lower-level functionaries during the colonial period. Only 29.9 percent of bureau directors in the South Korean government were college graduates.[63] The Americans tried to encourage the emergence of an elite group of highly trained bureaucrats who were dedicated to honest and efficient administration. Such public officials would stand in contrast to Rhee's corrupt administrators and shine as an example for aspiring civil servants.

Despite their generally low estimation of the South Korean government, U.S. officials did identify a small number of bureaucrats who seemed genuinely committed to national development. The Americans believed that this select few could become a potent political force through exposure to American political and economic institutions. They reasoned that after observing the workings of the U.S. government and the efficiency of American industry, South Korean bureaucrats would become more zealous in promoting national development and democratization at home. Americans also recognized that singling out specific officials for education in the United States would ensure their prestige among peers and swifter advancement in the ROK government.

After the Korean War, the United States introduced the Leader Program, which became one of the most direct and long-standing efforts to develop South Korean bureaucrats and political figures. This initiative invited promising government officials to the United States to observe American business and politics. Future South Korean presidents Kim Young Sam and Kim Dae Jung both participated in the program at different points in their careers. During the Rhee era, the Leader Program focused on building relationships with politicians and civilian leaders who could potentially assert themselves against the preponderant power of the central government and its executive branch. In the mid- and late fifties, the State Department invited a combination of assemblymen, local political figures, and business leaders to visit the United States under the program's auspices to study U.S. legislative bodies.

The Leader Program made awarding these grants to members of the National Assembly one of its key priorities. Although Rhee's Liberal Party generally maintained a majority in the assembly, it was the locus of the regime's most strident political opposition. The United States took a special interest in the younger, more dynamic members of the assembly who seemed committed to democratic principles. When the State Department first announced that it would award the grants, American officials noted that the plan "evoked great enthusiasm among National Assemblymen, many of whom are young and of unusual ability."[64] After the program had been in operation for several years, the State Department lobbied vigorously for its continuation and expansion on the grounds that it had "given an increasing body of Korea's legislative leaders, few of whom have had experience in the West, a better understanding of the United States and its policies and a broader perspective in facing legislative problems in Korea."[65]

In 1957 mayors and local political leaders became another major target of the program. Recognizing that since liberation there had been "only a slow relinquishment of authority to local communities" in South Korea, the United States tried to strengthen mayors of medium-sized cities and other local politicians who might eventually become a force for greater local autonomy. The Americans believed in the capacity of their own institutions to transform the mind-set of these politicians. If local political leaders were given the opportunity to personally observe U.S. democratic institutions in action, then "on their return their increased knowledge of the United States, its foreign policy and the way democracy works . . . should enable them to strengthen local government operations in their respective communities." The first group of local leaders to visit the United States under the Leader Program included the mayors of Chŏnju, Mokp'o, and Suwŏn, as well as a provincial assemblyman and a rural county chief. State Department officials considered the members of this group to be "independent politically" and expected them to remain so for the foreseeable future.[66]

The State Department designed an itinerary for the South Koreans that promised to improve their understanding of the functions of local government and leave them with an admiration for the United States. It was recommended that their "observation experience in the United States . . .

include visits to several small American municipalities with sufficient time in each community to gain understanding of all aspects of city government and community life." They should also have "an opportunity to see rural life as well as one or two of America's cities."[67] The Americans were convinced that this program would forge lasting ties between the United States and relatively independent South Korean leaders who were committed to democratic development.

The Leader Program did generate substantial enthusiasm for American political institutions among some participants. When Pak Haejŏng, a member of the opposition Democratic Party who represented North Kyŏngsang Province in the National Assembly, spent three months touring the United States in 1956, he was enthralled by the level of political freedom and economic efficiency that he observed. On returning home, he glowingly summarized his experiences in an article in *Kukhoebo*, the National Assembly's journal. Pak wrote that "the thing that I immediately felt above all was that the United States is a nation of freedom." Pak was also impressed by the 1956 presidential election, which occurred during his visit. He marveled at how "government interference in the election could not be found" and thought this was "enviable when compared to our country." The way that Americans lived made a lasting impression on Pak as well. "One could not but envy" their "cheerful private lives and the businesslike, yet free environment."[68] For relatively young political leaders like Pak, participation in the Leader Program fostered an awareness and even an envy of conditions in the United States that could easily be translated into a desire for socioeconomic change and a frustration with the failures of the Rhee government to produce it.

At the back of many participants' minds was how they could apply what they had learned for the benefit of their own nation. Im Songbon, the chairman of the Taehan Coal Corporation, reflected on this question after he had spent three months in 1956 touring American industrial facilities and interacting with technicians in his field. After returning home, Im expressed enthusiasm for American culture and society in a lengthy narrative of his travels. He believed that "among all civilized nations, there is not any other country which is as well protected by God and bestowed with natural benefits as the United States." But Im's visit not only increased his admiration for America but also stimulated him to think about the problems that confronted South Korea. He wrote that "crossing my mind whenever I made inspection of America's prosperity and development . . . was the question of how to plan the development of our Korean economy." Im explained that "we Korean[s] want our society to be good, to be better, both in material goods and spiritual ways." The road to prosperity in South Korea, he argued, could be found by emulating facets of American life. Im thought that "the most important contributing factor to America's greatness is *Freedom*" and concluded that "securing liberty, and economic and friendly ties between the Republic of Korea and United States of America" would likewise be "important in solidifying the foundation of economic independence."[69] Im later mailed a copy of his travelogue to President Eisenhower's press secretary, James C. Hagerty. Doubtless, his determination to forge a wealthier, more democratic nation with close ties to the United States gratified American officials even as it endorsed ideas that were increasingly at odds with the realities of Rhee's rule.

Private American foundations and think tanks organized additional programs for Korean bureaucrats that were as effective as the Leader Program, if not more so. These foundations shared the official U.S. commitment to train a new tier of highly skilled civil servants who would contribute to South Korean development. Through funding provided by the Ford Foundation, the Economic Development Institute (EDI) in Washington, D.C., had become an important training ground for leading public and private officials from developing countries aligned with the United States. The institute offered a six-month "general course" that drew students from the Free World nations of Asia, Africa, and Latin America. After hearing lectures by American development experts, participants would then discuss the problems confronting their own societies.[70] South Korea was among the many nations that sent its leading technocrats to the EDI during the 1950s.

One of the most prominent South Korean bureaucrats to attend the EDI program was Song Insang. Song had worked in the ROK Ministry of Finance during the Korean War and subsequently become vice president of the Bank of Korea. He was selected to attend the EDI in October 1956. Participation in the program proved an inspiring experience for Song, who recalled in his memoir how he had relished this rare chance to openly discuss approaches to development with leaders from other countries. He remembered studying the economic development plans that were being implemented in countries ranging from India to Brazil, noting that "he learned a lot from this discussion." Equally valuable were the EDI social hours in which Song schmoozed with leaders from other Free World countries. These leisure periods were "a great success" because they enabled participants to "talk openly with nothing to hide about the hardships facing developing countries" and to "discuss the best way of conquering backwardness."[71] When Song returned to South Korea he was appointed minister of reconstruction, a highly influential position. According to Song, many of the lessons he had learned at the EDI continued to influence his actions. In particular, the course gave him a new sense of possibility about Korea's future. It helped him realize that to "revitalize and develop an economy a goal must be fixed[,] and that through making effort and acquiring the consent of the people the goal could be accomplished."[72]

The passion for economic development and the interest in planning that Song acquired at the institute loomed large in his subsequent career. While listening to the luminaries invited to speak at EDI, he had become "firmly determined to try preparing a long-term economic plan upon returning to Korea."[73] As minister of reconstruction, Song was the driving force behind the creation of South Korea's first economic development plan. In 1957 he assembled the Economic Development Committee (Kyŏngje palchŏn wiwŏnhoe) for this purpose. The committee consisted of sixteen leading South Korean technocrats, some of whom had received education or training in the United States, and six American advisers. Through the committee, arrangements were made for a group of economic experts from the University of Oregon to travel to South Korea to assist Korean economic planners. Although collaboration between the Oregon team and South Korean planners was not as productive as originally hoped, the committee did manage to put forward a three-year economic plan in January 1959. The National Assembly did not approve the plan until a few days before the Rhee regime fell in April 1960, and it was therefore never implemented. Nevertheless, Song took pride in the accomplishment, which, he later argued, was a precursor of the more detailed economic plans that followed in the sixties and seventies.[74]

Song's admiration for the United States did not mean that he always agreed with American advisers. In some of the disputes between the Rhee regime and U.S. officials regarding American aid strategies, Song sided with Rhee. Song was highly critical of the plan for South Korean economic reconstruction drafted by Robert R. Nathan Associates and generally did not subscribe to the views of American officials on the issues of inflation and exchange rate reform. Song thought that American aid policy prioritized supporting U.S. security objectives and facilitating the economic resurgence of Japan. He genuinely believed that American advisers placed too much emphasis on agricultural production and not enough on stimulating the growth of South Korean industries. Song argued that this was because, unlike aid to Europe under the Marshall Plan, which was dedicated entirely to economic recovery, U.S. assistance to the ROK was designed in part to support the Mutual Security Agreement and UN troops in Korea. As a result, he contended, American aid programs focused on importing raw materials rather than industrial equipment.[75]

Despite these criticisms, Song was more eager to work with American officials and more willing to acknowledge the flaws of Rhee's policies than most other South Korean bureaucrats. Song took over the Ministry of Reconstruction after conflicts between the U.S. economic coordinator, C. Tyler Wood, and South Korean officials had grown so divisive that American aid funds could not even be disbursed. Song adopted a much more conciliatory approach in dealing with Wood's successor, William E. Warne. During their first meeting, Warne proposed that they "join together to eliminate the obstacles in front of them and swiftly free up and mobilize available funds." Song agreed and explained to his subordinates in the Ministry of Reconstruction that "it was important to create an environment in which American aid funds could be utilized directly or indirectly for Korea's economic reconstruction" and to avoid "opposition for the sake of opposition."[76] Although Song retained the view that South Korea's interests and autonomy needed to be protected from U.S. demands, American aid officials were gratified by his desire for a more constructive relationship.

Song also did much to promote further cooperation between American aid officials and South Korean bureaucrats. Throughout his career he advocated sending his colleagues for study and training in the United States. He hailed the technical training program established by the U.S. Operations Mission (USOM), which bore primary responsibility for administering American financial assistance in South Korea, as the "most successful of all American assistance programs" and proposed legislation to create special positions in the ROK government for its graduates. Moreover, Song worked to facilitate a public dialogue between Americans and South Koreans about the country's economic future. In 1957 he began hosting a weekly radio show, *Economics Talk*, that focused on issues confronting his country's economic recovery. Song often invited American aid officials on his program to explain their vision of economic progress in South Korea.[77] Thus despite his disagreements with U.S. officials, Song continued to cooperate with the United States on critical issues. And although he was a political ally of Syngman Rhee, he tried to stimulate public interest in economic development, which was dangerous to a regime that remained indifferent to increasing national prosperity.

While formal exchange programs provided a key mechanism for influencing Korean officials like Song, American advisers working in South Korea looked for more informal ways to build productive relationships with promising bureaucrats. In some instances, they tried to establish a private dialogue with potential allies in the ROK government who were willing to engage in an earnest discussion of the country's economic problems without the vitriolic accusations and counteraccusations that had always characterized relations with Rhee. Edwin Cronk, the U.S. economic counselor in Seoul, formed the "Thinkers Group" in the American embassy to serve this purpose. The group consisted of Cronk, four Americans working for the U.S. Agency for International Development (USAID) in South Korea, and four young South Korean government officials each from a different agency. All of the Korean officials were proficient in English, had received some education or training in the United States, and had risen swiftly in the ranks of the ROK bureaucracy. According to Cronk, they would "talk about issues, completely off the record" and promised that they "wouldn't report, or take any actions, as a result of these conversations." The purpose of these frank exchanges, Cronk recalled, was "to try to figure out what each of us, respectively, might do about a specific problem, or how [we] envisaged Korea's future." They often discussed officially taboo subjects such as the possibility of raising the exchange rates and the difficulties presented by Rhee on this issue.[78] Naturally, neither the U.S. nor South Korean participants in the Thinkers Group could overcome all of the obstacles created by Rhee's policies. But the South Koreans did leave these meetings with a renewed enthusiasm for development and a willingness to surreptitiously undermine the regime if doing so would benefit the country.

One of the Thinkers Group's regular participants was Yi Kihong (Daniel Lee). Yi had studied English in a Japanese high school during the colonial period and worked as a translator for the U.S. Military Government between 1945 and 1947. His connections with the USAMGIK helped him receive a scholarship in 1948 to study economics at Amherst College. He went on to earn a Master of Arts degree at Columbia University. On returning home, he became chief of the Department of Planning in the Ministry of Reconstruction. Yi was highly critical of the corruption that prevailed in South Korea, and the opportunity to converse with American officials and Korean colleagues who shared his views heightened his determination to push for economic reform. Yi recalled that "strengthened by their trust and cooperation, I managed my affairs in a way that emphasized the concepts of national economic development and the expansion of economic prosperity which were at the time alien to Korean society."[79]

Yi drew on members of the group for advice in driving forward measures to promote development and reduce corruption. He was one of the few South Korean officials whose participation in reconstruction programs Americans genuinely welcomed. During his two years of service in the Ministry of Reconstruction, Yi collaborated with U.S. officials in implementing a variety of projects, including a housing construction program, an urban renewal initiative, and the expansion of irrigation facilities in rural areas. At times, Yi acted boldly to reduce corruption and waste. He was well aware that the Rhee regime had been using American aid funds for political purposes and had frequently vented his frustration with these practices in meetings with U.S. officials. Yi was especially distressed by his government's distribution of raw sugar to allies in the business world who reaped windfall profits by importing the sugar at government-mandated exchange rates and then selling it at much higher prices for domestic consumption. He thought that this practice was wasteful in a poor country. Yi wrote that "for a rich country such as the United States sugar is a mass commodity," but for a "famine stricken" country like South Korea it should have been "an indulgence for only a part of the wealthy class." Yi worked privately with American officials to cut the amount of sugar provided by U.S. programs in half. Although he realized that doing so might hurt the regime's allies in the business sector, he "cared nothing about enterprises benefiting from the allocation of American aid funds." Instead, he was proud of his association with "a few people who rose above corruption and who carried out business with a spirit of impartiality in a dissolute society."[80]

The most eminent member of the Thinkers Group was Yi Hanbin. In 1949 Yi became one of the first South Koreans to participate in an American educational exchange program when he received a scholarship to attend the Harvard Business School. After returning to South Korea, he joined the Bureau of the Budget and swiftly rose through its ranks. By 1958, at the age of thirty-three, he had already become director of the bureau. Yi praised the Thinkers Group for encouraging his commitment to national development and for building solidarity among progressive South Korean bureaucrats. He later wrote that "the members of the group on both sides were free thinkers" and were therefore willing to talk about "not only the economic problems but also the political difficulties plaguing economic development in South Korea." Consequently, "among the four of us on the Korean side[,] there was a sense of thinking about and managing together the difficult tasks that faced our distressed country and during these meetings a close sense of kinship formed between us."[81]

Like his colleagues in the group, Yi became a determined economic reformer and proved willing to work with U.S. officials to implement more reasonable policies. Soon after joining the Budget Bureau, he earned praise from members of a visiting economic task force as "the best informed official in the ROK government."[82] David Kang's study of corruption and development in South Korea asserts that the Budget Bureau became an "island of innovation" in a sea of inefficiency and waste. Yi Hanbin forced the bureau to undertake important reforms, including budget reclassification, performance budgeting, and commercial accounting for state-owned enterprises. Kang's work also notes that Yi's bureau maintained a close relationship with American aid officials and aggressively promoted other young South Korean bureaucrats who had received training in the United States.[83]

By the late 1950s the number of American-trained bureaucrats available to Yi had grown dramatically. Through a variety of programs, the State Department had arranged for a substantial number of South Koreans to study in the United States. Between 1954 and 1967 the U.S. aid mission to South Korea spent over $12 million to cover the tuition and expenses of 2,936 students selected for training in public administration and a variety of other fields deemed necessary for economic development. The vast majority of ROK government officials who participated in these programs received their training before 1960. In the United States they studied economic planning, banking management, treasury accounting, and related fields. The U.S. aid mission also kept track of graduates after they returned to South Korea and attempted to ensure that they were placed in appropriate positions.[84] Participants echoed the enthusiasm for development expressed by Song Insang and other Koreans who had studied in the United States. Kim Yonggap spent one year learning about financial administration at Harvard University through a U.S. government–sponsored program before becoming a section chief in the Ministry of Finance. At Harvard, Kim discussed the difficulties of taxation and infrastructure development with aspiring bureaucrats from other Free World nations. He later reflected that "studying the financial troubles facing newly independent countries and pursuing their solutions" was a "truly meaningful task."[85]

South Korean bureaucrats who participated in these training programs gained a sense of group identity. On returning home they formed associations like the University Club, which sponsored discussions among high-ranking South Korean officials and scholars and American diplomats. Much as the Kwanhun Club was a means for continuing American influence over South Korean journalists, the University Club provided an avenue for continued interactions between Americans and ROK government officials.[86]

In addition to sending talented South Korean bureaucrats to the United States, American officials tried to improve the quality of training available in South Korea so that ultimately the country would be able to educate future generations of civil servants without U.S. supervision. In the late 1950s the American aid mission launched two new programs to strengthen the country's educational institutions in the fields of business and public administration. The first program created a partnership between Seoul National University and the University of Minnesota whose purpose was to establish a graduate school of public administration at SNU. The second arranged for business school faculty from Washington University in St. Louis, Missouri, to help Yonsei University and Korea University improve their schools of management.

SNU's Graduate School of Public Administration (GSPA) was the first of its kind in South Korea. Planning for the school began in 1957, and shortly thereafter the dean of SNU selected eleven faculty members to study for advanced degrees at the University of Minnesota.[87] These and subsequent program participants often returned to SNU with a more critical perspective on their own government and an admiration for the United States. The individual research they performed at the university built and reinforced such viewpoints. Kim Unt'ae, a member of the first group of SNU faculty to take part in the program, wrote a master's thesis on administrative structure and practices that sharply criticized the operations of the ROK government. Kim argued that bureaucratic decision-making processes in South Korea were "too slow" and often based on insufficient evidence. There was a need for "administrative reorganization and more effective organization and methods for coordination and control." He thought that such changes could best be made "by making use of the experience of other countries (particularly the United States of America)." Kim hoped that administrative reform conducted along the lines of what he had learned in the United States would favorably "affect the rate and nature of economic development" in South Korea.[88]

The University of Minnesota also sent several faculty members to Seoul to serve as advisers. These advisers encouraged South Korean faculty and students to participate actively in setting a direction for the school. One American adviser recalled that he saw his objective as creating "an atmosphere of warm friendship where an effective interchange of ideas can take place." South Korean faculty returning from the United States took part in joint discussions of matters such as developing course outlines and materials, improving teaching methods, and preparing research materials to support the school's programs. The first class of 103 students that entered the GSPA in 1959 was also involved in selecting activities and curricula.[89] American advisers were hopeful that fostering this kind of open exchange would prepare aspiring South Korean bureaucrats to govern in a democratic society.

Washington shared a similar optimism about the new schools of management at Yonsei and Korea Universities that the United States funded through its business administration program. The program provided for both the training of Korean professors in the United States and the hands-on assistance of American academicians in South Korea. More than two dozen Korean faculty members received instruction at Washington University in St. Louis, while twelve members of the university's business faculty served as advisers in South Korea. Until the mid-1950s business education in South Korea had a Japanese orientation, which placed heavy emphasis on commercial transactions. The Americans urged that the course content and teaching methods be revised at both universities. Under American guidance, the South Koreans introduced subjects like economics, personnel, accounting, and finance,[90] and they deemphasized lecturing and introduced the case study method. The new curriculum was intended not only to improve the skills of aspiring managers but also to stimulate critical thinking and discourage reliance on authority.

Although business education in South Korea remained somewhat disconnected from the country's corporations and businesses, the program energized many participants and deepened their commitment to change. Yu Sehwan, a professor at Korea University's School of Management, relished the opportunity to attend Washington University. He reflected that studying in the United States had been "a major turning point in his life" and a chance for him "to be born anew as a professor." Yu praised the transformation of business education at his university during the late 1950s and early 1960s. In 1960, he wrote, business education in South Korea had been "so far behind American business management studies that it had been endlessly shameful," but within a few years the first courses in management accounting and economics had been offered and the content of courses in other areas revised.[91] Even if academicians like Yu could not have an immediate impact on the economic climate of South Korea in the 1950s, they added to the ranks of pro-American managerial elites who were intent on combating the economic stagnation and corruption that was so prevalent during the Rhee years. The influence of this group of elites was growing rapidly and inexorably by the late fifties.

An educated South Korean elite determined to break the bonds of stagnation and authoritarianism of the ROK government emerged during the first five years after the Korean War. The country's burgeoning university system teemed with students who were earnestly committed to experiencing the democracy that they studied and were willing to challenge the government when it fell short of their ideals. The rapidly expanding mass media had become devoted to the principles of journalistic integrity and freedom of the press and regularly excoriated the Rhee regime for its failings. Finally, a new tier of reform-minded technocrats was asserting itself within the bureaucracy and, in some instances, taking actions that undermined the regime's agenda. The United States had not single-handedly created this wellspring of discontent but, by providing vital resources to key individuals and institutions, had encouraged it.

Americans hoped that the civil institutions that they helped build in the 1950s would give rise to South Korea's next generation of political leaders. But they did not. South Korea's new democratic elites earnestly sought to gain political power so they could promote socioeconomic change. The problem was that the country's new military elite wanted to do the same thing but in a very different way. And while America's investment in civil institution building in the ROK had been substantial, its commitment to organizing a modern, efficient military establishment, as the next chapter argues, had been even greater. Nevertheless, the civil institutions built during the 1950s would remain an important part of the political landscape. Even during the two decades of military dictatorship that would follow, they contributed to the creation of an informed, educated citizenry—a prerequisite for democracy—while, in some instances, perpetuating democratic ideals so that political liberalization at least remained a possibility.

Before 1945 few Koreans would have predicted that the political leaders who proved most successful at guiding South Korea's emergence as a modern, industrialized nation would come from the the military. The prestige of the military had declined throughout the nineteenth century, and no national armed forces had existed on the peninsula during the three and a half decades of Japanese colonialism. So how did South Korean military elites acquire the power, competence, and will to steer the country through a brutally swift process of industrialization? America's need for a powerful indigenous army to serve as a partner during the Korean War and as an ally once the war ended played the most important role in enabling them to do so.

Between 1946 and 1960 the United States transformed the military of the Republic of Korea (ROK) from a small, disorganized constabulary into the most dominant institution in South Korean society. Americans planned for this force to defend, not govern, the country, but the vast resources they invested in building it and training its officers made military rule a distinct possibility. The South Korean army became a political force not only because it possessed a near-monopoly over the means of coercion, but also because U.S. training programs imbued its elite officers with outlooks and levels of expertise that set them apart from the rest of society. The task of creating an efficient fighting force for the Cold War era meant instructing officers in how to carry out complex technical and logistical operations, skills that South Korea sorely lacked during these years. Moreover, U.S. training programs rigorously indoctrinated military officers with a sense of duty and patriotism.

American training programs helped forge elite officers with a strong sense of public responsibility and ardent faith in their ability to lead. At the same time, these officers were far less enthusiastic in their embrace of American ideals than their counterparts in civilian society. They tended to admire the U.S. military for its efficiency and power but did not necessarily profess a similar admiration for the United States and its political institutions. Many of the new South Korean officers had served in the Japanese army during World War II, and that experience continued to color their outlook. The practices and culture of the ROK military often nourished very undemocratic ways of thinking. Ultimately, South Korean officers came to share Americans' commitment to building their nation's strength and prosperity. But many wanted to attain these objectives in a way that would maximize the autonomy of both the military and the country and minimize U.S. influence.

The Origins of the ROK Army and Its First Officers

Although Korea had amassed a long and venerable military tradition over the course of the prior two millennia, the status of the army as an institution had declined dramatically by the late nineteenth century. In the twelfth and thirteenth centuries the Korean army had ruled over the entire peninsula before being overthrown by invading Mongols. But the Chosŏn Dynasty (1392–1910) was heavily influenced by the teachings of the Ch'eng-Chu school of Confucianism, which held the military in disdain and called for rule by scholar elites. For much of the Chosŏn period, the military declined in size and strength and was subjected to reorganizations that weakened its institutional cohesion. Efforts to modernize and rebuild the army during the nineteenth century failed to protect Korea's sovereignty against the predatory interests of foreign powers.[1]

Although there were no national armed forces in the Japanese colonial period, many Koreans first experienced service in a modern military during these years either by enlisting or being conscripted into Japan's imperial army. As Japan's need for troops surged during World War II, the empire forced thousands of Koreans into service. By 1945 approximately fifty thousand Koreans had served in the Japanese military and several hundred had become officers. A handful of Koreans who were able to attend the Japanese Military Academy or other elite officer training schools would eventually play a vital role in the formation and development of the ROK army.

Americans wanted to build an indigenous military organization from the time they first occupied southern Korea. General John Reed Hodge, the commander of U.S. occupation forces, explained that he was "very interested in establishing a Korean army from the beginning of the Occupation not only to relieve American troops of many details in handling Korean security, but to get a start for the future when we accomplished our mission of setting up a Korean government."[2] The U.S. Military Government in Korea (USAMGIK) was determined to pursue the creation of a Korean army even though they assumed that it would be a difficult task. Despite the significant number of Koreans who had served in the Japanese army, the Americans found on their arrival in 1945 that southern Korea was ill-prepared to found a modern military. One report maintained that "Koreans in 1945 were . . . totally unprepared to organize, equip and train an army of their own."[3] That statement probably underestimated the capabilities of Korean officers who had served in the Japanese forces, but it demonstrates how American advisers perceived their mission. They believed that they would have to take responsibility for introducing new methods of organization and training and compel the Koreans who had mastered Japanese techniques and strategies to adopt American ones.

When it came to building a formal South Korean army, however, U.S. State Department officials did not share Hodge's sense of urgency. Also fearing that the Soviet Union would condemn such a move, they forced Hodge to settle for a "Constabulary." Plan Bamboo, a compromise hammered out by the USAMGIK, the State Department, and the War Department, called for the creation of a 25,000-man constabulary to be used as a reserve police force. After the plan's approval in January 1946, the occupation force began recruiting nine light infantry regiments, one for each province in southern Korea.[4]

By December 1945 the USAMGIK had already established a Military English Language School, where the constabulary's first generation of officers received their training. The school's ostensible purpose was to teach English to Koreans who had some military experience so they could more readily assist American advisers. Koreans who attended the school remember concentrating primarily on English but also spending one hour a day engaged in military training. According to Paek Namgwŏn, one of the founding members of the constabulary, U.S. advisers forced Korean recruits to abandon the training methods they had learned from the Japanese and adjust to the American style of military discipline.[5] The USAMGIK drew the school's first entering class from the ranks of Koreans who had served in either the Japanese army or the Kwangbok army, a small group of Korean nationalists who had fought alongside Chinese forces against the Japanese during World War II.[6]

The nucleus of the new constabulary consisted of the first 110 graduates of the Military English Language School. These officers would dominate the highest positions in the South Korean military for the next two decades. Thirteen of the first fifteen ROK army chiefs of staff came from this group, as did eight generals, seven chairmen of the Joint Chiefs of Staff, and six future defense ministers. Among the group's best-known graduates were Yi Hyŏnggŭn, Paek Sŏnyŏp, and Chŏng Ilgwŏn, who were the first three South Koreans to be promoted to the rank of four-star general during the

Korean War; later they took turns serving as army chief of staff.[7] Although many in this first group of graduates were viewed as collaborators because they had served in the Japanese military, they were in their own way deeply nationalistic. Their experiences during the colonial period had convinced them that a strong military would be the key to building a modern, independent nation. They viewed joining the constabulary as an expression of their patriotism.

In the spring of 1946 the United States intensified its efforts to recruit and train Koreans for the constabulary. The organization's membership grew rapidly—from approximately 6,000 in November 1946 to 31,000 by December 1947 to almost 50,000 by the time a separate South Korean state was created in August 1948. Along with these increases in the constabulary's size went measures to improve the quality of officer training. American advisers converted the Military English Language School into the Officers Candidate School and revamped its curriculum to improve the combat skills of its cadets while fostering a sense of national responsibility. Courses were added in subjects ranging from tactics to Korean history. In the classroom, the Americans encouraged activities that would promote national unity. Yi Chiŏp, one of the original 110 members of the constabulary who instructed some of the earliest classes at the school, recalled teaching his students the Korean national anthem for the first time.[8]

The most important American figure in the expansion of the constabulary before 1948 was U.S. Army captain James Hausman. First dispatched to southern Korea as a military adviser in July 1946, Hausman acquired a keen grasp of the complexities of building indigenous armed forces. He made it possible to offer the constabulary a more thorough indoctrination in American training techniques by ordering the first translations of U.S. military handbooks and training manuals into Korean. Hausman has also been credited with keeping the expansion of the constabulary on pace through careful management of the limited budget provided by the U.S. government.[9] Most significantly, Hausman cultivated personal ties with members of the first generation of South Korean officers by opening his office to their complaints and concerns. He became widely regarded as a mentor by officers in the constabulary, which enabled him to exert enormous behind-the-scenes influence over the South Korean military as these officers assumed important positions.

Despite Hausman's lobbying for expanded training of the Korean forces during the U.S. occupation, it was not until the ROK government was inaugurated in August 1948 that the United States launched a more formal

The Military

effort to create a military establishment. This entailed sending a 100-man Provisional Military Advisory Group (PMAG) to South Korea. But PMAG's efforts had barely gotten off the ground when mutiny within the ROK Army sparked the Yŏsu uprising in October 1948, causing a major upheaval. The Americans had originally allowed Koreans to join the constabulary regardless of their ideological leanings. Once the rebellion had been suppressed, however, U.S. laxity in allowing Koreans with leftist backgrounds to join and infiltrate the establishment was blamed for the crisis. Korean officers then initiated a major purge of suspected Communists and leftists in the organization. More than 10 percent of the force, which had grown to eighty thousand troops, was dishonorably discharged, and between thirty and forty officers were executed.[10]

With the suppression of the Yŏsu rebellion and the elimination of dissident elements, the road was paved for more vigorous U.S. efforts to forge the South Korean military into a unified force. By the summer of 1949 this undertaking was well under way. PMAG had been converted into the permanent Korean Military Advisory Group (KMAG) and given a budget of $20 million. American military advisers in South Korea, who by this time numbered five hundred,[11] established a host of new schools to provide technical training for both officers and enlisted men. In September 1948 KMAG opened two artillery training centers that later became the foundation for the ROK Army's artillery school. The creation of infantry, signal, ordnance, and engineering schools with special courses for officers soon followed.[12] Finally, through arrangements made by James Hausman, the first group of six South Korean officers had received special training in the United States in August 1948. Hausman hoped that these officers would absorb American methods of training and organization and use them to improve military education in South Korea.[13]

The top ROK officers who completed this training shared the commitment to build a strong national military but differed in their attitudes toward U.S. influence. The divisions among them were based on both their military background and their native region. A salient divide existed between officers who had served in the regular Japanese army and those who had been members of the Japanese Kwantung Army. Koreans serving in the Kwantung Army had focused on suppressing rebellions against the Japanese imperial government in Manchuria and received a less rigorous indoctrination in Japanese military techniques. As a result, they often found it easier to adapt to American training methods than former members of the regular Japanese army, which had applied a more doctrinaire approach to military discipline.[14] Regional background also contributed to factionalism among the officers. A significant number of elite ROK Army officers were originally from northern Korea but had migrated south after World War II out of distaste for either the Soviet Union or the Democratic People's Republic of Korea (DPRK). Officers with northern origins tended to be more ardently anti-Communist and to show a deeper gratitude toward the United States than their southern colleagues.[15] Of course, such distinctions were not strict. The early South Korean military was characterized by constantly shifting factions and alliances. Officers harbored aspirations for their nation that were as varied as the officers themselves. Nevertheless, the incipient ROK Army's most well-known officers have made it clear in their memoirs that they approached the critical issues of building a military establishment and managing relations with the United States very differently.

Yi Hallim was among the members of the first generation of South Korean military officers with relatively close ties to the United States. Originally from Hamgyŏng Province in northern Korea, Yi was one of a handful of Koreans to attend both the Manchurian Military Academy and the Japanese Military Academy during World War II. Horrified by what he called the "cold starkness of politics in the north" under the Soviet occupation, he migrated to the American zone. In 1946 Yi became one of the original 110 members of the South Korean Constabulary and eventually rose to the rank of lieutenant general in the ROK Army. Yi embraced a commitment to soldierly ideals and national progress that was partially inspired by the United States. He was one of the first six Korean officers chosen to attend American training schools, and his visit to the United States had a powerful impact on him. Yi recalled that "when I went to America and saw, learned and felt various things, my eyes were opened to a new world." A visit to the U.S. Military Academy at West Point left a vivid impression on Yi. In contrast to the "militaristic way of thinking that emphasized giving one's life to the fatherland" that he had encountered at the Manchurian and Japanese military academies, West Point emphasized "a sense of responsibility to do one's duty while attaching importance to nation and honor." He became determined to use West Point as a model in developing South Korea's own military academy. Yi's sojourn in the United States left him with a profound respect for the American way of life. Indeed, he felt that the chance to "experience the true nature of a democratic society" was even more valuable than studying military science and strategy.[16]

Yet even figures like Yi Hallim accumulated grievances against some Americans. Occupying U.S. forces, including those responsible for building the South Korean military, frequently exhibited the haughtiness of a conquering army in their dealings with the indigenous population. This attitude aroused the ire of Korean officers who saw joining the military as a path to national strength and autonomy. Yi recalled "clashes of opinion" with American soldiers who "intended to lord it over us from above." Although many of these clashes started from "trivial quarrels," on one occasion they almost induced Yi to abandon the constabulary.[17] Despite these instances of conflict, however, Yi generally retained an outlook that gelled neatly with the objectives of the United States.

Although equally devoted to building a strong national army, Yi Hyŏnggŭn, another of the constabulary's founding officers, remained relatively indifferent to American guidance. Yi had attended the Japanese Military Academy and risen to the rank of captain in the Japanese army during World War II. His military background and English language proficiency were superior to those of most of the constabulary's other members. Highly regarded by the USAMGIK for these reasons, Yi was given the serial number *one* in the new constabulary. Despite this promising beginning, Yi's relations with American officers were often highly contentious. According to his memoir, "the difficulties and humiliation endured in the process of founding the army are not easy to express in writing." For example, he witnessed a U.S. adviser berating a Korean officer in front of a large contingent of Korean soldiers. The officer had been in the act of giving a "spiritual sermon" (*chŏngsin hunhwa*), a practice common in the Japanese imperial army, to troops under his command. The American commander declared that such sermons were "a practice of the Japanese army" and needed to be discontinued. Yi had an angry confrontation with the American, whom he insisted should not have embarrassed a Korean commander in front of his troops. He then ordered his compatriot to continue giving the sermons as planned.[18] Officers like Yi Hyŏnggŭn, who were comfortable with Japanese methods and reluctant to subordinate themselves to those of the United States, enabled such practices to persist despite their repudiation by U.S. advisers.

Incidents like the one described by Yi Hyŏnggŭn abounded during the early days of the South Korean armed forces. Other officers with similar military backgrounds were, if anything, more determined to continue Japanese training methods. Ch'ae Byŏngdŏk, a former major in the Japanese army and ROK Army chief of staff when the Korean War broke out, was a particularly strident opponent of U.S. methods of training and organization. Yi Chiŏp, to whom Ch'ae assigned the task of creating an education branch for the army operations section, remembered that Ch'ae specifically ordered him to ignore American models. Ch'ae "thought the American concept of combining operations and training within one staff section was incredibly stupid" and "made [Yi] question whether or not the 'damn Americans' really knew how to fight." Ch'ae directed Yi to make the branch "more like a Japanese organization."[19]

Even when they received preferential treatment from American advisers, Korean officers with prior Japanese training had difficulty working up much enthusiasm for American institutions and ideals. In contrast to Yi Hallim, who seemed genuinely moved by his experiences while studying in the United States, Yi Hyŏnggŭn, who attended the same training program, wrote that when he heard the news that he had been selected he "did not particularly welcome it," in part because he had already gone to an artillery school in Japan. Although the training he received was in the end "very satisfying," he was far less enamored of the United States and far less interested in modeling South Korea's military on its American counterpart than the more pro-American officers.[20] While concurring with the broader U.S. objective of preserving the security of South Korea against DPRK invasion or leftist subversion, Yi Hyŏnggŭn remained critical of many of the specific measures implemented by the USAMGIK and KMAG through much of his early career.

The contrasting experiences of Yi Hallim and Yi Hyŏnggŭn reflect the enthusiasm or ambivalence of South Korean military officers about American influence. But while the attitudes of some ROK officers did not coexist easily with U.S. hegemony, ultimately they did coexist because both the South Koreans and the Americans recognized the crucial need for a strong indigenous military that could defend the autonomy of the new nation. When North Korean forces stormed across the 38th parallel on 25 June 1950, the need for such coexistence, as uneasy as it was, rose to a new level.

The Korean War and the Americanization of Training

When the Korean War erupted, Americans had already trained a South Korean army of nearly 100,000 men and set up training schools that offered an increasingly thorough and sophisticated military education. But these measures paled in comparison to those undertaken during and after the war. Along with the United States's decision to defend the ROK went an extensive effort to rapidly expand and strengthen all branches of the ROK armed forces. In the wake of the invasion, the U.S. War Department began to expand KMAG and empowered it to build a military organization that was better equipped to handle the rigors of war. During the summer and fall of 1950, as U.S. and ROK forces retreated to the southeastern corner of the peninsula and then, buoyed by General Douglas MacArthur's famous Inch'ŏn landing, launched a counteroffensive, KMAG officers quickly established replacement training centers that prepared hundreds of new Korean recruits daily.[21] The United States also expanded the number of KMAG advisers in South Korea from a few hundred to nearly 2,000 and charged this strengthened contingent with the task of expanding and improving the ROK military. The rapid training of new recruits naturally spurred a dramatic increase in the size of the South Korean army, which by December 1950 had ballooned to 242,000 troops. When China entered the war, the Americans reinforced the ROK military even more vigorously. The South Korean army had grown to nearly 357,000 troops by June 1952 and stood at 492,000 by the time the armistice ending the war was signed in July 1953.[22]

As American commanders struggled to turn the ROK military into a larger and better trained force, they centered their efforts on the development of an elite officer corps. In 1951, when U.S. campaigns to implement wide-scale military training in the ROK intensified, General Matthew Ridgway wrote a memorandum to the U.S. Department of the Army explaining that an officer corps of "adequate professional competence, thoroughly imbued with the will to fight, capable of aggressive leadership and inspired of those essential spiritual qualities in which are included love of country, honor, integrity, devotion to duty and professional pride" was the "sine qua non" of any military organization. Ridgway emphasized that there was no such officer corps in South Korea and that the ROK army would not be an "effective fighting force" until one came into being. He believed that it was incumbent upon KMAG, which "virtually commands the ROK Army and is capable of strongly influencing its actions," to take the lead in creating this corps.[23]

Wartime efforts to develop the South Korean officer corps followed through on Ridgway's recommendation. The urgent need for close collaboration between the U.S. and ROK militaries made it possible for American advisers to supervise and instruct South Korean officers in both the heat of battle and the slightly more relaxed atmosphere of the nation's newly expanded military training schools. KMAG advisers focused on introducing their Korean protégés to American ideals of military efficiency, duty, and patriotism. They sought not only to train these officers as combat leaders but also to remold their character, making them more capable of independent judgment and more dedicated to serving their nation. These traits were, of course, vital for officers to have but, in a society without strong political leaders, could potentially encourage the military to do much more than fight its adversaries.

KMAG relied on the "counterpart system" to train officers for combat and to enhance their capacity for autonomous decision making. This would enable American advisers to monitor and direct the activities of the South Korean forces at nearly every level. Under the counterpart system, individual KMAG advisers were paired with ROK command or staff officers, with each being termed the other's counterpart. The chief of KMAG acted as a senior adviser to the ROK Army's chief of staff, while lower level advisers worked with ROK commanders at the corps or division level. Moreover, KMAG assigned advisers to specialized units such as signal corps, engineers, and tank companies. Advisers lived, trained, and fought with their assigned regiments. They were expected to become acquainted with every phase of their unit's activities and to evaluate the strengths and weaknesses of their counterparts. By acquiring intimate knowledge of their units and serving as models of efficiency, the KMAG advisers aspired to make South Korean troops replicate U.S. military discipline and organization.[24]

The exigencies of war demanded that U.S. advisers prioritize bolstering the combat efficacy of their counterparts. The battlefield became an impromptu classroom where Americans could educate Korean officers in how to command their troops. One KMAG adviser recalled that "when operations were being planned I went into great detail with my counterpart and then I had the ROK's [sic] hold a rehearsal of the action." After reviewing material with his counterpart, the adviser "would have him conduct briefings with superior officers." He believed that this kind of "attention to detail and rehearsing of the troops increased the chances of success and cut down the casualties."[25] Another adviser related that "I toured the front line with my counterpart inspecting gun positions" and "talked to my counterpart in depth about grazing fire, plunging fire" and "defense in depth."[26] Through this sort of close supervision, the Americans virtually forced South Korean officers to perform combat operations and administrative functions according to U.S. standards.

But improving how Korean officers handled themselves in combat was only part of the American agenda. KMAG advisers strove to ensure that their counterparts developed the personal and even psychological characteristics that they considered necessary for effective leadership. This meant strengthening the confidence and autonomy of the South Korean officer, whose self-image was often perceived as fragile. The KMAG "Advisor's Procedure Guide"

KMAG officers instructed their South Korean counterparts in both military and technical skills, as in this photograph of an American naval officer working with his Korean advisee. (Naval Historical Center)

explained that American advisers had to "criticize" their counterparts' mistakes "without causing them embarrassment or 'loss of face.'" Furthermore, the adviser "must teach them economy without seeming to deprive them of their needs. He must hold them to proven military methods and standards while still applauding their improvisation and, last but not least, he must do these things with a view toward building their confidence."[27] It was believed that this approach would make the advisers' South Korean counterparts more capable of leading their own forces and more willing to accept U.S. tutelage.

American attempts to remold the character of Korean officers were consistent with the broader philosophy that "self-help" was the best way for individuals or groups to change their destinies. KMAG advisers placed a premium on motivating their counterparts to overcome their weaknesses through their own efforts. In the final report of his tour of duty as a senior quartermaster adviser to the South Korean army, Colonel Max Drummond listed a range of negative traits that characterized the "average" Korean officer with whom he had worked. These traits included not "taking the initiative" and being "non visionary," "unable to foresee an impending crisis," and "weak on programming and planning." Drummond noted that the best tactic for improving their effectiveness was "encouraging them to do more for themselves on their own initiative and efforts." He explained that "if we as advisors would find and point out more mistakes, errors, faults, failures and causes of such deficiencies . . . and encourage the ROK Army to provide the impetus to the solution, much more rapid progress will be accomplished in stabilizing and increasing their supply and logistical posture."[28] Drummond's point was that enhancing the efficiency of the South Korean army involved more than just eliciting obedience to U.S. instructions. It also required making the Korean officers aware of their weaknesses so they would seek to redress them of their own volition. He hoped that, by taking into account their yearning for autonomy, KMAG would ultimately render ROK military officers amenable to American guidance.

The close interaction with American advisers that resulted from the counterpart system left a lasting impression on many South Korean officers. Some did strive to emulate U.S. standards of efficiency and discipline. Yi Tongsik, a graduate of the Korean Military Academy (KMA) who became a platoon leader during the war, recalled gaining an entirely new understanding of the Americans through his combat experiences. Yi said that when he first saw U.S. troops "chewing gum and walking frivolously," he thought they were just the "foolish children of a rich house." But when he observed how these soldiers methodically awoke every morning to groom their weapons and check on their ammunition and how they were never even one minute late when changing guard duty in front of their tent, he came to admire their professionalism. Yi felt that their "overall level of education, social atmosphere, trust in superiors and administrators and individual respect for the law" were all things that Korean soldiers "needed to have."[29] His contact with U.S. forces both taught him how a modern military organization should function and inspired him to work on perfecting the South Korean army.

But not all South Korean officers admired their American supervisors. Tensions between the two groups frequently arose over day-to-day issues such as the control of weapons and other equipment. Some ROK officers became notorious for stockpiling and selling extra supplies on the black market to supplement their salaries. Paid a mere fraction of what even American privates received, such individuals regarded these activities as necessary for the well-being of their families and resented U.S. interfer-

During the Korean War, the battlefield often became an impromptu classroom where KMAG advisers trained their South Korean counterparts. (Naval Historical Center)

ence.[30] More interested in economy, American advisers strictly monitored and restricted the amount of matériel that their counterparts received.[31] Korean officers found American restrictions not only insulting but also dangerous to the war effort. South Korean commander Chŏn Uyŏng complained that the severe limitations that his counterpart imposed on ammunition and supplies forced his troops to "fight with empty hands." He added that although Americans had "offered their lives along side Koreans" and fought together in an "alliance of blood," he "could not but become estranged" from his KMAG adviser during the last months of the war. Their relationship became so strained, according to Chŏn, that they could not even exchange greetings. Conflicts with Americans over issues like these could easily translate into a broader alienation from the United States. Chŏn recalled that wartime disputes with his KMAG adviser "planted the seed of nationalist feeling in him."[32] In Chŏn's case, nationalism developed in opposition to American influence as much as it did because of it.

Nor did wartime supervision by American advisers force senior Korean officers to completely relinquish the cultural practices they had absorbed during their service in the Japanese army. Social relations between officers and their troops often continued to reflect Japanese influence as they maintained an undemocratic and, from the American perspective, unprofessional character. Commanders in the wartime ROK Army demanded complete subservience from their subordinates and administered harsh discipline, including beatings and even shootings, when they did not receive it. Although American advisers disapproved of such practices, they seldom used their authority to prevent them. One KMAG adviser reflected that "the advisor may dislike the beatings that take place in ROK units but this is their way, and the Advisor shouldn't mess with it." Another adviser thought that KMAG "should concentrate on developing a fighting force and let [South Korean officers] handle the discipline."[33]

Ultimately, this intense supervision of South Korean officers strengthened the ROK military elite but did not Americanize it. Frustration with the United States led many officers to question or reject American practices and ideals. In a state of wartime emergency, however, Americans were content to accept the South Korean military as it was. Its leadership fiercely opposed Communism, and even U.S. advisers who took a critical view of their Korean counterparts acknowledged the growing efficiency of ROK forces in combat. When the war ended, the Americans were convinced that the South Korean military was vital to the country's future and offered it their continued support. Nor did they abandon their effort to professionalize leading Korean officers and inspire them to replicate U.S. standards. Their key instrument for pursuing this objective was South Korea's new system of military schools.

Military Education and Training Schools

The expansion of South Korean military education during and after the war was just as rapid as the growth of the military itself. Schools, like the KMA, that had been developed before the war were expanded and fine-tuned, while new institutions that could serve the needs of an increasingly professional military establishment, such as the National Defense College, were added. Americans modeled these institutions on similar schools in the United States. They designed the curricula to produce officers who were technically proficient, devoted to their nation's well-being, and receptive to American influence.

Before the war, KMAG had already begun to develop an extensive system of service or branch schools patterned after American ones. Among them were a signal school, an engineering school, an infantry school, and an artillery school. During the last two years of the war these schools were renovated and their curricula expanded. All of them provided courses in officer training. At many, officers learned new technical skills and gained experience commanding men with specialized training. Typical was the ROK Army Engineer School, based on the U.S. Army Engineer School at Fort Belvoir, Virginia. The school provided instruction in the operation of bull-dozers, cranes, and other equipment, as well as specialized classes in areas such as electrical engineering, stone masonry, and carpentry.[34] Other branch schools were more oriented to combat training, although some of the areas they covered had important civilian applications. At the armor school, for instance, preparation for tank combat included instruction in how to drive, fire, and repair tanks. According to the 1956 ROK *Military Education Annual*, because students at the armor school "received detailed education in the internal structure of tanks, they also acquired high level skills that enabled them to repair and maintain internal combustion engines and other compo-nents."[35] Rank-and-file South Korean soldiers no doubt saw the advantages of possessing such technical expertise primarily in terms of their employ-ment once they left the army. More importantly, these schools gave ROK officers more experience in overseeing projects that could benefit the econ-omy than any organization in the civilian sector.

Branch schools complemented their focus on combat and training with efforts to cultivate new personal qualities and a nationalist élan. The artil-lery school, for instance, saw its mission as extending far beyond simply preparing soldiers for combat. It listed among its goals "the cultivation of a noble character, nurturing firmness of purpose, superior military training and forging a strong body."[36] Officers who directed some of the branch schools came to see them as repositories for the aspirations of the South Korean nation and likely attempted to inculcate students with this view. The director of the ROK Army Infantry School explained in 1956 that "the expectations of the people of the nation are coming to be wholly concen-trated in the army infantry school."[37] By continuously turning out patriotic officers with finely honed technical skills, the service schools aimed to exert an enduring impact on South Korean society.

The branch schools graduated thousands of officers during and after the Korean War, but their programs were fairly short in duration. Perceiving the need for a special group of elite officers who would be trained much more rigorously in U.S. military doctrine, KMAG advisers founded the KMA. To a greater extent than any other military institution in the ROK, the KMA reflected American influence. In September 1951 KMAG officers had begun building the new academy around what was originally the Military English Language School. After the curriculum was revised and expanded, the institution was renamed the Korean Military Academy and reopened at Chinhae in January 1952.

From its inception, the military academy's four-year program attracted highly talented and motivated individuals. The KMA administered a series of rigorous mental and physical exams to all of its applicants. For the first class, which entered the program in 1952, the school accepted 200 cadets from 1,400 applicants; over time the selection process became even more challenging. As early as July 1952, the number of applicants for the second class had grown to 2,500 for the same 200 spots. Moreover, the academy had started making an extensive effort to attract a large field of applicants.[38]

The U.S. advisers who supervised its establishment modeled the KMA on the revered U.S. Military Academy at West Point. Many of them were themselves West Point graduates. Colonel Harry McKinney, the senior U.S. adviser to the KMA, received a degree from the academy in 1927 and worked there for twelve years.[39] McKinney and his staff imported manuals and books used at West Point and made them the basis for the policies and regulations of the KMA. They also based programs of instructional and tactical training, as well as an honors system, on those at West Point. Again, under the guidance of the American officers, the KMA adopted the Thayer System as the foundation for its curriculum. The Thayer System was the creation of Sylvanus Thayer, who served as superintendent at West Point during the early nineteenth century. It combined broad liberal education with socialization in a disciplined military culture. The system demanded that students be subjected to rigorous daily testing while demonstrating loyalty and integrity.[40] To ensure that the academy never went too far astray from the American standard, KMAG appointed numerous U.S. officers to monitor its development. One report on the KMA insisted that guidance be provided by a "carefully selected advisory detachment which maintains daily surveillance over the activities and administration of the academy." This surveillance would be supplemented by frequent visits from high-level officials; such visits were to be "punctuated by specific queries concerning points of progress and not be the occasion for ceremony and superficial briefing only."[41]

The regimen of instruction and training that Americans put into place at the KMA aimed to totally reshape the character of its cadets by inculcating them with self-discipline and devotion to their nation. The institution's official mission was thus to "develop physical, mental and moral character in the young cadet and to cultivate unselfishness and loyalty to country."[42] From the time they entered the KMA, cadets were exposed to the formal symbols and slogans that it had adopted. The academy chose as its motto the Sino-Korean characters *chi* (wisdom) *in* (mercy), and *yong* (bravery). The school flag, which consisted of a yin-yang symbol against a background of a hibiscus flower and a laurel tree, was intended to elicit loyalty from cadets to both army and country.[43]

Upon entering the academy, cadets found that their lives were subject to constant regulation by their instructors and superiors. The school's Tactical Department theoretically controlled the lives of cadets twenty-four hours a day, seven days a week. On a typical day students awoke at 5:30 A.M. and attended roll call by 6:00 A.M. After breakfast they spent the entire morning receiving classroom instruction. Afternoons were divided into periods of supervised study, training, and recreation, which generally consisted of orga-nized athletics. Cadets spent their evenings in supervised study sessions as well. The only time this schedule changed was during the summer, when cadets received more focused tactical military training for eight and a half weeks.[44] This regimen helped turn KMA graduates into one of the most disciplined groups in the new army.

Other dimensions of the KMA's curriculum paid greater attention to shaping the broader attitudes of students. As one brochure on the academy explained, the future South Korean officers were being trained to be "not only professional soldiers but also to be responsible citizens of their country and the world in which they live."[45] The curriculum served both of these purposes by offering a well-rounded, liberal education in addition to mili-tary training. Courses on subjects such as "Military Art and Engineering" were significant parts of the curriculum, but topics like culture, history, and philosophy were also well represented. During their first year, cadets stud-ied both the Korean language and Korean history.[46] Courses in these areas likely reinforced their sense of belonging to a single national people with a common culture, history, and language. The KMA's curriculum functioned in other ways to make cadets more sympathetic toward American influence. The cadets spent more time studying English than any other subject, taking five hours of instruction per week during their first year and six hours per week during their second and third years. Moreover, textbooks used in courses such as the "History of Civilization" and "Economics and Govern-ment" were based on those used at West Point and likely contained an American worldview if not blatantly pro-American content.[47]

Americans even tailored extracurricular activities at the KMA to influence the outlook of aspiring officers. Cadets participated in a wide array of ceremonies, parades, and associations. On National Army Day, for example, they paraded through a stadium in Seoul along with representatives from the rest of the army and the other branches of the military. When the ceremony was held for the first time, in 1956, dignitaries from both the U.S. and the ROK armed forces attended, and President Syngman Rhee gave a speech emphasizing the responsibility of the South Korean military to the ROK as well as to the Free World.[48]

Sports were another significant part of the academy's extracurricular life. Through athletic competition, cadets could be shaped into stronger and more efficient soldiers while gaining familiarity with American pastimes such as baseball, basketball, and volleyball.[49] In addition to engaging in organized activities on their own campus, KMA cadets formed teams that competed with other schools, especially the other military academies. At least one athletic competition between cadets from South Korea's three military academies—Army, Navy, and Air Force—was held annually.[50] By promoting teamwork among the cadets, such competitions fostered unity and esprit de corps within the KMA. At the same time, by bringing together students from the different service academies, these competitions instilled a common sense of national purpose among the country's future military officers.

The United States also organized institutions that could reeducate senior officers to supplement the emphasis of schools like KMA on finding the best young recruits. The command and staff colleges most specifically fulfilled this role. The Army Command and General Staff College was established in December 1951 and patterned after the U.S. Army Command and General Staff College at Fort Leavenworth, Kansas. Air and Navy Command and Staff colleges were added in the mid-1950s. All of these schools offered ten- or eleven-month courses for mid-level officers to prepare them for duty as commanders and general staff officers of divisions and higher units by teaching them to use their staffs more effectively.[51] At the same time, these institutions sought to produce broader changes in the outlook of students by emphasizing subjects that would bolster officers' commitment to either the South Korean state or the global struggle against Communism. For instance, the ROK Army Command and General Staff College stressed the concepts of patriotism, loyalty to the service, and avoidance of politics.[52] The Air Command and Staff College provided courses on "Free World Powers," "Communist Powers," and "National Security."[53]

The ROK National Defense College was another important training ground for elite officers. Opened in October 1956, it was patterned after the U.S. National War College. The National Defense College offered ten-month intensive courses to members of the armed forces and government agencies. Six U.S. officers from the army, navy, and air force together planned almost the entire curriculum, emphasizing topics that would provide a broader understanding of national security, the organization and function of the military services, and the international aspects of national policies. The college offered courses in military strategy, joint planning, international affairs, and other areas.

In addition to providing instruction on military subjects, the National Defense College sought to enhance students' capacity for independent judgment, improve work efficiency, and increase respect for freedom of expression.[54] The Americans insisted on teaching methods geared to recast the way that officers thought. Generally, students were not given "school solutions" to problems. Instead, they were presented with materials on a particular topic and encouraged to "think over and discuss the pertinent issues." The primary objective of these exercises, one report explained, was to "stimulate thought processes." By "inviting full discussion" in class, officers would be "encouraged in the formulation of independent judgment." Students pursued both committee and individual studies at the college. Committee studies were intended to promote "integrated thinking" and, through mandatory group discussion, offer "a positive means of arriving at logical conclusions." Individual studies required students to apply "original and creative thought" to projects that would ultimately be their own. Such projects aimed to stimulate objective analysis and self-evaluation. The college directed its students to apply their newfound skills to the goals of national development and resistance to Communism. To enable and motivate officers to contribute to the nation's prosperity and security, it offered courses in areas such as "Korean Economy and Foreign Trade," "ROK National Policy Formulation," and "Korean Foreign Policy." A course on the "Analysis of Communism" focused on "examining the doctrine of communism" to provide an understanding of the need for "consideration of the world-wide influence of Communism."[55]

But KMAG was not convinced that even this elaborate system of indigenous military schools would be able to adequately train elite South Korean officers. The group decided that the highest-ranking officers required special training in the United States. No South Korean military men received a more thorough introduction to U.S. military methods than these officers. KMAG sent a small number of them to the United States before the Korean

War broke out, but after 1951 the figure jumped from under 30 men per year to nearly 1,000. Under the CONUS (Continental United States) program, more than 7,000 South Korean officers received special training at American military schools between 1950 and 1957. This number included 4,729 from the army, 920 from the navy, 189 from the marine corps, and 1,503 from the air force.[56] During the war itself, the majority of South Koreans selected to participate in the program attended combat arms schools at Forts Benning (Georgia), Sill (Oklahoma), and Belvoir (Virginia). But after the war ended, the military advisers placed an increasing emphasis on training officers at technical and administrative service schools where they were more likely to acquire skills and knowledge that could be applied to national reconstruction and development.[57]

Perhaps more than any of KMAG's other training programs, CONUS strove to produce South Korean officers who embodied the discipline and patriotism of the modern military. One KMAG officer called the CONUS program "a package plan to provide maximum instruction at the least possible expense in the least possible time." From the American perspective, the program had unique advantages. First, by studying in the United States Korean officers received the benefit of learning from leading U.S. instructors who were considered too valuable to send to distant countries like South Korea. Second, they had access to state-of-the-art training equipment, which could not be duplicated in South Korea without enormous expense. Finally, South Korean officers sometimes but not always improved their English as a by-product of their training in the United States, thus facilitating their communication with KMAG advisers when they returned home.[58]

Like most training devised by KMAG, the CONUS program aspired to do more than simply enhance combat skills and technical knowledge. It also strove to instill in participants a commitment to social and economic progress in South Korea and a desire to emulate the American way of life. The officers enrolled in the CONUS program typically received invitations to live with American families for short periods and had the opportunity to tour American cities during their vacations. U.S. advisers were confident that the ROK officers would be impressed by America's abundant wealth represented by the vast number of cars on its highways, the size of its buildings, and the modernity of its lifestyle.[59] They believed that through exposure to U.S. technological prowess, South Korean military elites would realize their own nation's backwardness, gain a new appreciation for democratic values, and form favorable impressions of the United States.

The Americans were so certain of the CONUS program's effectiveness that they began creating similar programs that sent Korean officers to civilian universities during the mid-1950s. One such program was designed specifically for KMA instructors, who received postgraduate education in engineering and mechanics at universities like Stanford and Purdue. KMAG envisioned that participants would help train other instructors in their departments to maximize their influence on the academy.[60] Of course, such programs were expensive and therefore limited in size. But they helped to increase the technical superiority of the South Korean military to the country's civilian educated elite.

KMAG regarded training Korean officers in U.S. military schools as a way to ensure that the entire ROK Army adhered to higher standards of discipline and organization. One American general expressed hope that the techniques taught in the United States would be "placed into effect in Korea by Koreans themselves when they return." He reasoned that if this occurred, it was logical to expect that those standards would "snowball throughout the ROK army and its training centers," enabling South Korea's military to become "more nearly self-supporting in its training."[61] As the ROK armed forces began to voluntarily adopt American procedures, the United States would be able to reduce its own expensive commitment to training the indigenous forces. Meanwhile, KMAG advisers made a concerted effort to maximize the impact of training conducted in the United States. They presided over the student selection process and demanded assurances from the ROK adjutant general that on completing the program the participants would be assigned to specific positions in the South Korean military. As a result, many graduates of U.S. service schools became staff officers or school instructors and exerted an influence that went far beyond their limited numbers.[62]

This extensive system of military education had a transformative effect on ROK officers, but it was an effect that ultimately defied American expectations. The South Koreans were often most impressed with the rationalism and efficiency of their American counterparts. They exhibited a determination to improve the fortunes of their nation that was, at least during the 1950s, at odds with the country's apathetic political leadership. But trainees were not as enthusiastic about American cultural and political values. In some instances this was a reflection of lingering Japanese influence on the military, especially at the top levels. In other cases South Korean officers were so overwhelmed by the social and material differences between the United States and their own country that they doubted America's political or economic system could be transplanted to South Korea. Finally, their ambivalence about the United States sometimes reflected the very success of the U.S. programs. As ROK officers gained a sense of self-confident nationalism, they became increasingly eager to assert the autonomy of their own military establishment and nation.

The newfound self-confidence demonstrated by South Koreans trained at elite U.S. and ROK military institutions was stunning. They praised the new system of schooling for boosting their faith in their own capabilities as soldiers and leaders. For officers such as Yi Tonghŭi, these institutions inspired a new sense of possibility. Yi was among the first to attend the revamped KMA and eventually became one of its deans. He explained that "we didn't start our classes with too much enthusiasm, but we certainly started to become serious students once we realized what the penalties might be." At the KMA, he learned that he was "much smarter than [he] thought"; during his time at Chinhae he became a "real soldier and a serious student."[63] Yi embodied the discipline, confidence, and independence that the Americans attempted to instill in ROK military leaders.

Self-confidence was often accompanied by a feeling of superiority to other groups in Korean society. Military officers trained at elite institutions were well aware that their education was more advanced than most civilian schools in South Korea could provide. Han Muhyŏp, who attended the National Defense College and later became an instructor there, remembered with great pride being told by an officer who had studied at the prestigious Seoul National University, that students at the National Defense College learned in one year what their counterparts attending the best civilian institutions learned in three or four.[64] After hearing such praise for the college, graduating officers naturally believed that their competence in critical fields exceeded even that of the country's civilian elite.

Graduates of institutions like the KMA and the National Defense College thus viewed themselves as the most qualified group to lead the transformation of South Korean society. Student essays in the KMA's newspaper, *Yuksa Sinmun*, argued that cadets at the academy needed to play a special role in reshaping their country. An editorial appearing in March 1958 described "The Mission and Special Characteristics of the Military Academy." Its author contended that if a "country and nation seeks to become powerful and strong, first the nation's constitution and spirit must be strong." The nation required "independent enlightened individuals who were diligent and maintained the social order." The KMA's cadets had an obligation to take the lead in building this new national spirit. Indeed, "students at the military

The Military

academy had the responsibility of displaying the nation's soul, guarding the country and becoming a national symbol." These students comprised an "elite youth" that was capable of playing this role because "in Korea the military cadets were the foremost model of physical vigor and possessed the greatest spiritual and moral strength."[65]

Despite the political and economic problems that plagued South Korea after the war, graduates of the KMA tended to be ambitious and optimistic. Another editorial in *Yuksa Sinmun* exhorted cadets to be the "vanguard of the people." Just as young Koreans had been at the forefront of the movement seeking independence from Japan beginning in 1919, youth would once again need to play a major role in postwar reconstruction efforts in South Korea. Moreover, "among these youths, the country's development and society's reform would have to be the responsibility of cadets."[66]

Korean officers who traveled to the United States for training were often amazed by the contrast between the affluence of the United States with its well-equipped schools and war-devastated South Korea. Experiencing this disparity firsthand sometimes prompted officers to shift their broader devotion to making Korea a stronger nation to a more specific yearning to achieve economic development. Song Yoch'an, a lieutenant general who became prime minister of the ROK after a military coup in 1961, recalled how his training at the Command and General Staff College in Kansas influenced his thinking. "While studying I thought deeply about Korea's future," he noted, as war still raged in Korea. Song concluded that "what was required for reconstructing war-torn Korea was first of all the spiritual armament of the people against Communism and positive cooperation for economic rebuilding."[67] His studies in the United States may not have single-handedly created Song's commitment to national development, but they certainly intensified it.

The international environment that prevailed at U.S. military training schools sometimes sparked nationalistic sentiments among South Korean officers. Upon arriving at the artillery school in Fort Sill, Oklahoma, in 1953, ROK Army general Yi Kwangho observed that among the students were generals from many Free World countries and that the school therefore constituted a "sort of international stage." In this context, Yi saw it as the mission of the Korean generals in attendance to "preserve their dignity, confirm their military spirit and labor not to be inferior in comparison to the generals of other countries." Along with this reinvigorated sense of nationalism went a more pragmatic desire to study harder and acquire the knowledge and skills needed to improve conditions at home. Yi added that "our foremost purpose in studying here is to learn things that will be useful and practical for our nation."[68]

Some of the Korean officers who traveled to the United States under the CONUS program admired and envied the abundance they saw in the United States and dreamed of emulating the American standard of living in South Korea. Chŏn Chehyŏn, an ROK Army commander who attended the artillery school at Fort Sill in 1952, described that period of his life with particular enthusiasm. In his autobiography, Chŏn wrote that the training gave him both an understanding of combat maneuvers and the confidence to show his fellow officers what he had learned. More than anything else, however, "living for seven months in a nation of freedom, democracy, individualism, rationalism and science" gave him an "enormous cultural shock." He remembered thinking, "Don't our people have to do things like this? Doesn't our nation have to live like this?" He believed that the recipients of such training could "not avoid feeling that the seeds of a new patriotism and a powerful ambition had been planted."[69] Chŏn expressed the precise attitudes that Americans hoped to cultivate—a commitment to military discipline, patriotism, and a strong pro-Americanism.

But while the budding nationalism of ROK officers inspired them to strengthen their nation, it was in other ways a double-edged sword that produced resentment toward the United States and American dominance over the South Korean military. The resentment was prevalent even among the high-ranking officers who received special training in the United States. Pak Kyŏngwŏn, a lieutenant general who would later become minister of home affairs in the ROK government, recalled that when he traveled to America in September 1952 his contingent of one hundred officers was divided into three groups of roughly equal size. One of these groups was "extremely pro-American" and one was "extremely anti-American"; the members of the third group "maintained their distance" from both positions.[70] Of course, the "anti-Americans" that Pak spoke of rarely possessed any sympathy for Communism or opposed the presence of U.S. forces in South Korea. Indeed, they shared the basic strategic assumptions of their American advisers. Their "anti-Americanism" was rooted not in ideology but rather in a desire for greater autonomy. The very closeness of the relationship between U.S. advisers and South Korean officers often sparked hostility toward what some Koreans perceived as the Americans' overbearing presence.

Many Korean officers who attended elite military schools like the KMA and the National Defense College worried about the contradictions inherent in institutions that had been charged with the task of forging a new national Korean spirit but at the same time had been so thoroughly modeled on American military schools. One KMA graduate wrestled with this issue in an article entitled "Spirit of the Cadet" appearing in *Yuksa sinmun*. The author ruminated on where cadets could find a guiding philosophy to strengthen their spirit. He thought that this was a difficult problem because Koreans could "not simply make West Point's traditions [their] own." Instead, Koreans needed "a unique and independent character."[71] Contemporaries who attended other institutions had similar reflections. Brigadier General Sim Hŭngsŏn, in an essay he wrote as a student at the National Defense College analyzing armed forces training and education in South Korea, praised the U.S. system but cautioned against too hastily emulating American institutions and practices. He argued that the educational process at South Korea's officer training schools should move "in a more Korean direction."[72]

Although the Americans had envisioned training ROK officers in the United States as a way of fostering goodwill between Koreans and Americans, in practice the military leaders who studied in the United States sometimes became more ambivalent about American influence. At the U.S. schools, ethnic clashes between nationalistic South Korean officers and American commanders, who occasionally made disparaging comments to Korean soldiers, produced disillusionment with the United States. Some Koreans became so distraught as a result of these clashes that they decided to abandon their training and return home. Such conflicts had a particularly strong effect on younger South Korean officers, who began to look down on senior officers who showed too much respect for their American commanders.[73]

Furthermore, the chance to travel freely in the United States exposed ROK officers to the worst as well as the best features of American life. Many military training schools were located in the Jim Crow South, and Koreans who attended them were at times disturbed by the racial discrimination that they witnessed, even if it was not directed specifically at them. Pak Chŏngin, a division commander who studied at the artillery school at Fort Benning, Georgia, found the "democracy and orderliness" that he encountered in America admirable. But "the discrimination against Negroes in the Southern region" gave him a "shock" and was "terribly distasteful."[74] Witnessing this sort of racism did not necessarily turn officers like Pak into anti-Americans, but it dimmed their enthusiasm for emulating the United States.

Other officers worried that the emphasis on education and training in the United States would undermine the success of the very institutions that Americans had helped build in South Korea. Yi Pyŏnghwa, a graduate of the KMA who spent one year as a graduate student in engineering at Purdue University, became convinced that his compatriots were too eager to learn English and study in America. He criticized young South Koreans who had been "infected with America fever" and raced blindly to the United States. Instead, he contended, they should "assume responsibility for leading their nation in a better direction." Doing so would ensure that their juniors would "not get infected by America fever" and enable them to receive a better education in their own country.[75]

Finally, some South Korean officers found training in the United States to be neither inspiring nor alienating but simply something they needed to endure in order to advance within the ranks of the ROK Army. This seems to have been the case for the most well-known participant in these programs, future South Korean president Park Chung Hee, who attended the artillery school in Fort Sill in 1954. According to one biography, there was little difference between what Park learned in the United States and what he had already studied in South Korea. His letters and diaries written there are replete with ennui and a longing to return home. He wrote to his wife that at Fort Sill "it was difficult to tell spring from summer" and that when he thought of her and his daughter "from his secluded quarters he was filled with homesickness." Although Park in many ways reflected the ideals of martial discipline and modernizing nationalism that the Americans sought to instill in South Korean officers, he never developed a taste for the American way of life.[76] Despite the role of the Korean War and the CONUS program in fostering bonds between the two countries, some Korean officers could never fully embrace the United States.

Such guarded attitudes did not mean that these Koreans failed to acquire skills and beliefs that Washington sought to engender. But their growing self-confidence could also make them defiant when it came to accepting American guidance or replicating American institutions and practices. They had their own vision of what South Korean society should be like, and that vision did not necessarily embody American values and ideals. As the military's importance in South Korean society continued to grow during the years after the Korean War, the demeanor of its officer corps toward both the rest of Korea and the United States would play a decisive role in shaping the country's destiny.

The ROK Army, the United States, and the Rhee Regime

The United States was clearly not happy with all of the traits exhibited by South Korean officers that emerged as a result of the Korean War. Their ambivalence toward American influence was easy to discern, as was their lingering attachment to practices that gave the military an undemocratic flavor. But the war had forged what many called a bond of blood between the U.S. and ROK armed forces, and Americans remained supportive of the ROK military even after the armistice. Washington could tolerate the occasional truculent nationalism exhibited by the officer corps because the military as a whole remained staunchly anti-Communist and committed to national progress. Although ROK military leaders clashed with Americans over specific issues and programs, their common aspirations prevented these clashes from destroying the relationship.

By the mid-1950s both Washington and its allies effusively praised the South Korean military for serving the purposes that the United States had intended with efficiency and zeal. Americans had come to regard the ROK military and its officers as vital not only to South Korea but also to the entire strategic balance in the Pacific. In 1955 William Lacy, the U.S. ambassador to the ROK, argued that cuts in the South Korean military establishment should not be considered because it was "undoubtedly the strongest single stabilizing force in Korea" and a "highly significant political factor in the general Far Eastern situation." Lacy maintained that the ROK military represented "a goal towards which the other Asian countries . . . aspire, as we wish them to."[77] America's allies held the South Korean military in similarly high regard. Reporting in 1957, the British military attaché in South Korea observed that "considering the short time the ROK Army has been in existence and the comparative youth of the senior officers . . . a surprisingly high standard of military efficiency has been reached." The attaché also found that the officers were "patriotic and loyal" and that morale was "basically good."[78] Pleased with the progress made by the South Korean military, Americans worked to boost its reputation and prestige.

The ROK armed forces had gained American respect at a time when the Eisenhower administration was taking a growing interest in using military establishments that received U.S. assistance to accelerate economic development in Afro-Asian bloc nations. In 1956 President Eisenhower assembled a special committee to study the U.S. Military Assistance Program. In its final report, published two years later, the committee recommended that American military and economic planners give armed forces in developing countries their full support as "a 'transmission belt' for economic progress." The committee's final report stated that "an officer corps which has acquired, through training and educational programs, many engineering and administrative skills and an understanding of economic planning, can supply the reserves for meeting the expanding needs of a national economy." Given the existence of highly skilled officer corps in many developing nations, the report argued, American military and economic assistance programs should "encourage the new military elites to assume greater responsibilities in promoting economic progress as well as attending to the immediate needs of internal security."[79]

The United States made a concerted effort to follow this advice in South Korea. Shortly after the Korean War ended American military commanders began dispatching South Korean forces on "civic action" missions as "a means of benefiting the Korean economy and of creating a positive and friendly image of ROK [forces]."[80] These forces often worked with the ROK Army's corps of engineers to rebuild bridges and pave roads that had been destroyed during the war. U.S. commanders also arranged for the U.S. Operations Mission (USOM) to supply South Korean units with asphalt-laying equipment with the expectation that they would initiate such projects independently. In some instances, the Americans identified particular projects that could benefit the South Korean economy and released ROK military units to work on them. General Carter B. Magruder, the commander of United Nations forces in South Korea between 1959 and 1961, recalled that when he assumed the post, coal production in mines in the eastern part of the country was low because there was no way of transporting the coal to either railroad lines or ports for shipment. Magruder enabled ROK engineering units to construct new roads so that more coal could be extracted.[81] Throughout the Rhee regime, the scope of these activities continued to broaden. Irrigation and land reclamation projects carried out by the South Korean military during this period called on thousands of officers and enlisted men, as did work in areas such as forest conservation and disaster relief.

By involving the ROK military in these undertakings, Americans tried to channel the nationalistic energies of South Korean officers toward the task of economic reconstruction. In doing so, they inevitably strengthened the confidence of the military elite in their ability to lead the country. As Korean officers assumed control over operations that enhanced the well-being of their society, they could not have failed to notice how the discipline and efficiency of their organization contrasted with the civilian govern-

The Military

ment's indifference to the urgent task of economic reconstruction. They realized that with their training they possessed a stronger will and a greater capacity to strengthen their country than any other group in South Korean society. Although the Americans had long preached the need for the military to remain aloof from politics, stirrings of political discontent among elite officers became increasingly apparent. Yi Hallim remembered that "under these political and social conditions it became impossible to uphold the military's dignity, independence and separation from politics."[82]

While discontent with the Rhee government mounted within the military, the ROK president did his utmost to ensure that its leaders did not become a political threat. Rhee adeptly exploited the divisions that existed among elite officers from different geographic backgrounds to prevent them from uniting against him. He continuously rotated the post of army chief of staff between rival factions, the first led by General Paek Sŏnyŏp and the second by General Chŏng Ilgwŏn. Although both generals had been born in northern Korea and served in the Manchurian Army, they came from different provinces and generally aligned themselves with officers who shared their provincial backgrounds. Numerous changes in military leadership at the highest levels occurred throughout the Rhee era, while the president's policies stymied any political ambition that the officer corps might have harbored.[83]

Rhee's manipulation of high-ranking generals temporarily staved off their participation in national politics, but it added to other officers' frustration with South Korea's economic situation. His machinations eventually led to the creation of a new division within the officer corps between the most senior officers who benefited from Rhee's patronage and ambitious junior officers who were increasingly alienated by the complicity of their superiors in the regime's corrupt behavior. Many of these younger officers had received more extensive training and a more thorough education in the United States than the more senior staff and were eager to assume top positions in the armed forces. By the late fifties, the resentment of these junior officers against both their status in the military and Rhee had become a potential source of political instability. It was clear that even Rhee, with all of his skills in political manipulation, could not restrain them indefinitely. The question was not *if*, but *when* they would enter the political arena.

The South Korean military grew swiftly in size, power, and ambition during the decade after World War II. U.S. training programs had imparted skills and attitudes that ensured its progression as a political force.

But while American officials had succeeded in turning the ROK Army into an efficient fighting force and stirring up military nationalism among the elite officers, they had never managed to fully imbue this group with a faith in democratic politics. Despite their rigorous exposure to U.S. training regimens and, in some cases, to the United States itself, Korean officers remained ambivalent about holding America up as a model for their own nation. U.S. policies had yielded a group of elite officers who believed that they and only they had the ability and resolve to enable South Korea to become wealthier and stronger. The mentality that existed among many South Korean officers by the late fifties was one that boded well for security and economic development but was much less auspicious for democracy.

Between 1948 and 1960 the United States supported Syngman Rhee's highly autocratic regime despite its minimal commitment to economic progress. At the same time, however, the Americans had done much to foster demand for modernization and democracy among different groups in South Korean society. By the late fifties the results of these policies were readily apparent. Conflicts between the South Korean state and elites who called for socio-economic change were shaking the very foundations of Rhee's rule. As the possibility of renewed military conflict on the peninsula receded, his government lost the confidence of South Koreans and Americans alike. U.S. policymakers felt increasingly comfortable with the security situation but were deeply troubled by South Korea's failure to make economic progress despite hundreds of millions of dollars of American assistance.

The result of this turmoil was successive political revolutions led by the two groups that had received the most direct exposure to American influence—students and military officers. A student-led revolution in April 1960 forced Rhee to leave office and replaced him with a new, democratic government headed by members of the opposition Democratic Party. Within thirteen months, however, another revolution, directed by a group of young army officers, ended South Korea's brief democratic experiment. Each of these uprisings embodied in its own way both attitudes that Americans had promoted in the Republic of Korea (ROK) during the fifties and the criticisms of U.S. influence that had emerged.

The United States played a pivotal role in determining the ultimate course of South Korean politics. The Kennedy administration's interest in promoting tutelary elites that could spur rapid economic development shaped American understandings of the evolving political situation in the ROK. U.S. officials viewed the combination of economic hardship and political turmoil that prevailed in South Korea as a threat to the stability of a critical anti-Communist buffer state. The weakness of the democratic government installed in the spring of 1960 was worrisome. The new leadership cringed at taking actions that might alienate the constituencies that put it in power, and Americans doubted that it would be strong enough to tackle the tough decisions required for economic development. When the military junta seized control in May 1961, Washington initially protested but soon recognized the new leaders' zealous determination to promote economic growth. The United States decided to support military rule rather than insisting on the restoration of democratic government and, by doing so, paved the way for developmental autocracy.

Rhee and American Foreign Policy

U.S. foreign policy had played an indispensable role in bringing Syngman Rhee to power and enabling him to survive armed challenges to his rule. Within five years of the conclusion of the Korean War, however, American support for Rhee had weakened dramatically. Washington's main reason for backing Rhee had always been security, but by the late 1950s the issue seemed less urgent in the South Korean context. U.S. policymakers still worried about Communism and leftist insurgency but not as much as they had before and during the war.

Changing U.S. perceptions of the security situation on the Korean peninsula were readily apparent by the mid-1950s. Washington continued to regard North Korea as dangerous, but it was less concerned about the possibility of another invasion. A 1956 memorandum prepared by the National Security Council (NSC) explained that there were "no indications of communist intentions to attack in Korea or of communist willingness to accept free world conditions for the unification of Korea." Although this meant that the stalemate between North Korea and South Korea, which was "highly unsatisfactory for the United States," would persist, it also made it clear that the threat of a renewed invasion by the Democratic People's Republic of Korea (DPRK) no longer seemed imminent.[1] Moreover, Americans had grown confident that if North Korea did launch an offensive, South Korean forces would be able to repel it. One NSC report of 1959 stated that the "ROK armed forces, together with U.S. forces now in Korea, are sufficiently combat ready to resist [an] initial attack from North Korean forces."[2] Though the report indicated that American backup would be needed for a sustained assault by Chinese and North Korean forces, it painted a far more optimistic picture of the security situation than the one that had prevailed a few years earlier.

American fears of internal subversion subsided along with those of a renewed DPRK invasion. Although U.S. policymakers remained concerned about the issue, from the mid-1950s onward their reports on the subject tended to indicate that it was not one of South Korea's most salient problems. A 1955 State Department document, entitled "Report on the Counter-Subversive Capacity of the Republic of Korea," argued that the

By the mid-1950s the ROK Army was emerging as a powerful, disciplined force, making Americans less anxious about security. (U.S. Army Collections, Eisenhower Library)

"threat of Communist control of the ROK through subversion is at present a potential, rather than an actual, danger." It added that the "North Korean directed guerilla elements in the ROK" active before and during the war had been "almost totally annihilated" and there were "relatively few manifestations of internal Communist activity."[3] Although two years later an increase in such activities was reported, "there has been no evidence . . . indicating that the integrity of the ROK government or the ROK military establishment or other ROK institutions was endangered by Communist subversion."[4] The point was not that U.S. officials no longer worried about invasion or subversion but that, with an improved security situation, suppressing Communism in South Korea no longer eclipsed other American objectives. Threats to national security, while still taken seriously, could no longer justify the kinds of political repression carried out by Rhee's government.

While Washington's anxiety about security on the peninsula eased somewhat, its angst about South Korea's economic direction grew exponentially. North Korean economic recovery programs after the war had been far more successful than those carried out in the South, and Americans were well

Toward Developmental Autocracy

aware of this fact. By 1956 the U.S. Central Intelligence Agency (CIA) had already reported in great detail how the DPRK was moving ahead of South Korea in terms of industrial development, per capita income, and many other key economic indicators. One 1957 report noted that "in spite of tremendous war damage, insufficient manpower, lack of adequately trained technicians and poor crop harvests in 1953–1955, the economic rehabilitation of North Korea is progressing steadily as a result of the continued assistance of the Sino-Soviet Bloc." Moreover, the report voiced fears common among U.S. policymakers that this "fact can be advertised and used as a propaganda weapon both in South Korea and in other Asian countries."[5] Potential comparisons between the stagnation that existed in the South and the steady progress occurring in the North worried Americans, who saw the peninsula as a showcase for liberal capitalism in Asia.

Economic development had also received renewed emphasis during the second Eisenhower administration because academic experts on the subject like Walt Rostow were gaining greater influence in policy circles. Rostow and other prominent scholars maintained that development would be the key to defeating Communism in the postcolonial world. In seeking ways to rid countries like the ROK of barriers to progress, these experts stressed the importance of an indigenous leadership committed to change. Rostow had argued in his well-known book, *The Stages of Economic Growth*, that to prepare a "traditional society for regular growth . . . a new elite—a new leadership—must emerge and be given scope to begin the building of a modern industrial society." Although such elites could potentially be found in all segments of a given society, Rostow tended to emphasize the significance of the role of political leaders. The government of a developing country needed to "lead the way through the whole spectrum of national policy—from tariffs to education and public health—toward the modernization of the economy and the society of which it is a part."[6]

American analyses of the political situation in South Korea often echoed Rostow's concern about the ability of indigenous political leaders to bring about meaningful change. They usually found Rhee lacking in this regard. In 1957 two U.S. diplomats stationed in South Korea contended that "President Rhee's role in domestic affairs since 1948 has achieved the short range goal of preserving order, but he has not furnished the country with the leadership necessary for the development of a viable society."[7] Along similar lines, an annual summary of the situation in South Korea prepared at the end of 1957 griped that "the President and his Administration . . . failed to supply real inspiration or imagination for social and political development."[8]

Out of their growing conviction that his government had become an obstacle to development, American officials began placing more pressure on Rhee to modify his economic policies while continuing to encourage opponents of his regime.

After 1957, U.S. assistance policies changed in ways that weakened Rhee's administration. Americans slashed economic aid to South Korea from a high of $382,893,000 in 1957 to $321,271,000 in 1958 and $222,204,000 in 1959. Rhee had become so reliant on the United States's largesse as a tool for rewarding his allies that cuts in its assistance inevitably weakened his political position. Washington struck another blow to the economy by demanding that Rhee initiate a stabilization program that would force the regime to limit budget deficits and discontinue the inflationary currency expansion that had been a hallmark of its economic policy since 1948. The stabilization program was devised and implemented by the Combined Economic Board (CEB), which had been formed in 1952 to enable American and South Korean officials to consult on policy issues. The board had been relatively idle during the first few years of its existence, but after 1956 the Americans worked hard to reinvigorate it as a mechanism for dictating policy.[9] By stripping the regime of its ability to print more currency, the CEB's stabilization program deprived Rhee of yet another means of controlling national politics. U.S. officials did not deliberately seek to weaken Rhee's authority by taking these measures. But with an improved security environment, they were simply less inclined to spend hundreds of millions of dollars to bolster a political economy that enabled Rhee to remain in power.

Feeling threatened by the cuts in aid, Rhee began taking increasingly desperate measures to ensure his political survival. In December 1958 he forced through the National Assembly an amendment to the National Security Law giving the government broad new powers to curtail freedom of the press. The fearlessness of opposition newspapers in criticizing his regime had made the press one of Rhee's most urgent concerns. The measure passed only because his security forces physically prevented members of the opposition from voting. For South Koreans in the media and other fields, the president's action constituted a dangerous move toward outright authoritarianism and the nullification of the limited freedoms they still enjoyed.

The constitutional revision alerted U.S. policymakers to the growing conflict between the government and civil society. U.S. ambassador Walter Dowling worried that South Koreans would become disillusioned with both democracy and the United States if the regime continued such tactics. He warned that "the mood of the Korean people is no longer such that it will passively accept and submit to undemocratic and authoritarian measures of political control." Government efforts "to stifle freedom of the press, to curtail opposition political activity, or to tamper with the Constitution" would ultimately produce "a strong popular reaction, including violent actions against those responsible for these measures." In this context, Dowling believed that it was essential that the United States not allow the regime to dominate its opponents. To protest the government's high-handed tactics, he recommended such actions as sending members of Congress to Seoul in an attempt to "psychologically influence" Rhee, reevaluating American assistance for the South Korean police, and delaying economic aid payments.[10] It was hoped that this strategy would enable the country's growing democratic forces to gradually ease Rhee from power.

But with the approach of the South Korean presidential election, scheduled for March 1960, Rhee seemed more determined than ever to prolong his time in office. In July 1959 his regime abruptly executed Cho Pongam, a member of the left-leaning Progressive Party who had received one million votes in the 1956 presidential election, on tenuous evidence that he was involved in Communist plots against the government. The State Department viewed the action as part of a "slow but steady tightening at every level of the Administration's governmental and political controls." Several months after Cho's death a State Department memorandum argued that "the time has come when we must take action in Korea to prevent further deterioration of the political situation." The most pressing objective, according to the memorandum, was "to halt and reverse the trend to a totalitarian regime in Korea and assure as far as possible that a fair and free election for President will be held in 1960." It recommended following through on Ambassador Dowling's earlier suggestions to reevaluate American assistance programs and look to the U.S. Information Service for the "dissemination of information on the basic requirements of free elections and democratic processes."[11] As the 1960 election drew nearer, the Americans took increasing risks to make sure that Rhee's opponents had a fair chance to assume power. It was clear to Washington, South Korea's burgeoning democratic forces, and the regime alike that the spring of 1960 would determine the nation's political future.

The April 19 Revolution

With the March 1960 presidential election close at hand, the Rhee regime seemed to be on its last leg. Syngman Rhee, who stood as the Liberal Party's presidential candidate, was by this time eighty-five years old and bordering on senility. The party's vice presidential candidate, Yi Kibung, who suffered from advanced locomotive ataxia, needed to be helped in and out of his chair and had trouble speaking coherently for more than a few sentences. Nevertheless, the regime decided to make one last grasp at retaining power. On election day the Liberal Party implemented its secret plans for group voting, ballot stuffing, and the removal of opposition ballots. The implausible results gave Rhee 88.7 percent of the vote and Yi Kibung 8,225,000 votes to Chang Myŏn's 1,850,000.[12]

The fraudulent election set off a chain of events that would lead swiftly to the demise of Rhee's government. It actually began on the eve of the balloting, when police in Masan, a small city near the southeastern coast, fired on a group of Democratic Party supporters, killing eight. On 11 April the body of a student who had been tortured by police was found in the harbor, and Masan erupted into three days of spontaneous mass protests that produced further clashes with the police. Despite the regime's efforts to censor news of these events, word had clearly reached Seoul by 18 April, when students from Korea University launched a large, peaceful protest against police violence and demanded that new elections be held. On the way home, however, the students were attacked by gangs called upon by the police chief. The next day, tens of thousands of student protesters gathered before the presidential mansion and were dispersed only when police fired point-blank into their ranks. By 25 April even larger protests threatened to throw the country into complete anarchy. Before this happened, Rhee finally resigned. A few days later Vice President–elect Yi Kibung committed suicide with his wife and two sons, leading to the collapse of the Liberal Party. During the weeks that followed, an interim government led by Hŏ Chŏng, an old associate of Rhee who had distanced himself from the Liberal Party, was established with American approval. The interim government began drawing up plans for new elections and a new constitution that diminished the power of the president. Free elections that turned the government over to the opposition Democratic Party were held on 29 July.[13]

The students who had led the revolution represented their actions, first and foremost, as an effort to replace authoritarianism with democracy. One prominent leader explained that "for twenty years the anger of the people at the government's authoritarianism had accumulated" and that the revolution had been an expression of the people's suppressed anger.[14] Another student leader emphasized that, unlike the revolts in past centuries, the April 19 Revolution was not "a class conflict of the bourgeoisie or the proletariat but a people's rights revolution."[15] But the fact that the students

Toward Developmental Autocracy

did not view their revolution as a class struggle did not mean that they held no hope that it would bring sweeping changes to South Korea. As a student from Yonsei University declared, "we must look at our situation and make the April 19 Revolution into a tool for bringing about reforms that spread across the whole of society."[16] Emboldened by their dramatic victory over a seemingly implacable foe, these young revolutionaries saw themselves as the social and political vanguard of their nation.

Although students had played the most pivotal role in overthrowing Rhee, it was politicians who gained control of the government. In the national elections of July 1960, the opposition Democratic Party won a majority in the General Assembly. Chang Myŏn, the new prime minister of the ROK, was Catholic, pro-American, and generally a liberal Democrat. He had managed to get elected vice president in 1956 despite running as a Democratic candidate and had been the most important member of the political opposition during the subsequent four years. The new leadership was sincerely committed to the development and democratization of South Korea and proved much more amenable to working with the United States to achieve these objectives than had the government it replaced. But given the longtime dominance of the Rhee regime, it had limited experience, if any, in governing the country and was unprepared to meet the high expectations of the electorate.

Governance was never an easy task for Chang's administration because it had to balance the varying agendas of the United States, reformist groups who demanded rapid change, and more conservative Koreans whose cooperation was needed for economic development. In the months following the election, Chang's government struggled to achieve needed reforms while maintaining political stability. Despite their limited experience, the new leaders did have some success in reforming South Korea's political system and instituting financial reforms. In December 1960 the first local elections in Korean history were held to choose the provincial governors and a new mayor of Seoul. And thanks in part to pressure from the United States, some necessary economic measures were passed. The Chang administration established a new exchange rate, consolidated power companies, and increased rates for heavily subsidized government services. It also created a National Reconstruction Program that promised to improve living standards nationwide.[17]

Despite these achievements, Chang's government was not always able to maintain stability. Public security became a significant problem. The police system, which had been a major instrument of political repression during the Rhee years, was left in shambles by the revolution. In 1960 several hundred police officers who had served the Japanese still occupied key positions in the ROK's security operations, but the majority of them were forced to quit or become subject to retribution from the general population. Without the police, however, crime rates skyrocketed in many South Korean cities. Gangs flourished and the government could muster few resources to protect citizens from theft and violence. Frequent demonstrations advocating or opposing a wide variety of issues occurred at the end of 1960 and the beginning of 1961. These included student demonstrations in support of North-South talks and conservative counterdemonstrations that were peaceful yet tense. Although most of these rallies were small and rarely dangerous, they nevertheless produced fear that the country was about to descend into chaos.[18]

Especially worrisome to both the Americans and South Korean conservatives were leftist student organizations such as the Mint'ongnyon. According to Mint'ongnyon, Korea's division into North and South was a byproduct of Great Power imperialism, and the only way to solve the problem of national division and advance economic development was to rid the peninsula of foreign influence. Radicals claimed that South Korea's economic underdevelopment had been exacerbated by U.S. economic assistance and that for modernization to take place, American influence needed to be eliminated. They argued for reunification by direct negotiations between the North and South and tried to arrange student conferences, some of which were publicly endorsed by North Korea, where the issue of reunification could be discussed. Although few if any members of these radical groups had direct contact with North Korea, they envisioned rapid reunification of the peninsula.[19] The number of South Koreans supporting this agenda was small, but their calls for more radical social change drew the attention of both the Korean media and the United States.

As South Korea's political situation deteriorated, it became clear that Chang Myŏn did not enjoy solid support from either the members of his government or the general public. As soon as the Democratic Party gained power, a factional struggle arose between Chang's supporters and those of President-elect Yun Posŏn. A subsequent split in the party left Chang with a plurality rather than a majority in the General Assembly. Although Chang was able to rebuild his majority during the following months, he remained in a relatively vulnerable position and consequently became extremely hesitant to use force of any kind to reduce crime or control demonstrations. Beleaguered by political factionalism and criticism for its inability to resolve pressing social and economic problems, the Chang government saw its popularity plunge. In a cabinet-sponsored poll taken several months after Chang assumed office, only 3.7 percent of respondents unreservedly supported him, while 51.5 percent said they would "wait and see."[20]

Within a few months of the time it was formed, Chang's administration was unable to provide the kind of leadership that South Korea needed to overcome substantial problems. In its excessive reluctance to use force to maintain order, the new government failed to understand the basic truth that James Madison had pointed out in the Federalist Papers—that good governments must learn first to control the governed and then to control themselves.[21] Although sincere in his determination to bring democracy to South Korea, Chang was too easily bullied into unwise policy choices by the sectors of the population that had helped him gain power. Because his government could not make the difficult decisions necessary to maintain order, develop the economy, and reform the political structure, it quickly lost credibility with both South Koreans and American policymakers.

The United States and Chang Myŏn

Washington's initial enthusiasm about the April 19 Revolution swiftly turned to consternation as the new government's efforts to preserve stability and promote economic development faltered. With fears of a North Korean invasion decreasing, U.S. officials sought above all political leaders who could develop South Korea's foundering economy. More often than not, they found the Chang Myŏn government lacking. Although pleased with its democratic proclivities and amenability to working with the United States, they worried that Chang would be unable to keep "traditional" obstacles to economic development such as corruption and factionalism under control. This viewpoint became especially prominent after January 1961, when John F. Kennedy took office.

In the weeks after 19 April 1960 State Department reports were full of excitement about the new possibilities for democracy in South Korea. Under Secretary of State Douglas Dillon wrote that he "look[ed] forward to gains in ROK prestige in the world, and in concomitant advance in principles which we consider we are defending in having fought in Korea in the first place."[22] American policymakers tried to boost the momentum toward democracy that had been generated by the revolution. In June 1960 President Eisenhower visited South Korea, addressed the National Assembly, and met with leaders of the Democratic Party. Eisenhower's appearance

Toward Developmental Autocracy

so soon after the takeover was in many ways a powerful statement of American support for the new government.

Despite the democratic movement that was taking hold in the ROK, however, American policymakers still had reservations about Chang. Early evaluations of the new South Korean prime minister emphasized his honesty but expressed concern about his capability to lead. In a telegram shortly before the July elections, Secretary of State Christian Herter felt that Chang's "personal integrity and broad understanding of international affairs" would enable him to become a good President, but Herter hoped that a "younger man of more dynamism as well as political and executive ability" would be elected to the more powerful position of prime minister.[23] The U.S. ambassador in Seoul, Walter McConaughy, agreed but wrote that "apart from Chang, no individual comes readily to mind who, among leadership ranks in either faction, is qualified by experience and age to fill [the] Prime Ministership." Resigned to the fact that the political leadership would be inadequate, McConaughy thought that the direction of the ROK government would depend "more on [the] emergence of a working team of younger leaders than upon any individual." The United States would need to encourage the development of new political leaders by supporting "those many Koreans[,] particularly younger citizens and gov[ern-men]t officials[,] . . . who are fired by genuine desire to set [the] country's political economy in order."[24]

In the months after Chang became prime minister, American officials continued to worry about the inability of his government to make urgent social and economic reforms. In August 1960, one month after Chang's election, Assistant Secretary of State J. Graham Parsons sent a lengthy telegram explaining that "there has not been a leader or group in Korea with the imagination, vision and energy to give the nation the definite believable national ideals, goals and programs" that were necessary "to end the Korean spiritual and social confusion, to ameliorate the discontent and even spiritual hunger which underlies so many of Korea's problems, and to give the country a sense of unity, direction and destiny." In the absence of national leadership that could stimulate these social changes, he added, "the economic and technical progress which is also essential to the national welfare" would be impossible.[25]

As the Chang government continued to struggle with its own internal problems and to bring order to South Korean society, U.S. officials became more pessimistic about its prospects. They thought that the leadership was

Toward Developmental Autocracy [111]

too steeped in the country's cultural milieu to overcome its stultifying effects. In December 1960 Ambassador McConaughy explained that "lacking a parliamentary tradition and limited by an opportunistic political opposition," the new regime was "further affected by traditional concepts of personal family and regional loyalties." Although the Chang government had made some progress, he remained skeptical that it could achieve economic growth.[26]

Such criticisms became more pronounced under the new American president. Deeply influenced by modernization theory, which faulted the cultural traditions of underdeveloped countries for their economic poverty, the Kennedy team regarded Chang's leadership as overly "traditional" in its outlook. One report written in the early days of the new administration made note of Chang's poor judgment in making appointments, particularly for not giving leadership posts to young officials who were "pledged to integrity and austerity in Korean life." Yet the "pervading effects of [the] oriental family system and traditional respect for elders" would make it difficult for even the most able and forward-looking South Koreans to gain positions of responsibility in the Chang government.[27] Such analyses overemphasized the role of Korean culture in the government's ineffectiveness under Chang, but they were more accurate in their characterizations of his appointees. These concerns did not entirely eclipse American respect for Chang's adherence to democratic principles, but they did lessen confidence in his ability to cope with the crises that surrounded him.

U.S. policymakers now feared that instability brought about by Chang's weakness would undermine America's position in the ROK. They were taking notice not only of the Chang government itself, but also of the radical groups whose demonstrations it seemed unable to control. American officials were troubled by rumors about possible uprisings that were circulating even if they were not entirely convinced of their validity. One widely read report pointed to the "dangerously deteriorating" situation in South Korea and to the fact that the government was "increasingly powerless to take necessary actions." It added that "the reaction against the government, possibly even revolution, would be strongly anti-American."[28] Along similar lines, an intelligence report of March 1961 expressed concern that "design, incident or a combination of accidents" would "ignite street demonstrations, converting them into destructive mob action and a major crisis" and that "a major explosion of some kind" was possible during March or April. Although the odds were against such an "explosion" occurring that spring, the report continued, given the ROK's political instability "internal crisis or threat of crisis will be the norm, not the exception, over the years ahead."[29] Despite these apprehensions, Kennedy officials did not seek the overthrow of a democratically elected government that was closely aligned with the United States. On the other hand, they saw little reason to stand by it if more promising alternatives emerged.

Park Chung Hee's Military Revolution

South Korea's first experiment with democracy ended on 16 May 1961, thirteen months after it had begun. Chang's government did not topple because of an "explosion" or through Communist subversion, as Americans had feared. Instead, it fell to a brief, virtually bloodless military coup d'état carried out by 3,500 troops assembled around a corps of 250 officers. Although both the CIA and Prime Minister Chang had been warned that a coup was in the making a few weeks before it occurred, Chang did not take the threat seriously, and for most of the country the takeover came as an almost complete surprise.[30]

The leader of the coup, Park Chung Hee, was a forty-one-year-old major general whose sensibilities were shaped by his experiences in both the Japanese and South Korean militaries. During the Japanese colonial period, Park attended Taegu Teacher's College and taught briefly in a primary school before deciding to pursue a long-desired career in the military. Park passed the test for the Manchurian Military Academy and, based on his performance there, was one of a handful of Koreans selected to attend the Japanese Imperial Military Academy near Tokyo. After graduation in July 1944, he was posted to a Japanese army regiment in Manchuria, where he fought until the end of World War II. Park emerged from his experiences in the Japanese army with a fervent belief in using the military as a tool to reshape society.[31]

Upon liberation, Park returned to Korea and became involved in the country's incipient armed forces. In 1946 he entered the constabulary and attended the Military English Language School. But for Park, joining the new U.S.-created military establishment was far from a statement of support for the U.S. Military Government in Korea (USAMGIK) or its objectives. During his first few months in the constabulary, numerous disagreements and minor conflicts flared between him and American advisers. Perhaps more significant was Park's brief affiliation with the Korean Workers Party. The trigger was probably the death of his brother, Park Sanghŭi, who had been a leader in the anti-Japanese movement during the colonial period and sided with the left after liberation. He was killed by the Korean

National Police in October 1946 while leading a demonstration that took over the Myŏn office and police station in his hometown, Kumi. Although Park Chung Hee had exhibited few ideological attachments at this time, he blamed the Korean right and to a lesser extent the United States for his brother's death. After this personal tragedy Park moved closer to members of the Korean Workers Party, who had infiltrated the constabulary and acquired a reputation for being anti-American.[32]

Park's involvement with the left came to a dramatic end in the autumn of 1948. After a mutiny in the army, the ROK government declared martial law and conducted a purge of leftists in the military. Park himself was arrested and interrogated. He saved himself by disclosing the names of some leftists whom he knew in the army. Many of his associates were executed, and Park himself was sentenced to life imprisonment but the judgment was subsequently reduced and then suspended. Park survived only because of good references from his superior officers and the sympathy of Paek Sŏnyŏp, the ROK Army intelligence chief who was responsible for carrying out the purge. Although Park did not serve time in jail, he was suspended from holding an official military post for roughly one year.[33]

For Park, getting back into the graces of his superior officers took some doing, and it is not clear that he ever entirely succeeded. Nevertheless, his fortunes improved significantly during the early months of the Korean War. When DPRK troops crossed the 38th parallel in June 1950, Park remained in the South, although he might have easily crossed the border. After this demonstration of loyalty, he was reinstated in the military and began to thrive as an officer with a reputation for diligence and efficiency. Yet his early affiliation with the left continued to haunt him. He was generally slow to rise in the ranks and often received a "temporary" promotion to prove himself worthy of the post before being formally advanced.[34] Park probably felt a mixture of gratitude and resentment toward his superiors in the South Korean military. They had spared his life and enabled him to thrive in his career as an officer. But they also limited his advancement and probably continued to mistrust him.

Park first began contemplating a military coup during the spring of 1960, when Rhee was making his last stand before the April 19 Revolution swept him away. The motives of Park and his co-conspirators arose from an intricate web of nationalistic and personal ambitions. Both in public and in private, Park condemned the corruption and inefficiency in government and came to see the military as the only institution capable of saving the nation. Park was sympathetic toward the leaders of the student revolution but not

Toward Developmental Autocracy

toward the political leaders they brought to power in the summer of 1960. That year he wrote in his journal that "the established politicians who look upon themselves as the leaders of the country are deplorable because of their unrestrained, ignorant and shameless behavior. Most of the people are watching the reform policy of the Second Republic with great expectations and concern for improvement in their lives. However, the political situation is chaotic and disordered, increasing the disappointment of the people."[35] These frustrations provided sufficient inducement to overthrow the existing political leadership.

But Park and his cohort were also motivated by concerns about their own status in the armed forces and by conflicts with their superior officers. American military personnel in South Korea wrongly suspected Park and his closest allies of involvement in a failed plot against the ROK Army's leadership and were pressuring the Chang Myŏn government to discharge them. Many of Park's co-conspirators came from the eighth graduating class of the Korean Military Academy, a tightly knit group within the ROK Army that included Park's brother-in-law and future chief of the Korean Central Intelligence Agency, Kim Chongp'il. When the ROK government implemented military reduction programs, the army's leadership began forcing officers from the eighth graduating class to retire. Having served as field commanders during the Korean War, many of these officers protested that they had been treated unfairly and came to resent both elite officers and the government. Although Park and others had talked about attempting a coup since early 1960, organization of the uprising proceeded much more rapidly after Kim Chongp'il was discharged in February 1961.[36]

After months of careful planning, the junta finally sprang its coup during the early morning hours of 16 May 1961. Marine and airborne brigade units stormed across the Han River into Seoul and seized control of army headquarters and the government radio station. Although Park's forces constituted only a small fraction of the total enlisted in the ROK armed forces, they encountered little resistance from senior officers or the rest of the military establishment. The highest-ranking officers were afraid to assemble troops to suppress the revolt because they believed that their subordinates would side with Park. Although not all of the units that had agreed to participate in the revolution mobilized exactly as planned, in the absence of any serious opposition, the junta captured Seoul within two hours and secured the rest of the country within three days.

News of the coup first spread on the morning of 16 May, when the Military Revolutionary Committee seized the national radio station and announced that it had assumed control of the legislative, executive, and judicial branches of government. The committee explained that its motives were to terminate corruption and overcome the difficult situation facing the nation. It promised that the new regime would seek to prevent the spread of Communism, observe the provisions of the United Nations (UN) Charter and all international agreements, stabilize the national economy, and eventually turn over the government to "honest and competent political leaders." Later that day, the committee announced that the entire nation had been placed under martial law. It subsequently prohibited all public gatherings and travel to foreign countries, set new curfew hours, froze all bank assets, closed all airports and harbors, and established censorship of all publications.[37]

Three days later the Military Revolutionary Committee renamed itself the Supreme Council for National Reconstruction (SCNR). As the SCNR consolidated its control, it initiated aggressive campaigns to stamp out Communism and eliminate corruption while, at the same time, using them as an excuse to purge potential opponents. Within six days of gaining power, the SCNR placed more than 2,000 politicians, including Chang Myŏn, under arrest. By the end of the summer an additional 17,000 civil servants and 2,000 military officers had been taken into custody, dismissed, or retired. The SCNR also sought out and arrested Mint'ong student leaders regardless of whether evidence of their actual crimes existed. To impose order in major cities, the new government rounded up so-called thugs and gangsters and imprisoned more than 13,000 of them. In the early days of the Park regime, civilians could be arrested for violating traffic or curfew laws, and regulations were placed on luxuries such as coffee and entertainment like night club dancing.[38]

Despite these extreme measures, the SCNR was initially not entirely unpopular. South Koreans had grown disillusioned with the failure of Chang's government to curb the continuous political and economic instability that plagued the country. The military committee's rapid extirpation of gangs and hoodlums doubtless earned it the approbation of citizens from various walks of life. Similarly, the Park regime's early emphasis on eliminating corruption appealed to those who had come to resent the opulent lifestyle enjoyed by their politicians.[39] Furthermore, a substantial number of intellectuals and students, many of whom possessed moderate-to-leftist views, had supported the coup.[40]

The junta's military background strongly influenced its posture toward both the rest of South Korean society and the United States. Its leaders deeply believed that the military alone could foster meaningful social change in the country. Often they attempted to use Korean history to legitimate this belief. About a year after gaining power, the regime published a book under Park Chung Hee's name, entitled *Our Nation's Path*, that explained the SCNR's agenda. This volume presented a withering excoriation of much of Korea's history and culture, blaming them for the country's poor track record in economic development. It proclaimed that "our present national traits of reliance upon others, truckling, and blind obedience to the ruler all have their history in five centuries of the Yi dynasty."[41] The book also offered a detailed analysis of the ways that Yi dynasty traditions contributed to Korea's low productivity, claiming that "the Korean form of laziness derives from the Yangban concept (a concept deeply ingrained throughout our history in the minds of the nobility), privilege consciousness and the desire for unearned income."[42]

Our Nation's Path argued that the people should look to military rather than Confucian traditions for guidance on the nation's future. Counting Korean military heroes among the few segments of the country's "worthy heritage," it called Admiral Yi Susin, whose naval forces repelled a sixteenth-century Japanese invasion, "the greatest prototype of the national hero." Over the course of history, "the real national image of the great man was not that of a weak pedant but rather of a patriotic fighter who would readily die on the battlefield in defense of his country."[43] Soldiers, rather than scholars or government officials, were and always had been the ones who could strengthen and improve the nation, according to South Korea's new leadership.

While the junta demonstrated the sense of military nationalism that the Americans had helped imbue in South Korean officers, it also reflected the ambivalence toward the United States that was typical of officers with Japanese backgrounds like Park Chung Hee. Park recognized the necessity of continuing U.S. assistance and, indeed, tried to extract as much aid as possible when it supported objectives that meshed with his own agenda. But he worried about the implications of the country's reliance on the United States. Park's autobiography, *The Country, the Revolution and I*, expressed some of the regime's mixed feelings on this issue. The book noted that South Korea was "under the influence of the United States—whether she likes it or not." It went on to say that "we thank the Americans one hundred times for their aid during the dark days of our fighting. But our grief over the misery of Korea, perennially left at the mercy of others is almost fathomless." Commenting on U.S. financial assistance, Park asserted that "we [Koreans] highly appreciate the ideals of democracy and enthusiasm with which foreign aid is given, but the United States should not, through this vehicle, expect to Americanize the Korean society."[44] Park's writings demonstrated how extensive exposure to American ideas and institutions simultaneously fueled the military's ambitions to lead the country while alienating it from certain dimensions of American hegemony. Clearly, however, the success of the junta's leaders would hinge in part on how U.S. policymakers responded to them.

Park Chung Hee and American Foreign Policy

Park's rapid seizure of power in many ways presented American policymakers with a fait accompli. Once the coup occurred, it would have been difficult for Americans to overturn it without causing complete political chaos. But the United States still wielded enormous influence on South Korea and could have undermined Park if it had been determined to do so. But this was generally not the course that America chose. Instead, U.S. officials opted to develop a closer working relationship with Park than they had had with either of his predecessors. Park enjoyed American support and indulgence despite his autocratic proclivities because of his earnest pursuit of economic development. U.S. policymakers recognized that the military regime's modernizing zeal was something that had been lacking in Chang Myŏn's civilian government. To the Kennedy administration, Park's military background and relative youth were both assets that would enable him to push forward with modernization and reform. Although American policymakers worried that Park's fervent nationalism would make him less amenable to U.S. influence, they were willing to overlook this difficulty because economic development had become their top priority.

U.S. officials did not come to this view of Park right away. When his junta first seized power in May 1961, they seemed uncertain how to deal with it. The coup itself had occurred at a somewhat inopportune time for the State Department. A new ambassador, Samuel Berger, had been appointed by President Kennedy but had still not arrived in Seoul. In the interim, chargé d'affaires Marshall Green had primary responsibility at the American embassy. Moreover, both Kennedy and Secretary of State Dean Rusk were visiting Canada, leaving Chester Bowles, who had very limited knowledge of South Korea, in charge of the State Department. The speed and certainty of the U.S. reaction to the coup were both circumscribed by these circumstances.[45]

The highest-ranking U.S. military leaders and diplomats stationed in the ROK were dismayed by Park's action and at first sought to restore the Chang government. Hours after the coup had been launched, General Magruder,

Toward Developmental Autocracy

the commander in chief of the UN forces, called upon all military personnel under his authority, which included the South Korean army, to "support the duly recognized Government of the ROK headed by Prime Minister Chang." He expected that the "Chiefs of the Korean Armed Forces would use their authority and influence to see that control is immediately turned back to the government authorities and that order is restored in the armed forces." At the American embassy, Marshall Green issued a statement that the United States concurred with Magruder's position. The junta countered by preventing both of these statements from being published in newspapers or broadcast on the radio.[46] But the stands taken by Green and Magruder had little effect because they were never officially endorsed by the U.S. State and Defense Departments. While the State Department privately agreed with Green, it refused to convey an official position and decided to adopt a "wait and see attitude."[47]

As the Kennedy administration took stock of South Korea's new leadership, however, this "wait and see" posture slowly shifted to more open acceptance of the new government. A national intelligence report written two weeks after the coup observed that its leaders would "inject a new sense of drive and discipline into the ROK Government's economic and administrative efforts" and perhaps would have some success at "curbing corruption." On the other hand, the report asserted, the coup's leaders were

a new and different breed from the civilian and the more senior military people with whom the US has had most contact. Their authoritarian and nationalistic stamp suggests that they will be less receptive to US guidance. Furthermore, they will be tough, determined, and difficult to deal with. They will probably continue South Korea's alignment with the US, recognizing their country's dependence on the US, but at the same time will seek to assert South Korea's independence in military, economic, and political affairs. ROK-UN military command relationships will probably be a source of continuing difficulty.[48]

Such characterizations of the regime reflected U.S. fears that the junta's commitment to the country's autonomy would diminish American influence, while suggesting the underlying attraction of the junta. Being "new and different" from other South Korean officials, as well as being "tough and determined," were doubtless positive traits in the eyes of some U.S. officials.

As Park consolidated his power during subsequent months, American officials began to recognize the new regime as a force that could promote development while becoming less concerned about its nationalistic, authoritarian character. When Ambassador Samuel Berger arrived in Seoul, he drafted a somewhat more sympathetic appraisal of the regime's activities. In October 1961 Berger told the U.S. secretary of state that the military government had "taken hold with energy, earnestness, determination and imagination albeit with certain authoritarian and military characteristics which have hampered its public image." He believed that Park had instituted a "genuine revolution from the top trying to introduce sweeping reforms of a most fundamental kind." If the new regime could keep threats to South Korea's stability under control, it might do something that few U.S. officials had thought the previous government capable of—stimulate economic development. And if it averted threats to its authority, "there could be established a stable political and economic environment in Korea. In this event, basic economic growth which has top priority in their thinking could be rapid."[49]

Over time American policymakers became convinced of Park's leadership abilities in part because he was committed to eliminating what they viewed as the pernicious effects of Korean traditions such as corruption and factionalism. In describing initiatives that he had undertaken, they often contended that Park's dynamism was countering the influence of traditional forces. In one telegram, Berger wrote that "the government is energetically rooting out and exposing past corruption." In another, he claimed that "the vigor with which Park has fought against factionalism in the Supreme Council has so far served to keep this endemic disease under control."[50] Even those with reservations about the Park government sometimes acknowledged its capacity to contribute to national development. Contrasting the present government with the one it had replaced, a U.S. official observed that with the Chang Myŏn "regime we were more confident about its good intentions than about its political capabilities. In the case of the new military regime we are somewhat more confident about capabilities, at least to initiate reform measures, and less confident of intentions."[51]

By the fall of 1961 the Kennedy administration was far more receptive to the regime. In November Kennedy invited Park to visit the United States, where the two leaders discussed the pressing issues of military security and economic development. The news conveyed to Park during his meetings with Kennedy and other U.S. officials was not entirely good. Washington had decided that the huge costs of waging the Cold War throughout the world, including an increasing American commitment to Vietnam, would force the United States to reduce the level of economic assistance that it could offer Korea.[52] Nevertheless, Kennedy's decision to invite Park to the

The military background of the Park government loomed large during South Korean president Park Chung Hee's first meeting with President John F. Kennedy in 1961. (John F. Kennedy Library)

United States played a significant role in stabilizing and legitimizing the South Korean regime.

Park's military background heightened his appeal to U.S. officials and helped convince them that he had the potential to succeed as a nation builder. Key members of the Kennedy administration seemed to be particularly attracted to military leaders. They were fond of pointing out that they belonged to the generation that had fought in World War II.[53] The president consistently associated himself with the U.S. armed forces by resurrecting the U.S. Army Special Forces and becoming closely identified with the elite counterinsurgency unit, the Green Berets.[54] South Korean army officers, with their intimate connections to the U.S. military, naturally garnered the understanding and respect of American officials with military backgrounds. The U.S. Department of Defense showed sympathy toward the military coup from the beginning and criticized General Magruder for supporting Chang during the hours after the coup had occurred. Marshall Green attributed this attitude to the fact that "many of the old-time military who had served in the Korean War and who were very dedicated to the Korean armed forces . . . automatically sided with them [the junta's leaders]."⁵⁵

U.S. military leaders who had served in Korea played an important role in shoring up American support for the junta. During a business trip to South Korea in July 1962 General James Van Fleet, who had been a strong advocate of building up the ROK military during the Korean War, met with key members of the junta. In subsequent meetings with State Department officials, Van Fleet gave a strong endorsement of the Park government. He told the deputy secretary of state that the leaders of the military coup were "good boys." Van Fleet then reminisced about his wartime experiences, noting that the Korean military had been "very eager to have American guidance and approval." Since then, the "Koreans had matured" and "wanted to do things in their own way," but they still "wanted and needed American approval." Van Fleet recommended that the United States publicly endorse the Park regime.⁵⁶ The enthusiastic if slightly patronizing backing of prominent military figures like Van Fleet carried significant weight with the Kennedy administration and helped cement American support for Park.

Moreover, key advisers on development policy, such as Walt Rostow, advanced the argument that the militaries of developing countries were potential agents of economic and social change. Shortly after the Kennedy administration assumed political leadership, Rostow had discussed the possibility of encouraging local indigenous military establishments that received U.S. financial aid to make "radically enlarged contributions" to the economic development and modernization of their nations. Rostow reasoned that local militaries often contained "a high proportion of the administrative and engineering talent of their societies" and could "lead the way in the construction of public works." He had also proposed that military training periods be used to "expand literacy and the acquisition of technical skills essential to civil life" in order to promote the diffusion of organizational and administrative capabilities acquired in the army to the society as a whole.⁵⁷ Doubtless, South Korea, whose military personnel had been trained in skills with civilian applications by U.S. officers, was one of the countries that Rostow had in mind when he advocated this approach.

American development experts dispatched to South Korea often saw the applicability of Rostow's notion of the military as a modernizing force to the Park regime. Joel Bernstein, who served as director of the U.S. Agency for International Development (USAID) between 1964 and 1967, recalled being impressed with the discipline exhibited by South Korean officials from military backgrounds. He said that regardless of where he traveled in the

Toward Developmental Autocracy

country, meetings with government officials always began in the same way. He "would be sat down in a chair, and tea was served, and then they [the government officials] would begin a briefing with a flip chart and graphs around the wall, and the briefing was straight out of the U.S. military briefing manuals." Bernstein thought that the organizational skills demonstrated by these government officials was a by-product of the fact that "there had been inculcated throughout Korea a sort of problem-solving approach which is not in its traditional culture." The military, he added, "obviously had a great deal to do with that."[58] For officials like Bernstein, the military origins of the Park regime elicited confidence and respect.

Well attuned to the positive attitudes of U.S. officials toward the ROK armed forces, high-ranking members of the SCNR emphasized their military origins in efforts to curry favor with the Kennedy administration. In public speeches and conversations with American diplomats, they frequently pointed to their backgrounds as evidence that they were equipped to govern the ROK. When Kim Dongsŏng, a foreign ministry official, visited the United States in 1963, for instance, he gave an address explaining the motives and policies of the coup's leaders. Kim boasted that "in the military coup we have the situation of the military personnel who have been associated with the American military personnel for many years following the American methods of military thought." Such statements served to reassure Americans who had qualms about the regime and generate a favorable impression of Park's government among those with more limited knowledge of South Korean politics.[59]

Park also embodied the new sort of political leadership that the Kennedy administration hoped would gain power in developing nations. Even before he was elected president, Kennedy had expressed his hope that a new generation of dynamic "men" who would reform the world's traditional societies would emerge. In his nomination speech, he proclaimed that "all over the world, particularly in the newer nations, young men are coming to power—men who are not bound by the traditions of the past—men who are not blinded by the old fears and hates and rivalries—young men who can cast off the old slogans and delusions and suspicions."[60] Within several months of the coup, American policymakers had come to believe that Park might well be one of these "young men."

American officials often emphasized the youth and dynamism of the junta's leaders in their discussions of U.S. relations with the ROK. In one conversation between President Kennedy, Rostow, and other high-ranking administration officials in June 1961, Kennedy said that the economic situation in South Korea seemed "hopeless." Rostow, however, disagreed; he noted, among other things, the presence of "young, aggressive, capable people" in the ROK government as the basis for optimism.[61] Ambassador Berger sometimes emphasized the vigor of the regime's leadership as well. In a telegram of 15 December 1961 to Secretary of State Dean Rusk, Berger wrote that members of the junta had "established themselves as a group of capable, energetic, and dedicated men determined to make genuine reforms, to lay the foundations for honest and effective government and devoted to the return of representative government." Given the junta's vigorous commitment to change, Berger argued, the administration could tell Congress that "our continuing massive support is well justified."[62] Even the highest-ranking members of the Kennedy administration had come to regard the junta in these terms. When Park visited the United States in November 1961, for instance, Vice President Lyndon B. Johnson praised him for his "display of ability, energy and dedication."[63] Such descriptions of the junta's leadership helped it to garner sympathy from the White House.

It is significant that long after Park's assassination in 1979, many American officials continued to evaluate him according to the same logic. During an interview in the late 1990s, Richard A. Ericson, who served as a political counselor to the American embassy in Seoul between 1965 and 1968, offered an opinion of Park that epitomizes the way American officials balanced their distaste for the regime's authoritarianism with their attraction to its dynamism. Park, Ericson contended, "was one of the great men of recent Asian history." He went on to explain that:

> . . . this isn't to say that he [Park] didn't have blemishes, warts, even cancers. The man was terribly flawed, but he also had a fixation on being the one who brought Korea into the modern era, and economic development was the key to that and he pursued this with extraordinary vigor for his first two terms in office over eight years. I think he has never been given adequate credit for that. The American press always portrayed him as an autocratic little monster of some kind that stifles all Christian and democratic elements unmercifully and was cruel and supported cruelty, etc. And to a certain extent some of those charges are reasonably accurate. The point with Park was that he also had this burning intent to take Korea where he thought it should go and he had the conviction that he alone was the one who could do it. And you know, he may very well have been right.[64]

Toward Developmental Autocracy

Ericson's analysis acknowledges Park's flaws, but it also portrays him as a vigorous, even heroic figure who could lead South Korea to modernity. During the Kennedy and Johnson administrations, such evaluations made U.S. officials more eager to support Park and assist him in the vital tasks of governing and promoting economic development. America's decision to recognize Park rather than seeking to restore South Korea's democratically elected leaders paved the way for developmental autocracy.

Development over Democracy

When South Korea's brief, undistinguished first experiment with democracy ended in 1961, a new consensus on the need for a strong government that could forge ahead with economic development quickly formed in Washington and Seoul. Americans and South Koreans agreed that improving the country's economic situation was so crucial that it needed to be achieved even at the expense of democracy. But despite this broad understanding of the political future of the Republic of Korea (ROK), important questions remained: How powerful should the government be? How much dissent would be tolerated? What type of economic model should be adopted? Americans and South Koreans did not always arrive at the same answers.

They resolved their disagreements in different ways at different times. As South Korea's economy improved during the 1960s, it became less dependent on the United States and Park Chung Hee gained greater leverage to resist U.S. influence. Between 1961 and 1963 American officials used the influence that economic aid bought them to force the recalcitrant junta to amend its economic policies and hold free elections. Once Park triumphed in an open election and transitioned to a civilian government, however, relations between the two governments improved. While Americans had insisted on a democratic government that allowed some measure of dissent, they also wanted the South Korean state to be strong enough to implement unpopular but necessary reforms. During the mid-1960s U.S. support for Park at critical junctures facilitated the emergence of a developmental autocracy. By the end of the decade, political and economic centralization within Park's government went far beyond what the Americans considered necessary, however. U.S. officials in Seoul looked for ways to move the Park regime away from its increasingly authoritarian tendencies. But they found their influence limited by both the declining importance of American economic aid and the reluctance of policymakers in Washington to undermine Park at a time when they were focused on other parts of the world. A South Korean state that was strong but tolerant in the sixties thus gave way to virtually unrestrained authoritarianism by the 1970s.

Civilizing the Military

Although the Kennedy administration welcomed Park's exuberant commitment to economic development, the two years after his junta seized power were fraught with tension between U.S. and South Korean officials. The junta's leaders were bold, nationalistic, and determined to improve conditions in their country. But at the same time they were truculent, autocratic, and mistrustful of American advice. Their military regime imposed strict limitations on civilian life and formulated economic plans that veered toward autarky. These policies sparked a series of conflicts between American officials and the ROK government over how the South Korean political economy would be structured. The Americans used their considerable leverage to push the junta away from military rule and economic nationalism toward political and economic liberalization.

Washington generally wanted to see Park remain in power and was willing to tolerate a junta-controlled government that was not fully democratic. At the same time, they needed assurance that the regime had at least nominal credibility as a democracy and some popular support. This meant ending the military dictatorship and creating a new civilian government that Park could lead but not completely control. Convincing the junta to abandon military rule proved an arduous task. Hard-liners like Kim Chongp'il, Park's nephew-in-law and one of the engineers of the coup, warned that holding any elections could lead to the junta's demise and the return of political instability. The question of whether Park would govern through a strong civilian government or a military dictatorship created serious frictions between the junta and the United States.

A pledge made by Park, shortly after seizing power, to hold elections and restore civilian government after two years provided an important basis for U.S. policy between 1961 and 1963. Washington made it clear that while it considered the fulfillment of this pledge essential, it could accept a formally civilian government that Park would lead or indirectly control. In the summer of 1962 Ambassador Samuel Berger, in a communication to the State Department, explained the kind of political evolution that he considered desirable. The United States should "work on the assumption that [the] transition and election will be carried out on schedule and [that the] successor government will have some measure of constitutional legitimacy." But Washington could "also assume that [the] revolutionary leadership will seek to perpetuate its objectives and control in any new government." This, he thought, was "not necessarily an undesirable project."[1] For Berger, Park and his military cohorts were really the only South Koreans capable of ensuring stability in the country.

The State Department shared Berger's view that South Korea's interests would be best served if Park retained leadership of a more open political system. Discussing the possible outcomes of the elections that Park had promised to hold, Secretary of State Dean Rusk wrote that "it is not realistic for us to insist on full-blown democracy and complete disappearance of the military leadership in 1963." The United States should therefore be prepared to accept Park or an individual selected by him as South Korea's leader, but "this leadership must be legitimated by the people through processes sufficiently free and fair to be acceptable in Korea and the world." Rusk also acknowledged that the "continuation of the KCIA [Korean Central Intelligence Agency] in some form" was probably inevitable. Nevertheless, the United States had to accept such limitations because Park was the "only figure . . . who seems to possess sufficient intelligence, vision, breadth of contact, forcefulness, personal reputation and access to power to fulfill present leadership requirements."[2] In the South Korean context, the secretary preferred a political system that met the basic requirements of democracy but could be strictly controlled from the center.

The junta was less eager than the Americans for elections, despite their potentially legitimating effect. As the date of the promised balloting approached, Park attempted to postpone the return of civilian rule. In March 1963 he informed Berger that he planned to hold a referendum on whether to continue the military government for four more years. Elections would be held only if voters rejected the proposal. Berger objected, for he could not see how such a referendum could amount to anything other than a continuation of military rule, and requested guidance from Washington. The State Department came closer to openly opposing Park over this question than it did at almost any other time during his long tenure in power. Secretary Rusk told Berger that the United States could "not possibly approve and might be compelled openly to oppose continuation of [the] military government for four more years." He also warned that if Park carried out his plan to indefinitely postpone free elections that the United States would have to "review in [a] most fundamental way [the] degree and character of its support of Chairman Park's government." The State Department was willing to consider actions such as public condemnation of Park and the suspension of economic development aid and military assistance.[3]

Clashes over economic policy in 1961 and 1962 deepened American misgivings about Park's leadership. The Kennedy administration emphasized some of the same reforms that Washington had long urged on Park's predecessors, such as improving agricultural productivity, increasing exports, and normalizing relations with Japan. But the Kennedy team was far more insistent than representatives of either Truman or Eisenhower. Under Kennedy, the United States slashed economic assistance and threatened further cuts if its advice was ignored. The U.S. Operations Mission (USOM) reduced economic development grants to the ROK from $177.5 million in 1961 to $92.5 million in 1962.[4] The aid that was offered was to be used to implement specific policies. A "Report of the Korea Task Force," prepared by the National Security Council (NSC) in June 1961, recommended that U.S. influence in South Korea be reinforced by "making economic development assistance available in increments which can be withheld in the event of Korean failure to carry out agreed programs."[5]

The Kennedy administration insisted that the junta consult closely with newly dispatched American advisers in devising economic plans and policies. The NSC task force report stated that "U.S. representatives should insure close consultation in the development of plans including annual budgets and their acceptability to the United States as a condition for granting developmental assistance." After the two sides worked together to formulate such policies, "American influence would be applied to make sure that the agreed plans, policies and programs were carried out."[6] U.S. officials in Seoul took it upon themselves to tutor members of the junta in the principles of economic development and to impose their economic prescriptions.

But South Korea's new leadership mistrusted American advice and undertook several important initiatives without consulting the United States. With great fanfare, the Park government released its "First Five-Year Economic Plan" in January 1962. Reflecting the economic nationalism of the junta, the plan virtually ignored the recommendations that Park had received from leading aid officials in Washington. When Park visited the United States in November 1961, he had been advised to boost agricultural production and develop small export industries. Walt Rostow had told him that "Korea's foremost requirement was to increase the productivity of the Korean farmer."[7] Luther Hodges, the secretary of commerce, had explained that "by starting with certain small industries (e.g. handicrafts)," South Korea could "develop a small export business to build up reserves."[8] Instead, Park's economic plan called for the rapid creation of heavy industries through an import substitution strategy that was fairly similar to the one used by Syngman Rhee.[9] No doubt this approach appealed to the junta's

Development over Democracy

leaders because it gave the state the power to nurture or enfeeble domestic businesses while promising economic autonomy.

American advisers were deeply critical of the First Five-Year Plan, which had been "based on political expediency rather than on economic reality" and was "better described as a collection of goals rather than as a plan for achieving established goals."[10] They subsequently forced the South Korean government to revise it under the close supervision of U.S. economic experts. The junta reluctantly shelved its plans to rapidly build new factories that could produce steel and machine goods and agreed to pursue objectives that Washington considered realistic.

The Park regime triggered a more severe clash with American officials in 1962 when it enacted a major currency reform without alerting the United States. Accordingly, all units of the old currency, the hwan, had to be converted into the new currency, the won, at an exchange rate of ten to one. But only a small amount of the new currency was made available for living expenses; the rest was frozen to finance future industrial investment.[11] The currency reform was the brainchild of Yu Wŏnsik, who some Americans suspected of Communist leanings. Yu had envisioned the reform as a means of providing capital to domestic industries, but U.S. officials worried that the reform would lead to inflation, which they had been pressuring the Park government to curb. On learning of the action, James Killen, the director of the USOM in South Korea, immediately demanded a meeting with Yu. At the meeting Killen accused Yu and the ROK government of violating the terms of the economic aid agreements and threatened to withhold further assistance. As in the case of the First Five-Year Plan, American advisers got their way in the end and the currency reform was abandoned. In the aftermath of the conflict, Yu was asked to resign from the Supreme Council for National Reconstruction (SCNR).[12]

By the summer of 1963 Park's foot-dragging on the question of holding elections and his open defiance on economic policy issues had dampened American enthusiasm for the junta. In July, Ambassador Berger complained to the State Department about the junta's apparent determination to remain in control of South Korea at all costs and refusal to accept American guidance. Berger was particularly critical of "the small group that constitutes [the] core of the original revolution," by which he meant Park, Kim Chongp'il, and some of their close allies. This group was characterized by "a 'will to power' and a willingness to be ruthless" and by a "touchy ultra-nationalism and barely concealed anti-Americanism." Berger worried that Park would cancel the promised elections. Moreover, "if events unfold as now appears likely," the United States would be "unable to support the junta."[13]

But Park recognized the need to accommodate American demands before he lost the support of the United States. In addition, the failure of the junta's initial economic reforms gradually made it more willing to accept U.S. guidance. Extremely poor harvests in 1962 and 1963 resulted in an increase in food imports and food prices. The currency reform exacerbated the ROK's economic difficulties much as American advisers had predicted. The reform failed to turn up money that could finance investment, while many enterprises had difficulty getting loans. This led to a drop in output and even greater inflation.[14] Under intense pressure from the United States, the Park government replaced many of its more nationalistic economic advisers who came from military backgrounds with civilian economists. In the summer of 1962 and the spring of 1963 Park reshuffled his cabinet and appointed American-trained technocrats to positions in the Ministries of Commerce and Finance.[15] These new bureaucrats worked with U.S. advisers in "a fairly cooperative fashion," according to Berger.[16]

More importantly, Park finally yielded to U.S. pressure that he allow free elections to take place in October 1963. In a referendum that American officials generally deemed to be orderly, fair, and efficient, Park pulled off a narrow victory over his closest rival, Yun Posŏn.[17] Park then crafted a new civilian government to suit his purposes. It had a strong executive and a weak legislature in which Park's Democratic Republican Party (DRP) gained the majority. Although the new government restored basic political freedoms, the KCIA had been built into a powerful organization that could be used to monitor and at times intimidate Park's potential opponents in the name of national security. The political system formed in 1963 satisfied American demands that the South Korean government have some measure of popular legitimacy even while it contained safeguards that made it virtually impossible for Park's political opposition to gain power. It was a system that both Park and U.S. officials had a vested interest in sustaining, and during the next few years it allowed for much more cooperative relations between the two countries.

Foreign Policy and Developmental Autocracy

Once Park had restored some semblance of civilian rule and adopted—in the U.S. view—responsible economic policies, Washington became preoccupied with ensuring that his political opponents did not undermine the government's efforts to promote economic development. During the years

Development over Democracy

between 1963 and 1966, the United States pressured the South Korean government to undertake an array of initiatives that were both extremely unpopular and, in the American perspective, absolutely necessary to stimulate the economy. These included foreign policy measures such as normalizing relations with Japan and sending ROK forces to Vietnam, as well as domestic policy measures like promoting exports and devaluing the won. The regime's opponents vociferously fought many of these actions. Park's willingness to accommodate the Americans on these issues in the face of strident opposition bolstered U.S. support for his government while forging a rift between American officials and Park's opponents. Believing that Park was genuinely interested in economic progress and that his opponents acted as a barrier to meeting this objective, Americans strengthened the South Korean state at the opposition's expense.

Rifts between Park and his domestic opponents were the sharpest on foreign policy. The normalization of relations between South Korea and Japan proved particularly contentious. As described in Chapter 1, American officials had sought such a move since the end of World War II but could never overcome lingering Korean animosity stemming from the bitter legacy of Japanese colonialism. The Kennedy administration believed, as its predecessors had, that reconciliation between the two nations was vital to South Korea's economic future. As American expenditures in Vietnam escalated during the early and mid-1960s, U.S. officials were more determined than ever to get Japan to assume part of the economic burden of supporting South Korea. Robert Komer, an NSC staffer who played a key role in setting policy for the ROK, explained in 1962 that American interests dictated "an early resolution of this issue in a manner which will bring Japan to assume a greater share of the burden of subsidizing South Korea."[18] The NSC foresaw economic benefits for the Park government in normalized relations with Japan. A settlement would mean that "rapid Korean economic development . . . would be materially accelerated by Japanese economic aid," and "Korea would gain greater access to Japanese markets for her exports."[19] In the early sixties both the South Korean and Japanese governments showed an increasing willingness to negotiate, and the United States pressured both sides to do so.

But Park's efforts to negotiate an agreement were disrupted by popular protests. Intellectuals, students, and members of the opposition could not set aside their painful memories of the colonial period to achieve better state-to-state relations with Japan. During the spring of 1964 Yun Posŏn, Park's opponent in the 1963 election, launched a campaign against the proposed normalization treaty, and on 3 June large-scale student demonstrations swept across major university campuses. In meetings with U.S. officials in Seoul, Park repeatedly warned that such demonstrations posed a serious threat to the ROK government. A sympathetic American embassy informed the State Department that these demonstrations were a threat not only to the U.S. agenda in South Korea but also to the stability of the country. In late May Ambassador Berger wrote that the "situation in Korea has again reached a peak of uncertainty, unrest and disarray." When he met with Park after the first student demonstrations had erupted, the two agreed that the situation "had become serious."[20]

As the protests against normalization continued, American officials condemned Park's opponents and grew more dubious about whether further democratization in South Korea was desirable. They feared that the opposition was endangering economic growth and became more comfortable with supporting Park's system of formal but very limited democracy. Robert Komer found it "regrettable that [the] irresponsibility of a minority of the students, egged on by an irresponsible opposition, is undermining the ROK's real future hopes." These actions led him to conclude that "this country isn't ready for democracy yet, any more than it was for Rhee-style dictatorship in the Fifties."[21] Of course, Komer did not want to see a return to military dictatorship, but he doubtless thought that South Korea had already gone as far toward democracy as it could for the time being.

When Park declared martial law to suppress the demonstrations, the Americans attempted to dissuade him but later accepted his decision and even offered their tacit consent. In a meeting held at 10:30 on the evening of 3 June, Ambassador Berger cautioned Park that "martial law was no solution" to the widespread demonstrations that had begun that day and encouraged him to consider other measures to deal with popular grievances. But when Park requested that two divisions of the United Nations (UN) Command be released to deal with the situation, Berger acquiesced.[22] In the days that followed the United States pressured Park both to end martial law and to take actions that would boost public confidence in his government. In particular, they urged him to dissociate himself from Kim Chongp'il, whom they blamed for the intensity of the opposition to Park's stand on normalization. American officials then made it possible for Kim to depart gracefully from the scene by arranging for him to study at Harvard University.[23] Although these steps aimed to prevent the regime from returning to full-fledged authoritarianism, their ultimate objective was to strengthen rather than weaken Park's position. By encouraging the South Korean leader to break with his unpopular nephew-in-law while allowing him to strong-arm his opposition, the United States sought to stabilize the country so Park could undertake economic reforms.

After the first wave of demonstrations over normalization had subsided, Park continued to look for U.S. political support on the issue. In July 1964 he told the American ambassador that if the United States "could involve itself more openly and actively in negotiations it would make it possible for him to overcome domestic, political and student opposition."[24] Recognizing that Park's ability to deflect public criticism would be crucial to effecting a rapprochement between South Korea and Japan, U.S. diplomats in South Korea and Japan sought assistance from the State Department. One of them was Edwin Reischauer, the American ambassador to Japan, who was deeply invested in negotiating a settlement. In August, he wrote Walt Rostow that "to get normalization over the very great hurdles of party conflict and opposition in Korea," the United States would "have to push more openly for it in Korea than it had in the past."[25]

In subsequent months the State Department attempted to help Park legitimate his diplomacy in the eyes of the South Korean people. In November 1964 it drew up plans for him to visit the United States the following spring, reasoning that given the magnitude of U.S. influence in South Korea, the invitation would confer additional prestige upon Park, intimate American support for his diplomatic agenda, and weaken the opposition at home to his stand on an emotional and unpopular issue. Winthrop Brown, who had become U.S. ambassador to the ROK in July 1964, recommended tying Park's trip to progress in negotiations with Japan. If Park managed to conclude an agreement with Japan before the spring, then the visit itself could "help gain public acceptance [for] normalization and give Pak [an] extra boost in overcoming this difficult problem." On the other hand, if continuing popular opposition made it impossible to reach a settlement by that time, then the visit "could be used to improve [the] prospects [of] early normalization."[26]

When Park traveled to Washington in May 1965, the final details of the normalization treaty were still being negotiated. News that an agreement was close at hand had set off another wave of protests by South Korean students and opposition leaders. The timing of Park's trip had been carefully deliberated by American and Korean officials. As Ambassador Brown explained, the visit had been "strategically placed between [the] first shock of opposition moves now underway and [the] final struggle over ratification," and the South Korean government was counting on the United States "to provide [a] boost to Pak's position at this most important moment."[27] When Park met with President Lyndon Johnson, Johnson offered economic inducements to make a normalization agreement more palatable to the opposition. In a joint communiqué signed by the two presidents, the United States pledged to continue financial assistance to South Korea after it normalized relations with Japan.[28] The announcement seemed geared to mitigate popular fear that the United States favored normalization as a way of encouraging Japan to reestablish economic control of the ROK.

Taking advantage of the momentum created by his trip, Park pushed forward with negotiations on returning home. He agreed with American advisers that his country had reached a "psychological moment for the settlement which must not be lost."[29] By 22 June 1965 South Korea and Japan had drawn up a Treaty on Basic Relations. Park's opposition made one last-ditch effort to stall the agreement when it came up for ratification in the National Assembly in August. The Park government faced both student demonstrations and threats by opposition leaders in the assembly to resign and force new elections before the treaty could be ratified.

Against this background of raucous protest that threatened to derail the normalization agreement, Americans again focused on containing the opposition. On 12 August U.S. officials responsible for East Asian affairs met to consider the problem. They believed that it was essential to prevent Park's adversaries "from paralyzing National Assembly procedures and from increasing opposition sentiment in the population." According to American officials, opponents of the treaty could be divided into two factions: one that was irreconcilably opposed to the treaty and a more moderate group. The American officials discussed potential measures that would "diminish the number of fanatics and to dampen the opposition of the moderates." What actions, if any, the United States ultimately took to accomplish these objectives are unknown since records on the meeting remain classified.[30] The South Korean National Assembly did, however, ratify the treaty two days after the 12 August meeting, with most members of the opposition abstaining from the vote. But even as this ballot ended the controversy over normalization, U.S. pressure had already incited another foreign policy dispute between Park and his opposition.

Before the settlement between South Korea and Japan had even been reached, the United States was calling upon the Park government to undertake another controversial foreign policy initiative: dispatching ROK armed forces to Vietnam. When the Johnson administration requested troops from its Asian allies in 1965, South Korea was the only country that showed

Development over Democracy

an inclination to supply them. Its motives for assisting the United States apparently were a combination of economic opportunism and a strong belief in personal sacrifice for the greater good of the nation. Publicly American and ROK officials represented South Korean participation in the war as an expression of Free World solidarity, but both sides tacitly understood that it would be rewarded with opportunities for South Korean businesses to manufacture goods for U.S. forces in Vietnam. South Korean officials later expressed this understanding quite bluntly. In his autobiography, Yi Tongwŏn, a former ROK foreign minister, recalls telling Park that "Vietnam was a battlefield but it was also a market. Because of that we should use this chance to get everything we can from the United States."[31] For Yi, sending South Korean forces to the area was an amoral transaction that bartered blood for treasure.

Opponents of the Park government resisted their nation's entanglement in the conflict. Although they did not make their case with the same vehemence with which they had fought normalization of relations with Japan, they nevertheless questioned Park's motives for taking part in a distant conflict. When his government proposed sending the first contingent— 2,000 noncombat personnel—to Vietnam in January 1965, the opposition immediately raised a hew and cry in the National Assembly. Some members argued that the move would alienate neutral countries and run the risk of weakening South Korea's security. Frustrated by the opposition's so-called obstructionism, American diplomats tried to persuade its leaders to change their minds. On 22 January 1965 Ambassador Brown met with Yun Posŏn, one of Park's leading political opponents, and "tried to persuade Yun to reconsider his position." When Yun refused to budge, Brown approached Yun's allies.[32] On 26 January Park finally managed to convince the assembly to ratify his proposal but only by relying heavily on support from the Democratic Republican Party.

After such a hard-won victory, members of the party remained apprehensive about the political ramifications of the assembly's decision. Two days after the vote, DRP chairman Chŏng Kuyong voiced these concerns in a meeting with U.S. embassy officials. Chŏng said that there was "widespread opposition" to the deployment of ROK troops among intellectuals, the students, the press, and even members of Park's own party. He warned that the issue was "politically dangerous for the government and its party" and that reports of South Korean casualties would inevitably lead to "emotional antigovernment demonstrations." These demonstrations would "create a situation of instability and crisis which will be extremely difficult to deal with."

Chŏng then tried to sound out the Americans on how they would view measures of his government to counter and perhaps suppress the opposition if such a scenario unfolded. He asked specifically "what moves the United States might be willing to take to meet such a crisis and what steps it would approve on the part of the ROK [Government]." Ambassador Brown emphasized that dealing with any potential political crisis stemming from the dispatch of troops would be "essentially a Korean problem." He encouraged the South Korean government to try to engage the opposition on the issue, but by stressing that this was a "Korean problem" he was also offering tacit approval for more severe measures if they became necessary. Moreover, he promised that the United States would help the regime justify participation in the Vietnam War to the public. The United States was "prepared to assist the government in this task by making clear its support for the Park administration and its deep interest in the sending of forces to Vietnam."[33]

Before long, close collaboration between Park and the United States on the issue became even more crucial. As American involvement in Vietnam continued to expand, the Johnson administration pressured the Park government to deliver a combat division in addition to the noncombat forces it had already sent. The South Korean president recognized that these new troops would be a party to dangerous fighting, but, anticipating economic rewards that would boost development programs at home, he willingly accepted the risks. As his regime planned to take on an even greater share of the burden in Southeast Asia, Park's opposition once again became a potential stumbling block. American and South Korean officials coordinated their efforts to manage the issue politically. They were of one mind that before any public discussion of the proposal, the U.S. embassy, the UN Command, and the ROK government would have to agree on the "same story and [the] same way of putting it to the public."[34]

Ultimately, Washington chose to offer concrete economic benefits to the South Korean people as an incentive to support the government's controversial decision. Ambassador Brown saw the need for a measure that would both "meet the political objections which the [government] faces in seeking to send combat troops to RVN [Republic of Vietnam]" and "contribute at least partially to the solution to the economic problems which the government faces."[35] Brown persuaded the White House to suspend South Korean's funding requirements for the Military Assistance Program (MAP). When the program was established after the Korean War, the United States procured equipment for both UN and ROK forces in South Korea to reduce U.S. expenditures and improve South Korean industry. But over time,

Washington had required South Korea to assume the burden of procuring these items from its own defense budget. Since American efforts to transfer these costs to South Korea had long been an item of contention between Washington and Seoul, eliminating them had the potential to provide a political boost for President Park. Brown foresaw that this measure would be "represented by the ROK [Government] as a political victory" and would ensure "united DRP support for dispatch of a division to [the Republic of Vietnam]."[36]

The American offer of economic rewards did expedite the dispatch of ROK combat forces, although Park's opposition never supported the action. Park shrewdly included the proposal to send combat troops to Vietnam in the same National Assembly session as the ratification of the treaty normalizing relations with Japan. By doing so, he forced the opposition to spend most of its energy protesting the treaty, leaving scant time to debate the wisdom of sending troops to Vietnam. Thanks to American promises of increased aid, Park's allies in the DRP were united in their support to assist South Vietnam and approved the proposal to do so over the protests of a confused and weary opposition.[37]

It was not long, however, before another round of clashes between Park and his domestic critics on the Vietnam issue erupted. As the Johnson administration further entangled the United States in what proved to be an intractable conflict, it began calling on its allies for further contributions to the war effort. Once again, South Korea was among the few American allies to show any hint of enthusiasm in its response to Johnson's requests. Park entered into negotiations with the United States hoping to barter the dispatch of a second ROK combat division for new economic opportunities. Managing the potential opposition in South Korea remained his greatest obstacle. Thus, when Washington asked for a second division in December 1965, it immediately began talks on how to deal with probable dissent in the ROK. Ambassador Brown met with South Korean prime minister Chŏng Ilgwŏn to consider "tactics for handling political problems" that would inevitably result from a proposal to send more ROK troops. Chŏng requested a visit by either the U.S. secretary of state or secretary of defense to "assure [the] Korean public of continuing deep concern and support of US leadership for [the] ROK [Government]."[38] In a later meeting, Chŏng suggested that the United States arrange a trip to Vietnam by journalists and members of the National Assembly so that they "could be indoctrinated" on the need for ROK forces.[39]

The Johnson administration soon launched a public relations offensive in

South Korea calculated to give Park more leverage. In February 1966 Vice President Hubert Humphrey arrived in Seoul to underscore that the ROK government had America's blessing and to offer new types of economic rewards. During his brief stay, Humphrey met with government officials and members of the opposition party specifically to discuss the war effort in Vietnam. Prime Minister Chŏng later told him that these meetings would "be of great assistance to the government in winning both public and national assembly for the deployment of additional forces."[40] A week later, Park announced his proposal to send one additional regiment and another combat division to Vietnam. Once again members of the opposition fiercely protested and eventually voted against the measure, but with his hand strengthened by U.S. support Park was able to secure its passage on 20 March 1966.

Crucial to convincing members of Park's own party to vote for the proposal was the package of economic benefits that the United States offered in exchange for an expanded Korean contribution to the war effort. The Johnson administration not only continued its suspension of ROK funding requirements for the MAP program but also created opportunities for fledgling South Korean industries. The United States agreed to procure supplies from South Korea for American and South Vietnamese forces as well as for U.S. assistance agencies engaged in rural reconstruction and pacification projects in Vietnam. In addition, it began providing opportunities for South Korean contractors to participate in construction projects undertaken by the U.S. government and American contractors in Southeast Asia.[41] For a regime that relied heavily on economic development for legitimacy, these trade-offs had an almost irresistible appeal.

Many Koreans criticized Park's diplomacy on the issues of Japan and Vietnam for subordinating the will of his people to the imperatives of the United States, Japan, and global capitalism.[42] These criticisms did have some validity. For Park, however, the benefits of integrating South Korea into the world economy outweighed the costs. His government reaped economic windfalls from its policies toward both Japan and the Vietnam conflict. Under the terms of the normalization treaty, the Japanese government agreed to provide the ROK $30 million in unconditional grants and an additional $20 million in low-interest loans. Moreover, the treaty produced a dramatic increase in trade between South Korea and Japan. Within two years of the time it was signed, Japan had become the ROK's largest trading partner and a significant source of both foreign investment and technology transfer.[43] Along similar lines, between 1965 and 1968 the ROK earned $402 million through exports to Vietnam, sales to the U.S. military, and other arrangements deriving from its decision to send troops to the country. Moreover, South Korea began selling products to Vietnam that it was not yet exporting to other countries, such as steel, transportation equipment, and nonelectric machinery. The Vietnam War proved invaluable for the development of all of these export industries.[44] But while these two pivotal foreign policy choices created the framework for rapid economic expansion, they did not guarantee that it would occur. The Park government's domestic policies needed to be even more farsighted than its foreign policies were.

Domestic Policy and Developmental Autocracy

Like the international setting, the domestic environment in South Korea challenged the Park government to make critical but unpopular decisions. The country needed to mobilize its resources, spur exports, and take full advantage of the opportunities created by its foreign policy. None of these objectives could be achieved without causing short-term hardships for some sectors of the population. The United States supported a large team of economic advisers in Seoul to keep the pressure on Park to make what they considered the appropriate policy choices. Robert Nathan, who was a private consultant in South Korea at the time, explained that these advisers "worked hand in hand with the Korean government in running the economy in a kind of joint venture."[45] American advisers generally admired the reformist zeal of Park and his cohorts but feared that without guidance and support from the United States they would be unable to overcome formidable barriers to economic progress.

After Park made the transition to civilian government, American advisers found a new tier of bureaucrats who were much more open to U.S. guidance than their predecessors had been. Although military officers remained in control of many bureaucratic positions, Park appointed talented civilian administrators to top posts in the most important financial ministries. These included Chang Kiyŏng, who was appointed director of the Economic Planning Board (EPB) and entrusted with broad powers over economic development planning; Yang Yunse, who had earned a master's degree in economics at Cornell University and became deputy director of the EPB; and Pak Chunghun, the new minister of commerce. A zealous but apolitical commitment to economic development enabled members of this group to work comfortably within the state apparatus that Park had created while embracing American guidance.

Relations between the EPB and the USOM were particularly close during the mid-sixties. The EPB's building was located across the street from the USOM in downtown Seoul, and the geographic proximity of the two institutions facilitated interaction between their personnel.[46] Many South Korean officials were eager to learn from U.S. advisers who were schooled in cutting-edge economic development theories. Ch'oe Kakkyu, a former assistant director of the EPB, recalled that in "in the process of conferring" with Americans who worked in different branches of the ROK government, Koreans "could study and absorb many things." Ch'oe credited the USOM with introducing EPB planners to new concepts such as present value and the floating exchange system. He wrote that "to the extent that we were adept and skilled it was from the beginning because we were next to our family teacher the USOM."[47]

American advisers collaborated closely with South Korean planners to implement a new stabilization agreement signed by the two countries in April 1963. The pact emphasized increased savings through tax collection and reform of the monetary and fiscal structure by tightening the money supply and floating the exchange rate.[48] The Americans believed that these reforms would permit reductions in aid to South Korea. Implementing the stabilization agreement became one of the cornerstones of U.S.-ROK economic cooperation during the mid-1960s. The USOM sent David Cole, a Harvard University development expert, to Seoul to supervise a team of economists from both countries who monitored the Korean economy and made sure that the agreement was faithfully executed. Although the USOM kept a close watch over ROK policies, relations between Americans and South Koreans on the stabilization committee were amicable. Vincent Brown, who served as assistant director for program and economic policy in the ROK between 1964 and 1967, later said that "psychologically, this joint programming was palatable to Koreans because their U.S. colleagues were considered blood brothers."[49]

The most significant dimension of the stabilization committee was the fact that its meetings occurred in a virtual political vacuum. U.S. and Korean economists made crucial decisions about economic policies with little or no popular input. After these decisions were made, Americans often worked with the Park government to foresee and manage the political ramifications. U.S. officials recognized that implementing the committee's most important decisions necessitated tolerance for a stronger South Korean state even if it alienated the United States from the opposition.

One of the most critical elements of the stabilization agreement was domestic resource mobilization. The government needed resources that could finance investment, but financial savings were not increasing in real terms and tax revenues had failed to keep pace with GNP growth.[50] American advisers thought that this posed a significant obstacle to economic development. One USOM country plan called the expansion of domestic savings the "key bottleneck which will limit the rate at which the Korean economy will grow and progress toward self-support."[51] But the policy measures required to alleviate this problem were unpopular and, the Americans feared, destabilizing. Tax increases seldom fail to inspire popular antipathy, and South Korea was no exception. Many Koreans still associated modern modes of tax collection with the repressive Japanese colonial government and had few ethical qualms about tax evasion. Higher interest rates were opposed by the business sector, which believed that they led to an increase in the cost of bank loans and a rise in inflation.[52] Thus, although USOM advisers urged South Korea to "push all the specific savings-inducing policies that it can," they acknowledged that, "politically," this was "a very difficult prescription."[53]

The United States and the Park government worked together cautiously to build support for the necessary policies. The USOM shipped teams of high-profile advisers to Seoul to signal American support for these politically controversial measures and to pressure the Park government to implement them. The first of these teams, led by noted Harvard University economist Richard Musgrave, focused on rationalizing the ROK tax system. Musgrave suggested a variety of measures to bolster tax revenues, such as reclassifying urban lands, increasing property tax rates, merging local taxes with the basic national taxes, and strengthening the administration of inheritance and gift taxes.[54] At roughly the same time Washington sent a team of well-known gurus on money and finance to provide guidance on interest rate strategy. This group helped persuade the Park government to legislate dramatic increases in the maximum interest rates on savings deposits and bank loans.[55] South Korean newspapers closely scrutinized the comings and goings of these eminent American academics, and their presence no doubt added legitimacy to government efforts.

With U.S. backing, the Park regime succeeded in dramatically increasing tax revenues and tackling major interest rate reforms. In 1966 it implemented what some American advisers approvingly labeled the "quiet revolution in tax administration."[56] President Park created an Office of National Tax Administration (ONTA) in which to centralize authority for collecting taxes and investigating tax fraud. The new office was followed a year later by a tax law reform that raised assessments on the wealthiest individuals and corporations. Consequently, tax revenues surged from 29.2 billion won in 1964 to 156.4 billion won by 1968.[57] The interest rate reforms of 1965 were equally striking. The Monetary Board of Korea raised the maximum interest rate on time deposits from 15 to 30 percent per annum while hiking the interest rate on bank loans from 16 to 26 percent. Because the government combined this reform with an expansive public information campaign to promote greater savings, the reform's objectives were achieved much more rapidly than expected. Economist Kwang Suk Kim calculates that, as a result of this reform, adjusted household savings climbed from less than 1 percent of disposable income in 1965 to 4.1 percent in 1966 and remained higher than 3.4 percent for the remainder of the decade. Gross domestic investment as a percentage of GNP registered a similarly dramatic increase, growing from 15 percent in 1965 to 29 percent by 1969.[58]

The successful implementation of these critical reforms in the face of domestic opposition further strengthened U.S. support for Park. Policymakers praised him for overcoming popular opposition on both tax law revisions and interest rate reforms. After Park completed the first stage of his so-called quiet revolution in tax administration, Frank Landers, the USOM public administration adviser in South Korea, lauded the "strong leadership and positive support from top echelons of the ROKG[overnment]" for revising the tax structure. He noted that there had been and would continue to be difficulties caused by "resistance from vested interests, both public and private, . . . [the] political climate, commercial intrigues, and resistance to change from age old customs and practices." In light of these problems, Landers thought, "the achievements of the immediate past become more impressive and spark an optimistic view of future prospects."[59] From his perspective, the Park government's strong leadership was having a positive impact on the South Korean economy and therefore needed to be perpetuated.

American policymakers had similar praise for the interest rate reforms. In a lengthy report of November 1965 to Assistant Secretary of State William Bundy, Ambassador Winthrop Brown lavishly commended the regime's willingness to face down its political opposition on critical economic policy measures. The Park government had "taken a number of quite unpopular decisions which were economically necessary." Among other things, it had "raised the price of electricity and coal[,] . . . restricted the amount of credit," and "completely reorganized the interest rate structure of the money market." These measures had been undertaken "in the face of violent protests from the vested interests and most of the business community plus the political opposition and most of the newspapers." Whereas the regime's success earned the ambassador's respect, the opposition's stance on these issues only left the Americans more convinced that it was irresponsible and unworthy of U.S. support. Brown wrote that Park's willingness to risk "unpopular decisions, such as those made in the name of preventing inflation" had turned him into a "different and stronger man than he was before." This contrasted with "the inept performance of the opposition, which has completely disintegrated and provides no reasonable alternative to which the public can turn."[60]

Although they viewed Park's efforts to mobilize domestic resources as a sterling success, U.S. policymakers still believed that more needed to be done to stimulate the economy. In particular, South Korea would have to increase exports, an objective that required its own set of unpopular policy measures. American economic advisers insisted first that the ROK devalue the won, because it would make Korean exports cheaper to prospective buyers. But the government's subsequent decision to change the official exchange rate from 130 to 256 won per U.S. dollar met with widespread criticism and protest. According to the State Department, after the announcement "members [of the] National Assembly, [the] press, and other[s] in academic and business circles uttered cries of alarm." A major South Korean newspaper contended that the devaluation would lead to a "vicious price spiral," while members of the assembly called the decision a "complete mistake" and contended that it would cause the people great hardship.[61] The apparent ubiquity of such resistance aroused concerns in Washington that the Park government would be unable to implement the reform.

Once again the United States helped Park manage the opposition. Most criticism of currency devaluation stemmed from apprehension that it would raise the cost of imports and therefore cause inflation. The American embassy reported that there was "considerable discontent in [the] country over price inflation" and a "fear that devaluation would aggravate price rises." To counter the potential rise in food costs, the USOM agreed to make 250,000 additional tons of grain available to South Korea through the Public Law 480 program. The Operations Mission argued that these "additional grain supplies would make [it] easier for [the] ROKG to tackle the two problems of devaluation and ROK-Japan settlement." The announcement of this increased assistance became a critical part of the USOM's strategy for gaining popular acceptance of currency devaluation. The U.S. embassy observed that "since [the] act of devaluation will automatically result in some increase in domestic prices . . . from [a] tactical point of view it would be useful for [the] government to announce availability at [the] time devaluation is put in effect."[62] Secretary of State Dean Rusk lent further support to the measure by issuing a formal statement on the day that devaluation was enacted, praising it as "an important step toward the strengthening of Korea's foreign exchange earning capability and the establishment of equilibrium in her external accounts."[63] The Americans hoped that such pronouncements from high-ranking officials would convince South Koreans that the reform was in their country's best interest.

The combination of American economic assistance and South Korean policies did, in fact, limit the inflationary impact of currency devaluation. Although prices initially rose, within a month they had declined and stabilized. The USOM attributed this to U.S. economic assistance, bumper crop harvests, and efforts made by the South Korean government to control supplies of money and credit and restrict nonessential imports. American policymakers saw the ROK's success in implementing the measure while averting negative political ramifications as a cause for optimism and a reason for offering Park further support. A report in August 1964 stated that the "prospects for continued expansion of trade and investment under conditions of relative price stability appear encouraging" and that the regime was attempting to implement policies emphasizing export promotion, control of inflation, and industrial production.[64] With each difficult but necessary decision that it made, the Park government deepened American trust in its economic stewardship.

Yet despite its importance, currency devaluation was not in and of itself enough to increase exports. Actions to stimulate individual firms to manufacture and export goods were also essential. In this area, too, the regime made policy choices that were politically controversial but staunchly supported by the United States, at least initially. South Korea originated a distinctive system of export promotion that combined strategies used by the Japanese colonial government with those pushed by American advisers. Like the Japanese, President Park nurtured a select group of favored firms through tax concessions, special rates on railway transportation, and bank loans at preferential interest rates. The last of these policies proved especially controversial. The majority of the companies receiving the preferential treatment were large firms that would later become world renowned business conglomerates, or *chaebŏl*, such as Samsung and Hyundai. These firms are widely believed to have repaid the government's generosity by making contributions to Park's political party, the DRP.[65] This reciprocal exchange of financial largesse tied the strength of the state to the economic success of the chaebŏl.

To Park's political opposition, however, this symbiotic relationship smacked of corruption. In 1965 members of the opposition in the National Assembly launched an investigation of the regime's lending practices after allegations appeared in the media that a few privileged firms had received large-scale preferential loans on orders from high-ranking government officials. They targeted two leading chaebŏl: the Samho Group, a diverse financial organization with interests in textiles, banking, and the media, and the Hwasin Group, which was engaged in the manufacture of textiles for export. As a result of the probe, the assembly recommended that the government adopt measures that would tighten control of bank financing.[66]

Such protests against Park's increasingly collusive economic policies garnered little sympathy from the United States. Americans were far more worried that the assembly's protests would slow exports than they were about corruption or the growing economic power of the South Korean state. Although the economic counselor at the American embassy recognized that the Park government's use of preferential loans "encourage[d] favoritism and corruption," he saw few alternatives to it. He argued that "various political factions" had "seized upon the preferential loan controversy to discredit the Administration and Individual personalities for political, economic or purely personal reasons." Ultimately, the preferential loan system was essential to South Korea's future, as "large companies form the backbone of the Korean economy and they will undoubtedly continue to require access to financial resources which, if not forthcoming on financially justifiable grounds, could easily frustrate economic growth prospects."[67] Although Park was laying the basis for a highly centralized economic system, Americans initially saw little reason to protest because the system achieved the most critical objective: economic growth.

The series of politically difficult decisions made by the regime during the mid-1960s did bring clear benefits to South Korea which soon became readily apparent. By mobilizing domestic capital and promoting exports, the ROK had managed to dramatically increase economic growth rates after nearly two decades of futile efforts to do so by American and Korean policymakers alike. Exports soared from $54.8 million in 1962 to $250.3 million in 1966; in the same period the economy grew at a remarkable 8.3 percent, exceeding even the most optimistic projections.[68] These achievements served not only to solidify U.S. support for the Park government but also to boost the president's popularity among South Koreans. Park had staked his political legitimacy on economic growth, and by producing it he created a compelling reason for the public to support him. In 1967 he won easily a presidential election that most observers considered fair and in which "freedom of political discussion was prevalent."[69] The combination of economic development and American support had paradoxically enabled the South Korean state to become more powerful even while operating within the framework of a formal democracy.

Park's success in spurring economic development elicited highly favorable American evaluations of his governance and deepened U.S. support for him. In 1967 Ambassador Brown hailed the South Korean president as "the prototype of the new political figure in Korea." He had been "exposed to the ways and ideas of the outside world" and had "seen and experienced the implications of modern science and technology and has recognized that these must be appropriately introduced into Korean life if Korea is to survive."[70]

Although American policymakers generally waxed enthusiastic about Park's economic achievements, by the late sixties concerns about his growing political dominance began to creep back into policy documents. U.S. officials did not want Park's opponents to derail his strategies for economic development, but they also did not want him to use these strategies to create a political economy in which the state was too dominant. Even as Americans continued to praise Park, it was becoming increasingly clear that this was exactly what was happening.

American Resistance to the South Korean System

The United States had tolerated, even encouraged the South Korean state to strengthen itself at the expense of civil society in the years between 1962 and 1967. After Park's reelection in 1967, however, Americans working on the ground in South Korea began to worry about an easily discernible trend toward excessive concentration of power by the government. These officials became increasingly focused on reversing this trend, although their efforts often received lukewarm support from Washington.

Park moved toward greater authoritarianism for a variety of reasons, some of them related to security. The late 1960s were troubled times for South Korea's relations with allies and adversaries alike. North Korea suddenly seemed to be on the offensive. In January 1968 the Democratic People's Republic of Korea dispatched a group of highly trained operatives to assassinate the South Korean president. The mission failed, but the North

Koreans followed with other provocative acts—most notably the seizure of the uss *Pueblo*, an American spy ship that had malfunctioned in international waters near the peninsula's eastern coast. These offenses heightened South Korean anxieties about security at a time when the United States was seeking to reduce its commitments in Asia. Several months after taking office, new U.S. president Richard Nixon issued the so-called Nixon Doctrine, declaring that the United States would assist in "the defense and development of allies and friends" but would not "undertake all the defense of the free nations of the world."[71] The Nixon Doctrine was succeeded by National Security Decision Memorandum (NSDM) 48, which ordered the withdrawal of one full division of U.S. combat forces (approximately 20,000 troops) from the ROK.[72] The evolving international situation shocked Park into clamping down on potential subversion at home, while making him less inclined to heed American protests when he did so.

Park's decision to push ahead on heavy industrialization further necessitated a highly centralized power structure. Much as the Japanese governor-general had done in Korea in the 1930s, the Park government sought to create a spurt of industrialization by granting preferential access to raw materials and providing credit on highly favorable terms to a few large firms. Implementing such a plan demanded even closer collaboration between the state and major manufacturers than previously. Production of steel, machine tools, and ships required the government to channel larger sums of capital into a select group of companies whose performance could be closely monitored. Moreover, only a powerful state could deter or suppress labor activism while discouraging the chaebŏls' potential competitors.

Park's creeping efforts to further strengthen the state created a dilemma for U.S. policymakers. While recognizing that he was leading South Korea in a direction that threatened its prospects for democratization, they remained apprehensive at the prospect of anyone other than Park governing the ROK. Americans still doubted that the opposition had the ability or the temperament to assume power. U.S. diplomats and advisers in South Korea often responded to this difficult situation by seeking to develop alternative sources of economic and political power. They hoped that by encouraging small and medium-sized businesses and cultivating more viable political opponents, they could promote decentralization without threatening economic development.

This strategy was far less assertive than the one adopted by the Kennedy administration in the early sixties. After 1967, American officials never threatened to withdraw political support for the ROK government or withhold economic assistance to pressure Park to abandon his growing authoritarianism. Part of the reason for this change in strategy was that, in the span of a few years, America's ability to influence South Korean politics had declined precipitously. As the country's economy took off, the United States had reduced the level of economic assistance and encouraged the ROK to become more self-supporting. As it cut off economic aid, however, Washington lost a valuable mechanism for pressuring Park.

In the late 1960s U.S. doubts about South Korea's economic model surfaced with increasing regularity. As American advisers gained a better understanding of how this model functioned and what it held for the future, they started criticizing practices that they had encouraged during the first half of the decade. For one thing, Park's approach to economic development had genuine weaknesses that could undermine efforts to promote long-term growth. Furthermore, South Korea's foreign debt was increasing too rapidly, imports were expanding faster than exports, and the exchange rate had once again become unrealistically low. But Americans also worried about the implications of the evolving patterns of state-business interaction for democracy.

In the mid-sixties U.S. officials had been virtually unmoved by opposition complaints about Park's use of preferential loans to large corporations. By the end of the decade, however, they had grown wary of the deleterious impact this practice might have on both economic and political freedom in South Korea. In 1969 William J. Porter, who had become the American ambassador in 1967, reviewed loan distribution practices in the country. He found that whereas "government-sponsored loans tend to go to relatively larger and more politically powerful firms" at low interest rates, "small enterprises and those without political pull" were forced to pay high-curb market interest rates. This "polarized interest structure" strengthened the tendency toward economic concentration in South Korea. Unlike his predecessors, however, Porter believed that the United States should pressure the Park government to abandon this two-tiered system for one in which smaller firms would be treated more equitably. A unified capital structure would "lend encouragement to competitive smaller and younger enterprises" and give rise to "a larger and more vital entrepreneurial class whose political interests would pretty much coincide with ours." Porter argued that this type of economic change was instrumental in the eventual emergence of democratic government in South Korea, for it "allows greater freedom for private economic decisions and is therefore consistent with the growth of political liberalization."[73] Porter's analysis marked an important

Development over Democracy

shift in the perspective of U.S. policymakers toward the South Korean economic model. Whereas during the mid-sixties the Americans had endorsed South Korea's nonunified capital markets as a necessity for economic growth, by the end of the decade they worried that this structure gave the state too much power.

But Porter's resolve to encourage economic liberalization came at a time when America's capacity to influence policy making in South Korea was on the wane. Washington had noted the decline in its economic influence as early as 1965, when South Korean troops first arrived in Vietnam. By guaranteeing future economic aid in return for South Korean participation in the conflict, the Americans had lost one of their principal mechanisms for putting pressure on regime. When in October 1965 USOM director Joel Bernstein informed his supervisor at the U.S. Agency for International Development (USAID) that he intended to continue using a "combination of 'carrot and stick' approach" to influence Park on economic issues, his supervisor was dubious that this approach would still work. He wondered "what bargaining power" the agency would have "if the Koreans differ substantially with our recommendations." The USAID official ended by asking, "With Korean troops in Vietnam and U.S. troops in Korea[,] have we any bargaining power?"[74] It would not be long before American fears were realized.

In the process of developing their "Second Five-Year Economic Plan," which began in 1966, South Korean officials were increasingly recalcitrant to accept U.S. advice. Their concerns related less to the structure of the South Korean economy than to the potential rate of economic development. Having shattered U.S. projections of what was possible under the First Five-Year Plan, South Korean planners now wanted to push forward more aggressively than did their American advisers. Ironically, when U.S. officials tried to temper what they considered to be unrealistic ambitions, the Park government cunningly invoked the well-known American economic guru Walt Rostow to validate its position. The USOM director complained to Rostow: "You are being quoted as saying that conventional economists always underestimate demand for the products needed in a growing economy, that Korea should not worry about overcapacity because demand is always underestimated, that estimates of requirements should be made in the ordinary way and then everything should be doubled, and that economic development is too serious a matter to leave to economists who do not understand it adequately."[75] This episode marked only the beginning of a steeper, more dramatic decline in U.S. influence over the planning process in South Korea.

In the late sixties, as the Park government began to formulate its "Third Five-Year Economic Plan," covering the period 1971–76, South Korean officials limited the role of American advisers to preparing special reports that the government could choose to disregard. Confident that his regime could develop a feasible program on its own, Park charged a South Korean team of experts with responsibility for drafting the Third Five-Year Plan. At the same time, he reduced the involvement of the EPB, which had been the primary conduit of American influence in previous years. Much of the advice that Park did receive came from the newly established Korean Development Institute (KDI), whose creation the USOM had proposed but the ROK government had decided to fund and turn into an official government research institution. The relatively autonomous way in which the Third Five-Year Plan took shape ensured that it would include provisions that the USOM and other international financial institutions cautioned strongly against.[76]

With the South Korean government refusing to consider American guidance and the United States possessing fewer means of forcing it to do so, U.S. agencies working in South Korea began seeking other ways to influence the overall structure of the Korean economy. The USOM tried to promote small and medium-sized businesses as a means of fostering greater economic freedom. In the late sixties and early seventies the mission launched two new programs that attempted, though not very successfully, to change the course of economic development in South Korea.

The USOM's Industrial Development Program was inspired by American concern that the ROK's ever-increasing control over economic activity was distorting the process of industrialization in South Korea. According to one USAID report, the "large government role has led to excessive ROKG influence in the industrial sector, beyond that normally required in a developing economy, and has . . . actually stifled the growth of the important private segment of industry." To address this problem, the USOM planned "to promote small and medium industries, to spread the benefits of economic growth and to counter the pervasive effect of government control of Korean industry." By spearheading the privatization of industry, the USOM believed that it would enable the country "to benefit from more of the long-range social and political benefits that can accompany economic development."[77]

Through the Industrial Development Program, the USOM attempted to foster an environment that would allow small and medium-sized companies to flourish. Program staff worked closely with an indigenous organization known as the Korean Productivity Center (KPC) to improve their man-

agerial efficiency at smaller firms throughout the country. American officials believed that helping such companies improve their operations would
strengthen them and give them staying power in an economy that was
dominated by large conglomerates. Rather than assigning U.S. technicians
directly to the firms that needed extra support, the USOM sent advisers who
offered special training for South Korean consultants in the KPC. The USOM
then paid for the U.S.-trained Korean consultants to visit the targeted
companies in various provinces.[78] The Americans hoped that such activities
would build the KPC into an organization that could make long-term contributions to the diversity of private industry in South Korea even in the
absence of U.S. assistance.

In 1970, as the Industrial Development Program began to wind down,
the USOM began implementing a Private Enterprise Development Program
that had similar objectives. The program's philosophy was premised on the
idea that government control of domestic industries was an impediment to
political democratization and social change. One strategy paper noted that
the Park government had become a "partner in a number of industrial and
business enterprises" and voiced concern about the long-term effect of this
trend. U.S. officials worried that, because it "fostered the concentration of
wealth in the hands of a very limited elite," it not only had "an unhealthy
effect on the nation's economy" but also, by "restricting the participatory
base of the economy," seemed likely to "impede social development."[79]

Under the Private Enterprise Development Program, the USOM made a
concerted effort to reform South Korea's capital markets so all types of
private industry would have access to loans at lower interest rates. The
United States funded short-term specialists in the field to assist the ROK
in implementing programs that would offer credit to private businesses.
American officials argued that, if successful, such efforts would both permit
"better allocation of investment resources" and give South Korea's rapidly
developing urban middle class greater investment opportunities. In the long
term, the USOM hoped that these reforms would have "a welcome diffusing
effect on the ownership of industry and business." The program also continued efforts to improve the quality of private sector management. The
USOM selected promising entrepreneurs from leading small and mid-sized
firms for training in the United States. Arrangements were made for them
to "observe money and capital market operations in the U.S., and receive
training in American business know-how and industrial practices for adaptation in Korea."[80]

The USOM also used the development loan program to strengthen the independence of private industry and improve management at small firms. Originally a relatively small part of U.S. assistance to South Korea, the program expanded during the late sixties as the amount of grant aid that the United States could offer dwindled. Development loans supported agencies and institutions that needed capital to undertake significant infrastructure projects, especially but not exclusively in areas such as transportation, communication, public utilities, and mineral resource development. In the early and mid-1960s the bulk of these loans had been awarded to government agencies and public corporations, but by the late 1960s an increasing number of loans went to support private industry. In 1966 the USOM entered into a multiyear loan agreement with South Korea's Medium Industry Bank. The bank received more than $8 million to help it meet the demand for long-term loans. The USOM expected the bank to make "subloans" of less than $100,000 to "small and medium privately owned firms" seeking to undertake projects that could contribute to national economic development. In 1968 the United States extended a similar loan of $5 million to the Korea Development Finance Corporation. Like the Medium Industry Bank, the corporation was expected to extend subloans to private enterprises in the manufacturing and processing industries.[81]

American policymakers expected these loans to bolster the companies that received them and to serve as a catalyst for the development of a larger class of private industrialists. One USAID report boasted that the program was "being used to help create a vigorous class of local entrepreneurs as well as serve as a training ground for professional personnel such as engineers, economists and managers."[82] Frequently, companies and organizations that did receive loans through the program were expected to hire American consultants to offer advice and monitor their activities. The USOM hoped that these consultants would provide doses of American business expertise that could strengthen and modernize local South Korean firms.[83] By strategically selecting loan recipients in the private sector, the mission strove to build a business class that would be more independent from the state.

But by the time the USOM got around to implementing these programs, changing the trajectory of South Korean development had become extremely difficult. The Park government was supremely confident that its own development model would best suit South Korea and showed little inclination to accept American tutelage. Although the regime made some of the changes that mission officials had pushed for, economic power in South Korea became, if anything, more concentrated in the hands of a few firms.

By the 1970s private loans from the United States, Japan, and Europe were more readily available to South Korea, whose economic growth caused global money lenders to see it as a relatively safe bet. In this environment the Park government could easily funnel billions of dollars in foreign loans to its favored conglomerates at negative interest rates. This practice helped generate the economies of scale required for the heavy industrialization undertaken in the 1970s.[84] Throughout the late 1960s ties between the state and large conglomerates strengthened while the prospects for small and medium-sized companies dimmed.

USOM efforts to promote economic decentralization also suffered because they were not well supported in Washington, especially after Richard Nixon was inaugurated in 1969. The Nixon administration was generally indifferent to the nuanced evaluations of South Korea's political economy produced by U.S. officials working in the country. As long as Park did not move to the left, which he showed absolutely no sign of doing, Nixon and his top advisers paid scant attention to the subtle but significant changes occurring in South Korean politics. In some ways, Nixon made it more difficult for the USOM to pursue its agenda by winding down economic aid to South Korea and thereby further reducing American leverage in negotiations.[85]

USOM and other agencies' officials hoped that if they could not counter the trend toward economic centralization, they might at least stand in the way of the state's efforts to monopolize political power. As American evaluations of South Korea's economy slowly shifted during the late 1960s, so did analyses of its politics. A USAID country plan written in mid-1966 was one of the first U.S. policy documents to articulate concerns about the growing dominance of the South Korean state. The plan did not share the anxiety of many previous analyses of the country's prospects for stability. To the contrary, it noted that the government's power appeared "more secure than at any other time since 1963." Instead, the USAID voiced new concerns. The agency worried that if the Park government did not "use its superior strength over the Opposition judiciously," it might "drive the latter into complete frustration or . . . create a permanent cleavage between the 'ins' and 'outs.'" To avoid such an eventuality, Park would have to at least give the opposition "certain vestiges of influence in its dealings with the Government." In particular, there was a "need to develop overall a more constructive and meaningful role for the Assembly" and to reduce the dominance of the executive branch.[86] This was hardly a call for drastic political change. At the time, the USAID remained predisposed to the sort of developmental autocracy that was in place. But Washington was beginning to question whether by constantly siding with Park against his opposition it had enabled him to become too strong.

Motivated by these doubts, the Americans began seeking to identify and develop alternative sources of political leadership. In 1967 and 1968 the USOM drew up more concrete plans to strengthen democratic institutions in South Korea. One lengthy report, which the mission presented to Congress in 1968, laid out the rationale for such efforts and proposed a range of new projects that could foster political change in the ROK. The report explained that previous U.S. assistance programs had the unintended effect of disproportionately helping the military, the bureaucracy, and big business because these groups had the expertise and organizational ability to benefit from economic development. But "the time has now come for [US]AID programs to focus on ways of assisting workers, farmers, small business, the intellectuals and students who hitherto have been ancillary to the ruling coalition."[87] The USOM had no intention of doing anything to undermine the Park regime; rather, it tried to find ways to integrate broader segments of the population into the existing power structure.

Over the next few years the USOM worked closely with the Asia Foundation and other private American organizations interested in strengthening democratic institutions in South Korea to develop programs that could reach out to different sectors of the population and give them greater opportunities for political participation. One group that the United States paid growing attention to was the working class, which had grown rapidly during the 1960s along with industrial development. Between 1965 and 1969 the number of manufacturing employees in the country tripled from 291,000 to 829,000.[88] But this growing segment of the population remained weak politically, and the USOM saw the necessity of promoting "more effective representation of worker interest in the political and economic process of Korea." As a possible avenue for accomplishing this objective, the mission proposed offering assistance to the Labor Management Institute at Sŏgang University, which conducted labor-management training and research programs, as well as to the Federation of Korean Trade Unions.[89] Beginning in 1968, the USAID contracted with the Asian American Free Labor Institute (AAFLI), an agency of the AFL-CIO, to assist in the development of labor unions in South Korea along with several other Asian countries in the Free World. AAFLI helped arrange for workshops that were held in cooperation with indigenous labor unions. These workshops offered leadership training for union administrators, who took courses in areas such as organizing, collective bargaining, and union administrative procedures.[90] U.S. efforts to build up labor unions were cautious. The goal was to strengthen South Korean democracy by making it more participatory without encouraging the kind of labor radicalism that could, in the American perspective, endanger economic progress.

Another focus of USOM efforts to promote political liberalization was South Korea's legal system. Legal institutions in the ROK had been less subject to American influence than almost any other governmental organ in the country. Although the U.S. occupation had imposed some Anglo-American legal practices on South Korea, the system that existed in the late 1960s still resembled the one that had been established under Japanese colonialism. Courts did not function independently from the executive branch, while the rigorous examinations required to practice law severely limited the number of lawyers and made it difficult for ordinary citizens to find legal representation.[91] In this context, Americans viewed strengthening the rule of law as one means of restraining the executive and fostering public trust in the government. With encouragement from the USOM, the Asia Foundation made reforming the legal system in South Korea one of its top priorities from the late 1960s onward. The foundation paid for American legal experts to study ways to improve the Korean court system and to offer advice to the country's law schools on how to strengthen legal education. These experts could only take a first, tentative stab at reforming a complicated system, but they were among the first Americans to gain access to the records of South Korea's legal institutions and to have at least some Koreans in the field heed their advice. The State Department used the Fulbright Program and the Leader Program to supplement the Asia Foundation's work. Through the Fulbright Program, a small number of grants were arranged for law faculty at Yonsei University and Seoul National University, while more than eighty South Korean judges, attorneys, and prosecutors visited the United States in the mid-1960s.[92]

The Americans made a similar attempt to strengthen the National Assembly vis-à-vis the executive. The Leader Program continued to send members of the assembly from both the DRP and the opposition to the United States on observation tours. Such visits were intended to give the South Koreans a better understanding of how the legislative branch functioned in a democratic society and heighten their confidence to deal with an executive whose encroachments on the prerogatives of the legislature seemed to be growing. As a complement to the Leader Program, the Asia Foundation began sending assembly staffers to the United States to participate in the Congressional Intern Program. The foundation hoped to enhance legislative efficiency in the assembly and thereby bolster the institution.[93]

But U.S. measures to build alternative sources of political leadership were not implemented soon enough to hold back the swelling tidal wave of state repression. Park's intentions to move toward a more authoritarian political system became apparent in 1969, the first year of the Nixon administration, when he proposed a constitutional amendment that would allow him to serve for a third term as president. From the outset, this was a hotly contested issue with the opposition party and other dissident groups fiercely protesting the proposed change. Park raised the political stakes by threatening to resign if the amendment did not pass. After Park's party sneaked the amendment through the National Assembly in a secret, predawn meeting held in September 1969, opponents of the government mounted a last-ditch effort to derail the amendment in a national referendum, which was the final requirement for modifying the constitution.[94]

American policymakers realized that adoption of the amendment would raise questions about the credibility of South Korean democracy. Nevertheless, fear of the instability that might result from Park's resignation prevented them from criticizing or discouraging the amendment. U.S. officials still had doubts about the capacity of the political opposition to govern the country. Indeed, only several months before Park proposed the constitutional revision, the American ambassador had observed that "Korea's opposition political parties could hardly be less effective," for the current opposition leaders had "displayed little of imagination or initiative in meeting the challenges of a dynamic, rapidly growing nation."[95] Americans envisioned debilitating chaos and turmoil if the referendum failed. One intelligence memorandum prepared in October 1969, when debates over the issue were reaching a climax, predicted that if Park resigned "the ensuing developments could range from a relatively orderly transition to a new and weaker government on the one hand to near chaos on the other."[96] American policymakers, who remained convinced that Korea required a strong government to sustain economic development, did not welcome either of these outcomes.

Ultimately, the United States did not get in the way of Park's efforts to modify the constitution. When pressured by demands for action, American officials claimed that the issue pertained strictly to South Korea's internal affairs and that the United States needed to refrain from intervention. After a group of fifty Americans involved in church-related activities in South

Korea appealed to the U.S. embassy to make known its interest in the "removal of repressive controls" and an "honest referendum," the ambassador explained that America's policy was one of "strict neutrality and non-involvement" and that measures had been taken to avoid appearing to favor either side.[97] In the absence of any public U.S. opposition to the amendment, it captured 65 percent of the vote in the October referendum, paving the way for Park to seek another term as president. The outcome was, in all likelihood, a result of Park's popularity and the fact that his party had far more resources to mobilize popular support than its opponents.

In the aftermath of the amendment's passage, Washington could discern new tendencies in the Park government toward the arbitrary and excessive use of power. Ambassador Porter noted that the president's latest triumph had "left him inclined to more direct personal rule based on his feeling that he had the support of the people," and the management of national affairs seemed "more inclined to extreme reaction based on the personal feelings of Park himself." As Park changed his leadership style, Porter thought that a "continuing problem for the Embassy and the [State] Department will be critics, both American and Korean, of the authoritarian tendencies in the country which undoubtedly exist." Although these tendencies were dangerous, Porter believed that it would be futile for the United States to exert "corrective pressures." As he explained, "Even with the best of intentions it is obvious that we can have little if any direct influence on the evolutionary processes at work."[98] The U.S. ambassador did not recommend forcefully pressuring Park to restore democracy, as Kennedy had in 1962 and 1963. But at the same time, he did not offer backing for Park's political maneuvering, as the Johnson administration had during the mid-sixties. His strategy recognized South Korea's increasing autonomy while avoiding actions that could undermine its security, stability, or economic growth.

In the absence of diplomatic pressure, U.S. disapproval was not enough to prevent Park from taking further steps toward authoritarianism. But while American foreign policy created a more permissive context for his political ambitions, it was the 1971 presidential election that drove Park to completely suspend democracy. Park's opponent was future South Korean president Kim Dae Jung, a young, energetic crusader against continued military domination of South Korean politics. Despite both vast financial resources and a powerful nationwide network of pro-government political organizations at his disposal during the campaign, Park won by a much narrower margin than he had anticipated, receiving 53 percent of the vote to

Kim's 45 percent.[99] Kim's ability to capture the popular imagination and nearly pull off an upset troubled Park. Indeed, he believed that if he did not take drastic measures, his political dominance would slip away.

In October 1972 Park suddenly ended what remained of South Korean democracy. He declared martial law, banned political parties, dissolved the National Assembly, and closed the country's universities. When martial law was lifted on 13 December, Park announced the new Yusin (meaning literally "revitalization") constitution. Under the Yusin system, the president had the authority to appoint one-third of the assembly, to designate and dismiss all members of the cabinet including the prime minister, and to issue emergency decrees that would become law immediately. Presidential elections were removed from the public sphere and assigned instead to an electoral college. Moreover, the president could now serve an unrestricted number of six-year terms.[100] Park had essentially created a system of one-man rule that could be perpetuated indefinitely.

The Nixon administration responded to Park's sudden shift to total authoritarianism with disappointment but also with great restraint. In a telegram from Seoul to the State Department, written as the Yusin constitution was being created, Ambassador Porter lamented that Park had "turned away from the political philosophy which we have been advocating and supporting in Korea for 27 years." But despite his rejection of American political ideals, "an effort to persuade Park to abandon completely this course of action and return to the old constitution" had to be "discarded from the outset as impractical." Instead, the United States should pursue a policy of "disassociation," meaning that once Park formally announced the new constitutional amendments, the American embassy would state publicly that the ROK government was "taking actions with which we are not associated." By refraining from taking any sort of disciplinary action against the regime, the United States would be "accepting the fact" that it "cannot and should no longer try to determine the course of internal political development in Korea." This approach went along with the fact that Washington had, in the words of the ambassador, "already begun a process of progressively lower levels of U.S. engagement with Korea." Porter called for this process of disengagement to be "accelerated" as a result of the changing political situation in South Korea.[101]

American officials' unwillingness to use what remained of their influence in South Korea to pressure Park to reverse his course paved the way for fifteen years of continued military dictatorship that were interrupted only briefly by Park's assassination in 1979. Under the Yusin system, the country would continue and even accelerate the rapid economic growth that had begun during the 1960s by combining an economic program centered on heavy industrialization, export growth, and infrastructural development with a large-scale campaign known as the Saemaŭl, or "New Village," movement, which aimed to mobilize the rural population and augment agricultural productivity. South Korea would continue to move toward autonomy and economic development—goals that the United States had long hoped it would achieve—but in a much more authoritarian manner than the Americans had envisioned.

Between 1961 and 1972 Washington invested a significant portion of its own resources and energy into shaping a South Korean state that could strengthen the country's economy. These efforts brought both satisfaction and disappointment. The United States had recognized the need for a strong government that could make the difficult decisions required for economic reform without excessive interference from the civilian population. But American policymakers also expected the South Korean government to tolerate dissent even if it did not give it much consideration. In the early and mid-sixties, U.S. officials were fairly successful in keeping the Park regime within the broad political parameters that it could publicly endorse. If the ROK was not fully democratic between 1963 and 1967, it at least allowed for honest debate of key policy decisions.

To the frustration of many Americans working in South Korea, Park abandoned this quasi-democratic system during the late sixties. The relative indifference of President Nixon and his key advisers to the political character of the ROK government facilitated but did not determine Park's choices. Park's understanding of the political economy of rapid industrialization was shaped in part by the model introduced by the Japanese colonial government. Park recognized that this system, given its emphasis on close ties between large business conglomerates and the state, was more capable of satisfying his political ambitions. Ultimately, the more South Korea succeeded in achieving economic autonomy, the more its leaders were free to make their own decisions about how to govern the country. As American influence waned, Park veered toward greater authoritarianism.

The new state that Park forged through Yusin was an inordinately powerful one, but its ultimate demise was in many ways predetermined as soon as it was formed. With its emphasis on rapid economic growth, the state would inevitably create new forces that would demand democratization. Moreover, even while the Americans acquiesced in the establishment of

Yusin, they had already helped nurture some of the forces that would lead the resistance to it. As South Korean politics slipped into an authoritarian nightmare, groups that would provide much of the guidance for democratization, such as intellectuals and students, emerged partially but not entirely as a result of American influence.

Although the United States formally supported what could at best be called a quasi-democratic system of government between 1961 and 1972 and even helped derail its opposition on key issues, Americans working on the ground in the Republic of Korea (ROK) still hoped to broaden the scope of participation in national politics and pave the way for more genuine democracy. South Korea's influential community of intellectuals became vital in this regard. U.S. officials thought that the involvement of scholars and journalists in the process of nation building would add legitimacy to the state's development programs and encourage the country's political evolution. By fostering enthusiasm for economic progress among Korean intellectuals, the Americans hoped to quiet a potential source of dissent while giving the government a reason to trust this key sector of the population and incorporate its insights into the decision-making process.

But Americans also believed that for academics to become meaningfully involved in promoting national development, they would need new ways of thinking about the process. Official and private organizations made a concerted effort to stimulate discussions on development among leading South Korean intellectuals. They tried in particular to promote modernization theory, which offered a social scientific explanation of how emerging nation-states could develop their economies and political systems—a major preoccupation of U.S. social scientists during the Cold War. Americans hoped that studying modernization would instill in Korean scholars a new participatory ethos and enable them to play a more significant role in public affairs. Moreover, because modernization theory and its intellectual sibling, area studies, contained an intrinsic critique of Communism, Americans believed that it could foster a sense of nationalism that would not identify with North Korea.

Many South Koreans came to share America's enthusiasm for modernization theory, although they rejected its assumptions of Western superiority. The theory's optimistic faith that any state could follow a path to national prosperity captured the imagination of these scholars, who themselves craved higher standards of living. Even while becoming deeply committed to studying and precipitating national modernization, however, intellectuals adapted the concept to their own aspirations and goals. They eventually derived a hybrid conception of modernization that emphasized the possibility of achieving rapid socioeconomic change while preserving Korean traditions and culture.

Although the idea of a distinctly Korean version of modernization did promote a dialogue between intellectuals and the state, the dialogue was short-lived. The state's move toward greater authoritarianism in the late 1960s made exchanging ideas an increasingly one-sided process and divided the academic community. Some intellectuals continued to embrace the Park regime because its developmental agenda embodied their vision of a modernization process that differed from the one employed in the West. These scholars even provided some of the philosophical basis for the creation of the Yusin system. Other South Koreans, however, argued that even a distinctly Korean version of modernization needed to be accompanied by democratization and, as Park turned toward authoritarianism, became an important source of opposition to the regime.

The Problem of Intellectuals and Modernization Theory

The relationship between intellectuals and the state was a pressing concern to both the United States and the ROK from the time Park gained power in 1961. Early connections between academics and the new regime were fraught with tension and boded ill for their long-term cooperation. The junta's tight control of publishing and the media in the wake of the coup naturally alienated many intellectuals, and few, if any, scholars voluntarily assisted the revolutionaries. But Park had his own methods for mobilizing the academic community. On more than one occasion he sent armed soldiers into classrooms or offices of professors whose assistance he desired and then forced them to work on various committees. Park coerced academic experts in constitutional law and politics to help draft a temporary constitution and many of its emergency decrees.[1]

Intellectual alienation from the regime peaked in the summer of 1963, when Park flirted with the possibility of postponing the elections he had promised to hold that year until 1967. American officials felt that an irreparable rift between the government and the country's intellectuals was being created. In a report written at the time about the most influential South Korean journal, *Sasanggye*, they warned that a group of "younger Korean politicians and intellectuals in opposition to the Military government has been coalescing around the management of" the journal, seeking "the complete departure of Chairman Pak and the Revolutionary Mainstream from power." The Americans feared that the group would accomplish this by "whatever means feasible," though it seemed to be leaning toward "some type of popular uprising in which the university students would play a leading role and which would be actively supported by the United States government." U.S. officials, of course, flatly refused any involvement in such a scheme. Although, the report argued, "an air of unreality" pervaded the thinking of *Sasanggye* intellectuals, they would continue to play a "significant role" in South Korean politics.[2]

Americans worried that the growing estrangement of intellectuals from the Park government would prevent them from participating in the economic development process. Since intellectuals were a traditional source of political authority in South Korea, the growing rift between scholars and the state could be destabilizing. U.S. officials began working with private agencies to look for ways to promote a reconciliation between the two groups and to motivate Korean intellectuals to play an active part in facilitating socioeconomic change. A U.S. report prepared just after the military coup in 1961 had contended that the United States should "encourage the evolutionary process of social change" and that "in its encouragement special attention needs to be paid to the intellectuals." Among other things, the report called for "radio forums which would bring together students, intellectuals and government leaders for a free exchange of views."[3]

To increase cooperation between intellectuals and the state, the Americans sought to introduce South Korean scholars to new epistemological viewpoints that explained how economic development occurred and emphasized the need for enlightened elites to contribute to the process. They paid special attention to the younger generation of intellectuals. Edward Wagner, a professor of Korean history at Harvard University and one of the first U.S. experts in Korean studies, thought that the rising generation of scholars was more likely to benefit from contact with the United States because it sought "to apply Western methodology" and stood in contrast to the older generation which was "traditionalist."[4] Wagner helped select Korean visiting scholars for the Harvard-Yenching Institute and advised the Ford Foundation, so his views were influential.

Modernization theory was at the heart of this new American effort to influence Korea's intellectual community. By the late fifties the concept and its potential application to the less developed nations of Asia, Africa, and Latin America was the research focus of hundreds of U.S. scholars working in a range of disciplines. The theory's best-known proponents included economist Walt Rostow, sociologist Daniel Lerner, and political scientist Lucian Pye. Modernization provided a new, social scientific approach to understanding and managing the problems of underdeveloped areas that countered the Marxist conception of how socioeconomic change occurred. The basic precept of modernization theory was that the world could be divided into "modern" and "traditional" societies. It assumed that the traditional mores and customs of less developed nations prevented them from acquiring the rationalistic outlook essential for modernization. Contact with advanced societies such as those of Europe and America, however, could initiate the process of social change in traditional societies. This process, according to American social scientists, would encompass an array of interrelated social, economic, and political changes that would ultimately produce mature industrial capitalism and liberal democratic governments.[5]

In their contacts with South Korean intellectuals, Americans tended to emphasize the corollary idea that, in traditional societies, new indigenous elites who could serve as agents of change had a special role to play. Rostow had written in his well-known book, *The Stages of Economic Growth*, that in order to prepare a "traditional society for regular growth . . . a new elite—a new leadership—must emerge and be given scope to begin the building of a modern industrial society."[6] Modernization theorists argued that it was this elite stratum of society that was most likely to have access to the advanced ideas and technologies of the West, and that elites therefore needed to disseminate these new ideas to the rest of the population.

Americans viewed popularizing the concept of modernization as the ideal mechanism for capturing the imagination of South Korean scholars, inspiring them to contribute to national development and fostering a more productive relationship between scholars and the state. They hoped that modernization theory's optimistic emphasis on the possibility of change would counter the pessimism about the country's future that prevailed among some intellectuals. Asserting that a new elite must emerge for meaningful socioeconomic change to take place, Americans called on South Korean intellectuals who were reluctant to cooperate with the government to seek out greater involvement in national politics. Finally, Americans believed that analyzing how modernization might occur in Asia could prod South Koreans to confront their country's underdevelopment while subtly indoctrinating them in U.S. views of the Cold War. American faith that the theory could transform the outlook of Korean intellectuals led to expansive efforts on the part of U.S. officials, scholars, and cultural organizations to stimulate discussions on modernization.

The U.S. Information Agency (USIA) played an important role in organizing such discussions by arranging contacts between South Korean and

American scholars. The local branch of the USIA in South Korea—often referred to as the U.S. Information Service (USIS)—was among the most active branches of the organization in Asia. South Korea's USIS made building a relationship with the country's intellectuals a high priority. In one USIS plan, contributing to the "modernization of the ROK by promoting awareness and understanding of the requirements for economic growth, democratic social development and political stability" was among its major objectives, and "University faculty" was high on the list of targets to achieve it. The USIS was determined to spread the idea that "the academic community has a responsibility to study, articulate and disseminate practical ideas on the modernization process."[7] The USIS published magazines targeting Korean intellectuals, paid for translations of books, and arranged for scholarly exchanges between the United States and South Korea.

The USIS's translation program made the works of several modernization theorists available to Korean students and intellectuals. By 1964 Rostow's *Stages of Economic Growth* had already been through two printings and was credited by visiting American economists with widely influencing their South Korean counterparts. The USIS also printed a low-cost series of book translations for students that included titles such as Max Millikin's *The Emerging Nations*, Edward S. Mason's *Economic Planning in Underdeveloped Areas*, and Robert J. Alexander's *A Primer for Economic Development*. In the first printing, the USIS produced two thousand copies of each title, all of which sold out within six months. A translation of John Kenneth Galbraith's *Economic Development in Perspective*, also popular, went through several printings.[8] In addition to translating books into Korean, the USIS published a quarterly journal, *Nondan* (Forum), which contained translations of the most recent American scholarship in fields such as economics, history, and sociology. Its articles, by well-known Korean as well as American scholars, canvassed a wide range of subjects. Essays on modernization theory appeared with marked regularity, including Lester M. Salamon's "Comparative History and the Theory of Modernization," David E. Powell's "Social Costs of Modernization," S. N. Eisenstadt's "Intellectuals and Tradition," and Robert Fluker's "Regional Cooperation and the Modernization of Southeast Asia."[9]

In one of its more ambitious ventures, the USIS teamed up with the staff of Chungang, a South Korean television network, to create a weekly news program on "Modernization in Korea." The program, which began airing in December 1965, attempted to convey to its audiences "all aspects of the modernization process that is taking place with accelerated speed in Korea."

Initial segments consisted of twenty-five-minute roundtable discussions by prominent South Korean professors of economics. Subsequently, the series focused on a broad array of issues such as national planning, educational development, sociological change, and rural development. American experts in different fields appeared frequently. Among them, Oswald Nagler, an Asia Foundation–sponsored adviser to the ROK government, hosted a series of episodes on national physical planning that covered—among other subjects—community development. Although only a fraction of the South Korean population owned televisions when the series first appeared, it was probably viewed by 70,000 to 100,000 people each week.[10] Perhaps more important to the USIS than the number of viewers was the fact that the program prompted Korean scholars to discuss modernization with their American colleagues and to think about how they could contribute to the process.

Through exchange programs managed by the USIS, prominent American modernization theorists taught or lectured at South Korean universities and Korean scholars studied in the United States. Academic exchanges occurred in a wide variety of disciplines, but the U.S. Educational Commission (USEC) often provided lecturers in fields, such as political science and economic development, in which modernization theory was in vogue. Many of these lecturers discussed modernization during their tenures in the ROK. In 1963, for instance, political scientist William Douglas traveled to South Korea as a Fulbright lecturer and delivered an address on "The Role of Political Parties in the Modernization Process" at a conference held in Seoul. Although most of the American professors who participated in the exchange program for a full year or a semester tended to be relatively unknown, some of the most famous modernization theorists traveled to South Korea for short periods under the USIS's "American Participant" program. In 1964 the USIS invited Walt Rostow to speak at Seoul National University (SNU) and asked him to comment on where the ROK stood in terms of his "stages of economic growth."[11]

American private and philanthropic organizations made even more enduring efforts to develop the social sciences in South Korea and to integrate the study of modernization into these disciplines. The Ford Foundation's program was particularly sophisticated and long standing. Throughout the Cold War, the foundation supported the objectives of U.S. foreign policy by promoting international academic exchanges.[12] In South Korea, the Ford Foundation provided funding to strengthen the Asiatic Research Center (ARC) at Korea University. The center had been formed in 1957 as an adjunct research institution to advance social science research on Korea and East Asia. By the early 1960s it had already become home to a budding crop of Korean experts on Asian studies, some of whom had been trained in the United States. Among its core researchers were Min Pyŏnggi, an authority on Japanese politics who had studied at the University of Chicago, and Han Kisik, a specialist in Southeast Asian studies with a Ph.D. from the University of California at Berkeley. The Ford Foundation's grants to the ARC in 1962 and 1968 totaled nearly $700,000. The grants supported research on contemporary North and South Korea, Korean history, modern China, and other subjects.[13]

The Ford Foundation had several motives for backing this research agenda. Foundation officials believed that promoting studies of Asia and Korea could stimulate Korean scholars to think about the relevance of modernization to their own region and nation. Within American academia, modernization theory and area studies—including Asian studies—had become deeply intertwined. Area studies complemented modernization theory's broad effort to delineate a solution to economic backwardness with a specific emphasis on particular regions of the globe. Scholars often used modernization to measure and evaluate the countries that area specialists focused on. The research on Asia conducted by the ARC followed this trend. Funding proposals made it clear that many projects intended to use modernization as an analytic framework. The ARC's proposal to conduct "research on modern China," for example, asserted that "studies on the modernization process" of China and Japan were "absolutely prerequisite to the modernization problems in Korea."[14] Such funding proposals were as much the product of Korean initiative as they were of American guidance and reflected the genuine interest of South Korean intellectuals in modernization. At the same time, by framing their agenda in this way, South Korean scholars doubtless made their research seem more useful to the foundation and its American advisers.

Encouraging Korean scholars to look at Asia through the lens of modernization also served to indoctrinate them in American understandings of the Cold War. U.S. studies of modernizing Asia tended to reinforce the Cold War logic by using different methodologies to analyze American and Soviet spheres of influence. American scholars generally researched the process and problems of modernization in Japan, South Korea, and Free World nations while studying the nature of Communism in China, North Korea, and other Communist bloc nations.[15] Americans hoped that, if adopted in Asia, this intellectual bifurcation might make it possible to foster nationalistic aspirations for development in Free World states that were also parts of divided nations like South Vietnam, Taiwan, and South Korea.

Funding proposals for Korean studies approved by the Ford Foundation deployed this dichotomy. In 1962 the foundation provided support for a "Project for Research on Communist North Korea" to be supervised by the ARC. Eventually this project resulted in papers that included "A History of the Communist Movement in Korea," "The Ideology of the North Korean Communist Regime," and "Communist Ideological Education in North Korea." Although one paper was prepared on North Korea's "Seven-Year Economic Plan," terms like "development" and "modernization" were almost never used in the planning or implementation of this research. On the other hand, a "Project for Research on Contemporary South Korea" planned papers that included "A Study of the Modernization Process in Korea" and "Financing Economic Development in Korea—The Process of Capital Formation in Korean Society."[16] By having South Korean scholars perform these two very different types of studies on their own country and the Communist North, American funding attempted to create a modernizing nationalism that excluded North Korea.

By stimulating interest in modernization, the Ford Foundation also aspired to build a more cooperative relationship between South Korean scholars and their government. The funding proposal for the second research grant, which was awarded in 1968, made this point explicitly. The proposal contended that the polarization of intellectuals and the Park government had become "so extreme that university people tend to equate academic integrity with all out opposition to the government," while the regime failed to "make use of the specialized knowledge of the academic community." By contrast, support for research on Asia and the Communist World at the ARC could promote "a more constructive dialogue between the two."[17] When the Ford Foundation sent Colonel A. A. Jordan, a former economic adviser in Korea, to Seoul to evaluate the proposal, he echoed this logic. Jordan worried that the "government enjoy[ed] little genuine support among intellectuals and students" and that this "alienation" could "boil over into the streets." He recommended continuing exchange programs between American and South Korean scholars on the grounds that "efforts to bring Korean intellectuals into broader contact with American, Japanese, and other foreign scholars would not only broaden scholarship on all sides and strengthen an invaluable tie to the outside world" but also "reduce the alienation" of Korean scholars "from their own society and government." Jordan thought that such collaboration between American and South Korean scholars might take the form of "joint work on Korean development problems."[18]

Finally, the Ford Foundation supported research at the ARC with the hope of producing knowledge about an area of the world that had become increasingly important to U.S. foreign policy but about which little information was available. As Clarence Faust, a program officer at the foundation, noted: "In contrast to the substantial improvement since the end of World War II in American knowledge and competence in Chinese and Japanese studies, Korean studies remains [sic] almost completely undeveloped."[19] To enable Americans to benefit from the ARC research it supported, the foundation grants included funding for English translations of selected articles.[20] Thus many articles that appeared in the center's journal *Asea Yŏn'gu* had English-language abstracts or summaries.

The Asia Foundation joined the Ford Foundation in promoting studies of modernization in South Korea. The Asia Foundation was instrumental in establishing the Korean Research Center in Seoul in 1955; the center was meant to facilitate social science research in the ROK, particularly studies of Korean society, culture, and history. In the 1960s the Asia Foundation donated money to maintain the center's library, which contained a large number of English-language volumes, and to pay for annual research fellowships awarded to prominent South Korean scholars. Among the goals of these fellowships were "providing materials, foreign experience and services to enable Korean scholars to understand modern social science methodology" and "developing studies of modernization especially as they relate to the Korean experience." Studies conducted under the auspices of the center were later published in book form.[21]

Other institutions placed a greater emphasis on enabling Korean scholars to study or conduct research in the United States. Harvard's Yenching Institute managed an exchange program that offered South Korean scholars in the humanities and social sciences a year of study at the university. Here, they typically encountered luminaries who had been influential in introducing the concept of modernization to their respective disciplines. Although the number of individuals the institute could invite was limited, many of those it supported became important figures in their fields. For instance, Yi Kwangnin (1957–58) became a pioneer in the field of modern Korean history; Kim Chunyŏp (1958–59), a specialist on Chinese politics, later became director of the ARC; and Ch'oe Chaesŏk (1966–67), a sociologist, focused on Korean family institutions.[22]

The combined efforts of the USIS, philanthropic organizations, and American universities brought a significant proportion of South Korean social scientists into contact with the most recent U.S. scholarship in the field. By the mid-1960s there were numerous venues in which South Koreans could debate modernization and its application to their own country. They debated these issues both among themselves and with academics from the United States and Free World Asian countries. But although South Korean scholars discussed modernization, the questions of how they conceptualized it and whether it would motivate them to cooperate with the Park government remained.

"Koreanizing" Modernization

With American endorsement, modernization theory was a smash hit among South Korean intellectuals. These scholars examined modernization with more intensity and enthusiasm than even Americans could have predicted. The theory appealed to Korean academics because it enabled them to make sense of the dramatic changes that were occurring in their own society. Its popularity, especially among intellectuals who had had extensive contact with American scholars, was obvious by the mid-1960s. In 1966 Korean historian Han Ugǔn reported that "the problem of the 'modernization' of Korea" had been "much discussed in recent years both in individual articles and in various conferences and symposiums" and that such deliberations were not "limited to the academic research of historians, but discussed by scholars both at home and abroad as an urgent practical problem of Korean society."[23] The conferences and symposiums that Han mentioned had taken place at the most prestigious South Korean universities and appeared in the most respected journals.[24] Han himself was a member of a Visiting Scholars Association comprised of Koreans who had attended the Yenching Institute. The association held its own conferences on topics such as "Modern History of the Far East" and "Tradition and Change in East Asia."[25]

Even as South Korean academics embraced the concept of modernization, they rejected aspects that did not suit their own goals. With its assumptions that indigenous traditions were obstacles to economic growth and that the West needed to stimulate and guide the process of socioeconomic change in emerging nation-states, modernization theory privileged the Western experience. South Korean intellectuals developed their own hybrid conception of the theory, one that emphasized how their culture and tradition could enable the country to modernize in a way that differed from the processes that had unfolded in Europe and the United States. In an article appearing in *Sasanggye*, SNU law professor Hwang Sandŏk explained that "regardless of how much we strive to achieve modernization we can not walk the same path that the Anglo-Saxons have already walked." Modernization should not be a process of simply following the West but also of rediscovering "Eastern" and "Korean" things that possessed value.[26] Americans sometimes disputed but seldom tried to suppress South Korean approaches to modernization. They realized that by adapting the concept, Korean scholars were making it more appealing to their intellectual community and ultimately more influential.

South Korean intellectuals arrived at this distinctive version of modernization through a process of negotiation and debate with their American counterparts at conferences, symposiums, and seminars. A weeklong "International Conference on the Problems of Modernization in Asia," held at Korea University in 1965, was one of the most fascinating examples of how the two groups negotiated the meaning of "modernization." The conference, which received funding from the Ford Foundation and the Asia Foundation, was planned jointly by Korean and American scholars. They invited colleagues not only from South Korea and the United States but also from Japan, India, Hong Kong, and other Free World Asian countries. Well-known American academics, including Marion Levy and Lucian Pye, helped with the planning and attended the conference.[27]

In the opening session, participants wrestled with the "conceptual problems of modernization." Several Koreans on the panel emphasized the need to differentiate modernization from "Westernization" and the possibility that at least some aspects of Korean traditions could contribute to economic development. Ch'oe Chaehŭi, a professor of philosophy at SNU, argued that "it is our urgent duty to modernize numerous aspects of Korean traditional thinking and life." But, he emphasized, Korean modernization "does not represent simply Americanization." Instead, Koreans needed to develop a modern culture that was "peculiar to Korea."[28] Along similar lines, Kim T'aegil, Ch'oe's associate in the SNU philosophy department, insisted that the "modernization of Korea cannot be the same as its Westernization" and worried that "thoughtless imitation of Western civilization might poison the plan of Koreans to overcome the state of underdevelopedness."[29]

Like their American counterparts, South Korean scholars tended to impose order on religions and philosophies such as Confucianism and Buddhism that had played enduring roles in Korea's history by classifying them as "traditions." Their evaluation of these traditions, however, differed sharply from those of American scholars. Although willing to criticize them, Koreans argued that traditions possessed some facets that were worth preserving. They believed that traditions could infuse South Korea's modernization process with a moral dimension that was absent from Euro-American versions. In his presentation on "How to Harmonize Traditional Moral Values and Present Day Needs in Korea," Kim T'aegil contended that even if South Korea achieved "material richness" through modernization, it would "not suffice . . . for our human happiness." Koreans could find "something more in the Oriental traditions—the traditions of warm hearts and deep sentiments." For Kim, the "ideal stage of that humane sentiment" could be discovered in the Confucian concept of "Jen," which he defined as "an ideal state of character which enables a man to be fused into one with others."[30] In other parts of his talk, Kim had pointed to aspects of Confucianism that hindered economic growth. But in the end, he cautioned against throwing the baby out with the bathwater. If Confucianism had some dimensions that were antimodern, it had others that would enable Koreans to fashion an alternate version of modernity that they could embrace enthusiastically.

In another presentation, Yi Kiyŏng, a professor of religious studies at Tongguk University, spoke about the potential role of Buddhism in modernization. Yi criticized Max Weber's assertion that Buddhism ran counter to legalism, democracy, and the protection of human rights, and insisted that it was consistent with modernity. He pointed to specific ways that Buddhist philosophy could support modernization, contending that "if we take the trouble to look into the Bodhisattva ideal of Mahayana Buddhism, we find that it embraces teachings that help promote the development of science and technology and the betterment of the lot of mankind." Yi ended with a sharp critique of the Western model of modernization and offered hope that Buddhism would help South Korea avert the problems attached to the process in the West. He argued that "the materialistic atmosphere and worldly epicureanism that modernization has brought forth in Western countries has helped degenerate rather than advance the true posture of man." By contrast, the Buddhist ideal was to "lead man toward true happiness." In the Buddhist version of the process, Yi explained, "modernization must become eternal; law must become law in its true and full sense"; and "reason must be enhanced to the level of Tathata."[31] Yi was not entirely clear on precisely how this Buddhist ideal of modernization would lead man to true happiness, but his faith in its capacity to do so was unwavering.

At times American scholars at the conference disputed Korean contentions that their "traditions" were conducive to modernization but in the end seemed content to allow South Koreans to come to their own understanding of the process. Political scientist Lucian Pye from the Massachusetts Institute of Technology was perhaps the most vocal in questioning the Koreans' arguments. He wondered whether the emphasis on happiness and harmony in the Korean ideal of modernization was not, in fact, a contradiction in terms. Responding to Yi Kiyŏng's presentation on Buddhism, he argued that modernization might actually require "people who are driven and dissatisfied, agitated and neurotic." Pye thought that, for a creative individual, "coming into tune with his world may diminish his drive." He was also not convinced of Kim T'aegil's proposition that modernization needed to be informed by humane sentiments. Pye claimed that modernization required creative entrepreneurs who usually reflected "a very strange mixture of qualities," including "ruthlessness" and "the ability to persuade other people to come along with him."[32]

Other Americans were skeptical of whether Koreans would have sufficient agency in the process of modernization to ensure that it remained reflective of their traditions. Eminent sociologist Marion Levy, whose book on the family revolution in modern China had been a seminal work in demonstrating the relevance of modernization to the study of Asia, reminded Koreans that modernization was an inevitable process over which individuals had little control. In considering that process, Levy advised Asian scholars "to put aside what you would like it to be and examine with great care what it is likely to be." He bluntly cautioned them: "If you believe for a moment that in the process of modernization every society will have to make its own choice and can choose to preserve as many of its traditional moorings as it wishes, so long as it wishes, you are wrong."[33]

Although Americans questioned whether Koreans would actually be able to achieve their own unique version of modernity, they never really attempted to change the Korean perspective. At this abstract, philosophical level, they were willing to let their Korean colleagues work the issue out for themselves. Although Pye had carefully interrogated South Korean scholars, he prefaced his own paper by saying that "the problems of modernization of Asia will ultimately be resolved by Asians." He believed that he and the other Americans present could be most useful by sharing "some of our questions and some of our confusions," admitting that "we clearly do not have any answers."[34] The important thing for Pye and his colleagues was that Koreans were discussing modernization, not how they were conceptualizing the process.

In other sessions of the conference, the multinational contingent of scholars engaged in more concrete examinations of the problems of modernizing Asia. During these discussions, political scientists and economists considered the challenge of differentiating South Korea's modernization from that of the West and the role of Korean traditions in the process. Although Korean scholars did not reach a consensus on the specific actions that were needed to create a distinctively Korean version of modernity, they never doubted that it could be done.

The paper presented by Yi Ch'angnyŏl, an economics professor at Korea University, on the "Modernization of Korea's Finance System" exemplified how South Korean scholars envisioned their traditions thriving in a modernizing society. Yi touched on a subject that was at the forefront of the agendas of both the United States and the Park government. As described in the previous chapter, in 1965 President Park completely restructured interest rates to raise capital for investment. Like the numerous U.S. economic advisers working in South Korea at the time, Yi thought that it was necessary to raise interest rates to promote economic stability. But Yi also called for the preservation of "Kye," a form of private money market that had, according to Yi, originated in Korea "as far back as 10 centuries ago." Kye loaned funds to their members at interest rates that were generally higher than official rates. For small companies whose access to government-supported bank loans was limited, the Kye had become an important source of capital. Yi argued that Kye helped compensate for the limitations of South Korea's official capital markets and advocated that they be incorporated in financial reforms. And he hoped that "Kye activities [would] be assimilated to modern financial institutions along with the early implementation of rational financial policies."[35]

Yi's presentation was significant not only for what it revealed about how South Korean intellectuals envisioned modernization, but also because Yi could influence government policy. At the time of the conference, he had already been appointed to a committee of academics responsible for evaluating official policies and advising the government.[36] The advice of economists like Yi may well have contributed to the fact that private financial markets continued to exist in South Korea until at least the late 1980s, despite the dramatic economic changes in the country during the intervening years. Although Yi in many ways represented the prototype of the public intellectual whose emergence Americans hoped to foster, he also demonstrated how the priorities of such intellectuals could differ from those of the United States.

Despite the differences between American and Korean scholars that had surfaced at the gathering, the Americans were, on the whole, satisfied with the content and tone of the discussions. George E. Taylor, the director of the Ford Foundation, wrote that the "conference was, without question, a very successful enterprise." It was particularly important that "Asians were talking to Asians, even Koreans to Japanese, about their own problems" in ways that had been rare. Moreover, "the models of how to run a meeting, the role of the chairman, and the standards to be expected in discussions were quietly and effectively defused among the participants."[37] For the Americans, the ability of the South Koreans to take part in the give-and-take of an academic conference was significant in its own right, because it demonstrated a capacity for ordered debate that could prepare them to participate in talks with the Park government.

In other conferences and journals, South Korean scholars continued to develop their concept of a distinctively Korean version of modernization throughout the 1960s. When a group of them, including many of the same ones who had participated in the Korea University conference, assembled at Tongguk University in 1967, these scholars were more determined than ever to go beyond Western conceptions of modernization. In his opening address, university president Cho Myŏnggi expressed hope that modernization would be viewed "as the creation of a welfare society on so vast a scale that it involves the entire world and mankind rather than assimilation into the self-centered realities of life." Cho criticized South Korea's penchant for the "blind worship of Western ideas" and urged the panel that was scheduled to discuss "Western ideas for modernization" to "draw a conclusion through their discussion useful to 'our' modernization" by focusing "not only on the advantages and disadvantages of the western ideas but also on the way they are to be applied to and how they are to affect our tradition."[38]

Even if South Korean scholarship on modernization was going somewhat awry of U.S. expectations, its general outlook meshed with the goals of American social engineering. For the most part, Korean academics adhered to a conception of modernization that was firmly anti-Communist but at the same time deeply nationalistic. This conception created a framework of ideas that South Korean scholars could draw upon in seeking to influence a government with the same characteristics. The key questions that remained were how willing the state itself would be to enter into a dialogue with these scholars and how the relationship between the two would evolve over time.

Intellectuals and the State

The growing devotion of South Korean scholars to the idea of modernization motivated many of them to seek influence over government policy. Although Park Chung Hee had alienated much of the academic community during his first two years in office, after transitioning to a civilian government in 1963 he recognized the need to have at least some intellectual participation in policy making. During the mid-1960s the state created modest opportunities for select groups of intellectuals to work with the government on economic and political issues. Many scholars who had taken part in discussions of modernization sought to use their ideas and expertise to take advantage of these opportunities. Motivated by a desire to contribute to national development, these intellectuals became involved in government policy making in a variety of capacities.

Many academics became members of special advisory groups that assembled experts from different fields to make policy recommendations to the Park regime. Among the most prestigious and influential of these groups was the Modernization Research Group, which the president's secretary, Kim Chongsin, convened and presided over every week. The group was drawn from social scientists teaching at prominent universities in South Korea, including SNU faculty members like economist Pak Hŭibŏm and political scientist Ku Bŏmmo. Kim Chongsin recalled that the group's members would meet to "exchange opinions and debate the problems of politics, economics, society and the media." Afterward, detailed reports on the discussions were prepared for use as a reference when policy decisions were made.[39] Of course, the scholars in this group did not actually get to make crucial decisions. But they did familiarize Park and other key officials with the ideas of leading academics who shared the government's objectives, while building trust between the state and the intellectual community.

As the Park government's faith in academia increased, it started to make a greater effort to bring intellectuals into the government. After 1963 Park began appointing a small but significant number of academics to ministerial posts. The Ministries of Finance, Information, and Education were all directed by former professors at different points in time. Nam Tŏksŏk, an economics professor at Sŏgang University, became one of the most prominent ROK government officials with an academic background. In the early 1960s Nam had led a group of Sŏgang economists that offered advice on planning and other issues. Park appointed Nam minister of finance in 1966 and deputy prime minister in 1974. Because of Nam and other academicians' association with Park, the term "political professor" had come into frequent use in South Korea by the mid-1960s.[40]

Although cooperation between intellectuals and the state blossomed during the mid-sixties, this open-ended dialogue was short-lived. The government's turn to authoritarianism at the end of the decade created a dilemma for scholars who wished to contribute to national development. After the introduction of the Yusin system, they could no longer openly criticize or even discuss government policies. In this changing environment, South Korean intellectuals needed to either find ways of accommodating the regime or run the risk of resisting it. They soon discovered that the conceptions of modernization they had derived lent themselves equally well to either alternative. Many intellectuals began to rationalize that the Park regime, despite its growing authoritarianism, could best modernize the country in a way that was consistent with Korean traditions and culture. They argued that South Korean's unique historical and cultural circumstances required a strong political leader like Park. Other scholars, however, believed that democracy was rooted in Korean traditions every bit as much as authoritarianism was, and they viewed the state's efforts to eliminate dissent as the very antithesis of modernization. Not surprisingly, the intellectuals who held these very different perspectives experienced sharply divergent fates. Those who could reconcile the regime's new mode of governance with their vision of modernization found plentiful opportunities in both politics and academia. On the other hand, those who adhered to more democratic conceptions of modernization were dismissed from their teaching posts. Some of these scholars would become leaders of the unfolding campaign against military dictatorship.

Intellectuals who defended the Park regime after the commencement of Yusin often drew heavily on the conceptual tools provided by modernization theory. Kal Ponggŭn, a professor of law at Chungang University, helped Park in the drafting of the Yusin constitution and later became one of the most ardent defenders of the system. In an article published in the popular periodical *Sin tonga*, Kal defended the need for Yusin several weeks after the system had been put into place. He contended that the Yusin system had resulted in the "personalization of power" in South Korea. Once this phenomenon occurred, he explained, a single charismatic leader could become the driving force behind national change. As he put it, "among underdeveloped nations the personalization of power was not only the first step of development but also the best method of governing and achieving unity."[41]

While Kal played a significant role in laying out the official justification of Yusin, he was by no means the only scholar who supported it. Many other intellectuals who were genuinely interested in advancing the cause of national development embraced the logic of military dictatorship.

The career of journalist and scholar Im Panghyŏn offers one of the best examples of how the concept of modernization led many Korean intellectuals to support the Park regime in the 1970s despite its growing authoritarianism. In 1966, after working for several years as an editorial writer for the respected newspaper *Han'guk ilbo*, Im received an invitation to study for a year at Harvard University in the Nieman Fellowship Program. The program assembled leading journalists from the United States and around the world in an effort to promote a free exchange of ideas and improve the quality of journalism internationally. It was at Harvard that Im received his most intensive exposure to the thinking of leading American modernization theorists. The scholars who left the deepest impression on him were sociologist Edward Shils, whose work had helped define the concept of modernization; historian John K. Fairbank, who had utilized modernization as an interpretive lens to examine East Asian history; and Merle Feinsod, an expert on Russian politics.[42]

At Harvard, Im became especially interested in the role that intellectuals could play in the modernization process. During the year that he spent there, Im wrote his thesis on "The Role of Intellectuals and Political Leaders in Developing Countries." After reading the works of renowned Swedish economist Gunnar Myrdal, Im embraced the idea that intellectuals needed to share responsibility for national development. Myrdal's argument that intellectuals must become a force for modernization in backward countries led Im to ponder what sort of relationship between intellectuals and the military government would be appropriate. He decided that "although criticism was an important function of the intellectual . . . if people with expertise in modern specialized areas such as the economy, society, culture and political administration did not participate [in the government] the revolution could not succeed." He noted that in other advanced democracies like England and the United States, "intellectuals and political authorities did not always confront each other as they did in Russia." Rather, "people with specialized knowledge from the university and the media participated in the government as needed."[43]

Im's conviction that intellectuals needed to support national development was driven by a feeling of kinship with the Park government. He remembered that, like many others who had criticized the Park regime at home, when he left the country and tried to explain national affairs to outsiders, he felt a "sense of intimacy" with the South Korean government. At Harvard, Im often found himself defending Park despite the fact that he had usurped democracy. In his conversations with Koreans who had immigrated to the United States, he encountered many former countrymen who "looked dubiously" on Park's regime. Im was compelled to remind them that South Korea's circumstances were very different from those of the United States and therefore the country's path to modernity and democracy were likely to be different. He explained that under the democratic government that had gained power in the wake of the April 19 Revolution, "the social order was in ruin [sic], poverty became more severe by the day and unemployment increased." These conditions, he contended, inevitably led to the military's seizure of power. Im argued that before democracy could take hold, certain "basic preconditions" needed to inhere. He told critics of the Park government that "if we do not reorganize into a modernized society[,] there can be no industrial and agricultural development and the middle class will not have room to grow." For Im, there could be no democracy without economic industrialization.[44]

In contrast to U.S. expectations that intellectuals' participation in South Korea's development would lead to greater democratization by slowly opening the policy-making process, after Yusin scholars like Im tended to form collusive relationships with the government in which they legitimated Park's policies while receiving favors from his regime. In the late sixties and seventies Im continued to praise the regime and to justify its policies in the name of "Korean style democracy." In a book entitled *Kŭndaehwa wa chisigin*, or *Modernization and the Intellectual*, published in 1974, Im dwelled on the responsibility of intellectuals while extolling the Park regime as worthy of their support. He attempted, in particular, to counter students and academics who criticized the Yusin system for undermining democratic institutions. In the book's opening pages, Im contrasted the "textbook" or "Western" version of democracy espoused by university students with the Park government's emphasis on productivity and harmony. He wrote that "in comparison to the style of democracy in industrialized nations with its emphasis on welfare and distribution . . . our democracy must emphasize efficiency rather than consumerism and harmony rather than decentralization." Im argued that this was the version of democracy that the Park government was already implementing through the Saemaŭl or New Village Movement, a broad-based campaign to increase rural incomes by mobilizing people in agricultural villages.[45]

By the time *Modernization and the Intellectual* appeared, Im was already participating very directly in public affairs. His ideas naturally found favor with the Park regime, which was trying to find a convincing rationale for nullifying the South Korean constitution and implementing the Yusin system. In 1970 Im had begun serving as a special adviser to the Park government. He later became secretary of information and a member of the National Assembly for the ruling party.[46] Like many other Korean academics, Im had been inspired by the idea that intellectuals could play a role in fashioning a distinctively Korean version of modernization. Yet he saw no contradiction between adhering to these ideals and faithful service to an authoritarian regime.

Other scholars writing about modernization did not initially endorse the idea that democracy, or at least Western democracy, needed to be deferred as strongly as Im did, but they nevertheless expressed some ambivalence about the capacity of democratic institutions to foster modernization that lent itself to alliance with military dictatorship. The highly regarded South Korean legal expert Ham Pyŏngjun exemplified how uncertainty about whether democracy and modernization could coexist eventually led to support for the military dictatorship. Ham attended the "International Conference on the Problems of Modernization in Asia" at Korea University in 1965, when he was a promising young assistant professor at the Yonsei University School of Law. At various times during the meeting, he opposed the idea of devising alternative definitions of democracy for the sake of political expediency. In one exchange he labeled "dangerous" South Korean scholars who "suggest that we should build our own form of democracy which would be quite different from Western democracy." But during his own presentation on "Modernization and the Demand for Social Justice," he was sometimes critical of the way democratic institutions functioned in developing countries like South Korea. In explaining the difficulty of undertaking social welfare programs in poor countries, Ham contended that the problem did not stem from the fact that laws were not passed by legislatures but that governments were not strong enough to enforce the laws. "Passing laws is a very popular pastime among the politicians of underdeveloped countries," he observed, because it "gives the legislators the appearance of 'doing something.'" But governments had difficulty enforcing these laws because democratic institutions had been formed in the absence of Anglo-American conceptions of the rule of law. Given these circumstances, "we cannot do enough to foster genuine respect for law and order among the people."[47] Of course, Ham did not mean that democracy should be forsaken for authoritarianism, and his assessment of the problems created by formally democratic institutions in areas of the developing world was, in many ways, accurate. But given his strong preference for governments that could enforce the law, it is not surprising that when faced with the choice between remaining loyal to the Park government and trying to replace it, he chose the former.

Ultimately, Ham decided to endorse rather than oppose the Park government's move toward greater authoritarianism during the late 1960s and reaped great political benefits from his choice. Few South Koreans from academic backgrounds gained higher positions in the bureaucracy. Ham served as ambassador to the United States between 1973 and 1978 and later became a national security adviser to President Chun Doo Hwan. Before his untimely death at the hands of North Korean terrorists in 1983, Ham argued that the restrictions placed by the Yusin system on personal freedom were necessitated by national security and Koreans' poor understanding of the rule of law. In 1978 he wrote that while the people of South Korea would "prefer a more relaxed and freewheeling lifestyle," the government had found it necessary to strike the balance "more in favor of national security than of individual freedom." He maintained that "non-violent and loyal dissent had been fully permitted" and that the government had prohibited only forms of dissent that were "illegal and disorderly."[48] For Ham, modernization was impossible unless the government could ensure security and control dissent. He could accept and support Yusin because Park Chung Hee seemed to be the only national political leader who could achieve these objectives.

While scholars like Im Panghyŏn and Ham Pyŏngjun attained high ranks in the breaucracy, many others whose work centered on the social sciences or different dimensions of modernization followed similar if somewhat less illustrious career paths. Under Yusin, Park gained the power to appoint one-third of the members of the National Assembly. During the seven years in which the system was in operation, the president named roughly two dozen assembly members with academic backgrounds. The majority of these appointees were social scientists or deans from the country's elite universities. Working with other members of Park's political party, these former academics helped draft legislation that could define and support the objectives of the Yusin system. But their participation in the Yusin government was not limited to fashioning legislation. Park also drew on the assistance of scholars to create some of the ideological and philosophical grounding for the Yusin system and the New Village movement. Academics trained in the social sciences and the humanities helped develop new educational curricula, create propaganda, and write speeches that could dissuade potential dissenters and build popular support for Park's agenda.[49]

But while the wide-ranging discussions of modernization in South Korea during the 1960s produced scholars who facilitated Park's growing authoritarianism, they also influenced many other intellectuals to become leading dissidents in the Yusin era. Some argued that respect for human rights and the dignity of the individual needed to be a part of any Korean version of modernization. Others, who had sought to build a dialogue with the government on issues of national development, could not accept the state's sudden insistence on intellectual conformity. Many scholars who had once been eager to work with the Park government began to oppose it, even at the expense of their careers and, in some instances, their lives.

The same notion of a distinctively Korean version of modernization that had elicited support for the Yusin system among some intellectuals also provided a philosophical basis for resistance to authoritarianism. Some scholars influenced by this idea even claimed that democratic ideals were an intrinsic part of Korea's historical culture. An article entitled "Will Korea's Modernization Be Westernization?," which appeared in a 1964 issue of the progressive journal *Ch'ŏngmaek*, made this point rather bluntly. While the essay acknowledged that modernity and democracy had first been fully realized in the West, it also contended that "the most purely modern value was human liberation" and that the "values of human liberation had by no means been absent from either the East or Korea." The "values of human liberation," according to the author, had been manifest in past events in Korean history, such as the farmers' protest movement that occurred during the Three Kingdoms period and the slave uprisings during the Koryŏ Dynasty.[50] Scholars who located progressive democratic values in Korea's past naturally tended to see them as vital components of national modernization. Such beliefs created friction between some scholars and the regime.

Historian Kang Man'gil was among the most eminent scholars who linked democracy and modernization and, as a consequence, came into conflict with the state. Kang achieved recognition for his sweeping reinterpretation of Korea's modern history as one of ongoing conflict between progressive forces, represented by the *minjung* (people), and conservative elites that resisted change. In the early 1960s Kang entered graduate school at Korea University, where he eventually became a professor. As student and teacher he came into contact with many well-known Korean social scientists who were interested in modernization and development. Although Kang did not have as close a relationship with American scholars as many of the more senior faculty members did, he inevitably became involved in debating what was perceived as one of the critical academic issues of his era.

Kang was associated with the "internal development" school of Korean history, which advanced the argument that a nascent process of capitalist modernization in Korea was occurring before the country ever came into contact with the West or Japan and that the intervention of foreign powers had obstructed, rather than advanced, this process. Kang paid special attention to the role of the minjung as a force for historical change. In an early essay, "The Changes of the Sixteenth Century," for instance, he argued that Korea had begun moving in the direction of a modern society in the sixteenth century, rather than in the seventeenth century as other historians had contended. After surveying the political, economic, and social changes that had occurred during this era, he concluded that the driving force behind these changes had been the people, or minjung. He wrote that "more than anything else the basic source [of these changes] occurred . . . when the minjung started to reject the Yi Dynasty's system of social dominance."[51] Kang's work shared the preoccupation with the origins and sources of modernizing change that had become widespread among historians in both South Korea and the United States. But at the same time, it channeled this preoccupation in a nationalistic and populist direction by placing the minjung, rather than the state, at the center of this historical process.

Ultimately, Kang's populist conception of how historical change occurred led him to reject the rationale for the Yusin system. Like other scholars who had believed that modernization would provide grounds for increasing participation in the political sphere, Kang was disillusioned when South Korean politics took a turn in the opposite direction: "When I saw the Yusin dictatorship I felt a severe sense of betrayal and could not study the history of the Chosŏn period any longer. I thought that as the present became more difficult it no longer made sense to study the distant past."[52] Kang began calling on South Korean scholars to pay more attention to the country's modern history and to use it as a means of shedding light on contemporary problems. In a series of essays on history writing in postwar Korea, Kang emphasized the need for scholars not to deploy modernization theory in a way that could contribute to authoritarianism. In one essay, he wrote that modernization was, in its most essential form, a "process of moving forward for the sake of human liberation and, as a result, a process of extending historical subjectivity to new groups in every region." He worried that if "the source of successful political modernization was sought only in the elite group of political actors," it would ultimately "limit historical subjectivity and produce an anachronistic form of hero worship."[53] Kang eventually became a significant figure in protest movements against the Park government. He stood by scholars whom the regime forced to leave their positions at universities until he too was finally compelled to abandon his professorship in 1980.[54]

Other academics with less distinctive philosophical viewpoints were troubled by the breakdown of honest dialogue between intellectuals and the state that occurred after Yusin. Many South Koreans who had been willing to work with the Park government when dissenting opinions were tolerated during the mid-sixties joined the opposition when the regime demanded that scholars support the state's agenda. Yu Kich'ŏn, a legal expert and chancellor of Seoul National University from 1965 to 1966, was among the most prominent scholars in this group. Yu claimed that when Park offered him the chancellorship, he accepted the post on the condition that the government would respect academic freedom for faculty and students at SNU. With this guarantee in place, Yu was highly supportive of some major items on the government's agenda, especially the normalization of relations between South Korea and Japan. Like American and South Korean government officials, he saw improved relations with Japan as a potential stimulus to economic development and worked to build a consensus in favor of normalization among faculty on his campus.[55] Although Yu has contended that he was suspicious of Park's motives from the outset, as long as a climate of relative academic freedom prevailed he felt comfortable cooperating with the government.

But as Park began to adopt an increasingly restrictive posture toward academic freedom in the early 1970s, Yu moved toward more open resistance of the regime. In the spring of 1971 he aligned himself with student protesters who had become very active at SNU after Park amended the constitution so he could seek a third term. After he saw a dissident student viciously attacked by police, Yu decided that he could no longer teach criminal law. He recalled explaining to his students that criminal law "protects the legal order whatever it may be," and that to avoid becoming an arbitrary instrument of state power "criminal law must abide by the rule of law which in the university means academic freedom."[56] Yu's denunciation of the government soon drew the ire of the Park regime. In January 1972 he became one of the dozens of scholars in the social sciences who were forced to leave their posts.

The regime's suspension or dismissal of academics who criticized its policies did not quiet them but, instead, helped build an important element of the opposition. Despite the restrictions that had been placed on what they could say or write, dissident intellectuals remained determined to encourage democratization in the country and found ways to voice their criticisms of the regime. By 1972 the state had managed to persuade a considerable portion of the intellectual community to support the renewed military dictatorship, but an equally significant portion was prepared for a protracted confrontation.

Americans realized that intellectuals would be one of the most influential groups in South Korea's nation-building process and tried to encourage them to support liberal capitalist development. Official and private U.S. organizations hoped that involving the country's academics in discussions of modernization would contribute to both economic growth and democratization. Intellectuals would become more willing to participate in national development programs, while the state would recognize their ability to contribute to policy decisions. This, in turn, would broaden citizen participation in government and contribute to the state's evolution toward democracy. Between roughly 1963 and 1967, a significant number of South Korean academics embraced the most critical components of the American agenda. They were eager to discuss ways of modernizing their country and to share their views on the subject with the Park government. Before the regime sought to suppress all dissenting opinions in the early seventies, a relatively open dialogue between intellectuals and the state did occur. The regime was willing to listen to the differing prescriptions that intellectuals presented even if it did not always follow them.

By the early 1970s, however, the relationship between intellectuals and the state had changed. This was not a result of any inherent flaw in U.S. programs. The concept of modernization held great appeal for South Korean intellectuals, and Americans proved accommodating when their Korean colleagues adapted the concept to suit their own aspirations and goals. The problem was that the state's turn toward authoritarianism in the late sixties and early seventies made it impossible for intellectuals to participate in the nation-building process on a purely liberal democratic basis. The evolving political situation forced scholars to choose between supporting a military dictatorship and resisting the state's encroachments on free expression. The version of modernization that Korean scholars had derived could justify either decision. It fostered support for the Yusin system among some intellectuals and therefore, in some ways, helped legitimize full-blown military dictatorship. But the experience of openly discussing South Korea's future also strengthened the faith of many Korean intellectuals in democratic development. Thus, American programs also helped build a group that was willing to fight for the reestablishment of civil society and a system of government that was consistent with liberal democratic ideals.

To succeed at nation building in the Republic of Korea (ROK), Washington tried to shape not only the country's present but also its future. And it was clearly the younger generation of South Koreans that held the key to the nation's economic and political evolution. The increasing proportion of youth in the ROK population, combined with the continuing influence of students in national politics, made this sector of the population a constant source of both hope and anxiety for U.S. nation builders. Americans hoped that youth could serve as the vanguard of a new South Korean society based on collective responsibility, self-help, and shared systems of allegiances and values. But they also feared that young people would embrace a more xenophobic nationalism that would endanger national development and the ROK's alliance with the United States.

A wide array of American official, private, and religious organizations became involved in efforts to steer South Korean youth toward ideals and values that would facilitate liberal democratic nation building. They cooperated with each other and with international and indigenous Non-Government Organizations (NGOs) involved in youth work. The U.S. Information Service (USIS), U.S. Agency for International Development (USAID), and the Peace Corps all worked with Korean high school and college students in different capacities. Christian missionaries from Europe and the United States sought to influence South Korean youth through a combination of educational and welfare programs. Both the U.S. government and private agencies contributed substantially to the development of youth organizations such as the 4-H Clubs, Boy Scouts, and Girl Scouts. These organizations had developed branches on the peninsula before the Korean War and expanded through further U.S. efforts in the 1960s.

Although these official and private agencies had varied programs and emphases, they shared an overarching objective: to instill in South Korean youths a civic-mindedness that would prepare them to participate in a democratic society. For U.S. officials, this entailed not only exposure to democratic practices in the political arena but also encouragement to contribute to national economic development and embrace Free World internationalism. Americans believed that the long-term success of their nation-building project hinged on future generations' acceptance of this nexus of ideals and values.

Americans managed to initiate dialogues with different youth groups on a variety of social, economic, and political problems. Persuading these young people of the merits of American viewpoints on certain issues was almost never easy. South Korean students were passionate in their devotion to democratic ideals and in their desire for higher living standards. But they were also deeply nationalistic and feared that embracing American influence too zealously would lead to cultural subordination. Moreover, given Korea's long history of student dissent, many youths felt a kind of moral obligation to be critical of government—both their own and that of the United States. Nevertheless, the dialogues that occurred were significant in and of themselves. They acquainted young South Koreans with open forms of debate and demonstrated that Americans were interested in hearing their views even if they found fault with the United States.

Ultimately, however, U.S. ambitions to make Korean youth the vanguard of a new democratic society were thwarted by the state's shift to greater authoritarianism in the late 1960s. Student dissent became a major factor in only one or two instances during the early and mid-1960s. Partially as a result of American programs, South Korean youths held out hope for a future in which they would have a voice. When the Park government began limiting the input of civil society after 1968, students naturally felt a sense of betrayal. While Park had been able to co-opt a significant number of intellectuals, he was much less successful in mobilizing the younger generation. American efforts to foster a participatory ethos among South Korean youths were conducive to political stability only when the state allowed open debate and dissent. When the regime embraced authoritarianism, this desire for political participation became a prescription for conflict.

Youths and Students in South Korea

When the military seized power in South Korea, both Washington and the new ROK government recognized that managing the younger generation, which had played a key role in overthrowing Syngman Rhee, would become a critical issue. Ten days after the military coup, an American embassy official assured the U.S. State Department that the "embassy-USIS" had "kept in close contact with student communities in order to ascertain as much as possible their reactions to military takeover." The official believed that any assessment of the student mood could "at best be tentative" but pointed to a general ambivalence among university students about the new political leadership. But there was a possibility of future protests, as the students saw themselves as the "principal segment of Korean society in which moral responsibility for [the] defense of freedom rests" and were likely to "make bolder statements and take actions calling for the return of political freedoms."[1] In the early sixties American officials tended to be sympathetic toward students' democratic aspirations but remained concerned about their potential to undermine political stability.

Student demonstrations continued to elicit deep concern among American officials during subsequent years. This concern intensified when the protests touched on issues involving the U.S. role in the ROK. After U.S. soldiers committed an unwarranted assault on Korean civilians in Paju in 1962, students at many South Korean universities demanded the termination of a Status of Forces Agreement. Ambassador Samuel Berger wrote that some of the participants probably had "malicious or subversive motives" and that such actions "cannot repeat cannot be tolerated." Berger viewed the demonstrations as a manifestation of a more enduring problem in U.S.-Korean relations; they could not be "brushed aside as of minor or temporary significance."[2]

More widespread demonstrations in 1964 protesting the normalization of relations between South Korea and Japan produced a similar reaction among U.S. officials. The embassy in Seoul reported that the students "had once again demonstrated their potential for intruding upon and for affecting the local political scene." They had managed to "contribute greatly to Korean political instability" and caused the government to virtually suspend the ROK-Japan negotiations. And although the "core of political students" was small, it was "nevertheless important for the effect it [could] exercise on the local scene."[3]

The restlessness of students was not simply a result of political issues, however. It was also a by-product of larger grievances caused by the failure of the United States and the Park regime to improve socioeconomic conditions. Both governments were acutely aware of this fact. From Seoul, an American official wrote that "the average student is still avowedly anticommunist in outlook but, perhaps, emotionally, more attracted to the left for possible solutions to his own and the nation's problems since, apparently, little if any progress has been achieved by the present system."[4] Similarly, a South Korean government minister told U.S. officials that whereas university students "aspired to positions with status and income appropriate to their higher education," they often ended up "living a meager hand to mouth existence looking for jobs and spending much of their time in tea rooms discussing politics."⁵ Constantly dogged by concerns about the capacity of students to wreak political havoc, the United States became increasingly interested in finding ways to influence them.

American Policy and South Korea's Youth

In the sixties American policymakers gave the U.S. Information Service explicit responsibility for reshaping the attitudes of South Korean youths. The USIS involved itself most directly with college and high school students. In sponsoring special clubs, student conferences, and publications, the agency sought to engage student leaders and give them a new view of their role in national and global affairs.

English conversation clubs proved to be perhaps the USIS's most effective tool for connecting with young South Koreans. These clubs arranged for regular meetings between student leaders from top Korean universities and American group leaders drawn from either the USIS or the military. The nominal purpose of these clubs was to develop a better understanding of the United States through English conversation. More often than not, however, American leaders steered the agenda of meetings toward subjects of national and international significance in order to influence students' perceptions of critical issues.

Young South Koreans were drawn to these clubs for a variety of reasons. First, the most savvy students realized that improving their English skills could also increase their chances of finding jobs in an economy where college graduates often could not find them. Second, whether or not they were pro-American in their orientation, many young people possessed a curiosity about American life that could at least be partially satisfied through participation in a conversation club. Finally, these clubs provided a social outlet for many students. Whereas South Korean high schools and especially colleges were strictly segregated by gender during the fifties and sixties, many conversation clubs were coeducational. Not surprisingly, the clubs were among the most popular USIS programs. By 1968 thirty-four clubs met regularly at the USIS center in Seoul alone. Dozens of English conversation clubs met at USIS centers in Pusan, Kwangju, and other major Korean cities.⁶

Barnard Lavin, a USIS officer stationed in Seoul, formed one conversation club that required participants to read and discuss books in English. One student who read the autobiography of Benjamin Franklin was particularly impressed by Franklin's formation of "the Junto"—a group of twelve Philadelphians who met every Friday to discuss public affairs. In considering

Franklin's "Junto," club members saw the merits of forming such a group of their own. The group soon began meeting weekly to examine different aspects of U.S.-Korean relations with Lavin. Several members of the Junto rose to prominence either as student leaders or in their later careers. The USIS selected one of its members, Yi Taesŏp, to meet with Dwight D. Eisenhower during a presidential visit to Seoul shortly after the April 19 Revolution. Yi became a near celebrity in the ROK for announcing to Eisenhower that "the Korean students made it possible for the government to be put into the hands of good people." The Junto's members also included Kim Chaeik, who became economic counselor to President Chun Doo Hwan in the 1980s.[7]

Over the course of the 1960s the USIS built upon its conversation clubs to create larger student leadership conferences. These conferences focused on preparing students to participate in a democratic society. In 1968, for instance, the USIS held a special two-day seminar for student journalists from around the ROK to "assist in promoting democratic concepts of the press and the role that can be played by student newspapers on campus." The meeting centered around discussions between seventy-five student journalists from leading Korean universities and a variety of panelists that included journalism professors from South Korea and the United States. The panelists tended to concentrate on topics that could heighten students' sense of their own social obligations, such as "New Directions and Roles for the Student Press in Korea" and "Responsibilities and Roles of a Student Press on Campus and in Society—The U.S. Experience." An American Fulbright scholar delivered a lecture on student journalism in the United States; he encouraged participants to "dig into . . . the real injustice and corruption that exist on and off campus," and he wondered how students could "claim to have a role as social critics if they do not express their opinions in student papers."[8]

Also in the late sixties the USIS in Seoul launched another series of "student leadership workshops" for elite groups of young Koreans who had been handpicked by deans at Seoul's top universities. The purpose of the series was to "introduce student leaders . . . to the techniques of democratic leadership and to encourage them to contribute more to community and national betterment." A typical workshop lasted several days and included a range of recreational activities and panel discussions on topics such as "Student Participation and Contributions in Community Betterment Programs in Urban and Rural Korea" and "Effective Student Participation in the National Development and Social Modernization of Korea." The USIS invited South Korean professors who had experience in "assisting student efforts in community betterment programs" to give lectures and lead panel discussions.[9]

Both the passion for democracy and the zealous nationalism of South Korean students were plainly evident at these conferences. At the end of one workshop in 1968, the participants drew up a set of resolutions that seemed to reflect the sense of progressive nationalism that Americans had sought to impress upon them. The students resolved, among other things, "to strive to cultivate democratic leadership in directing the affairs of other students and to enable more adequate contributions to the society, the community, and the nation." Similarly, most, but not all, of their brief responses to the conference, reprinted by the USIS, were enthusiastic. One participant hoped that such workshops would be "the birthplace of new creative leaders in our country."[10] But on some occasions students' self-confident nationalism worried the Americans. After one conference in 1968 a student from Seoul National University (SNU) complained that "many of the discussions were below the desired level" and wished that the USIS could have used "more 'made in Korea' rather than 'made in U.S.A.' products during the final reception."[11] In some instances, participants were more overtly anti-American or anti-Western. During a discussion of the question "Western influence, irritant or stimulant?" at the 1964 International Student Association Conference, nearly all of the delegates concluded that "Western influence was an irritant" and asked why "the East" had not made a more visible impact on "the West."[12]

South Korean students sometimes struggled with the contradictions between their burgeoning sense of nationalism and their attraction to liberal democratic concepts that were Euro-American in origin. At one USIS student leadership conference near Taegu in November 1967, a young Korean dressed in a Boy Scout uniform interrupted a session on democracy in South Korea, crying out "Yankee go home" and "Yankee is number ten!" The student later sent a letter to the USIS post in Taegu explaining his actions. During a discussion of how South Koreans could develop democracy, he wrote, "many examples were quoted from foreign countries such as [the] Magna Carta, George Washington, Thomas Jefferson and Lincoln." But he thought that "to develop our democracy we should quote and discuss our ancestors who fought for democracy along with examples from other countries," for "in our history we can find many traces of efforts to establish democracy." He then chastised the other students who had attended the meeting for failing to "mention inherent Korean democracy."

Though noting that "to construct a better nation and to make progress Korea needs friendly relationships with foreign countries," he also included a list of grievances against foreigners, especially Americans. He criticized foreigners who had "talked about Korea's dirty streets [and] beggars . . . without even mentioning one word about the good aspects of Korea" and referred to newspaper reports about a group of Korean prostitutes who had "made a demonstration at a U.S. army camp carrying one of their colleague's dead body who had been killed by an American GI."[13] Even while partially accepting the necessity of U.S. assistance, such students resented South Korea's subordinate status in its relationship with the United States.

When confronted with such manifestations of Korean nationalism, Americans reacted with a combination of hope and caution but never let go of the idea that it was essential for the United States to guide South Korea to capitalism and democracy. One USIS official asserted that the Boy Scout's letter exemplified what Koreans called *chu-chae-ui-sik*.[14] "When the term connotes a self-respecting sense of nationalism," he explained, "there is no reason to do anything except welcome the development"; however, the word also had "xenophobic connotations similar to those which were expressed by the freshman student [Boy Scout] at the seminar as well as authoritarian overtones." In response to the threat posed by such ideas, the USIS officer recommended that the post's youth leadership programs be restructured "to allow for a linking of democratic ideas and healthy progressive nationalism." It would enable them to impress upon young Koreans that "virulent, blind nationalism has been a destructive force for nations which have unleashed it" and that the "twentieth century requires awareness, competence and knowledge rather than emotionalism." This kind of "input," the officer added, "will permit legitimate American participation in these programs as well as allow relevant American experience to be shared."[15] The USIS sought not to quell the rising tide of student nationalism in South Korea but rather to channel it in directions that were in the U.S. interest and conducive to political democracy.

Other USIS programs aimed to instill a greater optimism about the nation's economic development. Agency officials tended to believe that much of the real impetus behind student radicalism stemmed from the fact that young people simply did not understand the progress that the ROK was making through U.S. assistance. A 1964 report observed that "the people of South Korea, particularly its student leaders, are not fully aware of either the progress that has been made in the Republic of Korea since 1945 . . . or the industrial base now existing in South Korea."[16] It concluded that if students were able to view Korean industrial development firsthand, they would become reconciled to American influence and be more eager to contribute to their nation's progress.

In 1964 the USIS initiated a series of "economic seminars and factory tours" designed to show Korean student leaders that economic change was on the horizon. Working in conjunction with the ROK's Economic Planning Board (EPB), the USIS developed seminars in areas such as "the development of power and industry in Korea," giving students the chance to discuss the subjects with Korean planners and U.S. technical advisers. USIS and EPB officials then led the participants on a guided tour of the Dong-In Power Plant. Through these activities, the USIS sought to "create a greater sense of confidence among these young leaders in the vitality of the Korean economy and of the breadth of its base."[17] This new confidence, they reasoned, could contribute to the emergence of student elites that wanted to participate in, rather than criticize, the South Korean economy.

Some USIS officials who observed the first tour seemed convinced that the series was having an immediate impact on the students. A report on the seminar stated that ROK planners' explanation of how South Korea's power production would soon equal and surpass that of North Korea made "a distinct impression on the students." During presentations by representatives of the U.S. Operations Mission (USOM), "what the U.S. had done was deemphasized and what Korea had done and was doing to develop a strong virile industrial base for continued economic growth was emphasized." These presentations and subsequent discussion had been "welcomed" by the South Korean students.[18]

But student responses to the "seminar-tours" were not always enthusiastic. Barnard Lavin recalled that while he was leading a group of sixty students on a tour of the Hankook tire factory, one youth began handing out "leaflets" to the workers. Lavin "gently took hold of the collar of his school uniform" and told him that this was "not the purpose of this tour."[19] Lavin's anecdote was typical of the difficulties that American officials encountered in trying to persuade young South Koreans that their country was moving in the right direction. Despite their best efforts, some students continued to embrace radical rather than moderate, capitalist solutions to the problem of national economic underdevelopment.

The USOM supplemented the USIS attempts to spark interest in economic development with a special intern program that directly involved youth in the nation-building process. Student interns worked in partnership with USOM specialists and their counterpart agencies in South Korea on problems related to the country's modernization. The program was limited to students (between twelve and twenty-five annually) from top Korean universities, such as SNU and Ewha Women's University, who were to be brought "into direct contact with the development process in Korea in a broad sense."[20] Interns generally worked with senior USOM specialists and the Korean businesses or agencies that their USOM adviser was assisting. After attending a general program that addressed development issues, students spent six weeks working on projects where they were trained to apply the most recent managerial concepts to specific problems. The intern program emphasized active participation to give the students a sense of their own potential agency in transforming their country. Clifford Liddle, the USOM's senior educational adviser, pointed out that "the students learn by doing and in the doing they develop a pride in personal professional achievement and increased confidence in the accomplishments of their nation."[21]

The nature of the projects depended on participants' major academic interests, but nearly all of them acquainted students with aspects of economic development. Interns frequently studied projects or institutions where they could directly observe the ways that the USOM was working with different groups of South Koreans. Such assignments were intended to build the students' faith not only in their nation's economic prospects but also in the benefits of cooperation with the United States. One intern was assigned to the Pusan and Chongp'yŏng thermal power plants, both of which were being constructed through USOM development loans. The intern studied documents that described the plants' progress and potential benefits to the country at large.[22] Another intern majoring in chemical engineering went on an extensive field trip that exposed him to government-run development projects and enabled him to meet with consultants working for the USOM-aided Korean Productivity Center. The student toured several industrial areas and was asked to identify factors that could both contribute to and deter economic development in South Korea.[23] Such projects encouraged students to apply their intellects and analytic skills toward solving national problems.

The students who participated in this program were a privileged few, and they generally came away with a sense of gratitude toward the United States. In his final report, one intern acknowledged that "the U.S. government has assisted our government," and he hoped that Americans would "continue their efforts . . . in the future."[24] Kim Syng-An, an economics major at Sŏgang University, had become "aware of the hard work involved in Korean economic development planning" and had come "to understand what the ROK government and USOM people are thinking and doing and trying to do for the construction of a better Korea."[25]

The intern program even seemed to awaken students to the possibility that they might participate in their country's economic transformation. One student wrote that "the essential point of our tasks is modernization whatever the field may be" and that "better development or modernization will be accelerated by the creative industrious effort of the enterprisers."[26] The student ended his report with a ringing declaration of the need for a broad spectrum of individuals to take part in national development efforts. He believed that "man can choose and determine the way to consistent and perpetual development." This "man," he proclaimed, "is the government policy maker, he is the industry-owner, he is the manager, he is the engineer and technician, and he is the laborer."[27]

Despite the sense of privilege that student interns gained from participating in the program, however, they could never entirely dispense with their concerns about America's enormous influence in South Korea. A theology student from Yonsei University, who interned in the USOM's rural development division in Ch'ŏngju, offered a generally positive picture of the mission's influence on that area. At the same time, however, because "our country has its own culture, customs and national character," in rendering assistance to South Korea, he told USOM officials, "you will have to understand them more." The student emphasized that it was necessary "to mutually understand each other rather than giving assistance without mutual understanding."[28]

American youth programs in South Korea focused not only on increasing optimism about the ROK's economic prospects but also on building a sense of solidarity between South Korean students and students from other Free World Asian nations. Americans wanted to build bridges between the rising generation of South Koreans and their counterparts in the Philippines, South Vietnam, and, most prominently, Japan. In conjunction with USIS posts in other Asian countries, the USIS in Seoul sponsored international student conferences that could achieve this objective. The agency held annual "Far East Student Leadership Conferences" in Hawaii, where student leaders from South Korea, Japan, and other free Asian countries discussed issues of international significance.[29] In addition to conducting its own meetings, the USIS assisted independent South Korean student groups whose purposes seemed to match its own. When the International Student Association of Korea organized a conference for representatives of several East and Southeast Asian countries in 1964, for instance, the USIS made its building available for forums and had one of its officers attend the conference.[30] These initiatives, however, had far more intractable obstacles to overcome than those that focused on democracy or economic development, and they never entirely achieved their objectives.

The greatest challenge for USIS officials was to persuade South Korean students to take a more positive view of Japan. The Americans desperately wanted to mitigate the protests against normalizing relations with Japan that swept across university campuses in the mid-sixties. The efforts of the USIS on this issue complemented broader American diplomatic attempts to promote diplomatic reconciliation between the ROK and Japan. In 1964 and 1965 the USIS arranged for South Korean student leaders and journalists to visit Japan, despite various technical problems stemming from the lack of official relations between the two countries. After touring the facilities of the U.S. Armed Forces newspaper *Stars and Stripes*, the students visited several Japanese universities including Keio University and Tenri University. The latter was known for having the best Korean Studies program in Japan. South Korean students met with their Japanese peers and had open discussions on a variety of political issues. One report on the program explained that while the "trip was publicly identified as a media observation tour, the real purpose again was to expose the Korean students to the realities of the new Japan in order to influence them to accept and support the Korean government's efforts to normalize relations with Japan."[31]

But Americans could not easily reduce either Korean resentment of Japan or Japanese racism toward Koreans. According to one USIS report, while a Korean student "was commenting on something of interest to him," a Japanese student behind him was heard to say "oh shut up you chubby little bastard."[32] After one group discussion, when students sang their national songs, the Korean youths sang *arirang*, a popular folk song associated with resistance to Japanese colonialism. One Korean student recalled being "really moved at that time" because "20 years ago Korea was a Japanese colony and now we sing in Japan as students from a sovereign nation."[33] The bitter feelings between the youth of these two countries were reflected in editorials that the young South Koreans wrote for their school newspapers after returning home.

Many South Korean students retained complex, and at times contradictory, feelings toward Japan. They were impressed by Japan's economic growth and sometimes observed that South Korea could learn from Japan's modernization program. But they remained suspicious of its political intentions and, in some ways, hostile toward the Japanese people generally. Yu

Imsuk, a student at Chungang University, thought that Japan was a "remarkable developed and mechanized country." Having viewed the accommodations for the 1964 Olympics in Tokyo, Yu wrote that when she "saw the Olympic Stadium's great and well provided facilities," she "felt even jealousy." But at the same time, Yu was troubled by what she perceived as Japan's lack of interest in and knowledge about Korea. She wondered, "Why do we Koreans have to make tremendous efforts for getting along with these Japanese who are not interested in Korea?" Nationalistic pride paired with anti-Japanese sentiment could be seen in her physical descriptions of the Japanese: "Most of the Japanese people are short, and Japanese males look feminine." After traveling to Japan she "newly recognized Korean men's continental masculinity," adding, "I don't think it is too much if I say that Korean women are more beautiful than their Japanese counterpart[s]."[34]

Yi Changsik, who attended Tongguk University, expressed a similar ambivalence. He told a USIS officer that "after seeing the great progress made by Japan, I think now we have to modernize our country through mutual cooperation with the neighboring countries." But though visiting the country heightened Yi's dedication to economic development, it did not leave him with much goodwill toward the Japanese, whom he considered hypocritical and inadequately penitent for the past misdeeds of their nation. In an editorial for his school newspaper, Yi wrote that Japanese students criticized South Korea for sending troops to Vietnam while Japan was "selling trucks and jeeps to the U.S. military and manufacturing even tanks and warships." Yi thought that this was because the Japanese "do anything they can if they can earn money." It was also disturbing that Japanese students "did not know what sort of bad things their ancestors did to the Korean people for 36 years." Yi and the other South Koreans had attempted to identify "those bad things including change of Korean names[,] deprivation of our farmland and elimination of Korean culture."[35]

The combination of admiration and hostility for Japan inspired by the visit led to mixed feelings about the prospects for improved relations between Japan and the ROK. Some students were mildly supportive of normalization but remained wary of Japanese intentions. One South Korean visitor conceded that "students should not engage in demonstrations against the ROK-Japan treaty" but nevertheless thought that the ROK needed to "do something to prevent our country from becoming a market for Japanese goods." Another student wondered "how the Korean people can check the flow of Japanese goods into Korean markets after the formal normalization of relations between the two countries."[36] Their impression of the Japanese people as self-interested and unrepentant for their country's imperial past made Korean students question whether relations between the ROK and Japan could be improved without reviving the economic subordination that had existed under Japanese colonialism.

Although South Korean students never fully accepted the rationale for improved relations with Japan, programs run by the USIS and the USOM were able to engage elite Korean youth by offering them avenues for expressing their personal and collective aspirations. But these programs had limitations. U.S. officials were always, to some extent, a source of authority and therefore suspect. Realizing this, the Americans began to think that young, energetic Peace Corps volunteers might have dramatic successes where government officials could muster only partial ones.

The Peace Corps and South Korean High Schools

Peace Corps volunteers assigned to South Korea beginning in 1966 were supposed to contribute to the country's development in many ways, but shaping the attitudes of Korean youths was perhaps their most pressing task. The official mission of the Peace Corps emphasized the modernization of traditional social values. The American volunteers taught English and science in high schools and established public health programs in rural areas. Through such activities, they were expected to make South Koreans aware of their backwardness and promote a desire for social change. One official report on the Peace Corps in South Korea explained: "Koreans do not often have to think for themselves; most situations are determined by a series of traditional patterned responses." Therefore, "the basic goal of the Peace Corps is fostering attitudinal changes—to get the Koreans to think for themselves." The Peace Corps was "taking aim at the whole elaborate social structure."[37] Americans anticipated that merely through interacting with Korean students, Peace Corps volunteers could awaken them to the possibilities of socioeconomic change. At a meeting with Peace Corps director Sargent Shriver, a South Korean official expressed the hope that the presence of young Americans in South Korea would "embarrass the Korean youth into action."[38]

Officials in the Peace Corps saw TESOL (Teaching English to Speakers of Other Languages) programs as an effective vehicle for changing the outlook of South Korean youth. The organization believed that English language classes would provide direct opportunities for the volunteers to communicate new ideas and forge friendships with their students.[39] The training manual distributed to the first group of volunteers in 1966 exhorted each of them to "be a good teacher and a dependable technical advisor" and at the same time to be "a good friend, an obliging neighbor and a well accepted member of the community." It concluded with the admonition, "Even if you fail in the first tasks, you must succeed in the last one."[40]

In some instances, Peace Corps volunteers did attempt to steer their students toward a progressive, nonrevolutionary sense of nationalism. In a salutation that he wrote for the yearbook at the high school where he taught, one volunteer offered instructions on how Korean youth could build "a new society." The volunteer noted that in the future South Korea's population would be "large and young in age" and therefore eager to effect social change. "The role of today's students," he argued, "is to learn how to bring about changes in a new society; economically, politically and socially." The volunteer did not reject the possibility that Koreans might build this new society on the basis of their "traditions," as Americans sometimes did; instead, he believed that to "make a new society . . . we need to know our past better so that we can choose the best of our tradition." Yet South Koreans needed to be open to "Western" ideas; building a new society would also require choosing "the best from modern societies." To "do this we must learn about Western civilization and experience."[41]

More frequently, however, the cynicism of Peace Corps volunteers limited their resolve to implement the institution's objectives. Rather than seeking to change the attitudes of their students, volunteers sometimes came to identify more strongly with aspects of Korean culture than they did with American culture. Some of them even concluded that, if anything, South Koreans could give young Americans a lesson on responsible citizenship. In the Peace Corps newsletter, a volunteer English teacher commented on how everyday he had watched "a crew of little girls don white aprons, pick up their stubby brooms and attack the day's accumulation of dirt in the school." He wondered, "Why don't American schools employ this positive method of instilling responsibility in their students?" He noted that "the major reason is the danger of injury to students and subsequent law suits against the schools"; nevertheless, he could not help "admiring the responsibility and maturity of these middle school students even as they hang out fifth story windows."[42]

Other volunteers went even further in rebuffing the developmental objectives of their organization. More than virtually any other group of Americans in South Korea during the sixties, Peace Corps volunteers exhibited a penchant for "going native," or taking on elements of Korean culture while rejecting their own. For some of them, life on the peninsula became a potential cure for the psychic ailments that plagued Americans. Volunteer Gary Katsel encouraged his colleagues to "walk the burning coals" by immersing themselves more deeply in Korean culture. Katsel wrote: "America is a nation of spiritually hungry people . . . who are getting their kicks from 'The Hillbillies,' deodorant advertisements, LSD and pot." He continued: "If we could have the life practicality of Korea without the search for kicks and trinkets, we could have much less insomnia and much more chance for building a truly universal society, more directed to man than to the accoutrements of man." Katsel could not understand the "Peace Corps' edict to retain one's cultural identity," since "only through shedding one's cultural clothes and assuming new ones in a new role" could one "get out of the awful straightjacket we have inherited from Western culture."[43]

Of course, not every Peace Corps volunteer in South Korea agreed with Katsel. For some, the country was a source of neither the amoral Confucianism described by policymakers nor the lost spirituality sought by some of their colleagues. Two volunteers even wrote a response to Katsel's piece criticizing his assumption that "one culture can be shed like a snakeskin and the other donned." They argued that "no culture has all the answers" and "perhaps both the U.S. and Korea could benefit from an eclectic approach."[44] But despite their disagreements, Katsel and his critics shared an indifference toward their organization's modernizing agenda in South Korea and in all likelihood did not consistently seek to implement it.

Practical difficulties as well as ideological and cultural issues weakened the determination of Peace Corps volunteers to achieve the objectives set out by the organization's leadership. Unlike diplomats or technical advisers who had often spent years working in underdeveloped countries, young members of the Peace Corps had few experiences that could prepare them for the rigors of everyday life in the ROK. After their arrival in 1966, the first group of 100 volunteers proved especially prone to health problems. Within ten months, members of the first group required 25 hospitalizations; there were at least 15 cases of amoebic dysentery, 4 cases of mononucleosis, 2 cases of typhoid, and 4 medical evaluations.[45] Other workers had difficulty understanding the resentment they sometimes encountered from South Koreans. Offering advice to an incoming group in 1971, one volunteer observed: "You'll love Korea one minute and you'll hate it the next minute . . . 'hello monkey' will greet you fifty times one day and the next smiles, giggles and salutes of your students will greet you." Even "washing your face and eating rice everyday, three times a day, is a major feat." Such realities combined with Korean resistance to change made "job and working objectives . . . difficult to achieve."[46]

Although Peace Corps volunteers showed little enthusiasm for the official approach to social engineering, their activities nevertheless encouraged some elements of democratization that American policy had not emphasized. The very cynicism of volunteers regarding the broader objectives of U.S. foreign policy enabled them to have a more honest dialogue with South Korean students than most other Americans could. Because they were younger than most Korean teachers and not always viewed as authority figures, they could, when at their most effective, engage in the kind of freewheeling debate with South Koreans that is the backbone of democratic society. More than most other Americans, Peace Corps volunteers allowed and even encouraged criticism of the United States. This was not what U.S. policymakers who devised the Peace Corps program had intended, but, in encouraging some forms of dissent, it helped develop a component of democratic thought that was just as important as the participatory ethos that stood at the center of other U.S. programs.

Missionaries, Religious Organizations, and Christian Youth in South Korea

Student radicalism was a source of anxiety not only for U.S. officials but for American missionary and Christian groups as well. Christian missionaries had been working in Korea since the late eighteenth century, and their religion had continued to spread throughout the nineteenth and early twentieth centuries despite persecution from the Chosŏn Dynasty (1392–1910) and the Japanese imperial government. Between 1910 and 1945, Korean churches had often resisted Japanese colonialism and sheltered dissidents. Koreans therefore tended to associate Christianity with resistance to colonialism rather than with foreign imperialism, as was the case in many other postcolonial societies.[47] But despite the advantage that Christianity enjoyed in postwar South Korea, as nationalism blossomed in the 1960s there was inevitable friction between young student nationalists and the foreign missionaries who exerted enormous influence over their churches and schools. American missionaries feared the impact of student nationalism on both their own work and South Korean politics.

The difficulties that student nationalism posed for foreign missionaries were exemplified by a dramatic confrontation between students and missionaries at Yonsei University in 1960. Yonsei was a prestigious Christian–

affiliated private school established by American missionary Horace Underwood in the nineteenth century. In August 1960 Yonsei's board of directors, which was chaired by Methodist missionary Charles Sauer, met to replace the university's outgoing president. The board selected Horace G. Underwood, a descendant of one of the university's founders, as acting president and agreed to dismiss two South Korean members of the faculty. The decision to discharge the Koreans while appointing an American to lead the institution provoked a series of faculty strikes and student demonstrations that lasted for an entire semester. These protests came to a halt only after students attempted to raid the houses of Underwood and Sauer and sparked a confrontation with the police.[48]

These events raised concerns about student nationalism among missionaries that were similar to those that troubled Washington. Like some U.S. policymakers, American missionaries regarded student nationalism as potentially constructive in that it could engender a sense of national responsibility among an important segment of the population. At the same time, however, they worried that it would produce hostility toward foreign, especially American, influence if it flowed in the wrong direction. A 1961 report of the U.S. Presbyterian Mission to South Korea noted that "the American missionary has been traditionally associated with the nation's nationalistic aspirations" but wondered how long the mission could "rely on its continuance." Of particular concern was "a strong tide among students to be, as Koreans, the pilots of Korea's destiny." This sense of nationalism, the mission contended, was "readily exploited by Communist propagandists." Even worse, appeals to nationalism could become "a tool of those who would disrupt the relationship of missionaries and those with whom they work."[49]

American missionaries and Christian organizations in South Korea relied on several mechanisms to prevent this scenario. One of these was providing funding and counseling to Christian student organizations. With financial aid from American and European denominations, a broad range of student Christian groups fanned out among South Korean high schools and colleges in the late fifties and early sixties. Some of them, like the YMCA, had been active on the peninsula for many years but were able to expand their operations through assistance from their American counterparts. Others, such as the Campus Crusade for Christ and the Intervarsity Fellowship, were relatively new and owed their existence in part to foreign support.

The most significant Christian student organizations, which included the Korean Student Christian Movement (KSCM), YMCA, and YWCA, received extensive American support. The KSCM had been formed in 1948 by representatives of already existing independent campus organizations with different denominational backgrounds. Although the KSCM's growth had been impeded by the Korean War, funding from the U.S. National Council of Churches and from the United Presbyterian, Methodist, and Canadian missions had enabled it to establish branches on 45 university campuses and in 174 high schools by 1967.[50] American largesse stimulated the growth of YMCAs and YWCAs in South Korea in the 1950s and 1960s as well. The Korean War had shattered the Korean YMCA's organization, but when the conflict ended the North American YMCA International Committee sent both financial aid and personnel to spur its revival. In the late 1950s the committee donated $500,000 to the Korean YMCA as part of its "Building for Brotherhood" project. This money financed the construction of a new YMCA building in Seoul and smaller building projects in Taegu and Pusan.[51]

American missionaries believed that such organizations could provide guidance to Korean youth and ensure that student nationalism remained a progressive rather than a destructive force. They frequently served as advisers to Christian student organizations, helping them to set their agendas and manage their affairs. Missionaries viewed their own leadership as vital to the success of South Korea's Christian student movements. One American missionary who worked with the KSCM wrote that Christian study groups that met on many campuses were "like sheep without a shepherd," and he tried to visit them frequently to "encourage and admonish them in their faith."[52] Missionaries also believed that their task of guiding Korean youth was deeply intertwined with the country's political evolution. Two years after Park Chung Hee seized power, Presbyterian William A. Grubb explained that student work was "a strategic and challenging area, in a land where collegiate demonstrations toppled a distinguished but corrupt regime three years ago and where the energies of youth are being marshaled by the military government of a new nation." Grubb added that the KSCM and a developing youth program in the Presbyterian Church were working to "channel these energies in a truly redemptive way."[53]

Youth conferences and retreats where missionaries and students discussed national development and world affairs were one of the key venues that missionaries used to exert this kind of "redemptive" influence. Many of the conferences and workshops arranged by the KSCM echoed the themes of those initiated by the USIS. During the summer of 1964, for instance, several local branches of the movement organized study conferences where the responsibility of students to the modernization of South Korea was explored.[54] The following year the KSCM held national conferences devoted to topics such as "New Humanity in a Changing World" and "Calling to Today's Korea." American or European missionaries served as speakers or discussion leaders at some but not all of these meetings.[55]

South Korean students who participated in Christian organizations often did embrace both spiritual faith and progressive nationalism. These students fused Christian concepts of individual responsibility for the welfare of other human beings with a commitment to improve the lives of their compatriots. They attempted to enlighten their peers not only about Christian doctrine but also about the need for national renovation. Among the listed goals of the KSCM was "participation in society" on the grounds that the "Christian concern for one's neighbor demands a responsible society and a welfare state." They also included "international concern," because the "Christian Gospel proclaims God's power which united the world in Christ" and therefore Christians were "by necessity concerned about the events which take place in all continents and nations, among all races of people and all cultures." In addition to religious activities like "regular worship services" and "Bible study," the KSCM required its members to participate in service projects such as "campus beautification" and "raising money to help needy classmates." During summer vacations KSCM members conducted enlightenment campaigns in which, for example, groups of students traveled to rural areas to teach reading or other basic skills.[56] YMCA and YWCA chapters generally had similar goals and sponsored similar activities. The YWCA at Ewha Women's University, the largest such chapter in South Korea, devoted itself to studying and promoting "societal responsibility." A brochure on the program stated that "we must expend our strength to make our society more just and a better place to live." It also called for members to participate in service activities such as "helping poor classmates" and paying visits to orphanages and old-age homes.[57]

The appeal of the Christian ideals of enlightenment and progress was also evident at many youth gatherings. One non-Christian student who attended a KSCM conference on the "Modernization of Korea" wrote that he usually did not go to such events, believing that Christian students were "concerned only for themselves." He attended this particular meeting because modernization was a "common issue" of significance to Korean students. At the conference, however, he had become aware of the fact that "Christian faith had relevance to the common issue[s] that our nation is feeling" and decided that he could "not stand without becoming a Christian" and joining the KSCM.[58] Missionaries hoped that such dramatic conversions

Molding South Korean Youth [207]

would ensure that young people saw both Christianity and capitalist modernity as relevant to their nation's future.

Although Christian organizations inspired many students to make a dual commitment to spiritual enlightenment and national progress, they could not completely eliminate anxieties about American influence. Both the success and the limitations of these organizations were apparent at a 1965 Methodist youth conference on "The Calling of Christian Youth in a New Society." The meeting devoted one evening to the presentation of a one-act drama, "Christ in the Concrete City," directed by an American Methodist missionary. The drama displayed the relevance of Christ's life story to contemporary social, especially urban, problems. A ten-member International Christian Youth Caravan Team, which included members from West Germany, Mexico, the United States, and Japan, also appeared at the conference to remind "the Korean young people that they were very much part of the larger world." In addition, Korean professors lectured on such topics as "Understanding the Present Situation" and "The Calling and Commitment of Christian Young People."[59]

In discussions at the conference, South Korean students argued that faith was relevant to their nation's social and economic problems. But they did so in a way that troubled Western missionaries because they stressed the need for autonomy with a tinge of hostility toward foreign influence. According to one missionary, the young South Koreans noted that when American Protestants had first begun proselytizing on the peninsula in the nineteenth century, "the protestant church in America was marked by the concept of the Christian west moving into the pagan east" and the missionary had "brought all of these concepts into Korea with him." These students also complained that "much of what the church says even today is more western than Christian and thus irrelevant to Korean culture."[60] When those students pondered the best way to alleviate Korea's political and social problems, they constantly criticized other South Koreans for uncritically accepting foreign values and attributed many of the country's political and social problems to "the influence of the west." They feared that "Korea might fall prey to a modern form of economic and cultural colonialism" and wished to "recover their self identity and renew their sense of national solidarity."[61]

Naturally such discussions sparked missionary fears about the direction of student nationalism in South Korea. But more often than not these fears were overstated. The ideals of Christian progress and enlightenment were universalistic enough in their message to overcome students' nationalistic concerns about how they were introduced. The number of Korean Christians and the percentage of Christians in the ROK population grew throughout the 1950s and 1960s, and during this period students were among the most frequent converts. There had been only 300,000 Christians on the entire Korean peninsula in 1945, whereas by 1974 the number had soared to 4.3 million in South Korea alone.[62] The relationship between student nationalism and Christian enlightenment ultimately proved to be a symbiotic rather than an antagonistic one. But Christian student organizations not only promoted a sense of nationalism that coincided with the objectives of a modernizing state; they also, by fostering open dialogues on key issues, fueled expectations for participatory democracy. As the South Korean state veered toward authoritarianism during the seventies, these organizations would, as described more fully in Chapter 8, stand at the forefront of the democratic movement.

4-H Clubs and South Korea's Rural Youth

While Americans hoped that their appeals to South Korean youth would transform the mind-set of the country's younger generation, many of their activities focused on educated urban students. Until the late sixties, however, the ROK was primarily an agricultural country and Americans realized the need to engage young people in rural communities and villages as well. Youths in rural villages were generally neither as radicalized nor as politicized as those in urban centers. Nevertheless, Americans placed a priority on molding their attitudes. No organizations made as ambitious an effort to do so as the country's 4-H Clubs. The products of American resources and Korean initiative, 4-H Clubs expanded at a remarkable rate during the fifties and sixties.

South Korea's 4-H Clubs were based on the rural youth organization established in the United States during the early twentieth century to promote education on agricultural issues. The four Hs on the club emblem stood for Head, Heart, Hands, and Health—which were sometimes translated into the Sino-Korean characters *chi* (knowledge), *dŏk* (morals), *no* (labor), and *ch'e* (body). These characters, or letters, emphasized the need for individuals to cultivate their intellects, refine their character, and adopt healthful living habits. Individual 4-H Clubs required their members to recite the 4-H pledge—"I Pledge my head to clearer thinking, my heart to greater loyalty, my hands to larger service and my hands to better living, for my club, my community and my country." The clubs even had an official creed that was regularly recited by members; one stanza of the creed read, "I believe in my country, my province and my community and in my responsibility for their development." Through such ceremonials, individual self-cultivation and improvement was linked to the betterment of the country as a whole.[63]

In the forties and fifties Americans had played a significant role in getting the organization started and helping it develop in South Korea. C. A. Anderson, an army colonel with the U.S. occupation forces, initiated the 4-H Club movement in Kyŏnggi Province in 1947. A 4-H Club member in his youth, Anderson sought to alleviate the confusion that prevailed in villages with the sudden demise of Japanese imperialism. Anderson and four of his Korean colleagues set up two clubs in each district of the province and presented short training courses for the leaders of each club. The membership of these clubs grew rapidly until the Korean War, when many club activities were temporarily discontinued.[64]

After the Korean War, encouragement from both the ROK government and U.S. officials who were administering economic aid enabled South Korea's individual 4-H Clubs to unite in a national organization. In 1952 the Ministry of Agriculture and Forestry officially made the 4-H Club movement part of its educational and training programs. In 1953 members of the ministry met with the U.S. officials and drew up concrete plans to sponsor 4-H Clubs in every province of South Korea. In November 1954 the Korean 4-H Club Central Committee (4-H Kurakpu Chungang Wiwŏnhoe) held its first meeting in Seoul. Both the U.S. Army and the American-Korean Foundation (AKF) provided funds for the meeting and sent advisers to make sure that it went smoothly. With American financial assistance, the 4-H Club Central Committee established itself as the 4-H Clubs' central governing body and began the critical tasks of organizing new clubs, holding regular national events for club leaders, and training the new leaders of local clubs.[65]

The 4-H Club movement in South Korea expanded rapidly in the fifties. By 1958 there were 3,729 clubs with a total membership of 142,595. Participation in the movement grew even more explosively during the Park Chung Hee period. In streamlining the ROK bureaucracy, Park established the Agricultural Development Agency (Nongch'on chinhŭngch'ŏng) and incorporated the 4-H Club movement into the new organization. Under this arrangement, control over the nation's 4-H Clubs became more centralized, but active government support for the organization enabled the number of clubs and the membership to expand. At the movement's peak in 1967, there were 29,821 clubs and 762,182 members, making South Korea's membership in the 4-H Club movement second only to that of the United States.[66]

During these years the nation's 4-H Clubs received continuous financial and technical aid from both official and private U.S. agencies. This assistance involved both teaching Korean adults how to coordinate and supervise the organization at the national level and giving Korean youth who participated in local clubs direct exposure to American ideas and organizational techniques. By supplying Koreans with the material and intellectual resources necessary for building and expanding their 4-H Clubs, U.S. agencies hoped that the ROK's movement would replicate the American model.

In the fifties and early sixties the Korean Civil Assistance Command (KCAC) had offered several kinds of assistance to 4-H Clubs. In 1953 the KCAC began working with Korean information specialists to translate leaflets and pamphlets supplied by American clubs and disseminate them to South Korean clubs. These materials provided an introduction to the goals and ideals of American 4-H Clubs while teaching practical skills that could facilitate the task of rural reconstruction. The pamphlets included titles such as "What Is the 4-H Club?"; brochures contained information on how to raise different types of crops and livestock. The KCAC even paid transportation costs when several 4-H Clubs in the United States donated livestock and other necessities to their South Korean counterparts.[67]

In the 1960s the USOM made support for 4-H Clubs a significant part of its efforts to increase South Korea's agricultural productivity. Agricultural advisers from the mission helped train club leaders and develop educational materials for their clubs. Grants from the USOM enabled small numbers of Koreans to travel to the United States and learn about 4-H Clubs firsthand. During the late fifties such programs had been sporadic and focused more on teaching adult leaders how to coordinate the 4-H program at the national level. Nevertheless, once the International Farm Youth Exchange (IFYE) program was initiated in 1962, small groups of Korean youth were selected annually to visit the United States for six months.[68]

The American-Korean Foundation played an especially important role in the expansion of 4-H Clubs in South Korea. Monetary donations from the AKF supported scholarships for club members who lacked the financial resources to attend middle school or high school, the participation of Koreans in international 4-H meetings and events, the transportation of donated materials and livestock from the United States, the publication of pamphlets and instructional materials, and even the establishment of a national

4-h project bank that lent money to individual clubs. The AKF also retained special "4-h club project advisers," usually Americans who had gained some expertise—through government or military service—in solving problems related to Korean agriculture. These advisers helped devise and coordinate new training and educational programs for club leaders.[69]

Perhaps the most extravagant AKF enterprise was the establishment of a 4-h training farm in Kyŏnggi Province. Beginning in August 1964, a short course on general agriculture was provided at the "Sosa farm" to club members from all districts of the country. Between August 1964 and November 1966 alone, 501 Korean boys and girls received training in 23 different areas. During the fall of 1966 the AKF revamped the program by improving the facilities, extending the duration of the training course to 18 days, and making concrete plans to offer training to 300 4-h Club members every year. The farm program sought to reform Koreans' "mental attitudes," offer them practical information, and improve their technical skills. All participants learned about leadership, earth-block housing, and the proper care and management of fruit trees, field crops, and livestock. Female club members took additional courses in cooking, sewing, and home improvement. To ensure that students applied what they learned during the training, the AKF devised a follow-up program that provided group project assistance to some of the participants' individual clubs.[70]

Americans associated with this program tried to ensure that participants gained an admiration for the United States. In a training manual for students, the AKF's 4-h program director cited Abraham Lincoln's proverb "I do the very best I know how—the very best I can; and I mean to keep doing so until the end." The trainees were instructed to make the proverb a part of their everyday lives and to strive to follow its dictates.[71] Americans hoped that such advice would not only cultivate habits of diligence and self-help among the young South Koreans but also ensure that they would come to associate these values with the United States.

Although the size and function of individual 4-h Clubs may have differed according to region and evolved somewhat over time, most clubs consistently sought to instill in their members a particular set of ideals and behaviors. Through instruction in agricultural techniques, 4-h Clubs, like numerous other organizations involved in youth work in South Korea, encouraged young people to contribute to the welfare of their nation and their communities. One Korean 4-h handbook listed the first goal of the clubs as "promoting the development of the ideas and standards that are necessary for a nation in the farm life, family life and social life of rural youth."[72] In this sense, 4-H Clubs saw themselves as harbingers of much broader changes in how rural South Koreans thought and lived.

Even as they worked to build a sense of national community, however, Korean 4-H Clubs generally stressed the need for greater contact with Free World nations, especially the United States. American 4-H Clubs were often presented as exemplars of the organization and diligence that the Korean clubs needed to replicate. Handbooks for members regularly included sections on the American origins of 4-H Clubs and the role that American groups and individuals had played in the development of the 4-H organization in South Korea. One manual noted that the U.S. movement was the "driving force behind America's increase in agricultural production" and "the basis for the development of today's advanced democracy." By mentioning that the 4-H Club movement had spread from the United States to sixty other countries, the handbook emphasized the organization's adaptability to different societies.[73]

Club activities quite deliberately aimed to reshape the attitudes of participants. These activities included "ceremonials" such as oaths and songs that members were expected to learn and recite, individual and group projects designed to improve a particular club's village or community, and research projects for university members. Individual and group projects were often the central activity of local clubs. These projects were, according to one handbook, the kind of works through which members could "learn by doing." The manual instructed clubs to hold "project selection meetings" at the beginning of each year, when their leaders were to present a list of projects. Leaders were to allow members to select their own projects and to steer them in an appropriate direction only if they could not carry out their projects by themselves. Members were expected to report on their projects at monthly meetings, when their leaders evaluated the results.[74] Possible projects listed in 4-H Clubs handbooks were calculated to contribute to the productivity of individual communities and the nation as a whole. Individual projects ranged from farming tasks such as eliminating harmful insects and cultivating fruit trees to home beautification projects like repairing furniture and planting flower gardens. Group projects included health and sanitation work such as cleaning a sewer system or eradicating roundworm, as well as safety projects like repairing roads and bridges or establishing traffic patterns.[75]

Projects such as these were expected to change the basic social outlook of 4-H Club members. Planning a project and attempting to implement it would teach members that they had the ability to change their environment.

Taking responsibility for earnings and expenditures would stimulate an interest in family and agricultural planning and later the desire to obtain the training required to formulate fixed, long-term plans. Finally, recording the progress of their projects would enable members to take on a scientific perspective and acquire the habit of volunteering their new skills to the larger society.[76] Americans hoped that by creating a youthful vanguard committed to the transformation of village life, 4-H Clubs would accelerate the development of rural society and prepare the citizenry for political democracy.

The combination of American funding and South Korean initiative that characterized the 4-H Club movement in the ROK made it an effective vehicle for influencing the lives and attitudes of the country's youth. Many rural young people were eager for the material improvements in their living conditions that the clubs promised. They found themselves deeply engaged by the ideas and activities promoted by the clubs, including public and community service. In essays written for national and regional 4-H Club events, members articulated a strong nationalism and a sense of communal responsibility. But even while embracing the movement's ideals, some Koreans were troubled by its American origins. They looked for ways to reconcile their budding sense of nationalism with their steadfast commitment to a transplanted organization.

As 4-H Club members carried out projects suggested by their handbooks, many expressed a new determination to contribute to the well-being of their communities. One youth submitted a story to a 4-H Club publication that related how his club had started a "pig-raising" movement in his village. The story reflected the impact of 4-H ideals. The inhabitants of the village had "for 5,000 years simply followed the farming methods that had been passed on from their ancestors," which had eventually led to horrendous living conditions. After earning profits from raising and breeding his own pig, however, the youth worked with members of his local 4-H Club to teach modern techniques for raising pigs to his neighbors. As a result of their efforts, all of the villagers began raising two or three pigs, boosting the prosperity of the community. The young man believed that his example offered hope for South Korea as a whole, asserting, if "we fix the attitudes of 4-H members and change the thinking of farmers, we too can become prosperous." Linking the prosperity of individual villages to the overall welfare of the country, he maintained that "if our villages can not become prosperous than our people [minjok] can not live well and if our people can not live well our country can not be prosperous."[77]

In some instances, Korean 4-H Clubs members went so far as to cite the United States as a paragon of the virtues that South Korean youth needed. Such sentiments were most common among individuals who had benefited directly from their contacts with Americans. Kim Kilchi, a 4-H Club member who had spent six months in the United States through an IFYE grant, returned to South Korea with an appreciation for the American work ethic. He wrote that Koreans should pattern their behaviors on the ways that Americans lived and worked. Kim related the example of an American youth he had met in Ohio; although his family was poor, he had managed to graduate from Ohio State University. Kim's American friend had "since the age of 14 used his time before school to deliver newspapers and worked on highway construction jobs during his vacations" to earn the money for his college education. This was an example "worth remembering and following." Such stories had an almost intrinsic appeal to young people in a country where severe poverty existed but education was deeply esteemed. Kim noted that there were many reasons why Korean youth "played without finding jobs" but worried that they had the "bad habit of not trying to find them from the beginning." He believed "deeply in his heart" that Korean youth should emulate the "proper spirit" of young Americans who "thought it was shameful to depend on their parents."[78]

The view that Americans had something to offer Koreans was not confined to those who had been privileged to travel to the United States. Other 4-H Clubs members whose acquaintance with American ideas was somewhat more distant sometimes expressed similar sentiments. Using Kennedy-like language, one youth wrote that 4-H Clubs needed to become a "frontier" like the one "that had made America a rich country." Another short essay focused on none other than Abraham Lincoln. The author described how Lincoln had polished his own shoes even after becoming president and scoffed at the idea that such a task was "too humble" for a president. He then asked, "Don't the majority of people in our society think the exact opposite?"[79]

While some club members had no problem following America's lead, others wrestled with the contradictions involved in looking to foreign examples to build a sense of national purpose. In an essay entitled "Let's Be the Pioneers of Construction as a United Group," one club leader contended that "the way for villages to live well is not to depend on foreign countries or the government or the people of other villages." Villages needed to rely "only on themselves."[80] Others were quick to point out that 4-H Clubs on the peninsula needed to adapt the American model to the requirements of

Korean culture and society—to somehow make 4-H Clubs their own. In a 1966 essay on the "Indigenization of 4-H Clubs," a young South Korean argued that "because our 4-H movement is imported from a foreign country and has simply transplanted foreign methods it is necessary to indigenize it so that it is appropriate for Korea's climate." The author noted that even after twenty years, aspects of the 4-H movement did not accommodate the realities of Korean village life. Another member stressed the need for Koreans to move beyond discussions of indigenization or autonomy and have the confidence to see that the "4-H Clubs is ours." He contended that "one who even talks of indigenization is a reactionary and one who proclaims autonomy has a meaningless existence and can not make the 4-H idea part of his life."[81]

Through such arguments, 4-H Club members tried to reconcile their attraction to the movement's ideas on self-help and rural development with their concerns about the foreignness of the clubs. They perceived a fragile boundary between benefiting from foreign influence and succumbing to foreign domination and at times became conflicted as they tried to avoid crossing it. This led them to use the clubs as venues to express ideas that might have surprised or even dismayed the Americans who had been so vital to the movement's expansion in South Korea. Nevertheless, Americans viewed the proliferation of 4-H Clubs and the real contributions they made to agricultural development as proof of their success and eagerly sought to promote other organizations that adhered to similar ideals.

The Boy Scout and Girl Scout Movements

Like the 4-H Clubs, the Boy Scouts and Girl Scouts in South Korea benefited from U.S. assistance but on a smaller scale. Both organizations had a history in Korea that went back to the years before World War II when the American presence on the peninsula was still relatively marginal. Yet their familiarity to Americans working in the ROK made them natural objects of sympathy and support.

Scouting had existed in Korea during the Japanese colonial period. Inspired in part by the international Boy Scout movement, groups known as the Chosŏn Young Men's Army (Chosŏn sonyŏn'gun) and the Chosŏn Scouting Club (Chosŏn ch'ŏkhudan) began working to advance the education of young men in order to prepare them for the country's independence during the 1920s. A much smaller group, whose name, Nangjagun, translates roughly into "Women's Army," became affiliated with the "Young Men's Army" during the same period. The Japanese military government kept all of these groups under strict surveillance and restricted their activities, ultimately causing them to disband in the 1930s. Moreover, because of Korea's status as a Japanese colony, its scouting organizations were not recognized by the international Boy Scout movement.[82]

During the months after liberation, Koreans who had been active in these groups sought permission from the U.S. military government to resurrect them. In 1946 the U.S. Army Command authorized the formation of Boy and Girl Scout organizations in Korea that could participate in international conferences and meetings. In the years that followed, Americans made continuous efforts to promote their expansion and to help them emulate their counterparts in the United States. After the Korean War assistance to Korean Boy and Girl Scouts flowed from U.S. military personnel in South Korea, private individuals in the United States, and American scouting groups. Although the South Korean Boy Scouts and Girl Scouts never achieved anything close to the popularity of the 4-H Clubs, they did train thousands of youths over the course of the 1950s and 1960s. Their memberships generally ranged between five and ten thousand for much of the sixties.[83]

American assistance to the Korean Girl Scouts was extensive and helped meet both the material and technical needs of the organization. The Girl Scouts of America and other American agencies and individuals supplied equipment and sometimes helped with fund-raising. After the war, when the impoverished Korean organization lacked the financial resources to equip its members with uniforms and manuals, the American Girl Scouts provided materials to make new uniforms and an AKF grant enabled Girl Scout manuals to be translated, adapted, and distributed in 1955.[84]

Individual Americans in South Korea played a more direct role in promoting Korean participation in the Girl Scouts. The Korean organization received perhaps its greatest financial boon after the State Department's appointment of Samuel Berger as ambassador in 1961. Berger's wife took a keen interest in the Korean Girl Scouts and assisted in their fund-raising activities. In May 1962 she enabled them to hold a commemorative function at the American embassy, where funds were collected for their organization.[85] American missionaries also provided support. Winifred Frei, a Presbyterian missionary, reported in 1961 that during the previous year "much of my time and attention had been oriented towards the Girl Scouts of Korea." She taught special courses for Girl Scouts on topics such as "methods of group work, group leadership," and "When You Go to America." Frei became coleader of a troop from the elite Ewha Girls High School and arranged for it to engage in joint activities with an American Girl Scout troop.[86]

In addition to providing material assistance, Americans sought to ensure that South Korean women gained exposure to the institutional philosophy that buttressed both American and international Girl Scout organizations. Throughout the fifties and early sixties the American Girl Scout Association frequently sent advisers to South Korea to evaluate the Korean programs. Concurrently, many leaders of the Korean Girl Scouts traveled to the United States to receive advice and training. In the 1960s, as an increasing number of American military families were stationed in the ROK, joint activities between Korean Girl Scout troops and their American counterparts on U.S. military bases were often arranged.[87]

The Korean Boy Scouts received similar financial aid and institutional support from the United States. In 1953 the Boy Scouts of America provided funding and the USIS in Seoul supplied paper for the printing of a new manual. The USIS also promoted Boy Scout activities through its short film, *We, the Korean Boy Scouts*, which was shown in movie theaters in every province in 1959. American military personnel in the ROK made persistent efforts to assist the country's Boy Scout organization. Many American military commanders who had formerly been involved in the Boy Scouts of America sought training and education for the ROK organization. One state department telegram noted that the U.S. Marine Corps had "donated much time and guidance to the programs of the Boy Scouts of Korea." Moreover, U.S. armed forces in South Korea both donated and helped raise money for the group. Exchange programs, whereby Korean Boy Scouts visited the United States and American Boy Scouts traveled to the ROK, enabled the young South Koreans to get a firsthand glimpse of the way scouting operated in the United States.[88]

The Boy and Girl Scout organizations in South Korea worked to cultivate a sense of progressive nationalism among the country's youth. Their manuals emphasized the need for young people to conceptualize themselves as citizens of a nation. In its opening pages the 1961 Boy Scout manual stated that "youth must do the work that has been entrusted to them for God and their country."[89] Similarly, the Girl Scout manual explained that "a Girl Scout must not spare respect, loyalty or service to her country."[90] Many scouting activities served to instill members with a sense of responsibility for national development. Girl Scouts participated in "service camping," which required individual troops to camp out in underdeveloped rural areas and teach the residents how to improve their living habits.[91] The Boy Scout organization sought to forge a sense of national solidarity through functions, known as "jamborees," that brought together youngsters from the country's different provinces. International jamborees, which assembled Boy Scouts from around the Free World, were intended to ensure that such nationalist sentiment did not produce hostility toward international cooperation or foreign influence.[92]

Although few written reflections of the experiences of Korean Boy or Girl Scouts are available, some members of troops organized by particular middle schools or high schools summarized their experiences in school yearbooks. One commentary on scouting, published in the Yangchŏng Middle-High School yearbook of 1963, described the writer's participation in a "World Jamboree" held in the Philippines. Activities such as singing the national anthem, raising the South Korean flag, and performing an "arirang dance" in an international culture show had served to "elevate the glory" of his country. Yet the South Korean scouts stumbled when it came to promoting more conciliatory attitudes toward Japan. One Japanese Boy Scout had asked the writer to "leave politics behind" and "to spend time together as friends" at the jamboree. Unable to put aside his "national consciousness," however, the South Korean decided that he did "not want to be in front of the Japanese [scout] any longer" and retreated to his tent. Such interactions did not necessarily diminish the enthusiasm of South Korean youths for these organizations. Nevertheless, they reflected the inability of institutions like the Boy Scouts to mitigate the lingering sensitivities that informed South Korean resistance to many components of the U.S. agenda. They also demonstrated the ways that young Koreans used these organizations to meet their own needs and desires, turning them into mechanisms for resisting or shunning, as well as simply accepting, the ideas that Americans sought to instill in them.[93]

The Radicalization of Korean Youth

Throughout the 1960s American policymakers and cultural organizations had tried to foster a new civic-mindedness among young South Koreans. These youths had struggled to reconcile their attraction to American ideals with their burgeoning nationalism and suspicion of foreign influence. More often than not they had been able to do so. The dissemination of democratic ideals created new expectations. As young people assumed a sense of responsibility for the national progress required to develop a democratic society, they hoped that the ROK would become more willing to open the decision-making process. When Park Chung Hee started taking steps to perpetuate his control over South Korea after 1968, the very beliefs that the Americans had counted on to produce cooperation between youth and the government became an important basis of student dissent.

Many students who had found Park's appeals for rapid economic development and national independence convincing during the early and mid-1960s turned against him when he began to amend the ROK constitution toward the end of the decade. The career of Kim Kŭnt'ae, a former leader of the prominent student resistance movement called the minch'ŏngnyŏn, provides one of the more dramatic examples of this phenomenon. Park had seized power when Kim was still in high school. Kim supported the junta because he found its emphasis on growth and self-sufficiency more appealing than the sloganeering of the opposition. He remembered that "during the 1963 election I didn't have the right to vote but if I did I would have supported Park Chung Hee." The president's promise to "solve the problem of the people's economic plight through developing an independent economy" made him contemptuous of the opposition, which seemed less determined to end South Korea's reliance on foreign aid. Like many students who sought to help the government achieve this goal, Kim decided to major in economics after his admission to SNU in 1965.[94] In the mid-1960s Kim's outlook was probably fairly similar to that of his fellow students who participated in the USOM student intern program or joined USIS clubs. He was eager to see national development but also wanted to be able to participate in and, eventually, influence the process.

But Kim was shocked by the inauguration of the Yusin system in 1972 and the ensuing crackdown on civil liberties and freedom of expression. He had first joined the student protest movement in 1969, when he was suspended for taking part in demonstrations against Park's efforts to amend the constitution. It was Yusin, however, that turned Kim irrevocably against the regime. As he watched the Park government issue new laws and proclamations that clamped down on dissent, he "became determined to stand at the forefront of the opposition." Over the next decade Kim did exactly that. He became a leader of the minch'ŏngnyŏn, which played a notable role in resisting military dictatorship throughout the seventies and eighties. In 1985, at the age of thirty-eight, Kim was imprisoned and tortured by the South Korean government under suspicion that he was playing a behind-the-scenes role in another radical opposition group know as the sammint'u.[95] When the period of military dictatorship ended, Kim still retained his commitment to democratic political participation. He eventually was elected a member of the South Korean National Assembly and in 2003 was appointed minister of health and welfare by the new president, Roh Moo Hyun. Kim's journey from advocate of the Park government in the 1960s to radical dissident in the 1970s and 1980s was emblematic of how Park's inability to relinquish power alienated many of his supporters, laid the groundwork for confrontation between pro-democracy forces and the state, and destroyed the possibility of a smooth transition from developmental autocracy to democracy.

While South Korea's intellectual community was divided fairly evenly between supporters and opponents of the regime, from the late 1960s onward, the majority of students either actively opposed or stoically endured the government's growing authoritarianism. Park was not entirely without allies among the younger generation of South Koreans. His support was strongest in the countryside, which was traditionally more conservative and politically passive than the country's growing urban population. Most 4-H Clubs were successfully incorporated into the New Village movement and renamed "Saemaŭl 4-H Clubs." The organization continued to expand during the 1970s while placing a greater emphasis on scientific experimentation.[96] But Park could claim far fewer successes when it came to mobilizing urban youth and university students on behalf of Yusin. Although the regime attempted to create pro-government organizations on campuses, such as the National Student Defense Corps, most students joined them only when coerced.

Participatory democracy remained a powerful motivator of the student population, which, during the late sixties and seventies, emerged as the most tenacious source of dissent to the Yusin system. The first significant flurry of student opposition to the South Korean government began at SNU on 12 June 1969, shortly after Park had begun seeking to amend the constitution so he could run for a third term, and slowly spread to other major campuses throughout the country. These protests died down after Park managed to ram the amendment through the National Assembly in September 1969 but resumed during the spring of 1971 as the presidential election approached. In April 1971 students from eleven leading universities formed the National Student Alliance for the Preservation of Democracy and worked to ensure that the election would be open and fair. Throughout the year, students closely monitored and fiercely opposed the questionable tactics deployed by Park to sway the election in his favor.[97] Once Park triumphed at the polls, the students found it virtually impossible to reverse the growing concentration of power in the hands of the state. At the same time, however, the battle lines between students and the state had been drawn. After Park declared martial law in October 1972 and introduced the new Yusin constitution two months later, he would face a determined student resistance that could never entirely be suppressed.

Youth and students had long comprised the boldest and most persistent group in South Korean society when it came to challenging the authority of the government. Even without American programs, it is likely that students would have resisted the Yusin system. U.S. policymakers had not anticipated Park's shift to authoritarianism in the late 1960s. Rather than encouraging the student resistance, U.S. programs had sought to build a dialogue between students and the state by encouraging a progressive nationalism and nurturing an admiration for liberal democratic principles. At the same time, by enabling discussion of the meaning of participatory democracy and the responsibilities it entailed, American programs had helped deepen the commitment of South Korean students to the concept. The United States had also done much to raise the expectations of Korean youth that one day they themselves would be able to participate in a meaningful way in their nation's affairs. By sponsoring forums in which young people could practice democratic forms of debate and dissent, Americans made the Yusin system's efforts to close off free expression at the university all the more painful and disappointing to students. The waves of student dissent that occurred during the late sixties and seventies were therefore not the purpose of American nation-building activities, but rather the unintended outcome of them.

When and how do developmental autocracies become democracies? History provides no obvious answer to this question. It is clear, however, that if an autocratic government succeeds in promoting rapid economic development, it will eventually encounter new socioeconomic groups that demand greater autonomy from the state and more freedom of action. These groups often include students, intellectuals, workers, entrepreneurs, and members of the middle class. When challenged by demands for change, the state generally can manage them in one of three ways. The first option is accommodation. This approach was exemplified by the Kuomintang government in Taiwan, which, throughout the 1970s and 1980s, carried out just enough political reform to foster a sense of political progress and prevent a debilitating confrontation.[1] The second alternative is co-optation. In some instances, politically savvy autocrats can head off demands for democratization by convincing key sectors of the population that their interests lie in continued alliance with the state. Often they have successfully used religion, ethnicity, or nationalism to secure the loyalty of potential dissidents. This was the case in Malaysia and Singapore, which have enjoyed rapid economic growth but where the state has restricted the growth of civil society. It also appears increasingly likely that the People's Republic of China will follow that pattern.[2] The final alternative, and the one chosen by the Republic of Korea (ROK), is repression. Under the Yusin constitution, Park Chung Hee used brute force to eliminate his critics until his assassination in 1979, when his regime was replaced by an even harsher military dictatorship.

But while South Korea possessed a particularly repressive version of developmental autocracy, it also had highly determined groups of democratic elites. Throughout the 1950s and 1960s Americans had made a concerted effort to instill democratic ideals in students, intellectuals, and other key groups. Koreans had embraced and adapted these ideals with as much if not more enthusiasm and creativity than any other people in Asia. Between 1972 and 1987 democratic ideals only became more influential among rising sectors of the population, especially the working and middle classes. The state's efforts to suppress demands for political liberalization after 1972 led to fifteen years of escalating confrontations with civil society, as democratic forces constantly grew larger and more powerful.

These confrontations between the South Korean state and society put U.S. policymakers in a difficult position. On the one hand, they did not want to abandon the ROK political leadership that had always proven a staunch Cold War ally. Nor did they wish to do anything that could raise the specter of political instability. On the other hand, Americans had encouraged the growth of democratic ideologies during the previous decades and were reluctant to be perceived as acting against the very aspirations they had nourished.

The United States attempted to resolve this contradiction by extending formal support and recognition to the South Korean government while quietly offering encouragement to leaders who might eventually move the country toward democracy. But America was much less capable of shaping events in South Korea than it had been during the sixties and seventies. The South Korean state now had access to many sources of capital aside from U.S. assistance and could carry out development programs without American guidance. Threats of withholding aid or support could no longer sway the actions of the South Korean government. With its resources concentrated on Vietnam and other parts of the world, the United States had also curtailed many of the cultural programs it had sponsored to build up civil society during the sixties. Americans were therefore much less capable of encouraging cooperation between dissidents and the state than they once had been. Although American policies certainly influenced the course of events in South Korea during these years, they did not determine the country's political destiny as completely as they once had.

Yusin, Dissent, and American Policy

When Park Chung Hee enacted the Yusin system in 1972, some groups in South Korean society immediately challenged the state's growing authoritarianism. Initially, this was primarily an elite protest by students, intellectuals, and influential Christian ministers centered in major cities. These groups generally issued proclamations or, in the case of students, held demonstrations to demand the restoration of democratic government.[3] Such forms of protest did little to change the behavior of the state. Under Yusin, the Park government had more than adequate means at its disposal to ignore or suppress dissident intellectuals and students. Scholars could be removed from their teaching posts, while universities could be shut down to curtail student demonstrations. It soon became painfully apparent to students and intellectuals that if their methods of resisting state power did not change, they would never be able to exert a meaningful influence on the country's political situation.

Pro-democracy forces in South Korea increasingly came to view the country's rapidly expanding population of industrial laborers as their most natural ally. In the 1970s the working class remained predominantly female, although the proportion of male workers increased over the course of the decade. Workers endured harsh, unsafe conditions because the state required cheap labor for its drive toward industrialization. Few provisions were made for the health or welfare of workers, while the state discouraged and, in some instances, outlawed strikes or other forms of protest. With the regime's support, some of South Korea's largest *chaebŏl* (conglomerates), such as Hyundai and Samsung, prohibited the formation of labor unions.[4] Laborers naturally grew frustrated and looked for outlets to express their discontent.

In the 1970s students, intellectuals, and Christian organizations aligned themselves with the rapidly growing class of industrial laborers to force Park to abandon Yusin and reestablish democratic institutions. As a new generation of Christian leaders emerged from the Korean Student Christian Movement (KSCM), YMCA, and other church-based organizations and assumed important positions within their denominations, churches began to figure much more prominently in the democratic movement. Religious organizations and student groups began working together to promote labor activism. They initiated new educational programs that taught organizational techniques while seeking to further an understanding of democratic principles. Christian groups such as the Urban Industrial Mission (UIM) were often staffed by university students and graduates who worked closely with workers. The UIM focused on female factory workers, organizing them into "small groups" of seven to nine women. Although the initial purpose of these covert groups was often recreational, participants eventually moved into discussions of issues such as labor law and organizing. In addition, students frequently taught in night schools whose original intent of preparing young workers for college entrance exams had changed over time to providing a forum for expressing concerns related to the workplace.[5]

During the seventies a pattern of confrontation developed between the state and workers who were aligned with students, churches, and human rights organizations. As strikes began to increase in number and intensity, the Park government often responded with draconian measures to isolate or punish those responsible. When workers organized their own unions, police were regularly sent into factories to disband them and arrest their leaders. The activities of night school teachers and organizations like the UIM constantly aroused suspicion and were closely monitored by the Korean Central Intelligence Agency (KCIA). The Korean police in many instances arrested and tortured UIM staffers while the KCIA blacklisted workers who participated in UIM activities, often causing them to lose their jobs. The state combined these measures to quell democratic unionism with efforts to censor and control the media. When editors and reporters from the leading newspapers, the *Tonga ilbo* and *Chosŏn ilbo*, protested these limitations on free speech, the Park government had them dismissed. Within a few years, the regime's determination to exact reprisals against those who criticized its policies or otherwise undermined its agenda had earned South Korea international notoriety for its disregard of human rights.[6]

The Nixon and Ford administrations took a somewhat passive stance toward the growing conflict between state and society in South Korea. Initially, U.S. officials underestimated the strength and determination of the democratic forces. In 1973 Philip Habib, who after several stints as a foreign service officer in the ROK, had been appointed the American ambassador, saw "no serious challenge to . . . Park's continued rule" and predicted that "the objective and the hallmark of this era will be harmony and consensus—old Korean virtues—rather than contention and challenge."[7] Despite Habib's extensive experience in South Korea, he still did not appreciate how firmly democratic ideals had taken hold among critical sectors of the population.

Even when it became apparent that Habib's predictions of harmony and stability were well off the mark, the United States avoided pressuring Park on questions of political democracy or human rights. William Gleysteen, who worked in the State Department's Division of East Asian and Pacific Affairs between 1974 and 1976, recalled that "as much as possible the [Ford] administration avoided confrontation over political and human rights issues, desisting from public criticism and generally relying on diplomatic and other traditional means to convey its views to the Park government."[8] One of the few notable exceptions to this strategy occurred in August 1973, when the American embassy in Seoul was informed that KCIA agents had kidnapped popular dissident politician Kim Dae Jung from a Tokyo hotel room with the apparent intention of murdering him. Ambassador Habib rushed to meet with Park Chung Hee and demanded that Kim be kept alive. In this instance U.S. pressure helped spare the life of a future South

Korean president. Nevertheless, overt American intervention on behalf of human rights or political freedom in the ROK was rare before 1977.

The reason for this inattention to human rights issues was partially a result of the low priority assigned to South Korea by the Nixon and Ford administrations. Both presidents focused their Asia policy on improving relations with China and ending the conflict in Vietnam. Because the Park government provided stability, promoted economic development, and was reliably anti-Communist, U.S. policymakers saw little reason to risk undermining it. Even American diplomats who were troubled by the Yusin system did not favor more aggressive criticism of the regime's human rights abuses. They believed that although Yusin constituted a serious setback to democratization, South Korea was still proceeding in the right direction. Paul M. Cleveland, who served as a political and military officer in Seoul between 1973 and 1977, explained that while he was "deeply sympathetic with the human rights movement in Korea," he feared that "public flogging of the government's record on human rights would only increase repression and tensions." Cleveland was convinced that even without U.S. intervention, South Korea would inevitably progress toward political democracy as its middle class expanded. During the seventies, he argued, the "the economic growth of South Korea almost guaranteed an ever increasing middle class." Members of the middle class "knew what they were doing" and would "eventually claim a seat or seats at the policy making table." He was therefore content to let democracy "evolve at the pace that this middle class itself set."[9]

Cleveland's approach placed a premium on minimizing friction with the regime but still offered quiet encouragement for democratic forces and, indirectly, restrained Park. Throughout his tenure in South Korea, Cleveland met regularly with members of the opposition, including Kim Dae Jung and Cardinal Stephen Kim. The purpose of such meetings was, to some extent, self-serving since they enabled the United States to monitor Park's opponents and remain aware of their activities. But at the same time, they were intended to alert the Park government that Washington had an interest in the welfare of certain dissidents and would take a dim view of arbitrary measures against them. Moreover, these informal contacts gave opponents of the regime a chance to openly express their concerns to the United States, something that would have been difficult to do otherwise.[10] Thus during the Nixon-Ford era, the United States almost never made public statements in support of particular dissident groups. It aimed instead to quietly sustain and influence leaders of the democratic forces and thereby contribute to the country's gradual political evolution.

The onset of the Carter presidency in January 1977 seemed to portend a more dramatic American campaign to restore political democracy and advance the cause of human rights in South Korea. Jimmy Carter was determined to elevate human rights to a more central position in U.S. foreign policy, and early in his administration he instituted new mechanisms for monitoring the policies of allies and adversaries alike. American embassies were instructed to make representations to foreign governments whenever they discerned human rights abuses. Even long-standing allies like South Korea were served notice that, in their dealings with the United States, human rights would be an important issue.

But despite Carter's interest in human rights issues, diplomats working in South Korea often found the president's agenda difficult to implement. Thomas Stern, the deputy chief of mission in the U.S. embassy between 1976 and 1979, recalled that "we used to get periodic messages reminding us of the importance of human rights to the U.S. and requesting us to make the appropriate representations to the Koreans, particularly about 'political' prisoners." Although Stern made an earnest effort to pressure the Park government to make concessions on these issues, his appeals were seldom taken seriously. In fact, "the [ROK] leaders turned a deaf ear, even if they knew to what we were referring. They would nod and try to go on to the next subject." Stern was convinced that it would be futile to exert more pressure on Park, because "by this time, we had very little leverage with the Koreans." He noted that whereas U.S. assistance programs had been terminated, America had "economic investments and trade with Korea that many forces in the United States did not wish to see interrupted." Without U.S. economic aid that could be used as leverage, "we did not . . . have any sanctions that we could rationally apply."[11] In contrast to the early 1960s when the Kennedy administration had used threats of withdrawing economic aid to force Park to hold free elections, by the mid-1970s there was little American policymakers could do to influence the South Korean president.

The impotence of American diplomats in this area soon became a source of friction between human rights specialists appointed by the president, who expected to exert an immediate impact on South Korean policy, and more seasoned diplomats, who thought that the demands of human rights groups were unrealistic. When William Gleysteen became the American ambassador in 1978, he was put on the "firing line" by human rights advocates in the Carter administration. He remembered that "I tended to consider the views of human rights specialists as naïve; they in turn tended to consider me as defensive of Asian authoritarianism." Although Gleysteen by no means sympathized with the Park regime's growing political repression, he was skeptical that America's position on human rights would have any effect given Park's conviction that "more liberal policies would only embolden his opponents."[12]

But the inability of the Carter White House to force changes in the regime's policies was not only a by-product of the limited leverage that American diplomats could apply on the ground. It also stemmed from the lingering concerns of top administration officials that U.S. intervention could endanger security or stability on the Korean peninsula. In a pinch, they almost always chose security over human rights if there was any chance that promoting the latter could jeopardize the former. Most of the policy alternatives that had genuine potential to influence the Park regime carried with them the threat of fostering instability and therefore could never be seriously considered. One measure proposed by human rights specialists in the State Department was to issue an official statement making it clear that the United States did not condone Park's disregard of human rights. They believed that this sort of personal criticism might weaken his regime and strengthen his democratic opponents, but Gleysteen and other East Asia specialists in the State Department convinced Carter that such a step would be too risky. The ambassador contended that the consequence of this course of action "could conceivably be another coup and another military leader not necessarily more enlightened than Park Chung Hee."[13] Worried that a personal assault on Park could either destabilize South Korea or further alienate his regime without producing any tangible benefits, the Carter administration never pursued this option.

Another option was to withdraw U.S. combat forces from South Korea. Two American divisions stationed there since the end of the Korean War had become an important symbol of the United States's commitment to the ROK. These forces made substantial contributions not only to the country's security but also, by employing thousands of Koreans and procuring services in South Korea, to its economy. Although the proximity of American GIs caused occasional friction, the Park government had consistently supported their presence. Putting the withdrawal of these troops on the table might have given the United States a negotiating tool in confronting Park on human rights questions. Early in his presidency Jimmy Carter began formulating plans to remove these divisions, claiming that they were no longer necessary for South Korea's security.

Ultimately, however, security concerns forced Carter to shelve the idea of troop withdrawals. In 1978 a new U.S. Army/Central Intelligence Agency (CIA) appraisal of North Korean forces reported that large numbers of previously undetected artillery units were forward deployed against the South. Under pressure from the intelligence agencies, Carter scuttled a plan to reduce U.S. forces by one brigade or 6,000 troops and settled for the withdrawal of only 800 troops. In the wake of this new intelligence, anxieties about the security implications of troop reductions were so high that even some of Carter's strongest allies in the human rights campaign started to oppose troop withdrawals. Democrats in Congress thought that withdrawing troops was strategically risky and felt slighted that the president had contemplated this major policy shift without consulting them. Dissident politicians in South Korea were no more enthusiastic about troop reductions than Carter's critics at home. Even though the U.S. president might have extracted concessions on human rights if he played this card, the withdrawal of U.S. troops would have given Park further license to take national security matters into his own hands. For dissidents in South Korea, this was virtually synonymous with increasing political repression.[14]

Although Jimmy Carter was sincerely committed to improving the human rights situation and strengthening democratic forces in South Korea, the policy options that might have enabled him to do so all had limitations or drawbacks. The only time during his presidency that pressure on human rights issues had any effect on Park was when Carter himself traveled to Seoul for a summit meeting in the summer of 1979. The atmosphere at the Carter-Park summit was initially fraught with tension as the American president had criticized Park's government far more often and more directly than any of his predecessors. But the meeting ended on much better terms. Carter formally agreed to freeze troop withdrawals, something he had more or less been forced to do already, while Park vaguely promised to liberalize his human rights policies. At first, Park did seem to take his pledge seriously. He informed the American embassy of a plan to release 180 political prisoners several days after the summit had concluded.[15] Whether this was a token gesture or the sign of a more genuine shift toward political liberalization is impossible to know. By the time Park made this move, a chain of events that would eventually bring about his demise had already begun.

From Park Chung Hee to Chun Doo Hwan

Although Park seemed to be making some concessions on human rights questions in the weeks after his summit with Carter, few Americans doubted his ability to remain in power. One CIA report in June 1979 concluded that

Park had "substantial assets in terms of bases of support, institutional development, and political-economic programs that make it likely that he will be able to hold on to power into the 1980s."[16] Even U.S. intelligence agencies did not realize how tenuous Park's position was becoming and how vulnerable his political system was to changing domestic and international circumstances.

The series of events that would bring a simultaneous end to Park's rule and his life began in August 1979. At the time the regime was suffering the political ramifications of a global economic recession that had dramatically slowed the country's growth rate and necessitated intervention by the International Monetary Fund. Many companies that had thrived during the sixties were crippled by the economic crisis and structural shifts within the South Korean economy. The YH Trading Company, whose workers would help to set in motion a major political crisis, was typical of such firms. In the 1960s it had prospered as a labor-intensive firm whose employees worked long hours for low wages. In the 1970s, however, the company, whose chief export had been wigs, started to decline as the government shifted preferential treatment to electronics exporters. After more than 75 percent of the firm's four thousand workers had been laid off, the remaining employees unionized and sought an agreement with the company president guaranteeing wage increases and protection against layoffs. Rather than accepting these terms, the president closed the plant on 7 August. When union workers occupied the plant, Park sent riot police to force them out of the factory.[17]

Park's decision to suppress the strike set off a series of escalating confrontations between the state and democratic forces. Seeking political support for their cause, the dismissed workers fled to the headquarters of the New Democratic Party (NDP), the opposition party in the National Assembly. The regime responded by dispatching riot police to NDP headquarters to remove the workers and force them into vans. In the wake of the incident, NDP leader Kim Young Sam roundly denounced the government and demanded that Park resign. Seeking to silence Kim, Park arranged for a special meeting of the assembly on 4 October 1979. During the meeting members of the ruling party locked out the opposition and voted to expel Kim from his assembly seat. Nine days later all sixty-nine remaining members of the NDP resigned their seats, destroying whatever shred of institutional legitimacy the National Assembly had retained.[18]

Over the next few days, near chaos enveloped Kim Young Sam's native Kyŏngsang Province in the southeast. On 15 October one thousand students began marching down the streets of Pusan, demanding that Park end his long tenure in power. But unlike other protests, which were carried out primarily by students and intellectuals, the demonstrations in Pusan were joined by significant numbers of middle-class citizens who battled with riot police continuously for two nights before Park finally declared martial law in the city on 18 October. But as the regime tried to clamp down on domestic dissent, antigovernment protests spread like wildfire to other parts of the country. With the declaration of martial law in Pusan, new demonstrations erupted in the nearby city of Masan, and when the government issued a "garrison decree" to contain the violence there, the confrontations extended to Seoul and several other major cities.[19]

Against this background of swirling chaos that was rapidly engulfing the entire country, disputes began to develop among key members of the Park regime over whether to respond with more repression or to ease constraints on freedom of expression. A fateful meeting of these individuals occurred on 26 October in the KCIA annex of the presidential mansion. Present at the gathering were President Park; Park's bodyguard and long-standing confidant on political issues, Ch'a Ch'ijol; KCIA director Kim Chaegyu; and Kim Kewŏn, the head of the presidential secretariat. During this conference Kim Chaegyu apparently argued for compromise and reform, while Park and Ch'a chastised the KCIA director for not predicting the uprisings. Park threatened to use paratroopers to put down the demonstrations. For reasons that are still unclear, Kim Chaegyu suddenly shot and killed both Ch'a and Park, ending the president's two-decade-long domination of South Korea. Prime Minister Ch'oe Kyuha assumed the presidency and immediately declared martial law.[20]

The next few months were a time of both cautious optimism about political liberalization and concern raised by disturbing maneuvers within the military. Attempting to move the country toward democracy, Ch'oe announced on 10 November that steps would be taken to liberalize the constitution and that new elections would be mandated. His government also moved to restore the civil liberties of Kim Dae Jung and other prominent dissidents. But ominous developments were occurring within the ROK military establishment. On 12 December 1979 Major General Chun Doo Hwan, one of the leaders of a secret military organization known as the Hanahoe or "One Association," led a surprise attack on the residence of Chŏng Sunghwa, the army chief of staff and martial law commander. Chun then announced that Chŏng was being placed under arrest for complicity in the assassination of Park Chung Hee and appointed one of his allies as the new martial law commander.[21] Chun now had complete control of the military. Although he did not formally seize the reigns of political power, it was obvious that he had the capacity and the will to do so.

Chun's actions created great political uncertainty in South Korea in the early months of 1980. At times it seemed as if the Ch'oe government might hold out and manage a successful transition to a more democratic system. At other times Chun appeared bound to reestablish military rule. The fluidity and ambiguousness of the situation was reflected in the thinking of U.S. officials. The Americans were troubled by Chun's power grab, in part because to pull it off he had ignored protocol jointly established by the U.S. and ROK forces. One day after Chun arrested the martial law commander, Ambassador Gleysteen wrote Secretary of State Cyrus Vance that "the December 12 incident is bad news from our point of view." While he was reluctant to predict its ramifications, Gleysteen was generally pessimistic. He explained that "although we may yet be delightfully surprised to find that they adopt a position on political liberalization that stiffens the back of President [Ch'oe] and pleases the politicians, the odds are that we will be disappointed."[22] Nevertheless, he still believed that American foreign policy should focus on trying to steer South Korea toward gradual political liberalization. The United States should seek both to "prevent a dangerous disintegration of army unity and to preserve the momentum toward broadly based democratic government under civilian rule." The latter goal, the ambassador noted, would "require buttressing the image of President [Ch'oe] and the Cabinet as much as possible."[23]

Following Chun's maneuver, the Carter administration held a major review of U.S. policy to consider measures that would make known Washington's displeasure with his actions. During the review officials seriously contemplated imposing economic sanctions and postponing the annual security meeting—another symbol of the U.S. commitment to South Korea. But leading policymakers regarded both of these options as too risky. Those opposing sanctions feared that such a course would worsen the already unstable economy and lead to additional authoritarian measures by the military. Representatives of the Defense Department nixed the idea of postponing the annual security meeting on the grounds that security policy needed to be separated from U.S. political objectives.[24] Ultimately, the United States chose to refrain from moving against Chun, vainly hoping that he would moderate his ambitions.

Three months later American policymakers continued to express a mixture of cautious hope, consternation, and uncertainty about how to proceed.

In a telegram of 17 March 1980, Gleysteen reported that the simultaneous release of Kim Dae Jung and promotion of Chun Doo Hwan conjured up "contrasting pictures of Korea." The first image was of "a country proceeding more or less on schedule with promises of political evolution and headed—rather unbelievably—for transformation from the authoritarian one-man rule of the yusin era to a fully democratic system." The other, "more sinister" picture was one in which Chun's "gradual aggrandizement of power" was reaching a point where "many feel he already controls basic government policy." According to the ambassador, the basic approach of American officials aware of these starkly contrasting possibilities for South Korea's future was generally to sit tight with their fingers crossed and wish that the country would follow a course that was conducive to both stability and democratization. "Hopefully," Gleysteen concluded, "General Chun and like-minded military elites will restrain themselves while politicians work out compromises that will allow at least some progress in the current ROK experiment in political liberalization."[25] At this point the Americans hoped that South Korean politics could evolve along liberal democratic lines, although they were not entirely sure this was possible.

Americans' desires for peaceful political evolution were rendered futile by events that began to unfold less than two months later. On 14 April 1980 President Ch'oe promoted Chun Doo Hwan to the rank of lieutenant general and appointed him acting director of the KCIA. South Koreans were well aware that these changes shifted the locus of political power from the civilian government to Chun's military cabal. Student protests exploded nationwide and were bolstered by strikes at several major industrial plants. The orderly transition to representative democracy envisioned by the Americans had become impossible, and a major confrontation between military leaders intent on seizing power and democratic forces was all but inevitable. U.S. policymakers now faced a decision that they had desperately wanted to avoid making. They had to either abandon their objective of promoting gradual political liberalization or run the risk of jeopardizing security by supporting protesters. Americans struggled with these conflicting sensibilities during the crucial days between mid-April and late May 1980 when South Korea's fate hung in the balance. Ultimately anxieties about security rather than hope for democracy guided the hand of American policymakers.

As the country veered toward conflict between the military and dissenters, U.S. officials initially attempted to moderate the actions of both groups in order to maintain the delicate status quo. They urged Chun to use restraint, warning that his failure to do so could jeopardize U.S.-ROK relations. Ambassador Gleysteen believed that America's objective "should be to slow [Chun] down so he does not go beyond what the Korean people—and even the Korean military—consider tolerable."[26] The State Department agreed and, the day before a scheduled meeting between Gleysteen and Chun, advised him "to convey to Chun that we have a shared interest in not having a student government clash destabilize the country or upset the possibilities for sound political development."[27] Several days after speaking with Chun, Gleysteen met with opposition leaders Kim Dae Jung and Kim Young Sam and encouraged them to exert any moderating influence that they could on student protesters.[28] By pleading with both the military and dissident leaders for restraint, the United States hoped to avoid a destabilizing confrontation between democratic forces and the state.

While the Americans tried first and foremost to prevent an escalation of tensions, they also let Chun know that they would not oppose the use of the military or other repressive measures if alternative means of controlling the protests failed. Prior to his meeting with Chun, Gleysteen informed the U.S. secretary of state that "in none of our discussions will we in any way suggest that the USG [U.S. government] opposes ROKG [Republic of Korea government] contingency plans to maintain law and order, if absolutely necessary by reinforcing the police with the army."[29] Although the ambassador took pains to convey that Americans did not endorse using the military to repress civilian dissidents, to Chun the fact that the United States would not prevent him from doing so was significant. Whether or not Gleysteen intended it as such, Chun understood the ambassador's statement as a green light to use the armed forces wherever and however he deemed necessary. Believing that he had U.S. approval, Chun clamped down violently on dissidents over the next two weeks.

Ten days after meeting with Gleysteen, Chun started a crackdown on dissident groups through which he would ultimately seize control of the government. Despite American calls for moderation, student demonstrations demanding the immediate dismantling of the Yusin system had continued to increase. By 15 May the number of demonstrators in Seoul had grown to more than eighty thousand and their level of violence had risen markedly. Although the protests subsided somewhat the next day, Chun used this latest round of demonstrations as an excuse to declare "emergency martial law" on the evening of 17 May. The military authorities ordered all universities to close and suspended the National Assembly. The government also arrested several of its most prominent political opponents, including Kim Young Sam, Kim Dae Jung, and Kim Chongp'il.[30]

American officials recognized that Chun had destroyed any remaining chance for gradual democratization in South Korea. Gleysteen cabled the State Department that "an all but formal military takeover may be in process." Gleysteen had promised that the United States would not interfere if Chun used the military to manage demonstrations, but Chun's drastic actions far exceeded what the ambassador had anticipated. He wrote that "our visceral reaction to what has happened is obviously negative" and that the embassy was "deeply concerned that this [is the] last in a sequence of events that will erase what little credibility Chun has concerning his liberalization program."[31] In the aftermath of the 17 May crackdown, U.S. officials tried but failed to restore the shattered momentum toward political liberalization. They warned Chun that "actions to frustrate the Korean peoples' hopes for democratic development will have a profound effect on our ability to work together" and that the United States's further actions would "be influenced especially by the fate of the three Kims and prospects for an early session of the National Assembly." As it had done so often in the past, the State Department issued a statement urging "all elements in Korean society to act with restraint."[32]

American efforts to encourage restraint were once again frustrated by the course of events. Although much of the country seemed relatively quiescent the day after Chun's new declaration of martial law, student protests in the southwestern city of Kwangju continued unabated. South Chŏlla Province, where Kwangju was located, had reaped the fewest benefits from South Korea's dramatic economic growth. (Park Chung Hee was a native of Kyŏngsang Province in the southeast, where he had built most of the country's major industrial sites.) Chŏlla was also the home of opposition leader Kim Dae Jung, whose arrest had inflamed popular opinion there.

The military's brutal reaction to continuing protests in Kwangju is widely remembered as one of the most infamous events in modern Korean history. On 18 May 1980 special warfare forces entered the city and began indiscriminately attacking young people who looked like students. Thousands of citizens who witnessed this display of naked aggression poured into the streets and joined the students. On 21 May, when paratroopers arrived and fired on protesters, citizens united in an effort to take back the city. Demonstrators seized armaments, took over government buildings, and declared Kwangju liberated from military dictatorship. As army units were temporarily withdrawn to the perimeter of the city, armed student patrols took responsibility for keeping order, transporting the wounded, and distributing food.[33] After the fierce confrontations on the twenty-first, a lull settled over the city for the next several days, and the military and a Kwangju citizens' committee began negotiations. The talks soon became stalemated, however, leading to a tense standoff between the military and dissidents.

While the negotiations were still in process, several key U.S. policy-makers met in Washington to discuss the situation in South Korea. Among those present were Secretary of State Edmund Muskie, Carter's national security adviser Zbigniew Brzezinski, and CIA director Admiral Stansfield Turner. As they had done in the past, American officials attempted to balance their desire for political liberalization in South Korea with their concerns about security. The meeting took place in an atmosphere of heightened anxiety about the security of America's allies stemming from the overthrow of the shah in Iran less than one year earlier. Officials now repeatedly expressed fear that South Korea could turn into "another Iran," meaning that a conservative pro-American government would be replaced by a radical one that was hostile to the United States. Given these concerns, the policymakers at the meeting decided that "the first priority is the restoration of order in Kwangju by the Korean authorities with the minimum use of force necessary." The United States would continue to "press the Korean government, and the military in particular, to allow a greater degree of political freedom to evolve," but it would do so only after the situation in Kwangju was contained. General John Wickham, who as commander of American forces in South Korea had operational control over joint U.S.-ROK military personnel, released the Twentieth Division of the ROK Army from its duties along the demilitarized zone. It was this division that ended the citizens' uprising on 27 May and paved the way for Chun's usurpation of political authority.[34]

By the time Wickham released the Twentieth Division, the Americans saw the restoration of stability as their most urgent objective in South Korea and were willing to alienate democratic forces to obtain it. On 26 May, the day before the Twentieth Division entered Kwangju and used force to stop the demonstrations, a group of dissidents occupying some of the government buildings requested that the American embassy broker negotiations between them and the martial law authorities. Ambassador Gleysteen, however, turned them down, in part because the ROK Army contended that it would be inappropriate for the United States to become involved in an "internal" matter and in part because he suspected that the protesters were dangerous radicals.

Not all U.S. officials agreed with Gleysteen's decision. According to James V. Young, then the assistant U.S. military attaché in Seoul, "some embassy members including myself were disappointed that Gleysteen did not pursue this matter more vigorously." The ROK Army's claim that the suppression of the uprising was an "internal" affair did not mitigate the fact that the Americans had "an obligation to do whatever we could to halt further blood shed." Ultimately, the U.S. decision resulted in "more casualties on both sides."[35]

When the dust finally settled in Kwangju, somewhere between two hundred and two thousand South Koreans had lost their lives. The Kwangju uprising and the role played by the United States in it became an important touchstone for the waves of anti-American sentiment that would wash through South Korea during the subsequent decade. The decision made by a panicked group of U.S. officials to prioritize security over democracy was an especially tragic one because it alienated many of the pro-democracy forces that Americans had helped nurture during previous decades. This decision differed in many ways from the ones that had been made to defer democracy in the fifties and sixties because, by 1979, South Korea had many of the elements that could have enabled a workable democracy to be formed.

During the crisis, U.S. officials acted out of exaggerated fear of dissident radicalism. Although Ambassador Gleysteen had always wanted to see movement toward political liberalization, he had also voiced a concern tinged with racism that the dissident movement had veered too far toward extremism. In the aftermath of Park Chung Hee's assassination, for instance, he wrote the State Department that there had been "ample reminders that this society of garlic and pepper eating combatants has not changed its basic nature." This was exemplified by "dissident elements and some of the political opposition, grooved over decades into extremist patterns by confrontation with authority" that had "rejected the acting governments proposed scenario for reform and reiterated their demands for the immediate dismantlement of the [Yusin] system."[36] At Kwangju, Gleysteen worried about the impact of "a relatively small yet influential group of hard-line radicals, including a few who apparently opposed any compromise and wanted to establish a revolutionary government."[37] The fear that hard-line radicals were leading the protests was a major reason that U.S. officials placed such a high premium on security.

American mistrust of South Korea's pro-democracy forces was both tragic and ironic. Although the protesters at Kwangju included some radicals, the demands put forward by dissidents during the standoff were more liberal democratic than revolutionary. They called for the lifting of martial law, an end to military interference in politics, Chun Doo Hwan's resignation, and the release of political prisoners.[38] Such an agenda was geared to correct the abuses of military dictatorship rather than incite class warfare or anarchy. Even if the uprising in Kwangju had spread to other cities and succeeded in overthrowing the government, which for American policymakers seems to have been the worst-case scenario, the new regime would in all likelihood have been headed by Kim Dae Jung or Kim Young Sam rather than the hard-line radicals whose influence Gleysteen was so afraid of. During the nineties both of these dissident politicians would get a chance to govern South Korea, and they would do so in a way that showed moderation. Although they might have had more difficulty winning the confidence of the business community in 1980 than they did in the 1990s, there is little reason to believe that they would have been unable to govern the country in a manner that promoted stability and democracy after the uprising.

But although the stand taken by American officials may have facilitated Chun Doo Hwan's rise to power, ultimately the actions of South Koreans—both inside and outside of the military—played a larger role in enabling this outcome than anything that the United States did. Once Chun gained control over the military, there was little Americans could have done to stop him from taking over the government. Even if they had opposed the release of the Twentieth Division or warned Chun more firmly against cracking down on political protests, he would have almost certainly used combat forces loyal to him to end the demonstrations at Kwangju and seize control of the government. American officials had few policy alternatives for containing the ambitions of ROK military leaders that would not have hurt the United States as much as they hurt Chun.

As significantly, the democratic forces in South Korea were still not strong or united enough to overcome the military in 1980. Although the vast majority of people quietly opposed the continuation of military rule, outside of Kwangju protests were generally limited to those of the pro-democratic elites such as students, intellectuals, and church leaders. Only in Kwangju did members of the country's growing middle class demonstrate their willingness to violently resist the military's seizure of power. Moreover, the business community had maintained its symbiotic relationship with the state and remained ambivalent about democracy. As a result, these increasingly influential sectors of the population accepted, albeit reluctantly, the extension of military dictatorship. In just seven years, however, many of the conditions that had made South Korea's middle and business classes, as well as the United States, willing to tolerate continued military rule would swiftly evaporate, paving the way for another round of confrontations between the state and civil society that would have a very different outcome.

The Birth of Democracy in South Korea

South Korea was left reeling by the sheer brutality of what had occurred in Kwangju in May 1980. Three months later, on 27 August, Chun Doo Hwan was formally inaugurated as president after his election by an essentially rubber stamp "electoral college."[39] American policymakers were left to find ways of balancing their concerns for security with their desire for political liberalization in a climate of escalating anti-American sentiment. Although U.S. support for Chun had been hesitant during the events at Kwangju, he had masterfully used his control of the South Korean media to create the impression that Washington condoned his actions. In the wake of the massacre, the United States continued to extend formal support to the Chun government and to emphasize "quiet diplomacy" when it came to promoting the country's political evolution. For South Korean dissidents, however, formal support of Chun's government was morally inexcusable.

During the first months after Chun took office, the United States attempted to influence the new ROK president by offering him the official recognition that he craved in exchange for compromises on key human rights issues. American actions to save the life of future president Kim Dae Jung epitomized this approach. Kim had been imprisoned arbitrarily during the Kwangju uprising, and the Chun Doo Hwan regime subsequently decided to prosecute him for subversion. After the trial was announced, many hard-liners in the regime and the South Korean military appeared determined to kill Kim, whose very existence they viewed as a threat. Kim's execution, especially on the basis of patently false accusations, would have dealt a serious blow to the country's democratic development. Both the Carter and Reagan administrations made protecting his life a priority.

Top U.S. officials let Chun know that Kim's execution would inevitably damage the ROK's relationship with the United States and the international community. Immediately after Chun's inauguration, President Jimmy Carter personally assured him that the United States would continue to maintain its security relationship with the ROK but urged him to be careful in how he dealt with Kim. Carter cautioned that "Mr. Kim's execution, or even a sentence of death, could have serious repercussions."[40] The Chun regime expected the incoming Reagan administration to be more sympathetic, given its announced support for hard-line anti-Communist autocracies, but officials in the new administration made it known that Kim's execution would not be tolerated. Richard Allen, one of Reagan's key advisers on foreign affairs, has said that he warned South Korean officials that the U.S. reaction to Kim Dae Jung's death would be "like a lightning bolt from heaven striking" them.[41] In the end, Chun promised to stay Kim's execution and allow him to seek political asylum in exchange for an invitation to the White House after Reagan's inauguration.

With its decision to allow an official Chun visit, the Reagan White House more or less accepted the perpetuation of military dictatorship in South Korea as a fait accompli. Administration officials now needed a policy for dealing with this repressive regime without completely alienating dissident groups. Reagan advisers doubted that the confrontational approach employed by the Carter White House would have any influence on Chun. Moreover, in an atmosphere of renewed Cold War challenges, they were more cautious about creating friction with one of America's closest allies in the global struggle against Communism. At first, the Reagan team placed a premium on reaffirming security ties and establishing more amicable relations between the two governments. Over time, however, the administration placed a greater emphasis on quietly offering encouragement to South Korea's democratic movement.

The administration's initial emphasis on security was readily apparent during Chun Doo Hwan's visit to the United States in February 1981. Chun was the first foreign head of state to enter the Reagan White House. William Gleysteen, who still served as ambassador to South Korea, urged the State Department to make democratization a part, if not a major component, of its agenda. He advised that "largely by means of commending helpful first steps, we should encourage internal trends toward greater freedom and moderation."[42] Key Reagan officials seemed partially attuned to this issue but were less straightforward in recommending U.S. action to restrain Chun. Before the two presidents met, new secretary of state Alexander Haig wrote that although Chun faced the "challenge" of moderating "his strongman-style of government enough to enlist more positive support without inviting a new internal confrontation," it was "basically an internal issue." Pressuring Chun to move toward political liberalization was nowhere among the administration's top priorities. The president's primary objectives in meeting with Chun should be "to restore normalcy to our relations with a valued ally" and "to underscore the constancy of the American commitment to peace and stability in Northeast Asia."[43]

During the visit the Reagan administration refused to endorse the

President Ronald Reagan's embrace of South Korean president Chun Doo
Hwan alienated democratic forces in the ROK and stirred anti-American sentiment.
(Ronald Reagan Library)

repressive measures that Chun had taken to seize power, but it nevertheless
offered more than tacit approval for his government. In a recently declassified memorandum of the conversation that took place between Haig
and South Korean foreign minister No Sinyong (some sections of which
have been excised), there is little evidence that Haig pressured Chun to use
moderation in dealing with the opposition. The discussion focused primarily on security and economic issues. Although Haig had denied the
South Koreans' request to include a paragraph in the joint communiqué
endorsing Chun's actions to restore political stability, he let them know that
he had done so on the grounds that "the U.S. action in inviting Chun spoke
louder than words."[44]

By the time Reagan visited South Korea two years later, placing "quiet
pressure" on the ROK government to ease restrictions on civil liberties had
become a more significant part of his administration's agenda, in part because of the intense criticism of Chun's regime by Democrats in Congress.[45]
The issues of human rights and civil liberties came up during one of Reagan's private meetings with Chun. When Chun blamed Communist insur-
gents for the repressive measures taken by his regime, Reagan responded—
in the frank, open manner that often characterized his discussions with

foreign leaders—that "the soul of democracy is freedom under law." He told Chun that "if dissidents can't win elections by persuading the people, that's fine, but he [sic] can still have his say."[46] The U.S. president also spoke out on behalf of democratization in a widely publicized speech at the National Assembly and at an embassy reception to which members of the opposition were invited. He was perhaps most straightforward in his address to the assembly, where he contended that "the continuing development of democratic political institutions . . . is the only way to build the national consensus which is the foundation of true security." As he would continue to do over the next several years, Reagan called upon Chun to carry through on the promise he had made soon after seizing power to hold open elections in 1988.[47]

For South Korean dissidents, Reagan's efforts to subtly guide Chun toward democratization were inadequate. As the Chun government grew more repressive, American calls for gradual liberalization increasingly rang hollow. Once in office, Chun had purged the bureaucracy and the KCIA of his political rivals, replacing them with individuals who had demonstrated their loyalty to him. By 1982, more than half the members of the National Assembly were former military officers. Chun also shut down 172 periodicals, fired 400 journalists, and dismissed from their posts eminent academicians who criticized his regime.[48] Unlike Park Chung Hee, who had always enjoyed some popular support despite his authoritarianism, Chun alienated most sectors of South Korean society by his use of naked force to control the opposition.

As the Chun government tightened its oppressive grip on the citizenry, leading dissidents became increasingly critical of the United States for supporting it. Kim Dae Jung, now a political exile living in in the United States, frequently voiced his disagreement with American policymakers. He recalled being told by Reagan administration officials that they were pursuing "quiet diplomacy" in contrast to the "open diplomacy" of the Carter administration that had produced few results. But Kim disagreed with this approach. He argued that the United States should pursue a combination of "quiet" and "open" diplomacy. "Quiet diplomacy" was "good in certain particular circumstances but when it came to basic principles such as democracy, freedom of the press and support for human rights they should use 'open diplomacy' so that there was no room for misunderstanding." Although Kim was deeply impressed by American democracy, his failure to sway the State Department left him highly disillusioned with U.S. policy. He wrote that "there was certainly democracy within the United States but when it faced outward, that democracy was not there." This was "America's tragedy and a hardship for the countries that had no choice but to align themselves with the United States."[49]

Such criticism of American policy from figures like Kim Dae Jung became very influential within South Korea's broader democratic movement. Some of Kim's contentions were clearly reflected in *minjung* (meaning literally "the people") ideology, which emerged as an important unifying force for opponents of the Chun regime in the mid-1980s. Minjung ideology was a constantly shifting combination of nationalism, left-Christian theology, dependency theory, and demand for democratization. It called for a major restructuring of South Korea's economy, politics, and foreign policy to favor the minjung, whose aspirations for democracy and reunification, it contended, had been suppressed by both the ROK military dictatorships and the United States. Dissident intellectuals such as Kang Man'gil, Han Wansang, and Paek Nakch'ŏng concentrated on illuminating the minjung's role in Korean history and culture and identifying how South Korean society could be transformed to fulfill the minjung's aspirations. With its emphasis on the role of American foreign policy in supporting dictatorships in South Korea, minjung ideology sometimes identified the United States itself as an enemy of the Korean people.[50]

The generation of students who came under the influence of minjung ideology in the 1980s was stridently and sometimes violently anti-American. Perhaps the most spectacular expression of anti-Americanism by this group came in November 1985, when seventy-three students occupied the USIS building in Seoul, demanding the withdrawal of U.S. forces from the peninsula and an apology from the United States for the deaths that had occurred in Kwangju. American diplomats were able to defuse the situation after negotiating with the protesters for several days.[51] But the incident shows the extent to which attitudes toward the United States had shifted by the mid-eighties. The USIS, once an important venue for dialogue between Americans and South Korea's budding democratic forces, had become a site of confrontation between the two. The takeover was also a sign of the growing hopelessness and desperation of South Korean dissidents who had wrung few concessions from Chun.

Yet prospects for democracy in South Korea were not as bleak as they appeared. While Reagan's "quiet diplomacy" seemed to be having little impact at best and indeed might have been strengthening Chun, other dimensions of American policy were fostering changes in the South Korean economy that promised to limit the power of the state and build support for democratization among the country's powerful but hitherto apolitical business class. In particular, the United States had begun pressuring Chun to allow economic liberalization. The Reagan White House pursued this agenda more out of faith in free-market capitalism than from a desire to promote democracy. But by the late 1980s U.S. pressures for economic liberalization were making South Korea's business class more eager to contest the state's power.

When Chun traveled to the United States in 1981, South Korea was suffering from a severe recession and most of the economic discussions focused on what could be done to help the country recover. But even during this first meeting some U.S. officials wanted to pressure Chun to improve the climate for foreign investment. His government had recently passed laws requiring foreign investors to pay a substantial tax on capital gains when investments were liquidated and repatriated. The Americans contended that this new legislation was a disincentive for potential investors and urged President Reagan to take up the issue with Chun's economic secretary.[52] There is no record that this issue was discussed during the conversations between Chun and Reagan, probably because the Americans saw preventing economic instability as their highest priority at the time. But the fact that this issue was raised at all is indicative of Washington's determination to push hard for economic liberalization in South Korea.

During Reagan's 1983 visit to Seoul, U.S. officials advocated the liberalization of trade and finance much more forcefully. Beforehand, Secretary of State George Shultz had told the president that the trip should "underline the importance of Japan and Korea strengthening their commitment to liberalize trade, resist protectionism, and advance market opening measures."[53] Although Reagan and Chun skirted around the subject in their face-to-face meeting, Shultz and other State Department officials held separate talks with their South Korean counterparts in which they made the case for the liberalization of trade, foreign investment, and the financial sector.[54] By the mid-eighties, the Americans left no doubt that they expected economic reforms in exchange for their continuing support.

The Reagan administration's efforts to get the Chun government to liberalize the economy were far more influential than its attempts to promote political reform. Unlike Park Chung Hee, who had launched his military coup with a distinct vision of national development, Chun did not really have an economic agenda in mind when he seized power. He knew far less than his predecessor about how the Korean economy functioned and was probably not fully aware of the political repercussions that would accompany financial liberalization. Chun's limited understanding of economic issues worked to the advantage of American officials, who found him more amenable to their advice than either Park or Syngman Rhee. Moreover, Chun's lack of economic vision led him to rely heavily on skilled technocrats in the bureaucracy, which was loaded with American-trained Ph.D.s. In fact, the vast majority of Chun's top economic advisers had earned advanced degrees in the United States. Among them was Kim Chaeik, a Stanford University Ph.D. who played a critical role in shaping the regime's economic policies.[55] Under pressure from the United States and counseled by his leading advisers to liberalize the economy, Chun started denationalizing commercial banks and reforming industrial policy to reduce the state's role in investment decisions. Although these steps were sometimes undertaken in a slow and halting manner, by the mid-1980s they were creating a new relationship between the state and big business.

These new policies helped South Korea to resume the rapid economic growth rate that it had achieved through much of the sixties and seventies, but it also enabled businesses to become more independent from the state. Opening the country to foreign investment created a new source of financing for the chaebŏl and left them less reliant on the state's largesse. The stock market grew an astonishing 900 percent in value between 1980 and 1989, making it the ninth largest in the world and greatly expanding the market capitalization of many ROK firms. No longer indebted to the state for capital, South Korean entrepreneurs became increasingly resentful of government intervention in the economy. Some of the most powerful business leaders began openly calling for greater autonomy of the financial sector. Although the chaebŏl never stood at the front of South Korea's democratic movement, they were by the late 1980s willing to tolerate a more democratic polity, especially if it meant moderating the state's control over business. As Jung-En Woo has observed, during this period the chaebŏl increasingly "eschewed a capricious political order that so casually mixed benevolence with terror." Instead, they "came to desire greater stability and the rule of law, even if that meant liberal democracy."[56] The newfound willingness of the business community to support democratization would play an important role in the last conflict between dissidents and the military, which finally brought democracy to South Korea.

As the entrepreneurial and middle classes came to sympathize with the political opposition, the military's grasp on power grew increasingly unstable. This instability was magnified when a popular revolution brought an end to the rightist dictatorship in the Philippines in 1986, causing many dissidents in South Korea to anticipate a similar chain of events at home. By 1987 Korean politics had become a powder keg that could be ignited by one mistake on the part of the regime. Chun made just such an error in the spring of that year. He had originally promised to serve only one term as president and then to allow free elections, but on 13 April he effectively annulled that pledge. Then on 10 June he called a meeting of the ruling party, which rubber-stamped the selection of Roh Tae Woo, Chun's hand-picked successor, to stand for indirect election to the presidency. Chun argued vaguely that the national debates needed to revise the constitution would waste the resources and energy needed to prepare the country for the 1988 Olympics to be held in Seoul.[57]

Not surprisingly, Chun's announcement set off a wave of popular pro-tests that far exceeded those in 1980. Antigovernment demonstrations that were sometimes violent occurred in twenty-seven South Korean cities in the days following Roh's de facto election as the next president. Participation in these confrontations was not limited to students and intellectuals, as it sometimes had been in the past. South Koreans joining these massive protests came from a wide variety of classes and backgrounds, with the middle class well represented. Chun initially seemed ready to use force to resolve the problem. After more than a week of continuous demonstrations, he ordered some military units to prepare to enter Seoul. As Chun contem-plated the use of force to crush the protesters, members of the opposition planned a "Great Peace March of the People" on 26 June. In contrast to 1980, when Chun had been able to consolidate his political power by overwhelm-ing a significant but limited sector of the population, there was no way that he could have ended the demonstrations of June 1987 without an all-out civil war between the state and the people that it ostensibly governed. Further-more, the decision of the middle and business classes to throw their political weight behind the democratic movement made it impossible for the regime to wage a civil war without endangering South Korea's economic miracle as well.[58] With the military on alert and the people prepared to expand their protests, South Korea stood on the brink of chaos.

American officials watched the events unfold in South Korea with great trepidation. Their response to the crisis shared some similarities with their handling of events in Kwangju seven years earlier, but it also differed in significant ways. Like the Carter administration in 1980, the Reagan White House was concerned about security on the peninsula, and one of its first actions was to warn the North Korean government in Pyongyang not to exploit the situation.[59] As in 1980, Washington tried to balance its concerns about internal stability with its desire for the development of democratic institutions. It called for restraint by the leaders of both sides and encouraged a process of negotiation. This time, however, U.S. officials made it clear that they did not endorse the use of military force. They were keenly aware that their ambivalence on this issue during the Kwangju incident had become a touchstone for anti-Americanism and were determined not to let it happen again. Moreover, in their efforts to balance security and democracy, Americans were more inclined to tip the scales in favor of democracy in 1987 than they had been in 1980.[60] With tensions between the United States and the Soviet Union on the wane, Americans felt less indebted to hard-line anti-Communist governments that used the Cold War as an excuse to defer political reform.

As the crisis escalated, the White House first attempted to defuse the situation by encouraging Chun to exercise moderation. In a personal letter to Chun on 19 June, President Reagan cautiously admonished him not to use violence to suppress the protesters. Reagan maintained that "political stability based on sound democratic institutions is critical to assuring the long term security" of the ROK. He added that "dialogue, compromise and negotiation are effective ways to solve problems and maintain national unity."[61] Of course, Reagan still considered Chun a friend and an ally, so he did not pressure him to resign or surrender power, but he was sincere in his efforts to dissuade Chun from using brute force against the demonstrators.

Over the next several days, however, the face-off between the South Korean regime and its critics continued with few signs of compromise. American officials decided that they needed to play a more active role in resolving the situation. Gaston Sigur, the assistant secretary of state for East Asian and Pacific affairs, became the administration's point man for handling the crisis. In an address several months earlier, Sigur had spoken of the need for the "civilianization of government" in South Korea. His comments had drawn widespread attention and speculation in the Korean media. Sigur had been traveling in Asia with Secretary of State Shultz to attend meetings of the Association of Southeast Asian Nations (ASEAN) and the Australia, New Zealand, and United States Security Treaty (ANZUS) when the demonstrations in the ROK began to draw international attention. At his own suggestion, Sigur arrived in Seoul on 23 June as an emissary of the U.S. president. During the visit, Sigur tried to be as even handed as possible, conferring with Chun Doo Hwan and Chun's hand-picked successor Roh Tae Woo, as well as opposition leaders Kim Dae Jung, Kim Young Sam, and Cardinal Stephen Kim. He called on both sides to refrain from violence, emphasizing that the United States opposed the use of military force to end the crisis. On returning to the United States, he stated publicly that "the problems Korea faces are political problems; lasting solutions must be political agreements that Koreans reach themselves. Military steps offer no solutions."[62]

In the face of insurmountable pressure from nearly all sectors of South Korean society, Chun finally agreed to step down. On 29 June, his appointed successor Roh Tae Woo presented a "Declaration of Democratization and Reform," which promised that democratic elections would be held in December of that year and proposed major reforms to the ROK constitution. In a staged meeting designed to give Roh public credit for pushing these reforms forward, Chun agreed to accept the proposals made in the declaration. Four months later far-reaching changes were made to the South Korean constitution through a set of amendments that provided for the direct election of the president, strengthened the National Assembly, and eliminated some restrictions on freedom of expression.[63] South Koreans were now guaranteed the chance to put democratic principles into practice through fair elections.

The country's first democratic presidential election held at the end of 1987 did not completely end military domination of South Korean politics. By allowing Roh to take credit for democratization, Chun had shrewdly boosted Roh's popularity and made him a viable presidential candidate. The opposition was allowed to participate in the election without harassment or intimidation, but once the reforms were announced, divisions had emerged within the opposition camp. Although Kim Young Sam and Kim Dae Jung had been allies in the struggle for democracy, they came from regions— Kyŏngsang Province and Chŏlla Province respectively—with a history of mutual antagonism. Both men decided to run for president, effectively splitting the opposition vote. The result was an electoral victory for Roh Tae Woo, who captured 36 percent of the vote, leaving Kim Young Sam with 28 percent and Kim Dae Jung with 27 percent. Nevertheless, by 1987 it was obvious that the days of military authoritarianism had ended and that full-blown democracy was inevitable. In only five more years political control of the country would be turned over to civilian leaders who had spent years contesting military dictatorship.

Liberal democracy, which finally arrived in South Korea in 1987, proved to be remarkably durable, weathering a severe financial crisis in 1997 and a transfer of power to Kim Dae Jung and the opposition party that same year.

But democracy was possible only after years of conflict between military dictatorships that stubbornly resisted calls for democratization and diverse sectors of the population that demanded they be allowed to share power. The problem for the state was that its very success in developing the economy made the middle, business, and labor classes stronger, more independent, and ultimately more likely to side with democratic elites in their efforts to liberalize the country's political system.

American influence was significant but far from determinative in shaping struggles between the state and civil society after 1972. In many ways, U.S. officials tried to moderate the conflict between a powerful state and increasingly influential groups of democratic elites, both of which the United States had helped build up during previous decades. American policymakers were not solely responsible for either the brutality of the ROK's military dictators or the eventual triumph of democracy during this era. Rather, South Koreans worked within and around the confines of American influence to forge their own destiny.

Conclusion

The transformation that occurred in South Korea during the three and a half decades after the Korean War was stunning and unpredictable. Among the dozens of nations to emerge from formal colonialism following World War II, South Korea was one of the select few to achieve economic prosperity and political democracy. Once deemed an economic basket case, the country was well on its way to becoming one of the ten largest economies in the world. Once deemed incapable of self-government, South Koreans would soon have a democracy that was perhaps the most vibrant in Asia. Only through an honest and judicious evaluation of what enabled this transformation to occur can the experience of nation building in South Korea be understood and learned from.

Autocracy, Development, and Democracy

During the Cold War the Republic of Korea (ROK) was governed by successive autocratic governments that were supported by the United States and, in some instances, would have perished without American assistance. The success of these regimes in achieving stability, promoting economic development, and even creating the social basis for democracy raises some vexing questions. Could South Korea have enjoyed the same measures of economic growth and democracy under governments that more directly reflected the popular will? Were South Korea's leaders more autocratic than necessary in pursuing these worthy objectives? To what extent was the United States responsible for both the successes and excesses of their regimes? Answering these questions requires an assessment of what the alternatives to these regimes were and how South Korea might have evolved under these alternatives. There were three critical junctures—1945–48, 1960–61, and 1979–80—when American actions proved vital to the assumption of power by autocrats at the expense of governments or political leaders who enjoyed stronger popular support. Revisiting each of these junctures offers the clearest perspective on the relative merits of the regimes that gained power and the alternatives that might have been.

At the first crossroads, the years between 1945 and 1948, Americans intervened in a civil conflict between the left and the right that seemed destined to tear the country apart. In the absence of U.S. intervention, leftist revolutionaries would, in all likelihood, have defeated their opponents and assumed control of the entire Korean peninsula. Bruce Cumings has contended: "Had the Americans and the Russians quit Korea, a leftist regime would have taken over quickly, and it would have been a revolutionary nationalist government that, over time, would have moderated and joined the world community—as did China, as Vietnam is doing today." In Cumings's scenario, the unified Korean state would have presumably been able to move in a more moderate direction than the Democratic People's Republic of Korea (DPRK) ultimately did because the social conflicts fostered by Japanese imperialism would have been resolved and the national division, one of the major causes of North Korean militarism, would not have existed. A civil war would still have occurred, but it would not have approximated the destructiveness of the Korean War in which millions lost their lives.[1]

I generally agree with Cumings's analysis and can understand some of the reasons why he believes the triumph of a leftist revolution was preferable to the actual course of events. Korea would not have been divided, and the civil conflict that Cumings describes would not have been as deadly as the Korean War. Thousands of Korean families would never have had to endure decades of separation imposed upon them by the stark realities of the Cold War. Korea would have likely aligned itself with international Communism but perhaps would have abandoned socialist models of economic development along with the rest of the world in the mid-nineties.

At the same time, it is extremely unlikely that a Korea unified by the left would have enjoyed the same levels of prosperity and freedom that exist in South Korea today. Leftist nationalist governments of the kind that Cumings refers to do not have a good track record when it comes to stimulating economic growth or moving toward genuine democracy. The tragedies that befell some of the Asian countries in which leftist nationalist governments gained power often rivaled those that befell Koreans during the Korean War. Ironically, China and, to a lesser extent, Vietnam have been able to improve their economies and moderate their policies in recent years only by emulating elements of the South Korean model of development. If the United States had not helped revive capitalism in the ROK, the Asian countries that turned to Communism during the Cold War would have had a more difficult time changing direction in the 1980s and 1990s. Whether a Korea unified by a leftist revolutionary government would have had greater success in developing its economy and liberalizing its political system than the other Asian nations where social revolution triumphed is debatable. It is worth keeping in mind, however, that none of the leftist revolutionary governments that gained power in the postcolonial world after 1945 has been nearly as successful as South Korea in achieving rapid industrial development and lasting democratic government.

This is not to deny that American intentions in overturning a revolution in southern Korea were self-serving and geared chiefly to safeguard the United States's immediate economic and strategic interests. But while I find it difficult to excuse Americans' callous disregard for the desires of the Korean people, I find it equally difficult to ignore the fact that some of the long-term consequences of U.S. actions in South Korea were better than the intentions behind them. Initially, the United States foisted Syngman Rhee's autocratic government on South Korea. Yet Americans saw Rhee as a short-term fix rather than a long-term solution to the country's problems. They hoped that broader contacts between American and Korean society would facilitate the emergence of more dynamic, forward-looking political leaders. Such contacts did occur and they proved vital because, at the most basic level, the United States could offer Koreans more of the resources, opportunities, and ideas that they needed to fulfill their economic and political aspirations than could Communism. Ultimately, only South Koreans can decide if they are better off because of the pivotal decisions made by Americans between 1945 and 1948. But in doing so they must carefully consider not only what was lost but also what was gained.

The second critical juncture in which the United States supported autocracy at the expense of democracy was in 1960–61, when the military junta led by Park Chung Hee overthrew Korea's first democratically elected government. Washington was ambivalent about Park at first but became a strong supporter of his government when the new president's zeal for improving the economy became apparent. During the early and mid-sixties, when Park was at his weakest, U.S. officials quietly helped Park to retain power and control dissent.

What would South Korea have looked like if Americans had pushed harder for the restoration of a civilian government? The Chang Myŏn regime that Park toppled showed signs of taking on elements of what Fareed Zakaria has called "illiberal democracy."[2] It would probably not have deliberately infringed on basic liberties such as freedom of speech, the press, and religion, but it might not have been strong enough to protect the liberties of the minority against the majority. Reluctant to use the police or other forms of state power to control the governed, Chang would have had difficulty maintaining stability, one of the most critical prerequisites for sustainable development and democracy. It is also doubtful that he could have initiated the types of economic development programs that were eventually implemented by Park Chung Hee. In the early and mid-1960s the Park government carried out numerous unpopular but necessary reforms with American backing, such as revising the interest rate structure and normalizing relations between South Korea and Japan. The Chang Myŏn government showed little of the charisma or leadership that would have been essential to overcome the opposition to these measures. The result would likely have been economic stagnation, which in turn would have prevented some of the socioeconomic changes that ultimately made democratic institutions durable.

Like the Rhee regime, Park's government often resorted to authoritarian expedients that far exceeded what was required to implement economic reforms. The Americans had more success, at least initially, curbing such measures than they had during the Rhee era. The Kennedy and Johnson administrations were particularly effective in this regard. Constant pressure from American diplomats after the military junta seized power in May 1961 was crucial to getting Park to end military rule and hold open elections in 1963. Although power remained highly centralized in South Korea during the mid-1960s, Americans managed to ensure that relatively fair elections were held and that dissenting opinions could be voiced. As the South Korean economy expanded over the course of the decade, however, the ROK gained greater autonomy and could more easily resist U.S. pressure. With the inauguration of Richard M. Nixon in 1969, the United States sought to reduce its commitments in Asia and the overall level of American engagement with South Korea fell. In the late 1960s and 1970s, as Park returned to full-blown authoritarianism, the Nixon White House stood in his way only in extreme circumstances. A strong government remained necessary for economic development during this period, but under Nixon's permissive gaze Park strong-armed dissent in ways that could not be justified by the demands of even the incredibly rapid industrialization that occurred in South Korea under the Yusin system. Although the country's startling economic transformation in the 1960s and 1970s would have probably been impossible without Park Chung Hee, Park's methods of dealing with dissent during his last seven years in office must be considered an irreversible stain on his historical reputation.

Washington's decision to support Rhee in 1948 and Park in 1961 deferred the possibility of democratic government but in doing so prevented outcomes—the unification of Korea by leftist revolutionaries in 1948 and economic stagnation during the 1960s—that would have had much more dire implications for South Korea's future. The same cannot be said for America's willingness to back Chun Doo Hwan during the third critical juncture, 1979–80. This decision constituted one of the gravest errors that the United States made in its decades of intimate involvement in Korean affairs. In the aftermath of Park's assassination, a new military regime, one with substantially less legitimacy than its predecessor, gained power. Rhee and Park had not governed the country democratically, but they had always had the backing of at least some segments of the population. Chun Doo Hwan, on the other hand, had few allies outside of the military. Moreover, Chun seized power at a time when South Korea had in place many of the institutions and social groups needed to sustain liberal democracy. Had American officials at the highest level paid more attention to the socioeconomic situation of one of their closest allies, they might have understood this. The U.S. decision to support Chun, albeit somewhat reluctantly, left a lasting scar on American relations with South Korea and remains a source of tension between the two countries to this day.

Americans erred in supporting dictatorships in South Korea for too long and, at times, by being too tolerant of their excesses. But for much of the Rhee and Park eras, insisting on democracy would have been unrealistic. By advancing this argument I do not seek to lend credence to the invidious claims that South Koreans were simply incapable of democracy, which were sometimes made by Americans to justify their sanction of Rhee and Park. History has proved such assertions to be spurious. I merely acknowledge that, as Sean Wilentz writes in his masterful study of antebellum American politics, democracy "must always be fought for by political coalitions that cut across distinctions of wealth, power and interests" and survives "only when it is rooted in the lives and expectations of its citizens."[3] Such conditions took centuries to evolve in Europe, and the fact that they were not present in Korea in 1945 was not necessarily a by-product of Korean culture. By fostering sharp divisions within Korean society and impeding political participation, Japanese colonialism prevented the formation of coalitions that would have incorporated different interest groups while discouraging the revolution in expectations that must occur before democracy becomes possible.

How, then, did democracy come to be rooted in the lives and expectations of South Korean citizens? Americans cannot take all or even most of the credit for this phenomenon. It is important to remember, however, that even while American policies sometimes inhibited democracy from the top down, American influence worked in other ways to encourage democratization from the bottom up.

Building Institutions and Shaping Ideals

Creating institutions and disseminating new ideas were integral parts of America's Cold War strategy for remaking South Korea. Washington sought in particular to cultivate enthusiasm for economic development and democratic government. In pursuing this objective, Americans from both official and private organizations worked on the ground in the ROK and established relationships with a rising generation of South Korean elites. These elites, in turn, adapted U.S. techniques and ideals to their own aspirations and goals. This combination of American influence and Korean agency was what enabled the nation-building process in South Korea to follow the distinctive path that it did.

Over the course of the Cold War, the ROK military was the most dominant and influential of the new institutions created by the United States. Through a vigorous program of technical assistance and training that reached its apex during the latter half of the Korean War, Americans built a powerful military establishment in South Korea that was modeled after their own. American advisers were able to turn ROK troops into a disciplined, efficient fighting force within a remarkably short period. But Americans were less successful at inculcating South Korean officers with respect for democratic political culture. The ROK military was built around a corps of elite officers who had served in the Japanese armed forces during the colonial period. Although they came to admire the rationalism and discipline of the U.S. military establishment, American training could never entirely erase the imprint that Japanese militarism and imperialism had left on the minds of these officers.

The military was important because throughout the 1960s and 1970s, its leaders dominated South Korean politics. The undemocratic nature of their governments and the highly centralized model of economic development they adapted reflected both the military elite's sense of superiority toward the rest of Korean society and the lingering shadow of the Japanese colonial era. Although the United States failed to build respect for democracy within the South Korean armed forces, America's broader influence on ROK officers did benefit the country's development. Military dictatorships governed South Korea brutally at times to be sure. But Park Chung Hee and his cohorts were guided by a sincere determination to improve the lives of their people by understanding and applying the rules of science and economics. In this sense, South Korea's political leaders differed sharply from their counterparts in the North who made fairly pragmatic policy choices in the decade after the Korean War but, over the course of the Cold War, increasingly abandoned rational economic policies for ones that glorified their regime at all costs.[4] The rationalism demonstrated by ROK military leaders was not entirely a product of American influence but was nourished by intensive exposure to American methods of military organization.

Moreover, America's social and cultural influence extended far beyond the military. Throughout the 1950s and 1960s the United States was deeply engaged in building up South Korea's schools, training its bureaucrats, and seeking to influence the thinking of its intellectuals and students. Americans constantly aimed to spread ideas that were conducive to liberal capitalist modernity. They strove to instill in South Koreans a participatory ethos that would enable them to become responsible democratic citizens. In doing so, they were often arrogant and ethnocentric, thereby stirring nationalist resentment. But they were never so overbearing that they caused Koreans to reject the ideas of modernity and democracy altogether. More often than not, Americans allowed Koreans to come up with their own versions of these hallowed ideals.

American institution building did not in and of itself create demand for development, higher living standards, and political freedom among South Koreans. But U.S. programs did encourage these demands at a critical time in the country's development. Although the United States had not intended to cause friction between the state and society, as the state grew more repressive during the seventies and eighties the ideals that Americans had promoted in earlier decades nevertheless inspired South Korea's democratic movement, even if U.S. policy sometimes contradicted these ideals. The role of elites such as students and intellectuals was, in turn, critical to the country's transformation into a democracy. South Korea needed a middle class before democratic political institutions could fully take hold. It is important to remember, however, that the emergence of a middle class does not guarantee the kind of vibrant democracy that exists in South Korea. Malaysia and Singapore both have a significant middle class, but neither of these countries has moved as far toward democracy as the ROK. In the case of South Korea, students, intellectuals, dissident politicians, and other elites, whose outlooks had been partially shaped by their exposure to American institutions and ideals, all played a crucial role in introducing democratic concepts to the rest of society.

South Korea's success in turning the ideals of modernization and democracy into lived realities has not been replicated by many other postcolonial nations during or after the Cold War. South Koreans were able to embrace and ultimately realize these ideals because their near and distant pasts facilitated a distinctive pattern of sociocultural interaction with the United States. Americans were genuinely seen as liberators by many South Koreans both because of the U.S. role in ending Japanese colonialism and because of the sacrifices made by the United States to extricate the ROK from Communist occupation during the Korean War. In this sense South Korea differed from postcolonial societies that viewed American efforts to transplant their economic or political systems as a new form of colonialism. Moreover, after centuries of experience at adapting religions and philosophies imposed by outside forces, Koreans realized that U.S. hegemony need not destroy their own values and culture. Americans, for their part, were products of a political culture that was based on compromise and negotiation. They recognized that South Koreans' adaptation of American ideals and values to fit their own aspirations made them acceptable to Korean society. It was only through this synergy of American influence and Korean agency that the sociocultural transformation necessary for capitalist development and democracy occurred.

Meanings and Implications

The ROK's remarkable transformation has been used as a justification for many different historical and political viewpoints relating to both the Cold War and the prospects for nation building in the twenty-first century. But when the complex process of negotiation between Americans and South Koreans that enabled this transformation is considered, the lessons that can be drawn from the Korean experience seem to defy the easy generalizations that have been made about it.

For many, the economic success of South Korea in comparison to the impoverished conditions that now prevail in North Korea is evidence of the superiority of free-market capitalism and the wisdom of American policymakers. President Ronald Reagan offered one of the earliest expressions of this viewpoint when he addressed the National Assembly in 1983. He told the South Korean lawmakers that "the rapid progress of your economy— and the stagnation of the North—has demonstrated perhaps more clearly than anywhere else on earth, the value of a free economic system."[5] But the actual processes of nation building and development that occurred in South Korea did not entirely justify such a straightforward claim for the superiority of free markets. It is true that South Korea's economic system was more dynamic than the North's and that the South benefited from American aid and, in some cases, advice. But it is also clear that South Korea's economic system differed markedly from those in Europe and the United

States. The ROK achieved rapid economic growth rates through a model that drew as much on the Japanese colonial experience and on Koreans' own ideas as it did on American expertise. The sharply divergent fortunes of North Korea and South Korea cannot be understood solely through the lens of global competition between Communism and free-market capitalism. They speak more to the ways that Koreans modified both of these systems than to the relative merits of the systems themselves.

Nor can South Korea's rapid success in achieving industrial development and political democracy be attributed solely to the wisdom of U.S. policymakers. Americans at times did show vision, insight, and compassion in helping the country build institutions that were essential to long-term development. But Americans made similar attempts to build institutions, and disseminate new political ideals in Vietnam, Iran, and numerous other places with much less positive results. Americans were fortunate that in South Korea they encountered a people who matched their proselytizing zeal with a genius for adapting to foreign influence. Ultimately, it was less American skill at extending their ideals than Korean ability to appropriate them that made South Korea into one of the few places where nation building came close to producing the intended outcome. The many historical contingencies that were involved in the country's success story should be sobering to those who advocate renewed U.S. efforts to transplant democracy to different parts of the globe.

But even if South Korea's evolution into a prosperous democracy cannot be attributed to the wisdom of U.S. officials, its transformation nevertheless does reflect the flexible nature of American hegemony. In attempting to build up their allies in the postcolonial world, Americans naturally wanted them to emulate institutions that existed in the United States. But in the case of South Korea, they were generally flexible when it came to determining the shape that these institutions would take. Sometimes for better, sometimes for worse, Americans allowed the ROK to come up with its own models of economic development and its own conceptions of democracy. This flexibility is what enabled South Koreans to embrace the ideals that Americans proselytized in ways that could be reconciled with their nationalistic sensitivities.

The dynamism of the exchange that occurred between Americans and South Koreans on key issues stood in contrast to the situation in the North, where Koreans could never fully reconcile Stalinism with nationalism. After following Communist models of development in the 1950s and early 1960s with a surprising degree of success, North Korea's political leaders grew resentful of the domineering attitudes of their more powerful patrons—China and the Soviet Union. In the 1960s the DPRK turned to *juch'e* (self-reliance) ideology and shut out both the Free and Communist worlds in an effort to free itself from foreign domination. But according to prominent North Korea expert Charles Armstrong, juch'e proved "almost as devastating for the North Korean people as the Korean War itself."[6] Unlike Stalinism, international socialism, or juch'e, which all were fairly rigid, American hegemony was flexible enough to allow the South Koreans to reap the benefits of their own diligence and creativity.

Scholars and observers who are relatively sympathetic toward North Korea have argued that, although the DPRK now lags far behind South Korean in terms of economic development and human rights, by shutting out all foreign influences North Koreans have been more successful in preserving the essence of Korean culture.[7] But these arguments do not square with Korean history. Over the centuries Korea has welcomed and transformed the influences of foreign powers more often than it has rejected them. Koreans have shown remarkable ingenuity in integrating foreign ideals and philosophies with indigenous ones and carving out new versions of Koreanness to meet changing times and circumstances. In this sense, the way that South Koreans have learned to thrive during the last five decades is much more in keeping with the broad sweep of Korean history than the obstinately reclusive course that their brethren in the North have chosen. Indeed, the DPRK's insistent pursuit of a chimerical ideal of pure Koreanness is, in its own way, profoundly un-Korean.

The ultimate significance of U.S. nation building in South Korea, however, lies not on the Korean peninsula but in other regions of the world. South Korea's transformation into a prosperous democracy demonstrated not only the inevitability of American power but also its limitations. Americans certainly influenced the process of nation building, but they never completely determined it. Today, the levels of political stability, economic development, and human freedom that have been achieved in South Korea continue to elude much of Asia, Africa, and Latin America. Americans remain determined to steer the development of these regions in ways that will protect their own security and serve their national interests. But though U.S. power will doubtless shape and constrain the options available to the poorer nations of the globe, it will never singlehandedly decide them. In the end, the peoples of these nations must choose their own destinies, much as South Koreans chose theirs.

Notes

Abbreviations

ARC   Asiatic Research Center, Korea University
CDF   Central Decimal File
CIA   Central Intelligence Agency
CMH   Center of Military History, U.S. Army
CREST   CIA Records Search Tool
DDEL   Dwight D. Eisenhower Library
FFA   Ford Foundation Archives
4-HC   Korean 4-H Club Association, Historical Materials Collection
FRUS   U.S. Department of State, *Foreign Relations of the United States*
GCML   George C. Marshall Library
HSTL   Harry S. Truman Library
HUA   Harvard University Archives
JFKL   John F. Kennedy Library
KSMY   Kidokkyo Sahoe Munje Yŏnguso
           [Christian Social Problem Research Center]
LBJL   Lyndon Baines Johnson Library
NA   National Archives
NSA   National Security Archives
NSC   National Security Council
NSF   National Security Files
OCB   Operations Coordinating Board
OF   Don Oberdorfer Files
PHS   Presbyterian Historical Society
RG   Record Group
RNP   Robert Nathan Papers
ROK   Republic of Korea
SNUA   Seoul National University Archives
UN   United Nations
UNA   United Nations Archives
UNKRA   United Nations Korea Reconstruction Agency
USAIDL   U.S. Agency for International Development Learning
           and Resource Center
USAMHI   U.S. Army Military History Institute
USARPAC   U.S. Army Pacific
USIAL   U.S. Information Agency Library

USOM   U.S. Operations Mission
VFP   Van Fleet Papers
WHCF   White House Central Files
WHO   White House Office Files

Introduction

1   Many definitions of nation building exist in the literature. Some have stressed the creation of a state and the formation of political institutions. Others have placed a greater emphasis on the creation of a cohesive national identity. Some, such as Charles Tilly, have argued that nation building should be considered a combination of both of these. See Tilly, "Reflections on the History of European State-Making." Recently scholars have also noted that since the end of World War II, nation building has often referred to a process being implemented in a particular state by external powers, which is an important dimension of the conception of American nation building presented in this book. See Talentino, "Two Faces of Nation Building," and Etzioni, "A Self-Restrained Approach to Nation-Building by Foreign Powers." Talentino discusses the existing literature at greater length than I can here.

2   The influence of nation building and development on American foreign policy has received growing attention from students of the history of U.S. foreign relations in recent years. See, e.g., Latham, *Modernization as Ideology*; Engerman et al., *Staging Growth*; and Cullather, "Damming Afghanistan."

3   On the pivotal importance of the two Germanys to their respective Cold War patrons, see Harrison, *Driving the Soviets Up the Wall*, and Schwartz, *America's Germany*.

4   Acting Secretary of State to Director of the Bureau of the Budget, 16 May 1949, *FRUS, 1949*, 7:1025.

5   On this point, see William Stueck, "The Korean War and the American Relationship with Korea," *Rethinking the Korean War*.

6   USAID, "Field Proposed Program for 1963: Korea," USAIDL.

7   Staff Memoranda, Walt Rostow—Foreign Aid, 21–23 February 1961, NSF box 324, JFKL.

8   A number of political scientists have written about U.S.–South Korean relations during this period and utilized some archival materials. Among the best of these works are Cha, *Alignment Despite Antagonism*, and Moon, *Sex Among Allies*. Both of these are fine studies that utilize Korean language materials. Neither of them touches on American nation building, which is the major focus of this study. Although it does not utilize Korean materials, Don Oberdorfer's *The Two Koreas* provides good coverage of U.S.-Korean relations since the 1970s. There is, of course, a significant body of excellent work on the Korean War and the years between 1945 and 1950. Among the most well known of these are Stueck, *The Korean War*; Matray, *The Reluctant Crusade*; and Cumings, *Origins of the Korean*

War, vols. 1 and 2, which will be discussed below. Finally, although it did not deal explicitly with U.S.-Korean relations and deployed a "mass society" theory that is somewhat dated, Henderson, *Korea: The Politics of the Vortex*, remains one of the most insightful studies of Korea during the 1950s and 1960s.

9 See, e.g., the essays in Yŏksa munje yŏn'guso, *1950 nyŏndae nambukhan ŭi sŏntaek kwa kulchŏl*, and Taegyun Pak, "1956–1964 Han'guk kyŏngje kaebal kyehoek ŭi sŏngnip kwajŏng."

10 Cumings, *Origins of the Korean War*, vols. 1 and 2.

11 Zakaria first introduced this idea in an article, entitled "Illiberal Democracy," that appeared in the February 1997 issue of *Foreign Affairs*. He later developed it at greater length in his book, *The Future of Freedom*, where he considers East Asian development in particular on pp. 55–58. Zakaria is, of course, indebted to the ideas of scholars like Seymour Lipset, who argued that a middle class needed to exist before democracy could develop, and, more indirectly, to scholars such as Chalmers Johnson, who maintained that "soft authoritarian governments" in Asia had been the most successful at fostering economic development. See, e.g., Johnson, "Political Institutions and Economic Performance: The Government-Business Relationship in Japan, South Korea and Taiwan," in Deyo, *The Political Economy of the New Asian Industrialism*, and Lipset, "Some Social Requisites of Democracy."

12 Chalmers Johnson first pioneered the concept of the developmental state in his work on Japan and then applied it briefly to South Korea and Taiwan. See Johnson, "Political Institutions and Economic Performance." For a more detailed look at the development of South Korea's distinctive economic model, see Woo, *Race to the Swift*. Chibber, *Locked in Place*, makes some interesting comparisons between South Korea and India, where the state had fewer means of controlling the business class. A key difference between Zakaria and these political econo-mists is that Zakaria more bluntly argues that developmental states laid the basis for future democracy. Johnson and Woo do not advance such claims, partially because their work was published before democratization in South Korea and Taiwan had fully occurred.

13 See, e.g., Halperin et al., *The Democracy Advantage*, which argues that democratic governments are more effective at promoting economic growth than autocratic governments.

14 On Iran and South Vietnam in particular, see Bill, *The Eagle and the Lion*, and Catton, *Diem's Final Failure*.

15 Westad, *The Global Cold War*, 404.

16 De Certeau, *The Practice of Everyday Life*, xiii. For a more detailed account of Korean historical development and the influence of these ideologies, see Eckert et al., *Korea Old and New*, which remains the most efficient survey of Korean history in the English language. Deuchler, *The Confucian Transformation of Korea*, is also interesting on this point because it shows how Koreans adapted Con-

fucianism to their own sociocultural needs. For the idea of Korea as a dolphin, I am indebted to Katy Kongdan Oh.

17 Cumings, *Korea's Place in the Sun*, 162–74.

Chapter 1

1 Tilly, *Coercion, Capital, and European States*, 99. The analysis in the preceding paragraph draws heavily on pp. 99–103 of this book.

2 A good, brief summary of these events can be found in Eckert et al., *Korea Old and New*, 327–39.

3 There is a substantial literature on Japanese colonial exploitation of Korea. A good starting point is Shin and Robinson, *Colonial Modernity in Korea*. See also Eckert, *Offspring of Empire*.

4 Cumings, *Origins of the Korean War*, vols. 1 and 2.

5 Quoted in "United Nations Temporary Committee on Korea: Sub-Committee 2, Verbatim Record of the Sixteenth Meeting," 7 February 1948, RG 319, entry 153, Plans and Operations Decimal File, box 88, NA.

6 Quoted in Cumings, *Origins of the Korean War*, 1:153.

7 Historians have disputed the character of the KDP. Bruce Cumings emphasizes the presence of collaborators in the organization. See Cumings, *Origins of the Korean War*, 1:151–58. Others such as Allan Millett acknowledged the presence of collaborators but have depicted the KDP in a more favorable light. See Millett, *The War for Korea*, 47–48.

8 For detailed coverage of U.S. campaigns to eliminate the People's Committees, see Cumings, *Origins of the Korean War*, 1:293–350.

9 Before the fall of 1946 Americans occupied the top posts. After December 1946 Koreans were appointed and Americans were retained as advisers.

10 Millett describes some of this in *The War for Korea*, 116–17.

11 Cumings, *Origins of the Korean War*, 1:188–93.

12 Stueck, *The Korean War*, 24–25.

13 "Intimate Report on Rhee Syngman," 9 February 1948, RG 59, CDF 1945–49, 895.00/2-948, NA.

14 "The Composition of the Present Korean Government," 24 March 1949, RG 59, CDF 1945–49, 895.01/3-2449, NA.

15 On this point, see Tilly, "Reflections on the History of European State Making" and "Food Supply and Public Order in Modern Europe," in *Formation of National States in Western Europe*, 71–73, 400–409. According to Tilly, this process occurred between 1500 and 1800.

16 These points are mostly derived from Cumings, *Origins of the Korean War*, 1:41–67.

17 McCune, *Korea Today*, 129, 132–33.

18 Ibid., 129–33.

19 Ibid., 137–39; Pak Myŏngnim, *Han'guk chŏnjaeng ŭi palbal kwa kiwŏn*, 486–87.

20 Pak Myŏngnim, *Han'guk chŏnjaeng ŭi palbal kwa kiwŏn*, 492–94.

21 This has become an almost standard assertion among American scholars. See, e.g., McCune, *Korea Today*, 134–35; Cumings, *Korea's Place in the Sun*, 270; and Lie, *Han Unbound*, 9–10.

22 See, e.g., "Annual Economic Report, Republic of Korea, 1949," RG 469, box 21, NA. The report states that as of January 1950 the reforms had still not been implemented, though it notes the possibility that they would be carried out "within the 'plowing season.'"

23 Pak Myŏngnim, *Han'guk chŏnjaeng ŭi palbal kwa kiwŏn*, 456, 503–9.

24 Lie, *Han Unbound*, 11–12.

25 On the effects of land reform on landlord political power, see Ch'oe Pongdae, "Nongji kaehyŏk ihu chongch'ijŏg chibae chiptan ŭi hyŏngsŏng."

26 These efforts are described briefly in USAID, "Land Reform in Korea," USAIDL.

27 "Comments on the Present Economic Situation," RG 469, box 17, NA.

28 Quoted in Pak Myŏngnim, *Han'guk chŏnjaeng ŭi palbal kwa kiwŏn*, 515–16.

29 Ibid., 495–96.

30 Ki Hyuk Pak, "Economic Effects of Farmland," in Brown and Lin, *Land Reform in Developing Countries*, 100–126. This essay views the reforms as beneficial to long-term development but notes that the small size of landholdings lowered overall productivity.

31 Tilly, "Reflections on the History of European State-Making," 42, 74.

32 Oh, *Korean Politics*, 31–37, has a good summary of these events.

33 "Political Summary for March, 1949," RG 59, CDF 1945–49, 895.00/4-1849, NA.

34 "Brief History of U.S. Military Assistance to the Republic of Korea," Truman Papers, WHCF, box 25, HSTL.

35 Cumings, *Korea's Place in the Sun*, 217–24, 243–47.

36 "Brief History of U.S. Military Assistance to the Republic of Korea," Truman Papers, WHCF, box 25, HSTL; "A Memorandum concerning United States Political Objectives in Korea," 30 November 1950, RG 59, CDF 795.00/12-150, NA.

37 "Inflationary Implications of E.C.A. Program in Korea," 22 December 1949, RG 469, box 17, NA.

38 Oh, *Korean Politics*, 36–37; Lie, *Han Unbound*, 30. On the NSL and the impact of war and the military on South Korea's social structure, see Shin, "Effects of the Korean War on Social Structures," 133–39.

39 "A Memorandum concerning United States Political Objectives in Korea," 30 November 1950, RG 59, CDF 795.00/12-150, NA.

40 John Muccio to Dean Acheson, 13 June 1949, RG 59, CDF 895.00/6-1349, NA.

41 William Stueck (*Rethinking the Korean War*, 181) notes that although frictions on

the peninsula remained once the armistice was signed, conditions surrounding the armistice made a "repeat performance" of the war unlikely.

42 A vast literature exists on the activities of American forces in the Korean War, including Hastings, *The Korean War*; Blair, *The Forgotten War*; and Toland and Blakemore, *In Mortal Combat*. By contrast, no monograph on the U.S. role in building up the ROK military during the war has been published since Sawyer, *Military Advisors in Korea*.

43 One report from the American embassy noted that the ROK government had been "encouraged" by the belief in the United States that the expansion of the South Korean military was in the U.S. interest. See John Muccio to Dean Acheson, 15 January 1953, VFP, box 86, GCML.

44 "Current ROKA Budgetary Developments," 17 August 1952, ibid.

45 Van Fleet to Commander in Chief Far East, April 1952, ibid.

46 Clark to Omar Bradley, 13 December 1952, ibid.

47 Pak Myŏngnim, *Han'guk 1950*, 351–54.

48 Oh, *Korean Politics*, 38–40.

49 Lightner, Oral History Interview, HSTL.

50 Lightner to Director of the Office of Northeast Asian Affairs, 5 June 1952, *FRUS, 1952–1954*, 15:305–8.

51 Acheson to John Muccio, 4 June 1952, *FRUS, 1952–1954*, 15:302–4.

52 Yong-Pyo Hong, *State Security and Regime Security*, 71–79. For the text of the agreement, see "The Acting Secretary of State to the Embassy in Korea," 11 September 1954, *FRUS, 1952–1954*, 15(2):1875–82.

53 "Fairless Group Briefing," 29 January 1957, Records of the U.S. President's Citizen Advisers on the Mutual Security Program, box 15, DDEL.

54 "Situation and Short-term Prospects of the Republic of Korea," 21 November 1957, RG 59, CDF 1955–59, 795b.00/11-2157, NA.

55 "Report on the Counter-Subversive Capacity of the Republic of Korea," *FRUS, 1955–1957*, 23(2):74–75.

56 Se-Jin Kim, *Politics of Military Revolution in Korea*, 73–74.

57 On 15 July 1950 Rhee wrote a letter formally placing all ROK forces under the operational control of the UN Command. See "General Approach to and Possible Active Steps to Meet the Korean Internal Political Crisis," *FRUS, 1952–1954*, 15:336.

58 Yong-Pyo Hong, *State Security and Regime Security*, 24–31, 88–95.

59 Walter Robertson to Herbert Hoover Jr., 9 November 1955, *FRUS, 1955–1957*, 23(2):180–81.

60 "Discussion of the 334th Meeting of the National Security Council," 8 August 1957, DDE Papers, NSC Series, box 9, DDEL.

61 McCune, *Korea Today*, 38–40, 52–56, 114–15, 140–41.

62 UN Command, Office of the Economic Coordinator for Korea, *Stabilization and Program Progress*, 11, 74.

63 Millett, *The War for Korea*, 130–31; Mason et al., *Economic and Social Reconstruction of the Republic of Korea*, 167–80.

64 MacDonald, *U.S.-Korean Relations from Liberation to Self-Reliance*, 238–42.

65 UN Command, Office of the Economic Coordinator for Korea, "Organizations, Problems, Programs," Records of the U.S. President's Citizen Advisers on the Mutual Security Program, box 15, DDEL.

66 Arndt, *Economic Development*, 57–60.

67 Henry Tasca, "Strengthening the Korean Economy: A Report to the President," 15 June 1953, WHO, NSC Staff Papers, Disaster File, box 60, DDEL.

68 Robert R. Nathan Associates, *An Economic Programme for Korean Reconstruction*, xxiii.

69 Henry Tasca, "Strengthening the Korean Economy: A Report to the President," 15 June 1953, WHO, NSC Staff Papers, Disaster File, box 60, DDEL.

70 Robert R. Nathan Associates, *An Economic Programme for Korean Reconstruction*, 210.

71 "Observations of Agricultural and Fishing Conditions in South Korea, May and June 1957," 21 June 1957, RG 59, CDF 1955–59, 895b.00/6-2157, NA; Seoul to Secretary of State, 12 August 1957, RG 59, CDF 1955–59, 895b.00/8-1257, NA.

72 Edwin Cronk, Oral History Interview, in Bentley and Warner, *Frontline Diplomacy*.

73 "Annual Economic Review, ROK, 1956," RG 59, CDF 1955–59, 895b.00/5-2157, NA.

74 Woo, *Race to the Swift*, 63–64.

75 Edwin Cronk, Oral History Interview, in Bentley and Warner, *Frontline Diplomacy*.

76 "Annual Economic Review, ROK, 1956," RG 59, CDF 1955–59, 895b.00/5-2157, NA.

77 Rhee to Eisenhower, 29 December 1954, DDE Papers, International Series, box 37, DDEL.

78 Rhee to Walter Robertson, 1 August 1955, *FRUS, 1955–1957*, 22(2):131–33.

79 UN, Office of the Economic Coordinator for Korea, "Organizations, Problems, Programs," Records of the U.S. President's Citizen Advisers on the Mutual Security Program, box 15, DDEL.

80 Ibid.; UN Command, Office of the Economic Coordinator for Korea, *Stabilization and Program Progress*, 133–35.

81 *New York Times*, 9 November 1953.

82 Dennis Fitzgerald, Oral History Interview, DDEL.

83 O Wŏnch'ŏl, *Han'guk hyŏng kyŏngje kŏnsŏl*, 1:138–41.

84 Quoted in MacDonald, *U.S.-Korean Relations from Liberation to Self-Reliance*, 269.

85 Lie, *Han Unbound*, 33–34.

86 Quoted in MacDonald, *U.S.-Korean Relations from Liberation to Self-Reliance*, 255.

87 Cronk, Oral History Interview, in Bentley and Warner, *Frontline Diplomacy*.

Chapter 2

1　Seth, *Education Fever*, 21–26.

2　"Education in Korea: The Situation and Some of the Problems," 28 August 1947, RG 554, box 36, NA.

3　Seth, *Education Fever*, 37–38.

4　History of the Occupation of Korea, pt. III, chap. 9, file 8-5.1 BA, CMH.

5　Seth, *Education Fever*, 45–56.

6　"Activities of the American Advisory Staff since the Advent of the New Korean Government," RG 554, box 36, NA.

7　Korean Civil Assistance Command, *United Nations Command: Civil Assistance and Economic Affairs—Korea*, annual reports for 1 July 1952–30 June 1953, pp. 20–21; for 1 July 1953–30 June 1954, pp. 49–50; and for 1 July 1954–30 June 1955, pp. 54–55.

8　The American-Korean Foundation's annual reports from 1957 to 1959 list some of the schools that the foundation assisted.

9　"Help on Wheels," *Time*, 17 May 1954.

10　Korea Civil Assistance Command, *United Nations Command Civil Assistance and Economic Affairs—Korea, 1 July 1954–30 June 1955*, 54.

11　UN Command, Office of the Economic Coordinator for Korea, *Stabilization and Program Progress*, 97–98.

12　Im Taesik, "1950 nyŏndae miguk ŭi kyoyuk wŏnjo wa ch'inmi ellit'ŭ ŭi hyŏng-sŏng," 144–46.

13　"Progress 1959: United States—Korea Cooperation," booklet, SNUA; ROK, Ministry of Education, *Rebuilding Secondary Education in the Republic of Korea*.

14　"Rebuilding Education in the Republic of Korea," February 1953, 7, UNKRA Records, ROAG 2/5, box 15, UNA.

15　Ibid., 19.

16　Ibid., 21.

17　Ibid.

18　See "Progress in Educational Instruction under UNKRA" and "Monthly Activities Report for May, 1955" both in UNKRA Records, ROAG 2/3.1, box 45, and "UNESCO Report Recommendations," UNKRA Records, ROAG 2/5, box 170, UNA.

19　"UNESCO Report Recommendations," UNKRA Records, ROAG 2/5, box 170, UNA.

20　"George Peabody College for Teachers, Korea Project—Improvement of Teacher Training, Semi-Annual Report, March 1 through August 28 1959," SNUA.

21　Ibid.

22　Ibid. In a typical year 1,500 South Korean educators participated in the Peabody workshops.

23　Ibid.

24　Hŏ Hyŏn, "Kyoyuk mogchoke taehan hana ŭi koch'al [My Reflections on the Purpose of Education]," *Kyoyuk munhwa*, October 1954, 68–69.

25 Sŏng Naeun, "Pundan sidae ŭi hanmi kyoyuk kyoryu," 207–9.

26 Seth, *Education Fever*, 55.

27 Edman, *Primary Teachers of Korea Look at Themselves*, 79, 82–83, 100–101.

28 Korea Civil Assistance Command, *United Nations Command, Civil Assistance and Economic Affairs—Korea, 1 July 1954–30 June 1955*, 55–56.

29 See Han Man'gil, "1950 nyŏndae minjujuŭi kyoyuk ŭi sŏnggyŏk," 168–69.

30 "Kim Chŏnggang," in Han'guk chŏngsin munhwa yŏn'guwŏn, *Nae ka kyŏkkŭn minju wa tokchae*, 31–32.

31 "Yun sik," in ibid., 165–66.

32 Henderson, *Korea*, 170–72.

33 Schmid, *Korea between Empires*.

34 On the developments of mass media in Korea during the Japanese colonial period, see Robinson, "Mass Media and Popular Culture in 1930s Korea."

35 See "Sinmun yongjibul silsuyoja e paejŏng [The Supply of Newsprint to Users]," *Han'guk sinmun p'yŏnjibin hyŏphoebo*, 13 August 1957.

36 UNKRA, *Reports of the Agent General*, 1 July 1957 to 30 June 1958, UN General Assembly, Official Records, 13th session, supp. no. 16, 3.

37 Im Taesik, "1950 nyŏndae miguk ŭi kyoyuk wŏnjo wa ch'inmi ellit'u ŭi hyŏng-sŏng," 144, 150–52. The agency was known as USIS abroad but USIA stateside to distinguish it from the U.S. Immigration Service (USIS).

38 Henderson, *Korea*, 172–73.

39 "Cultural Projects: Progress Report," 7 July 1952, RG 59, CDF 1950–54, 511.95b/7-752, NA.

40 Im Taesik, "1950 nyŏndae miguk ŭi kyoyuk wŏnjo wa ch'inmi ellit'u ŭi hyŏng-sŏng," 179–81.

41 "Educational Exchange: Prospectus Call, Fiscal Year 1956," RG 59, CDF 1955–59, 511.95b3/6-155, NA.

42 "Educational Exchange: FY 1958 Foreign Specialists Group Project in Journalism," 10 March 1958, RG 59, CDF 1955-59, 511.95b3/3-1058, NA.

43 Ibid.

44 Kwanhun k'ŭllŏp, *Kwanhun k'ŭllŏp sasimnyŏnsa*, 17–18; "Educational and Cultural Exchange: Exchange Program Report FY 1963," 22 April 1964, RG 59, Bureau of Cultural Affairs, Planning and Development, Staff Country Files, 1955–64, box 220, NA.

45 "Educational and Cultural Exchange: Exchange Program Report FY 1963," 22 April 1964, RG 59, Bureau of Cultural Affairs, Planning and Development, Staff Country Files, 1955–64, box 220, NA.

46 Ibid.

47 Country Assessment Report, 25 January 1960, RG 306, USIA Records, Foreign Service Dispatches, 1954–65, box 1, NA.

48 "Educational Exchange: Leader FY 55, Kim Chang-chip," 29 October 1956, RG 59, CDF 1955–59, 511.95a3/10-2956, NA.

49 Kwanhun k'ŭllŏp, *Kwanhun k'ŭllŏp sasimnyŏnsa*, 15–20.

50 "Im Panghyŏn," in Han'guk chŏngsin munhwa yŏn'guwŏn, *Nae ka kyŏkkŭn han'guk chŏnjaeng kwa Pak Chŏnghŭi chŏngbu*, 343–44.

51 Kwanhun k'ŭllŏp, *Kwanhun k'ŭllŏp sasimnyŏnsa*, 16–17.

52 Ibid., 15–81.

53 For a complete list of articles that appeared in the journal, see ibid., 361–62. See also p. 61.

54 See, e.g., "Educational Exchange: FY 1958 Foreign Specialists Group Project in Journalism," 10 March 1958, RG 59, CDF 1955–59, 511.95b3/3-1058, NA.

55 "Ŏllon ŭi chayu was ch'aegim [The Freedom and Responsibility of the Press]," *Han'guk sinmun p'yŏnjibin hyŏphoebo*, 13 August 1957.

56 Kim P'albong, "Munhakin ŭi sahoejŏk palŏn: muŏshŭl hal kŏshin'ga? [The Testimony of a Scholar: What Is to Be Done?]," *Sasanggye*, December 1957, 104–13.

57 *Kyŏnghyang Sinmun*, 11 January 1959.

58 Henderson, *Korea*, 172–73.

59 Memorandum of Conversation, 3 June 1959, *FRUS, 1958–1960*, 18:556–58.

60 "Educational Exchange: Fiscal Year 1960 Country Program Proposal," 28 July 1958, RG 59, CDF 1955–59, 511.95b3/7-2858, NA.

61 "Country Assessment Report," 25 January 1960, RG 306, USIA Records, Foreign Service Dispatches, 1954–65, box 1, NA.

62 MacCorkle, "The Birth of a School," Materials relating to the Minnesota Contract, SNUA.

63 David Kang, *Crony Capitalism*, 71.

64 "Educational Exchange: Prospectus Call, Fiscal Year 1956," RG 59, CDF 1955–59, 511.95b3/6-155, NA.

65 "Educational Exchange: Fiscal Year 1960 Country Program Proposal," 7 July 1958, RG 59, CDF 1955–59, 511.95b3/7-2858, NA.

66 "Educational Exchange: FY 57 Leaders—City Mayors," 30 April 1957, RG 59, CDF 1955–59, 511.95b3/4-3057, NA.

67 Ibid.

68 Pak Haejŏng. "Nae ga pon miguk ŭi insang [My Impressions of America]," *Kukhoebo*, July 1957, 38–41.

69 "America as I Saw It," WHCF, General Files, box 821, DDEL. The word "Freedom" was capitalized and underlined in the original manuscript.

70 This course is described in Song, *Hoenam Song Insang hoegorok*, 128–32.

71 Ibid., 128–33.

72 Ibid, 136, 143–44.

73 Ibid., 143–44.

74 Ibid, 195–204. See also Taegyun Pak, "1956–1964 Han'guk kyŏngje kaebal kyehoek ŭi sŏngnip kwajŏng," 150–58.

75 Song, *Hoenam Song Insang hoegorok*, 87, 155–57. The "Mutual Security Agree-

ment" was used to refer to the Mutual Defense Treaty signed by the United States and South Korea in October 1953 and the subsequent "Agreed Minute" of September 1954.

76 Ibid., 157–59.

77 Ibid., 200–202, 210–13, 220–22.

78 Cronk, Oral History Interview, in Bentley and Warner, *Frontline Diplomacy*.

79 Yi Kihong, *Kyŏngje kŭndaehwa ŭi sumŭn iyagi*, 226–29.

80 Ibid., 184–201.

81 Yi Hanbin, *Ilhamyŏ saenggakhamyŏ*, 106–7.

82 Ibid., 79.

83 David Kang, *Crony Capitalism*, 69–70.

84 Landers, *Technical Assistance in Public Administration*, 43–44.

85 "Kim Yonggap," in Maeil kyŏngje sinmunsa, *Na ŭi yuhak sijŏl*, 74–128.

86 The University Club is described in Yi Kihong, *Kyŏngje kŭndaehwa ŭi sumŭn iyagi*, 224–26.

87 Stuart MacCorkle, "The Birth of a School," Materials relating to the Minnesota Contract, SNUA.

88 Woon-Tai Kim, "Administrative Structure and Practices in the Government of Korea," 175–77. The text gives the proper romanization of Kim's name.

89 Stuart MacCorkle, "The Birth of a School," Materials relating to the Minnesota Contract, SNUA.

90 Landers, *Technical Assistance in Public Administration*, 191–98; Hak Chong Lee, "American Role in the Development of Management Education," in Moskowitz, *From Patron to Partner*, 181–82.

91 Yu's reflections can be found in Koryŏ taehakkyo kiŏp kyŏngyŏng yŏnguwŏn, *Kodae kiyŏn sasimnyŏnsa*, 233–34.

Chapter 3

1 Kyung-Moon Hwang, "Bureaucracy in the Transition to Korean Modernity," 281–91.

2 Quoted in Cumings, *Korea's Place in the Sun*, 200.

3 Headquarters Provisional Military Advisory Group, "History of Department of Internal Security to 1 July 1948," RG 319, box 1, NA.

4 Millett, *The War for Korea*, 78–79.

5 "Paek Namgwŏn," in Han'guk chŏngsin munhwa yŏn'guwŏn, *Nae ka kyŏkkŭn haebang kwa bundan*, 185.

6 Cumings, *Origins of the Korean War*, 1:173–75.

7 Chi-op Lee, *Call Me Speedy Lee*, 215–16.

8 Se-Jin Kim, *Politics of Military Revolution in Korea*, 38–39; Chi-op Lee, *Call Me Speedy Lee*, 60–61. The translation of the book spells Yi's name differently from the proper McCune Reischauer romanization.

9 Clemens, "Captain James Hausman"; Millett, "Captain James Hausman."

10 Cho Kapche, *Nae mudŏm e ch'im ŭl paet'ŏra*, 2:236–38.

11 Captain R. D. Connolly, "KMAG," RG 338, Records of the USARPAC Historian, Organizational History Files, box 93, NA; Clemens, "Captain James Hausman," 188–89.

12 Kenneth W. Meyers, "KMAG's Wartime Experiences: 11 July 1951 to 27 July 1953," 206–40, RG 338, box 85, NA.

13 Hausman and Chŏng, *Han'guk taet'ongnyong ŭl umjigin migun taewi*, 160–61.

14 Cho Kapche, *Nae mudŏm e ch'im ŭl paet'ŏra*, 2:179–81.

15 Se-Jin Kim, *Politics of Military Revolution in Korea*, 56.

16 Yi Hallim, *Segye ŭi kyŏngnang*, 59, 113, 139.

17 Ibid., 65–66.

18 Yi Hyŏnggŭn, *Kunbŏn ilbŏn ŭi oegil insaeng*, 28–29.

19 Chi-op Lee, *Call Me Speedy Lee*, 84. Yi has romanized his name as Chi-op Lee, but the proper romanization is Yi Chiŏp.

20 Yi Hyŏnggŭn, *Kunbŏn ilbŏn ŭi oegil insaeng*, 37.

21 Sawyer, *Military Advisors in Korea*, 149–51.

22 Kenneth W. Meyers, "KMAG's Wartime Experiences: 11 July 1951 to 27 July 1953," part IV, chap. I, in RG 338, box 85, NA, contains a narrative of the steady expansion of the Korean army during the war. See also David Curtis Skaggs and Richard Weinert, "American Military Assistance to the Republic of Korea Army, 1951–1965," RG 319, Records of the Office of the Chief of Military History Publications, Unpublished Manuscripts and Supporting Records, 1943–77, KMAG in Peace and War, box 1, NA. According to the appendix to this volume, the ROK Air Force, Navy, and Marines possessed 7,500, 8,200, and 14,800 troops respectively in 1952 and 16,900, 14,300, and 27,100 respectively by 1955.

23 Ridgway to Department of the Army, July 1951, VFP, box 86, GCML.

24 Kenneth W. Meyers, "KMAG's Wartime Experiences: 11 July 1951 to 27 July 1953," part IV, chap. I, 23–27, in RG 338, box 85, NA.

25 Quoted in "The KMAG Advisor," 54, a study conducted by the Operations Research Office, Johns Hopkins University, copy, USAMHI.

26 Quoted in ibid., 41.

27 Quoted in ibid., 23.

28 "Final Report," 19 October 1955, RG 319, Records of the Office of the Chief of Military History Publications, Unpublished Manuscripts and Supporting Records, 1943–77, KMAG in Peace and War, box 8, NA.

29 Yi's recollection appears in Yukkun sagwan hakkyo che p'algisaeng hoe, *Nobyŏng dŭl ui chŭngŏn*, 706–7.

30 In 1952 a U.S. corporal earned an annual salary of $1,559 while an ROK Army corporal was paid just $8. Henry Tasca, "Strengthening the Korean Economy: A Report to the President," 15 June 1953, WHO, NSC Staff Papers, Disaster File, box 60, DDEL.

31 The complaints of numerous American advisers about the practice of stock-piling equipment and selling it on the black market are cited in "The KMAG Advisor," 76–77.

32 Chŏn Uyŏng, *Naemun naemu*, 193.

33 Both quotations are cited in "The KMAG Advisor," 18–19.

34 *Yukkun kyoyuk yŏn'gam*, 1956, 71–73.

35 Ibid., 68.

36 Ibid., 62.

37 Ibid., 57.

38 "Data on the Korean Military Academy," RG 338, Records of the USARPAC Historian, Organizational History Files, box 93, NA.

39 "Korean Military Academy," RG 338, Records of the USARPAC Historian, Organizational History Files, box 93, NA; Yukkun sagwan hakkyo, *Taehan min'guk yukkun sagwan hakkyo osimnyŏnsa*, 135–38.

40 Yukkun sagwan hakkyo, *Taehan min'guk yukkun sagwan hakkyo osimnyŏnsa*, 168–70.

41 "Special Report on the Korean Military Academy," 30 June 1955, RG 319, Records of the Office of the Chief of Military History Publications, Unpublished Manuscripts and Supporting Records, 1943–77, KMAG in Peace and War, box 7, NA.

42 "Korean Military Academy," RG 338, Records of the USARPAC Historian, Organizational History Files, box 93, NA.

43 Yukkun sagwan hakkyo, *Taehan min'guk yukkun sagwan hakkyo osimnyŏnsa*, 142–49.

44 "Korean Military Academy," RG 338, Records of the U.S. Army Commands, Records of the USARPAC Historian, Organizational History Files, box 93.

45 Ibid.

46 "Data on the Korean Military Academy," RG 338, Records of the USARPAC Historian, Organizational History Files, box 93, NA.

47 Ibid.

48 *Yuksa sinmun* [KMA Newspaper], 31 October 1956.

49 "Korean Military Academy," RG 338, Records of the USARPAC Historian, Organizational History Files, box 93, NA.

50 One such competition was reported in *Yuksa sinmun*, 31 October 1956.

51 David Curtis Skaggs and Richard Weinert, "American Military Assistance to the Republic of Korea Army, 1951–1965," chap. X, 19–23, RG 319, Records of the Office of the Chief of Military History Publications, Unpublished Manuscripts and Supporting Records, 1943–77, KMAG in Peace and War, box 1, NA; John Lovell, "The Military as an Instrument of Development in South Korea," in Nahm, *Korea and the New Order in East Asia*, 19.

52 Henderson, *Korea*, 354.

53 Lovell, "The Military as an Instrument of Development in South Korea," 19.

54 David Holovorsen, "National Defense College," *Korean Survey*, April 1957, 10–11;

"The National Defense College of the Republic of Korea," RG 319, Records of the Office of the Chief of Military History Publications, Unpublished Manuscripts and Supporting Records, 1943–77, KMAG in Peace and War, box 8, NA.

55 "The National Defense College of the Republic of Korea," RG 319, Records of the Office of the Chief of Military History Publications, Unpublished Manuscripts and Supporting Records, 1943–77, KMAG in Peace and War, box 8, NA.

56 "Status of Training of the ROK Forces," RG 319, box 11, NA.

57 David Curtis Skaggs and Richard Weinert, "American Military Assistance to the Republic of Korea Army, 1951–1965," chap. X, 19–20, RG 319, Records of the Office of the Chief of Military History Publications, Unpublished Manuscripts and Supporting Records, 1943–77, KMAG in Peace and War, box 1, NA.

58 Kenneth W. Meyers, "KMAG's Wartime Experiences: 11 July 1951 to 27 July 1953," 180.

59 Numerous South Korean officers have described this aspect of their training in the United States. See, e.g., an account of some of the military officers who were close to South Korea's future president Park Chung Hee in Cho Kapche, *Nae mudŏm e ch'im ŭl paet'ŏra*, 3:71.

60 "Instructor Training for Korean Military Academy," 19 March 1956, RG 319, box 8, NA.

61 Quoted in Kenneth W. Meyers, "KMAG's Wartime Experiences: 11 July 1951 to 27 July 1953," 180–81.

62 David Curtis Skaggs and Richard Weinert, "American Military Assistance to the Republic of Korea Army, 1951–1965," chap. X, 20–25, RG 319, Records of the Office of the Chief of Military History Publications, Unpublished Manuscripts and Supporting Records, 1943–77, KMAG in Peace and War, box 1, NA.

63 Quoted in Millett, *The War for Korea*, 67. Millett romanizes Yi's name as Lee Tong-hui.

64 "Han Muhyŏp," in Han'guk chŏngsin munhwa yŏn'guwŏn, *Nae ka kyŏkkŭn han'guk chŏnjaeng kwa Pak Chŏnghŭi chŏngbu*, 141–42.

65 *Yuksa sinmun*, 26 September 1958.

66 *Yuksa sinmun*, 30 March 1959.

67 "Song Yoch'an," in Hŭimang ch'ulp'ansa, *Sasil ŭi chŏnbu rŭl kisul handa*, 466.

68 Yi Kwangho, "Tomi yuhak changgyo tanwŏn ŭi pogo [Report of the Group of Generals Studying in the United States]," *Kukpang*, June/July 1953, 209.

69 Chŏn Chehyŏn, *Pogyŏl insaeng*, 44.

70 "Pak Kyŏngwŏn," in Han'guk chŏngsin munhwa yŏn'guwŏn, *Nae ka kyŏkkŭn haebang kwa bundan*, 254.

71 *Yuksa sinmun*, 31 October 1956.

72 Sim Hŭngsŏn, "Kukkun kyoyuk i chihyanghal mokp'yo [Aims of Armed Forces Training and Education]," *Kukpang yŏn'gu*, June 1959, 169–70.

73 Cho Kapche, *Nae mudŏm e ch'im ŭl paet'ŏra*, 3:75.

74 Pak Chŏngin, *P'ungun ŭi pyŏl*, 266–67.

75 Quoted in *Yuksa sinmun*, 30 March 1959.

76 Cho Kapche, *Nae mudŏm e ch'im ŭl paet'ŏra*, 3:69–73.

77 Lacy to U.S. Department of State, *FRUS, 1955–1957*, 27(2):104.

78 "Republic of Korea Army in 1957," FO 371/133692, Public Records Office, Kew, England.

79 "A Study of the U.S. Military Assistance Program in Underdeveloped Areas," Records of the U.S. President's Committee to Study the U.S. Military Assistance Program, box 12, DDEL.

80 "Civic Action—Republic of Korea," 21 September 1961, RG 59, CDF 1960–63, 795B.5-MSP/9-2161, NA.

81 Gen. Carter B. Magruder, Oral History Interview, USAMHI.

82 Yi Hallim, *Segye ŭi kyŏngnang*, 65–66.

83 Se-Jin Kim, *Politics of Military Revolution in Korea*, 56–60.

Chapter 4

1 Operations Coordinating Board, "Outline Plan of Operations with Respect to Korea," WHO, NSC Council Staff Papers, OCB Central Files Series, box 50, DDEL.

2 NSC, "Progress Report on U.S. Policy toward Korea by the Operations Coordinating Board," WHO, NSC Disaster File, box 61, DDEL.

3 "Report on the Counter-Subversive Capacity of the Republic of Korea," *FRUS, 1955–1957*, 23(2):75.

4 "Political and Socio-Political Developments in the Republic of Korea," 13 February 1958, RG 59, CDF 1955–59, 795b.00/2-1358, NA.

5 "Provisional Intelligence Report: Economic Rehabilitation of North Korea, 1954–1956," CREST Database, NA.

6 Rostow, *The Stages of Economic Growth*, 26, 30.

7 The telegram written by the chargé d'affaires at the American embassy in Seoul is quoted in Nes to J. Graham Parsons, *FRUS, 1955–1957*, 23(2):291.

8 "Political and Socio-Political Developments in the Republic of Korea," 13 February 1958, RG 59, CDF 1955–59, 795b.00/2-1358, NA.

9 According to the UN Command, Office of the Economic Coordinator for Korea, *Stabilization and Program Progress*, as of 1958 the CEB had held 95 of its 111 meetings after 1956.

10 Dowling to Robertson, 23 January 1959, *FRUS, 1958–1960*, 28:534–40.

11 Parsons to Christian Herter, 22 October 1958, *FRUS, 1958–1960*, 28:589–94.

12 Henderson, *Korea*, 174.

13 Ibid., 174–76.

14 "Chwadamhŏe: Nohan saja dŭl ŭi chungŏn [Roundtable: The Testimony of the Angry Lions]," *Sasanggye*, June 1960, 47. This article provides an interesting glimpse of the outlook of several student leaders of the April 19 Revolution shortly after they ousted Rhee's regime.

15 Ibid., 48.

16 Ibid., 49.

17 Henderson, *Korea*, 180–81.

18 Ibid., 179; Cumings, *Korea's Place in the Sun*, 344–45.

19 Seuk-Ryule Hong, "Reunification Issues and Civil Society in South Korea," 1251–53.

20 Henderson, *Korea*, 180–81.

21 The famous quotation comes from James Madison, *The Federalist*, no. 51, in Rossiter, *The Federalist Papers*.

22 Dillon to American Embassy, Seoul, 5 May 1960, *FRUS, 1958–1960*, 28:656–57.

23 Dillon to American Embassy, Seoul, 11 June 1960, *FRUS, 1958–1960*, 28:665–67.

24 McConaughy to U.S. Department of State, 3 July 1960, *FRUS, 1958–1960*, 28:673–74.

25 Parsons to McConaughy, 12 April 1960, *FRUS, 1958–1960*, 28:682–83.

26 McConaughy to Christian Herter, 24 December 1960, RG 59, CDF 1960–63, box 2181, NA.

27 McConaughy to U.S. Department of State, 11 April 1961, *FRUS, 1961–1963*, 22:442–47.

28 "The Situation in Korea, February, 1961," NSF box 127, JFKL.

29 "Special National Intelligence Estimate," 21 March 1961, *FRUS, 1961–1963*, 22:442–47.

30 Henderson, *Korea*, 182. CIA reports from late April 1961 demonstrate awareness of rumors that a coup would occur and knowledge of the coup's potential leadership. They also report that Chang was made aware of these rumors. See Dulles to Kennedy, 16 May 1961, in *FRUS, 1961–1963*, 22:456–57, which includes paragraphs of reports prepared in late April.

31 Cho Kapche, *Nae mudŏm e ch'im ŭl paet'ŏra*, 2:132–35.

32 Ibid., 174–209.

33 Ibid., 216–40.

34 Pak Myŏngnim, *Han'guk chŏnjaeng ŭi palbal kwa kiwŏn*, 429.

35 Quoted in Cho Kapche, *Nae mudŏm e ch'im ŭl paet'ŏra*, 3:229.

36 Ibid., 248–59.

37 "[Gen. Carter B.] Magruder to the Joint Chiefs of Staff," 16 May 1961, *FRUS, 1961–1963*, 22:449–51.

38 Henderson, *Korea*, 182–83.

39 On this point, see Cumings, *Korea's Place in the Sun*, 351–52.

40 See some of the views expressed in "Chwadamhoe: Miguk yuhaksaeng dŭl ŭi pon choguk ŭi p'yŏnmo," *Sasanggye*, November 1961.

41 Park Chung Hee, *Our Nation's Path*, 28. The Yi Dynasty had ruled Korea from 1392 until 1910, when the country was annexed by the Japanese.

42 Ibid., 80–81.

43 Ibid., 96.

44 Park Chung Hee, *The Country, The Revolution and I*, 153–55.

45 Marshall Green, Oral History Interview, in Bentley and Warner, *Frontline Diplomacy*.

46 Chester Bowles to American Embassy, Seoul, 16 May 1961, *FRUS, 1961–1963*, 22:455.

47 Marshall Green, Oral History Interview, in Bentley and Warner, *Frontline Diplomacy*.

48 Special National Intelligence Estimate, 31 May 1961, *FRUS, 1961–1963*, 22:468–69.

49 Samuel Berger to Dean Rusk, 28 October 1961, *FRUS, 1961–1963*, 22:522–26.

50 Berger to Rusk, 15 December 1961, *FRUS, 1961–1963*, 22:543; Berger to Rusk, 25 July 1961, NSF box 128, JFKL.

51 Robert H. Johnson to NSC Staff, 6 June 1961, *FRUS, 1961–1963*, 22:470.

52 For documents pertaining to these meetings, see *FRUS, 1961–1963*, 22:529–41. These meetings are discussed in more detail in the next chapter.

53 Halberstam, *The Best and the Brightest*, 39.

54 Dean, "Masculinity as Ideology," 49–50.

55 Marshall Green, Oral History Interview, in Bentley and Warner, *Frontline Diplomacy*.

56 Memorandum of Conversation, 24 July 1961, *FRUS, 1961–1963*, 22:585–87.

57 Rostow to Sorenson and Goodwin, 19 March 1961, NSF box 325, JFKL.

58 U.S. House, Committee on International Relations, "Hearings on Korean American Relations: Part 6," 95th Cong., 2nd sess., 54.

59 "Today's Korean Situation that Concerns the American Tax Payers," Kim Dongsŏng t'ŭksa miguk pangmun [Kim Dongsŏng's Visit to the United States], file 724.41US, Oegyo anbo yŏn'guwŏn.

60 Address of Senator John F. Kennedy Accepting the Democratic Party Nomination for the Presidency of the United States, http://www.cs.umb.edu/jfklibrary/jo71560.htm.

61 "Notes of the 485th Meeting of the National Security Council," 13 June 1961, *FRUS, 1961–63*, 22:480–81.

62 Berger to Rusk, 15 December 1961, *FRUS, 1961–1963*, 22:542–48.

63 "Vice President's Greetings at the Airport," NSF box 128, JFKL.

64 Richard A. Ericson, Oral History Interview, in Bentley and Warner, *Frontline Diplomacy*.

Chapter 5

1 Berger to U.S. Department of State, 23 July 1962, *FRUS, 1961–1963*, 22:581–85.

2 Rusk to American Embassy, Seoul, 5 August 1962, *FRUS, 1961–1963*, 22:591–95.

3 Ibid.

4 "United States Economic Assistance to the Republic of Korea, 1954–1973: Fact Book," USAIDL.

5 "Report of the Korea Task Force," 5 June 1961, NSF box 127, JFKL.

6   Ibid.

7   Memorandum of Conversation, 16 November 1961, NSF box 127, JFKL.

8   "Chairman Park's Call on the Secretary of Commerce," 15 November 1961, RG 59, CDF 1960–63, 795B.00/11-261, NA.

9   ROK, *Summary of the First Five-Year Economic Plan 1962–1966*, 24–29, 48–49.

10 "Country Assistance Program: Korea, FY 1966, Part III," USAIDL.

11 Kuznets, "Korea's Five-Year Plans." 47–48; Woo, *Race to the Swift*, 81–83.

12 Yu Wŏnsik, "Hyŏngmyŏng chŏngbu wa kyŏlbyŏlhada [My Departure from the Revolutionary Government]," *Chŏnggyŏng munhwa*, October 1983, 127–30.

13 American Embassy, Seoul, to U.S. Department of State, 15 July 1963, *FRUS, 1961–1963*, 22:652–56.

14 Kuznets, "Korea's Five-Year Plans," 47–48; Woo, *Race to the Swift*, 81–83.

15 An excellent analysis of this subject is provided in Pak Taegyun, "1956–1964 nyŏn han'guk kyŏngje kaebal kyehwŏek ŭi sŏngnip kwajŏng," 195–96.

16 Berger to U.S. Department of State, 27 July 1961, *FRUS, 1961–1963*, 22:589.

17 For the immediate U.S. reaction to the elections, see Berger to U.S. Department of State, 16 October 1963, *FRUS, 1961–1963*, 22:665–66.

18 Komer to Kennedy, 23 April 1962, *FRUS, 1961–1963*, 22:556–57.

19 "Memorandum Prepared in the Department of State," 17 May 1962, *FRUS, 1961–1963*, 22:567–68.

20 Editorial Note (first quotation) and Berger to Dean Rusk, 3 June 1964 (second quotation), *FRUS, 1964–1968*, 29(1):24, 26–28.

21 Komer to Walt Rostow, 3 June 1964, *FRUS, 1964–1968*, 29(1):25.

22 Berger to U.S. Department of State, 3 June 1964, *FRUS, 1964–1968*, 29(1):26–28.

23 Berger to U.S. Department of State, 6 June 1964, *FRUS, 1964–1968*, 29(1):31–34.

24 Ibid., 38–40.

25 Reischauer to Walt Rostow, 21 August 1964, *FRUS, 1964–1968*, 29(1):768.

26 Brown to U.S. Department of State, 23 November 1964, *FRUS, 1964–1968*, 29(1):779–80.

27 Brown to U.S. Department of State, 8 April 1965, *FRUS, 1964–1968*, 29(1):788–89.

28 Memorandum of Conversation, 18 May 1965, *FRUS, 1964–1968*, 29(1):101–5.

29 Brown to U.S. Department of State, 8 April 1965, *FRUS, 1964–1968*, 29(1):793–94.

30 Editorial Note, *FRUS, 1964–1968*, 29(1):796. The note quotes a document that remains classified. The author has requested that the document be declassified under the Freedom of Information Act.

31 Yi Tongwŏn, *Taet'ongnyŏng ŭl kŭrimyŏ*, 104–5, 109–10.

32 Winthrop Brown to U.S. Department of State, 22 January 1965, RG 59, CDF 1964–66, box 1654, NA.

33 Brown to U.S. Department of State, 28 January 1965, RG 59, CDF 1964–66, box 3015, NA.

34 American Embassy, Seoul, to U.S. Department of State, 8 April 1965, *FRUS, 1964–1968*, 29(1):120–21.

35 Brown to U.S. Department of State, 10 July 1965, *FRUS, 1964–1968*, 29(1):121–22.

36 Ibid.

37 Yi, "Alliance in the Quagmire," 109–10; Editorial Note, *FRUS, 1964–1968*, 29(1):125.

38 Brown to U.S. Department of State, 22 December 1965, *FRUS, 1964–1968*, 29(1):132–34.

39 Yi, "Alliance in the Quagmire," 166.

40 American Embassy, Seoul, to U.S. Department of State, 23 February 1966, *FRUS, 1964–1968*, 29(1):169–70.

41 A list of benefits that the United States offered South Korea in return for its participation in the Vietnam War can be found in American Embassy, Seoul, to U.S. Department of State, 27 January 1966, *FRUS, 1964–1968*, 29(1):156–60.

42 See, e.g., Kim Yongbok, "Hanil kwan'gye waegoktoen milch'ak [Strange Collusion in Japanese-Korean Relations]," in Han'guk chŏngch'i yŏn'guhoe, *Pak Chŏnghŭi rŭl nŏmŏsŏ*.

43 Ibid., 282–86.

44 Yi, "The U.S.-Korean Alliance in the Vietnam War," in Gardner and Gittinger, *International Perspectives on Vietnam*, 160–65; Woo, *Race to the Swift*, 94–97.

45 "Robert R. Nathan, Trip to Korea, June, 1966," RNP. In South Korea, the USAID and USOM were often used interchangeably during the 1960s.

46 Kim Hŭnggi, *Pisa kyŏngje kihŏekwŏn 33nyŏn*, 101–3.

47 Quoted in ibid., 103.

48 U.S. Congress, House Committee on International Relations, *Investigation of Korean-American Relations*, 166.

49 Vincent Brown, Oral History Interview, in Bentley and Warner, *Frontline Diplomacy*.

50 On savings rates and taxation, see Park Chong Kee, "The 1966 Tax Administration Reform, Tax Law Reforms, and Government Saving," in Cho and Kim, *Economic Development in the Republic of Korea*, 146–47, and Kwang Suk Kim, "The Interest-Rate Reform of 1965 and Domestic Saving," in Cho and Kim, *Economic Development in the Republic of Korea*, 247–48.

51 "Country Assistance Program, 1966," RG 286, Office of the Administrator, Office of the Executive Secretary, Regional, and Country Files, 1961–66, box 42, NA.

52 Kwang Suk Kim, "Interest-Rate Reform of 1965 and Domestic Saving," 140.

53 "Multi-Year Strategy Paper," 1965, RG 286, Office of Public Safety, IPS #1, Country Policy Guidance and Background, 1961–67, box 69, NA.

54 Landers, *Technical Assistance in Public Administration*, 137–38; "A Brief History of the Revenue Administration Improvement Effort," 2 May 1967, RG 286, Accession 72-A-3206, box 4, unprocessed records, NA.

55 Kwang Suk Kim, "Interest-Rate Reform of 1965 and Domestic Saving," 144–45.

56 "A Brief History of the Revenue Administration Improvement Effort," 2 May 1967, RG 286, Accession 72-A-3206, box 4, unprocessed records, NA.

57 Park Chong Kee, "1966 Tax Administration Reform, Tax Law Reforms, and Government Saving," 251–61.

58 Kwang Suk Kim, "Interest-Rate Reform of 1965 and Domestic Saving," 149–55.

59 Landers, *Technical Assistance in Public Administration*, 148.

60 Brown to William Bundy, 3 November 1965, RG 59, Bureau of Far Eastern Affairs, Office of the Country Director for Korea, 1952–66, box 2, NA.

61 American Embassy, Seoul, to U.S. Department of State, 6 May 1964, RG 59, CDF 1964–66, box 883, NA.

62 American Embassy, Seoul, to U.S. Department of State, 20 February 1964, RG 59, CDF 1964–66, box 568, NA.

63 Rusk to American Embassy, Seoul, 3 May 1964, RG 59, CDF 1964–66, box 567, NA.

64 "Quarterly Economic Summary—Republic of Korea—April–June, 1964," RG 59, CDF 1964–66, box 735, NA.

65 Good on these points are Woo, *Race to the Swift*, 106–9, and Kwang Suk Kim, "The 1964–1965 Exchange Rate Reform, Export Promotion Measures and Import-Liberalization Program," in Cho and Kim, *Economic Development in the Republic of Korea*, 108–12. Woo is particularly cogent on the reciprocal exchange of benefits between the state and the chaebŏl.

66 "Some Economic Aspects of the 'Preferential Loan' Controversy," 2 April 1965, RG 59, CDF 1964–66, box 882, NA.

67 Ibid.

68 Oh, *Korean Politics*, 62–63.

69 Winthrop Brown to William Bundy, 2 May 1967, *FRUS, 1964–1968*, 29(1):244–52.

70 Ibid.

71 LaFeber, *The American Age*, 638–39.

72 Kim, "Hanmi kwan'gye, chongsok kwa kaltŭng," in Han'guk chŏngch'i yŏn'guhoe, *Pak chŏnghŭi rŭl nŏmŏsŏ*, 333–34.

73 "Korean Economic Performance and U.S. Economic Policy," 28 March 1969, RG 59, CDF 1967–69, box 635, NA.

74 "Administrator's Review of the A.I.D. Program in Korea," 14 October 1965, RG 59, Bureau of Far Eastern Affairs, Office of the Country Director for Korea, box 2, NA.

75 Quoted in Woo, *Race to the Swift*, 99.

76 Kim Hŭnggi, *Pisa kyŏngje kihŏekwŏn 33nyŏn*, 208–10.

77 USAID, "Industrial Development," 24 November 1969, Document No. PD-AAD-435-A1, USAID Development Experience Clearinghouse, USAIDL.

78 Ibid.

79 "Private Enterprise Development," 24 August 1970, Document No. PD-AAD-456-B1, USAID Development Experience Clearinghouse, USAIDL.

80 Ibid.

81 USAID, "Project Budget Submission, FY 1970," USAIDL.

82 "Country Assistance Program: Korea, FY 1964–1965, Part II," USAIDL.

83 I have developed this point in greater detail in Brazinsky, "From Pupil to Model."

84 These economic developments are discussed in great detail in Woo, *Race to the Swift*. Chapters 5 and 6 focus on the late 1960s and the 1970s.

85 For details on the evolution of U.S. economic aid, see "United States Economic Assistance to Korea, 1954–1973: Fact Book," USAIDL. After 1970 South Korea received increases in assistance through Public Law 480, the so-called Food for Peace Act.

86 "Country Assistance Program: Korea, 1967," RG 286, Records of the USAID, Office of the Administrator, Office of the Executive Secretary, Regional and Country Files, 1961–1966, box 42.

87 "Congressional Presentation on Title IX," 26 February 1968, RG 286, Office of Public Safety, IPS #1, General Policy, Guidelines and Background, box 70, NA.

88 Nam, "Labor's Place in South Korea's Development," 430.

89 "Congressional Presentation on Title IX," 26 February 1968, RG 286, Office of Public Safety, IPS #1, General Policy, Guidelines and Background, box 70, NA.

90 USAID, "Asia Free Labor Union Development," Document No. PD-AAF-258-B1, USAID Development Experience Clearinghouse, USAIDL.

91 As an Asia Foundation representative in Seoul, David Steinberg did a lot of interesting research on this problem. One of his papers on the issue can be found in RG 59, CDF 1967–69, box 481, NA.

92 "Promotion and Utilization of Democratic Institutions for Development," 6 March 1967, RG 59, CDF 1967–69, box 481, NA. Asia Foundation activities are described in this document and in an attached paper by David Steinberg.

93 Ibid.

94 "Intelligence Note: Republic of Korea: Park's Prospects," 3 October 1969, RG 59, CDF 1967–69, box 2279, NA.

95 "The Political Opposition: An Assessment," 11 February 1969, RG 59, CDF 1967–69, box 2278, NA.

96 "Intelligence Note: Republic of Korea: Park's Prospects," 3 October 1969, RG 59, CDF 1967–69, box 2279, NA.

97 American Embassy, Seoul, to U.S. Secretary of State, 14 October 1969, RG 59, CDF 1967–69, box 2279, NA.

98 "U.S. Policy Assessment—Republic of Korea, 1970," 11 March 1970, RG 59, CDF 1969–73, box 2429, NA.

99 Oh, *Korean Politics*, 58–59.

100 A good summary of the political characteristics of the Yusin system is contained in Sohn, *Authoritarianism and Opposition in South Korea*, 46–65.

101 American Embassy, Seoul, to U.S. Secretary of State, October 1972, box 2, OF.

Chapter 6

1 Yi Sangu, "Che 3 konghwaguk ch'amyŏ kyosu dŭl [Professors Who Participated in the Third Republic]," *Chŏnggyŏng munhwa*, September 1983, 50–52.

2 "The Sasanggye Circle and Its Vision of Korea's Political Future," 16 August 1963, RG 84, box 40, NA.

3 "Report of the Korea Task Force, 5 June 1961," NSF box 127, JFKL.

4 Wagner to Barnett, 21 February 1961, Grant 62-230, reel 2557, FFA.

5 A good summary of the development of modernization theory in American universities may be found in Latham, *Modernization as Ideology*, 21–68. Latham and others have described modernization theory in such detail that I will not give a lengthy description here. See also Gilman, *Mandarins of the Future*.

6 Rostow, *The Stages of Economic Growth*, 26.

7 "USIA Country Plan for Korea, 1967," USIAL.

8 USIS Seoul, "Assessment Report—Korea, 1964," Educational and Cultural Exchange, USIAL.

9 Although *Nondan* is mentioned in USIS documents, few issues survive. The essays mentioned above were taken from issues published in the late 1960s and early 1970s and scattered throughout "Records of the USIA," LBJL.

10 "Inauguration of New USIS-Supported TV Series on Modernization in Korea," 29 December 1965, Korea—Incoming, USIAL.

11 Lavin, "Witness to Korean History." William A. Douglas's lecture on "The Role of Political Parties in the Modernization Process" is included in a book containing all of the lectures from the conference entitled *The Modernization Process in Korea* (prepared for a Congress of Cultural Freedom Seminar in Seoul, 29 June 1983), available in the Harvard Yenching Library.

12 On the general role of the Ford Foundation during these years, see Berghahn, *America and the Intellectual Cold Wars in Europe*.

13 Finkelstein to Ford Foundation, 6 May 1970, Grant 62-230, reel 2556, FFA.

14 "Application for Financial Support of the Second Special Research and Developmental Program of the Asiatic Research Center, Korea University," March 1965, Grant 62-360, reel 2556, FFA.

15 On this point, see Bruce Cumings, "Boundary Displacement: The State, the Foundations and the International and Area Studies during and after the Cold War," *Parallax Visions*, 173–204.

16 Final Report on the Second Special Research Program, Grant # 62-360, reel 2556, FFA.

17 "Application to the Ford Foundation for Funds for the Support of a Research Project," 7 September 1967, Grant 68-0056, reel 1526, FFA.

18 Col. A. A. Jordan, "Report on Korea Trip," November 1968, Grant 68-56, reel 1526, FFA.

19 Faust to Heald, 10 May 1962, Grant # 62-360, reel 2556, FFA.

20 "Application to the Ford Foundation for Funds for the Support of a Research Project," 7 September 1967, Grant # 68-0056, reel 1526, FFA.

21 Asia Foundation, *The Asia Foundation in Korea, 1964*, brochure, published by the Asia Foundation. A list of some of the grants awarded by the Asia Foundation in South Korea was supplied to the author by the local offices of the Asia Foundation in Seoul.

22 *Bulletin of the Korea Branch of the Visiting Scholars Association, 1972*, HUA.

23 *Bulletin of the Korea Branch of the Visiting Scholars Association, 1967*, HUA.

24 See ARC, *International Conference on the Problems of Modernization in Asia*; Tongguk taehakkyo, *Han'guk kŭndaehwa ŭi inyŏm kwa panghyang*.

25 *Bulletin of the Korea Branch of the Visiting Scholars Association*, 1967 and 1972 issues, 26.HUA.

26 Hwang Sandŏk, "Sadaejŏk k'arisŭma wa tongyang ŭi chaebalhyŏn: In'ganŭisik ŭi kŭndaehwa ŭi munje wa kwan'gyehayŏ [Subservient Charisma and the Rediscovery of the East as Related to the Problem of the Modernization of Human Consciousness]," *Sasanggye*, February 1959, 26–35.

27 Fairbank to Wood, 12 May 1964, Grant 62-360, reel 2556, FFA has some discussion of early planning for the conference.

28 ARC, *International Conference on the Problems of Modernization in Asia*, 83.

29 Ibid., 118.

30 Ibid., 114–24.

31 Ibid., 71–75.

32 Ibid., 75, 124–25.

33 Ibid., 113.

34 Ibid., 140.

35 Ibid., 551–57.

36 His name is listed in Yi Sangu, "Che 3 konghwaguk ch'amyŏ kyosu dŭl," 55.

37 Taylor to Wood, 15 July 1965, Grant 62-360, reel 2556, FFA.

38 Cho Myŏnggi, "Han'guk kŭndaehwa ŭi kaenyŏm.

39 Kim Chongsin, *Pak Chŏng Hŭi taet'ongnyŏng kwa chubyŏn saram dŭl*, 24–27.

40 Yi Sangu, "Che 3 konghwaguk ch'amyŏ kyosu dŭl," 55–59.

41 Kal Ponggŭn, "Yusin hŏnbŏp ŭi chŏngch'i chŏlhak kwa chidojasang [The Political Philosophy and Leadership Style of the Yusin Constitution]," *Sin tonga*, December 1972, 54–60.

42 "Im Panghyŏn," in Han'guk chŏngsin munhwa yŏn'guwŏn, *Nae ka kyŏkkŭn han'guk chŏnjaeng kwa Pak Chŏnghŭi chŏngbu*, 344–46.

43 Ibid., 348–49.

44 Ibid., 352–53.

45 Im Panghyŏn, *Kŭndaehwa wa chisigin*, ii–iii.

46 All of this is summarized in "Im Panghyŏn," 334–35, 356–61.

47 ARC, *International Conference on the Problems of Modernization in Asia,* 416–19, 436.

48 Pyong-choon Hahm, "Korea: In Search of Peace and Prosperity," in Jo, *U.S. Foreign Policy in Asia,* 285–89. The proper romanization of the name is Ham Pyŏngjun, but Ham sometimes spelled it "Hahm Pyong-choon."

49 Yi Sangu, "Che 3 konghwaguk ch'amyŏ kyosu dŭl," 63–64.

50 Im Hŭisŏp, "Han'guk ŭi kŭndaehwa nŭn sŏguhwa in'ga [Will Korea's Modernization Be Westernization?]," *Ch'ŏngmaek* 1, December 1964, 146–51. During the Three Kingdoms period, what is now known as Korea was divided into three competing states—Silla, Paekche, and Koguryŏ. This period lasted between roughly a.d. 300 and 676, when Silla assumed control of the entire Korean peninsula. The Koryo Dynasty was formed in 918, unified the Korean peninsula in 935, and remained in power until 1392. Peasant and slave uprisings in the twelfth century demanded changes in the hereditary status system.

51 The essay originally appeared in a 1968 journal published by Korea University. It was later reprinted in Kang, *Pundan sidae ŭi yŏksa insik,* 216–31.

52 "Kwŏndu int'ŏbyu: Kang Man'gil [Opening Interview: Kang Man'gil]," *Mal,* August 1997, 26.

53 Kang, *Pundan sidae ŭi yŏksa insik,* 46.

54 On Kang and others being forced to temporarily abandon their academic posts, see Kim Chunyŏp, *Changjŏng,* 211–24.

55 Yu Kich'ŏn, "Na wa Pak Chŏnghŭi wa hangmun ŭi chayu [Me, Park Chung Hee, and Academic Freedom]," *Sin tonga,* August 1988, 373–77.

56 Ibid., 379–80.

Chapter 7

1 Marshall Green to Dean Rusk, 27 May 1961, NSF box 128, JFKL.

2 Samuel Berger to Dean Rusk, 6 June 1962, NSF box 128, JFKL.

3 American Embassy, Seoul, to U.S. Department of State, 7 August 1964, RG 59, CDF 1964–66, box 2405, NA.

4 Ibid.

5 "Underlying Causes of South Korean Student Discontent," 8 June 1964, RG 59, CDF 1964–66, box 2401, NA.

6 "Monthly Highlights Report—May," 7 June 1968, USIAL. USIS cultural centers hosted similar clubs in several other South Korean cities.

7 Lavin, "Witness to Korean History"; "Country Assessment Report," 30 January 1961, RG 306, Foreign Service Dispatches, 1954–65, box 1, NA.

8 "Monthly Highlights Report—May," 7 June 1968, USIAL.

9 "Student Leadership Workshop," 15 November 1968, folder: EDX12 Youth Program Korea—1968, USIAL.

10 Ibid.

11 Ibid.

12 "The First Asian Student Conference: International Student Association of Korea," 25 June 1964, folder: EDX12 Youth Program Korea—1968, USIAL.

13 Sang-yon Kim to USIS Director—Taegu, undated, folder: EDX12 Youth Program Korea—1968, USIAL.

14 The standard romanization of the term is *chuch'e ŭisik.*

15 "USIS, Seoul, to USIA, Washington," 15 February 1968, folder: EDX 12 Youth Program Korea—1968, USIAL.

16 "Economic Seminar and Factory Tour for Fifty College Student Leaders," 12 October 1964, folder: Korea—Incoming—1964, USIAL.

17 Ibid.

18 Ibid.

19 Lavin, "Witness to Korean History."

20 USOM to Korea, *Second Intern Program,* introduction.

21 Ibid., 2.

22 Ibid., 10–11.

23 Ibid., 28.

24 Ibid., 14.

25 Ibid., 61.

26 Ibid., 27.

27 Ibid., 31.

28 Ibid., 116.

29 "Educational and Cultural Exchange: Far East Student Leader Program XIV," 16 January 1968, folder: EDX12 Youth Program Korea—1968, USIAL.

30 "The First Asian Student Conference: International Student Association of Korea," 25 June 1964, folder: EDX12 Youth Program Korea—1968, USIAL.

31 Lavin, "Witness to Korean History"; "Emphasis on Youth: Second USIS Sponsored Korean Student Journalist Visit to Japan," 7 September 1965, RG 59, CDF 1964–66, box 398, NA.

32 "Emphasis on Youth: Second USIS Sponsored Korean Student Journalist Visit to Japan," 7 September 1965, RG 59, CDF 1964–66, box 398, NA.

33 Ibid.

34 Ibid.

35 Ibid.

36 Ibid.

37 "Overseas Evaluation: Korea," 11 November 1961, RG 490, Country Program Evaluations, 1967, box 25, NA.

38 "Possible Peace Corps Program in Korea," 18 October 1961; Samuel Berger to Dean Rusk, 3 November 1961, RG 59, CDF 1960–63, 895B.00 A / 7-1461, NA.

39 Ibid.

40 "Peace Corps Training Manual," Peace Corps Collection, box 23, JFKL.

41 Mr. Travis, "Toward a New Society," Kyŏngmaek [Yearbook of Kyŏngbuk Middle-High School], 14 (1967).

42 "Uri Sŏnsaeng [Our Teacher]," *Yŏboseyo* [Hello], March 1968. The articles were in English but sometimes had Korean headlines.

43 Gary Katsel, "Walk the Burning Coals," *Yŏboseyo*, March 1968.

44 John Cushing and Ross Wiggins, "Katsel over the Coals," *Yŏboseyo*, June 1968.

45 "Overseas Evaluation: Korea," RG 490, Country Program Evaluations, 1967, box 25, NA.

46 Terry Quarles, essay, Peace Corps Collection, box 5, JFKL.

47 Clark, *Christianity in Modern Korea*, xi–xii.

48 Minutes and Reports of the Sixty-Seventh Annual Meeting of the Korea Mission of the United Presbyterian Church in the U.S.A., 1961, 81 (lent to the author by the mission).

49 Ibid.

50 "Report of the Korean Christian Student Movement," 1967, unprocessed materials, KSMY.

51 Mun-Kyu Kang, *The Korean YMCA Movement*, 25.

52 Annual Report: Peter Van Lierop, 7 May 1959, RG 140, box 10, PHS.

53 "Rev. William Grubb, Annual Personal Report," June 1963, RG 140, box 10, PHS.

54 Merwin to Billingsley [et al.], 30 July 1964, RG 140, box 14, PHS.

55 "Korean SCM Report for 1965: Renewing Life in the Academic World," unprocessed materials, KSMY.

56 "Report of the Korean Student Christian Movement," 1967, unprocessed materials, KSMY.

57 "Idae YWCA kyobon: Mokchŏk chojik p'ŭrogŭraem [Ewha YWCA Manual: Purpose, Function, Program]," unprocessed materials, KSMY.

58 Merwin to Billingsley [et al.], 30 July 1964, RG 140, box 14, PHS.

59 "Report of the First Korean MYF Convocation," 2 August 1965, unprocessed materials, KSMY.

60 Ibid. The quotations in this passage are from a summary of the students' discussions.

61 Ibid.

62 Oh, *Korean Politics*, 90.

63 "A.K.F. 4-H Training Manual," 4-HC.

64 Han'guk 4-H Yŏnmaeng, *Han'guk 4-H undong 50 nyŏnsa*, 71–76.

65 Ibid., 80–84.

66 Ibid., 91–95.

67 Ibid., 87–88.

68 Ibid., 88–89.

69 Ibid., 89–90.

70 "A.K.F. 4-H Training Manual," 4-HC.

71 Ibid.

72 "4-H Kurakpu chojik kwa unyŏng [The Function and Management of the 4-H Club]," 4-HC.

73 Ibid.

74 "4-H kurakpu chojik kwa unyŏng," 4-HC.

75 Ibid.

76 Ibid.

77 "Nokchong [Green Bell]," 4-HC.

78 "4-H hwaldong saryejip [A Collection of Examples of 4-H Activities]," 1965, 4-HC.

79 "K'ŭroba [Clover]," 4-HC.

80 "Nokchong [Green Bell]," 4-HC.

81 "4-H yŏn'gu" [4-H Research], 1966, 4-HC.

82 For a complete account of the development of Korean Boy Scout groups prior to 1945, see Han'guk poi sŭk'aut'ŭ yŏnmaeng, *Han'guk poi sŭk'aut'ŭ yuksimnyŏnsa*. On the early Korean Girl Scout groups, see Han'guk kŏl sŭk'aut'ŭ yŏnmaeng, *Han'guk kŏl sŭk'aut'ŭ osimnyŏnsa*, 142–51.

83 Han'guk poi sŭk'aut'ŭ yŏnmaeng, *Han'guk poi sŭk'aut'ŭ yuksimnyŏnsa*, 353, 365; Han'guk kŏl sŭk'aut'ŭ yŏnmaeng, *Han'guk kŏl sŭk'aut'ŭ osimnyŏnsa*, 228–29.

84 Han'guk kŏl sŭk'aut'ŭ yŏnmaeng, *Han'guk kŏl sŭk'aut'ŭ osimnyŏnsa*, 171, 178.

85 Ibid., 220.

86 "Personal Report, Winifred W. Frei," May 1961, RG 197, box 5, PHS.

87 Han'guk kŏl sŭk'aut'ŭ yŏnmaeng, *Han'guk kŏl sŭk'aut'ŭ osimnyŏnsa*, 184, 186, 199, 220.

88 Han'guk poi sŭk'aut'ŭ yŏnmaeng, *Han'guk poi sŭk'aut'ŭ yuksimnyŏnsa*, 239, 253, 258, 267; "Civic Action, Republic of Korea," 21 September 1961, RG 59, CDF 1960–63, 795B.5-MSP/9-361, NA.

89 "Yunyŏn taegyobon [Youth Manual]," 1961, Records Room, Boy Scouts of Korea.

90 "Kŏl sŭkaut'ŭ kyobon [Girl Scout Manual]," 1966, 6, Records Room, Girl Scouts of Korea.

91 Ibid., 164–66.

92 Some of these jamborees are described briefly in Han'guk poi sŭk'aut'ŭ yŏnmaeng, *Han'guk poi sŭk'aut'ŭ yuksimnyŏnsa*, 249–55.

93 Kim Chongbuk, "Poi sŭk'aut'ŭ manira kihueng [Boy Scout Trip to Korea]," Yungchŏng-yungchŏng chung-kodŭng hakkyo yŏn'gam [The Yungchŏng Middle-High School Yearbook], 1963, 64–65.

94 Kim Chonghwan, "Int'ŏbyu: Kim Kŭnt'ae chŏn minch'ŏngnyŏn ŭijang: Kŭraedo minjung kyŏt'ŭro kagetta [Interview with Kim Kŭnt'ae: Nevertheless I Will Go to the Side of the Minjung]," *Wŏlgan chosŏn*, August 1988.

95 Ibid., 290–99.

96 Han'guk 4-H Yŏnmaeng, *Han'guk 4-H undong 50 nyŏnsa*, 102–7.

97 For a summary of student activities during this period, see "1960, 1970 nyŏndae ŭi sahoe undong [The Social Movements of the 1960s and 1970s]," in Kang Man'gil et al., Han'guksa, 19:282–87.

Chapter 8

1 Excellent on this point is Roy, *Taiwan: A Political History*, 152–56.

2 See Bueno de Mesquita and Downs, "Development and Democracy." The authors call this pattern "sustainable autocracy."

3 "1960, 1970 nyŏndae ŭi sahoe undong [The Social Movements of the 1960s and 1970s]," in Kang Man'gil et al., *Han'guksa*, vol. 19, has a good summary of these activities.

4 Oh, *Korean Politics*, 65–66; Lie, *Han Unbound*, 98–100; Hart-Landsberg, *The Rush to Development*, 203–6.

5 A good source on this is Nam-Hee Lee, "Making Minjung Subjectivity," 378–432. See also Hart-Landsberg, *The Rush to Development*, 207–8.

6 See Lie, *Han Unbound*, 99–100, 104–5.

7 American Embassy, Seoul, to Secretary of State Henry Kissinger, 30 March 1973, RG 59, CDF 1970–73, box 2425, NA.

8 Gleysteen, *Massive Entanglement, Marginal Influence*, 14.

9 Paul M. Cleveland, Oral History Interview, in Bentley and Warner, *Frontline Diplomacy*.

10 Ibid.

11 Thomas Stern, Oral History Interview, in Bentley and Warner, *Frontline Diplomacy*.

12 Gleysteen, *Massive Entanglement, Marginal Influence*, 33–34.

13 Ibid., 33.

14 For a summary of Carter's efforts to reduce the level of American forces in the ROK and reactions to it both in the United States and South Korea, see Gleysteen, *Massive Entanglement, Marginal Influence*, 20–30.

15 Ibid., 45–50.

16 "The Outlook for President Pak and South Korea's Dissidents," CREST Database, NA.

17 The events surrounding Park's assassination have been well described in secondary sources. See, e.g., Hart-Landsberg, *The Rush to Development*, 211–13, and Oh, *Korean Politics*, 71–72.

18 Hart-Landsberg, *The Rush to Development*, 212–13; Oh, *Korean Politics*, 71–72.

19 Oh, *Korean Politics*, 72–73.

20 Cumings, *Korea's Place in the Sun*, 374.

21 Oh, *Korean Politics*, 74–78.

22 Gleysteen to Cyrus Vance, 13 December 1979, fully declassified and reprinted in Gleysteen, *Massive Entanglement, Marginal Influence*, 210–11.

23 Ibid.

24 Young, *Eye on Korea*, 84–86.

25 Gleysteen to Cyrus Vance, 17 March 1980, OF, box 2, NSA.

26 Gleysteen to Edmund Muskie, 7 May 1980, OF, box 2, NSA.

27 Edmund Muskie to Gleysteen, 8 May 1980, OF, box 2, NSA.

28 Gleysteen, *Massive Entanglement, Marginal Influence*, 118.

29 Gleysteen to Edmund Muskie, 7 May 1980, OF, box 2, NSA.

30 Oh, *Korean Politics*, 80–81.

31 Gleysteen to Edmund Muskie, 17 May 1980, OF, box 2, NSA.

32 Edmund Muskie to Gleysteen, 18 May 1980, OF, box 2, NSA.

33 Good accounts of these events are included in Oh, *Korean Politics*, 80–83, and Gleysteen, *Massive Entanglement, Marginal Influence*, 127–134.

34 The quotations in this paragraph are from Tim Shorrock, "The U.S. Role in Korea in 1979 and 1980," posted on *Korea Web Weekly*.

35 Young, *Eye on Korea*, 105–6.

36 Quoted in Shorrock, "The U.S. Role in Korea in 1979 and 1980."

37 Gleysteen, *Massive Entanglement, Marginal Influence*, 130–31.

38 Gleysteen to Edmund Muskie, 26 May 1980, OF, box 2, NSA.

39 Oh, *Korean Politics*, 85.

40 Carter to Chun, 27 August 1980, reprinted in Gleysteen, *Massive Entanglement, Marginal Influence*, 165–66.

41 Richard V. Allen, "On the Korean Tightrope, 1980," *New York Times*, 21 January 1998.

42 Gleysteen to Alexander Haig, 5 February 1981, OF, box 2.

43 "Your Meeting with Chun Doo Hwan, President of the Republic of Korea," 29 January 1981, NSA.

44 Haig to Gleysteen, 5 February 1981, NSA.

45 The domestic struggles between Democrats and the Reagan administration over support for Chun Doo Hwan are described by Thomas P. H. Dunlop, Oral History Interview, in Bentley and Warner, *Frontline Diplomacy*.

46 Meeting between Reagan and Chun, 13 November 1983, OF, box 5, NSA.

47 "Address of President Ronald Reagan before the Korean National Assembly," 12 November 1983, of, BOX 1, nsa.

48 Lie, *Han Unbound*, 122–24; Kim Chunyŏp, *Changjŏng*, 211–24.

49 Kim Dae Jung, "Miguk ch'eryu 2nyŏn ŭi hoego," [A Memoir of Two Years in America]," *Sin tonga*, July 1985, 217–18, 228.

50 There is a substantial literature on the minjung movement in South Korea. See, e.g., Abelmann, *Echoes of the Past*, and Nam-Hee Lee, "Making Minjung Subjectivity."

51 For a detailed account of the incident, see Thomas P. H. Dunlop, Oral History Interview, in Bentley and Warner, *Frontline Diplomacy*.

52 "Visit of President Chun—Deputy Prime Minister's Meeting on Economic Affairs—Taxation Question," 30 January 1981, NSA.

53 "Your Asian Trip," 1 November 1983, NSA.

54 "President Reagan's November 12–14 Visit to Korea," 14 November 1983, NSA.

55 Woo, *Race to the Swift*, 190–91.

56 Ibid., 201. Woo adds parenthetically that this was especially true if it meant "liberal democracy" along Japanese lines.

57 Oh, *Korean Politics*, 90–91; Lie, *Han Unbound*, 150–52.

58 Stueck, "Democratization in Korea," points to increased middle-class participation in the 1987 protests as a significant factor.

59 Oberdorfer, *The Two Koreas*, 168.

60 On the probability that the United States had "learned" a lesson from Kwangju and on changing American perceptions of the relative importance of security and democracy, see Stueck, "Democratization in Korea," 20–24.

61 Quoted in Oberdorfer, *The Two Koreas*, 168.

62 "Statement by A/S Sigur at White House," 26 June 1987, OF, box 1, NSA.

63 Oh, *Korean Politics*, 98–106.

Conclusion

1 Cumings, *Korea's Place in the Sun*, 199.

2 See Zakaria, "The Rise of Illiberal Democracy."

3 Wilentz, *The Rise of American Democracy*, xix.

4 Interesting on this point is Szalontai, *Kim Il Sung in the Khrushchev Era*, which shows how the DPRK regime became increasingly despotic during the 1950s and 1960s.

5 "Address of President Ronald Reagan before the Korean National Assembly," 12 November 1983, OF, box 1, NSA.

6 Armstrong, "Fraternal Socialism," 181.

7 In his recent book, *North Korea: Another Country*, Bruce Cumings notes that several South Korean student groups and novelists such as Hwang Sŏkyŏng have depicted North Korea as more purely Korean than South Korea (p. 154).

Bibliography

Archives and Manuscript Collections

KOREA

Kidokkyo sahoe munje yŏnguso (Christian Social Problem Research Center), Seoul
Kirok munsŏ pojonso (National Archives), Taejŏn, Pusan and Seoul
Korean 4-H Club Association, Historical Materials Collection, Seoul
Oegyo anbo yŏn'guwŏn (Center for Foreign Affairs and Security), Seoul
Records Room, Boy Scouts of Korea, Seoul, Republic of Korea
Records Room, Girl Scouts of Korea, Seoul, Republic of Korea
University Archives, Seoul National University, Seoul
    Materials Relating to the Minnesota Contract

UNITED STATES

Dwight D. Eisenhower Library, Abilene, Kansas
    Dwight D. Eisenhower Papers
    Oral History Interviews
    Records of the U.S. President's Citizen Advisers on the Mutual Security Program
    U.S. Army Collections
    White House Office Files
Ford Foundation Archives, New York, New York
Lyndon Baines Johnson Library, Austin, Texas
    Confidential Files
    Leonard Marks Papers
    National Security Files
John F. Kennedy Library, Boston, Massachusetts
    Confidential Files
    National Security Files
    Peace Corps Collection
    Records of Government Agencies
Carl A. Kroch Library, Rare and Manuscript Collections, Cornell University, Ithaca, New York
    Robert J. Nathan Papers
Ruth Lilly Special Collections and Archives, University Library, Indiana University–Purdue University, Indianapolis
    Annual Reports of the American-Korean Foundation
George C. Marshall Library, Lexington, Virginia
    James Van Fleet Papers
    Tyler S. Wood Papers

National Archives, College Park, Maryland
    Record Group 59: General Records of the U.S. Department of State
    Record Group 84: Records of the Foreign Service Posts of the U.S. Department of State: Korea
    Record Group 286: Records of the U.S. Agency for International Development and Learning
    Record Group 306: Records of the U.S. Information Agency
    Record Group 319: Records of the U.S. Army Staff
    Record Group 338: Records of the U.S. Army Commands
    Record Group 469: Records of U.S. Foreign Assistance Agencies
    Record Group 490: Records of the Peace Corps
    Record Group 554: Records of the General Headquarters, Far East Command, U.S. Armed Forces in Korea
National Security Archives, The George Washington University, Washington, D.C.
    Korea Declassification Project under the direction of Dr. Robert Wampler
    Don Oberdorfer Files
Naval Historical Center, Washington Navy Yard, Washington, D.C.
Presbyterian Historical Society, Philadelphia, Pennsylvania
    Records of the Mission to Korea
Ronald Reagan Library, Simi Valley, California
Harry S. Truman Library, Independence, Missouri
    Oral History Interviews
    Harry S. Truman Papers
        White House Central Files, Confidential Files
United Nations Archives, New York, New York
    Records of the United Nations Korea Reconstruction Agency
University Archives, Harvard University, Cambridge, Massachusetts
U.S. Agency for International Development Learning and Resource Center Library, Washington, D.C.
U.S. Army, Center of Military History, Washington, D.C.
U.S. Army Military History Institute, Carlisle, Pennsylvania
U.S. Information Agency, Declassified Materials Collection, Washington, D.C.

Periodicals: English Language
Korea Journal
Korean Information Bulletin
Korean Survey
Korea Times
Life
New York Times
Time

Periodicals: Korean Language

Asea yŏn'gu [Asiatic Research]
Chŏnggyŏng munhwa [Political-Economic Culture]
Ch'ŏngmaek ["Fresh Spirit"]
Haegun [Navy and Marines]
Han'guk sinmun p'yŏnjibin hyŏphoebo [Korean Newspaper Association Bulletin]
Hyŏndae munhak [Current Literature]
Kukhoebo [National Assembly Bulletin]
Kukpang [National Defense]
Kukpang yŏn'gu [National Defense Research]
Kyoyuk munhwa [Educational Culture]
Maeil kyŏngje sinmun [Economic Daily]
Mal [Language]
Pijinesŭ [Business]
Sae kyoyuk [New Education]
Sasanggye [World of Thought]
Sin tonga [New East Asia]
Tonga ilbo [East Asia Daily]
Wŏlgan chosŏn [Chosŏn Monthly]
Yŏwŏn [Women's Garden]
Yukkun kyoyuk yŏngam [Military Education Annual]
Yuksa sinmun [KMA Newspaper]

Published Reports and Documents

Asiatic Research Center. *International Conference on the Problems of Modernization in Asia.* Seoul: ARC, 1965.

Korea Civil Assistance Command. *United Nations Command, Civil Assistance and Economic Affairs—Korea, 1 July 1953–30 June 1954.* Prepared by Korea Civil Assistance Command, 1954.

———. *United Nations Command, Civil Assistance and Economic Affairs—Korea, 1 July 1954–30 June 1955.* Prepared by Management and Reports Branch, Headquarters, Korea Civil Assistance Command, 1955.

Republic of Korea. *Summary of the First Five-Year Economic Plan, 1962–1966.* Seoul: Republic of Korea, 1962.

Republic of Korea, Ministry of Education. *Rebuilding Secondary Education in the Republic of Korea: Summary Report on The National Survey of Secondary Schools.* Seoul: Central Education Research Institute, 1962.

Robert R. Nathan Associates. *An Economic Programme for Korean Reconstruction.* Prepared for the United Nations Korean Reconstruction Agency. New York: Robert R. Nathan Associates, 1954.

United Nations Korean Reconstruction Agency. *Reports of the Agent General of the*

United Nations Korean Reconstruction Agency, 1953–1958. New York: United Nations, 1953–58.

U.S. Congress, House Committee on International Relations. *Investigation of Korean-American Relations: Hearings before a Subcommittee on International Organizations,* 95th Cong., 2nd sess., 1978. Washington, D.C.: Government Printing Office, 1978.

U.S. Department of State. *Foreign Relations of the United States, 1952–1954.* Vol. 15: *Korea.* Washington, D.C.: Government Printing Office, 1984.

——. *Foreign Relations of the United States, 1955–1957.* Vol. 22, pt. 2: *Korea.* Washington, D.C.: Government Printing Office, 1993.

——. *Foreign Relations of the United States, 1958–1960.* Vol. 18: *Japan, Korea.* Washington, D.C.: Government Printing Office, 1994.

——. *Foreign Relations of the United States, 1961–1963.* Vol. 22: *Northeast Asia.* Washington, D.C.: Government Printing Office, 1996.

——. *Foreign Relations of the United States, 1964–1968.* Vol. 29, pt. 1: *Korea.* Washington, D.C.: Government Printing Office, 2000.

U.S. Operations Mission to Korea. *Student Intern Reports.* Seoul: USOM/Korea, 1967.

Books, Articles, and Unpublished Works: English Language

Abelmann, Nancy. *Echoes of the Past, Epics of Dissent: A South Korean Social Movement.* Berkeley: University of California Press, 1996.

American Education Team. *Curriculum Handbook for the Schools of Korea.* Published under the auspices of the United Nations Korea Reconstruction Agency and the American-Korean Foundation, 1956.

Armstrong, Charles. "Fraternal Socialism: The International Reconstruction of North Korea, 1953–1962." *Cold War History* 5, no. 2 (May 2005).

Arndt, H. W. *Economic Development: The History of an Idea.* Chicago: University of Chicago Press, 1989.

Asia Foundation. *The Asia Foundation in Korea, 1964.* Seoul: Asia Foundation, 1965.

Bentley, Marilyn, and Marie Warner, eds. *Frontline Diplomacy: The Foreign Affairs Oral History Collection.* Arlington, Va.: Association for Diplomatic Studies and Training, 2000.

Berghahn, Volker Rolf. *America and the Intellectual Cold Wars in Europe: Shepard Stone between Philanthropy, Academy, and Diplomacy.* Princeton, N.J.: Princeton University Press, 2001.

Bill, James. *The Eagle and the Lion: The Tragedy of American-Iranian Relations.* New Haven: Yale University Press, 1989.

Blair, Clay. *The Forgotten War.* New York: Times Books, 1987.

Brazinsky, Gregg. "From Pupil to Model: South Korea and American Development Policy during the Early Park Chung Hee Era." *Diplomatic History* 29 (January 2005): 83–115.

Brown, James R., and Sein Lin, eds. *Land Reform in Developing Countries: 1967*

International Seminar on Land Taxation, Land Tenure and Land Reform in Developing Countries. Hartford, Conn.: University of Hartford Press, 1968.

Bueno de Mesquita, Bruce, and George W. Downs. "Development and Democracy." Foreign Affairs 84 (September / October 2005): 77–86.

Catton, Phillip E. Diem's Final Failure: Prelude to America's War in Vietnam. Lawrence: University Press of Kansas, 2002.

Cha, Victor. Alignment despite Antagonism: The United States-Korea-Japan Security Triangle. Stanford, Calif.: Stanford University Press, 1999.

Chibber, Vivek. Locked in Place: State-Building and Late Industrialization in India. Princeton, N.J.: Princeton University Press, 2003.

Cho, Lee Jay, and Yoon Hyung Kim, eds. Economic Development in the Republic of Korea: A Policy Perspective. Honolulu: University of Hawaii Press, 1991.

Clark, Donald N. Christianity in Modern Korea. Lanham, Md.: University Press of America, 1986.

Clemens, Peter. "Captain James Hausman, U.S. Army Military Advisor to Korea, 1946–1948: The Intelligent Man on the Spot." Journal of Strategic Studies 25 (March 2002): 163–98.

Cole, David, and Princeton N. Lyman. Korean Development: The Interplay of Politics and Economics. Cambridge: Harvard University Press, 1971.

Cullather, Nicholas. "Damming Afghanistan: Modernization in a Buffer State." Journal of American History 89 (September 2002): 512–37.

Cumings, Bruce. North Korea: Another Country. New York: New Press, 2004.

——. Parallax Visions: Making Sense of American–East Asian Relations at the End of the Century. Durham, N.C.: Duke University Press, 1999.

——. Korea's Place in the Sun: A Modern History. New York: Norton, 1997.

——. The Origins of the Korean War. Vol. 2: The Roaring of the Cataract. Princeton, N.J.: Princeton University Press, 1991.

——. The Origins of the Korean War. Vol. 1: Liberation and the Emergence of Separate Regimes, 1945–1947. Princeton, N.J.: Princeton University Press, 1981.

Dean, Robert D. "Masculinity as Ideology: John F. Kennedy and the Domestic Politics of Foreign Policy." Diplomatic History 22 (Winter 1998): 29–62.

de Certeau, Michel. The Practice of Everyday Life. Berkeley: University of California Press, 1984.

Deuchler, Martina. The Confucian Transformation of Korea: A Study of Society and Ideology. Cambridge: Harvard University Press, 1995.

Deyo, Frederick C., ed. The Political Economy of the New Asian Industrialism. Ithaca, N.Y.: Cornell University Press, 1987.

Eckert, Carter. Offspring of Empire: The Koch'ang Kims and the Colonial Origins of Korean Capitalism, 1876–1945. Seattle: University of Washington Press, 1991.

Eckert, Carter, et al. Korea Old and New: A History. Cambridge: Harvard University Press, 1990.

Edman, Maron L. *Primary Teachers of Korea Look at Themselves: A Study of Role and Status*. Seoul: Ministry of Education, 1962.

Engerman, David, et al., eds. *Staging Growth: Modernization, Development and the Global Cold War*. Amherst: University of Massachusetts Press, 2003.

Etzioni, Amitai. "A Self-Restrained Approach to Nation-Building by Foreign Powers." *International Affairs* 80 (2004): 1–17.

Gardner, Lloyd, and Ted Gittinger, eds. *International Perspectives on Vietnam*. College Station: Texas A&M University Press, 2000.

Gilman, Nils. *Mandarins of the Future: Modernization Theory in Cold War America*. Baltimore: Johns Hopkins University Press, 2003.

Gleysteen, William H. *Massive Entanglement, Marginal Influence: Carter and Korea in Crisis*. Washington, D.C.: Brookings Institution, 1999.

Halberstam, David. *The Best and the Brightest*. New York: Random House, 1992.

Halperin, Morton, et al. *The Democracy Advantage: How Democracies Promote Prosperity and Peace*. New York: Routledge, 2004.

Harding, Harry. *A Fragile Relationship: The United States and China since 1972*. Washington, D.C.: Brookings Institution, 1992.

Harootunian, Harry. *History's Disquiet: Modernity, Cultural Practice, and the Question of Everyday Life*. New York: Columbia University Press, 2000.

Harrison, Hope. *Driving the Soviets Up the Wall: Soviet–East German Relations, 1953–1961*. Princeton, N.J.: Princeton University Press, 2003.

Hart-Landsberg, Martin. *The Rush to Development: Economic Change and Political Struggle in South Korea*. New York: Monthly Review Press, 1993.

Hastings, Max. *The Korean War*. New York: Pan, 2000.

Henderson, Gregory. *Korea: The Politics of the Vortex*. Cambridge: Harvard University Press, 1968.

Hong, Seuk-Ryule. "Reunification Issues and Civil Society in South Korea." *Journal of Asian Studies* 61 (November 2002): 1237–59.

Hong, Yong-Pyo. *State Security and Regime Security: President Syngman Rhee and the Insecurity Dilemma in South Korea, 1953–1960*. New York: St. Martin's, 2000.

Hwang, Kyung-Moon. "Bureaucracy in the Transition to Korean Modernity: Secondary Status Groups and the Transformation of Government and Society, 1890–1930." Ph.D. diss., Harvard University, 1997.

Jo, Yung-hwan, ed. *U.S. Foreign Policy in Asia: An Appraisal*. Santa Barbara, Calif.: ABC-CLIO, 1978.

Kang, David. *Crony Capitalism: Corruption and Development in South Korea and the Philippines*. Cambridge: Cambridge University Press, 2002.

Kang, Mun-Kyu. *The Korean YMCA Movement: Its History and Perspectives*. Seoul: National Council of YMCAs of Korea, 1990.

Kim, Ransoo. *Korean Education in Research Perspectives*. Seoul: Jog-Gak, 1984.

Kim, Se-Jin. *The Politics of Military Revolution in Korea*. Chapel Hill: University of North Carolina Press, 1971.

Kim, Woon-Tai. "Administrative Structure and Practices in the Government of Korea." M.A. thesis, University of Minnesota, 1959.

Krueger, Anne. *Studies of the Modernization of the Republic of Korea, 1945–1975: The Developmental Role of the Foreign Sector and Aid*. Cambridge: Harvard University Press, 1979.

Kuznets, Simon. "Korea's Five-Year Plans." In Irma Adelman, ed., *Practical Approaches to Development Planning: Korea's Second Five-Year Plan*. Baltimore: Johns Hopkins University Press, 1969.

LaFeber, Walter. *The Clash: U.S.-Japanese Relations throughout History*. New York: Norton, 1997.

——. *The American Age: American Foreign Policy At Home and Abroad, 1750–Present*. New York: Norton, 1994.

Landers, Frank. *Technical Assistance in Public Administration, USOM/Korea, 1955–1967*. Seoul: USOM/Korea, 1968.

Latham, Michael. *Modernization as Ideology: American Social Science and "Nation Building" in the Kennedy Era*. Chapel Hill: University of North Carolina Press, 2000.

Lavin, Barnard. "Witness to Korean History." Unpublished paper. In author's possession.

Lee, Chi-op. *Call Me Speedy Lee*. Translated by Stephen Tharp. Seoul: Woomin, 2001.

Lee, Nam-Hee. "Making Minjung Subjectivity: Crisis of Subjectivity and Rewriting History 1960–1988." Ph.D. diss., University of Chicago, 2001.

Lerner, Mitchell. "A Failure of Perception: Lyndon Johnson, North Korean Ideology and the Pueblo Incident." *Diplomatic History* 25 (Fall 2001): 647–75.

Lie, John. *Han Unbound: The Political Economy of South Korea*. Stanford, Calif.: Stanford University Press, 1998.

Lipset, Seymour. "Some Social Requisites of Democracy: Economic Development and Political Legitimacy." *American Political Science Review* 33 (March 1959): 69–105.

MacDonald, Donald Stone. *U.S.-Korean Relations from Liberation to Self-Reliance: The Twenty-Year Record: An Interpretive Summary of the Archives of the U.S. Department of State for the Period 1945 to 1965*. Boulder, Colo.: Westview Press, 1992.

Mason, Edward S., et al. *The Economic and Social Modernization of the Republic of Korea*. Cambridge: Harvard University Press, 1980.

Matray, James. *The Reluctant Crusade: American Foreign Policy in Korea, 1941–1950*. Honolulu: University of Hawaii Press, 1985.

McCune, George. *Korea Today*. Cambridge: Harvard University Press, 1950.

Millett, Allan. *The War for Korea, 1945–1950: A House Burning*. Lawrence: University Press of Kansas, 2005.

——. *Their War for Korea: American Asian and European Combatants and Civilians, 1945–1953*. Washington, D.C.: Brassey's, 2002.

——. "Captain James Hausman and the Formation of the Korean Army, 1945–1950." *Armed Forces and Society* 23 (Summer 1997): 503–40.

Moon, Katharine. *Sex among Allies: Military Prostitution in U.S.-Korean Relations.* New York: Columbia University Press, 1997.

Moskowitz, Karl. *From Patron to Partner: The Development of U.S.-Korean Business and Trade Relations.* Lexington, Ky.: Lexington Books, 1984.

Nahm, Andrew C., ed. *Korea and the New Order in East Asia: Proceedings of the Conference on Korea Held at Western Michigan University, April 6–7, 1967.* Kalamazoo: Center for Korean Studies, 1975.

Nam, Hwasook. "Labor's Place in South Korea's Development: Shipbuilding Workers, Capital and the State." Ph.D. diss., University of Washington, 2003.

Oberdorfer, Don. *The Two Koreas: A Contemporary History.* New York: Basic Books, 1997.

Oh, John Kie Chang. *Korean Politics: The Quest for Democratization and Development.* Ithaca, N.Y.: Cornell University Press, 1999.

Park, Chung Hee. *Our Nation's Path.* Seoul: Hollym, 1970.

——. *The Country, the Revolution and I.* Seoul: Hollym, 1970.

Rhodes, Harry A., and Archibald Campbell, eds. *History of the Korea Mission Presbyterian Church in the USA.* Vol. 2: *1935–1959.* Seoul: Presbyterian Church, Department of Education, 1965.

Robinson, Michael. "Mass Media and Popular Culture in 1930s Korea: Cultural Control, Identity and Colonial Hegemony." In Suh, *Korean Studies,* 59–84.

——. *Cultural Nationalism in Colonial Korea, 1920–1925.* Seattle: University of Washington Press, 1988.

Rossiter, Clinton, ed. *The Federalist Papers.* New York: Signet, 2003.

Rostow, Walt Whitman. *The Stages of Economic Growth: A Non-Communist Manifesto.* London: Cambridge University Press, 1962.

Roy, Denny. *Taiwan: A Political History.* Ithaca, N.Y.: Cornell University Press, 2003.

Sawyer, Robert K. *Military Advisors in Korea: KMAG in Peace and War.* Washington, D.C.: Office of the Chief of Military History, 1962.

Schmid, Andre. *Korea between Empires, 1895–1910.* New York: Columbia University Press, 2002.

Schwartz, Thomas. *America's Germany: John J. McCloy and the Federal Republic of Germany.* Cambridge: Cambridge University Press, 1991.

Seth, Michael. *Education Fever: Society Politics and the Pursuit of Schooling in South Korea.* Honolulu: University of Hawaii Press, 2002.

Shin, Eui Hang. "Effects of the Korean War on Social Structures of the Republic of Korea." *International Journal of Korean Studies* 5 (Spring/Summer 2001): 133–58.

Shin, Gi-Wook, and Michael Robinson, eds. *Colonial Modernity in Korea.* Cambridge: Harvard University Press, 1999.

Sohn, Hak-Kyu. *Authoritarianism and Opposition in South Korea.* New York: Routledge, 1989.

Stueck, William. *Rethinking the Korean War: A New Diplomatic and Strategic History.* Princeton, N.J.: Princeton University Press, 2002.

——. *The Korean War: An International History*. Princeton, N.J.: Princeton University Press, 1995.

——. "Democratization in Korea: The United States Role, 1980 and 1987." *International Journal of Korean Studies* 2 (Fall / Winter 1998): 171–80.

Suh, Dae-Sook, ed. *Korean Studies: New Pacific Currents*. Honolulu: University of Hawaii Press, 1994.

Szalontai, Balazs. *Kim Il Sung in the Khrushchev Era: Soviet-DPRK Relations and the Roots of North Korean Despotism*. Stanford, Calif.: Stanford University Press, 2005.

Talentino, Andrea Kathryn. "The Two Faces of Nation Building: Developing Function and Identity." *Cambridge Review of International Studies* 17 (October 2004): 557–75.

Tilly, Charles. *Coercion, Capital and European States, AD 990–1990*. Cambridge: Blackwell, 1990.

——, ed. *The Formation of National States in Western Europe*. Princeton, N.J.: Princeton University Press, 1975.

Toland, John, and Carolyn Blakemore. *In Mortal Combat: Korea, 1950–1953*. New York: Harper, 1993.

United Nations Command, Office of the Economic Coordinator for Korea. *Stabilization and Program Progress: Fiscal Year 1958, Korea*. San Francisco: United Nations Command, 1958.

Westad, Odd Arne. *The Global Cold War: Third World Interventions and the Making of Our Times*. London: Cambridge University Press, 2005.

Wilentz, Sean. *The Rise of American Democracy: From Jefferson to Lincoln*. New York: Norton, 2005.

Woo, Jung-En. *Race to the Swift: State and Finance in Korean Industrialization*. New York: Columbia University Press, 1991.

Yi, Kil J. "Alliance in the Quagmire: The United States, South Korea and the Vietnam War, 1964–1968." Ph.D. diss., Rutgers University, 1997.

Young, James V. *Eye On Korea: An Insider Account of Korean American Relations*. College Station: Texas A&M University Press, 2003.

Zakaria, Fareed. *The Future of Freedom*. New York: Norton, 2003.

——. "The Rise of Illiberal Democracy." *Foreign Affairs* 76 (September / October 1997): 22–43.

Books, Articles, and Unpublished Works: Korean Language

Ch'ae Myŏngsin. *Ch'ae Myŏngsin hoegorok: Sasŏn ŭl nŏmgo nŏmŏ* [The Autobiography of Ch'ae Myŏngsin: Beyond the Crisis of Life and Death]. Seoul: Maeil kyŏngje sinmunsa, 1994.

Ch'oe Pongdae. "Nongji kaehyŏk ihu chongch'ijŏg chibae chiptan ŭi hyŏngsŏng [The Formation of Dominant Political Groups after Land Reform]." In *Yŏksa munje yŏn'guso, 1950 nyŏndae han'guk ŭi sŏntaek kwa kulchŏl*, 228–67.

Cho Kapche. *Nae mudŏm e ch'im ŭl paet'ŏra 3: Hyŏngmyŏng chŏnhu* [Spit on My Grave: Before and after the Revolution, 3 vols.]. Seoul: Chosŏn ilbosa, 1998.

Cho Kijun and O Dŏkyŏng. *Han'guk kyŏngjesa* [An Economic History of Korea]. Seoul: Pŏmmunsa, 1962.

Cho Myŏnggi. "Han'guk kŭndaehwa ŭi kaenyŏm [The Ideas for Modernization of Korea: Opening Address]." In Tongguk Taehakkyo, *Han'guk kŭndaehwa ŭi inyŏm kwa panghyang.*

Chŏn Chehyŏn. *Pogyŏl insaeng* [A Second-Chance Life]. Seoul: Namgang munhwa chedan ch'ulp'anbu, 1989.

Chŏn Uyŏng. *Naemun Naemu: Chukkye Chŏn Uyŏng hoegorok* [The Memoir of Chŏn Uyŏng]. Seoul: Sach'o, 1989.

Chungang kyoyuk yŏnguso. *Minju simin ŭi kyoyuk: Haeinsa yŏrŭm ssemina rŭl chungsimŭro han yŏn'gu pogoso* [Democratic Citizenship Education: A Research Report Based on the Haeinsa Summer Conference]. Seoul: Chungang kyouyuk yŏnguso, 1962.

Han'guk 4-H Yŏnmaeng. *Han'guk 4-H undong 50 nyŏnsa* [A Fifty-Year History of the Korean 4-H Movement]. Seoul: Han'guk 4-H undong 50 nyŏnsa p'yŏnch'an wiwŏnhoe, 1998.

Han'guk chŏngch'i yŏn'guhoe, ed. *Pak chŏnghŭi rŭl nŏmŏsŏ* [Beyond Chung Hee Park]. Seoul: P'urŭnsup, 1998.

Han'guk chŏngsin munhwa yŏn'guwŏn, ed. *Nae ka kyŏkkŭn han'guk chŏnjaeng kwa Pak Chŏnghŭi chŏngbu* [My Experiences with the Korean War and the Park Chung Hee Government]. Seoul: Han'guk chŏngsin munhwa yŏn'guwŏn, 2004.

———. *Nae ka kyŏkkŭn minju wa tokchae* [My Experiences with Authoritarianism and Democracy]. Seoul: Han'guk chŏngsin munhwa yŏn'guwŏn, 2001.

———. *Nae ka kyŏkkŭn haebang kwa bundan* [My Experiences with Liberation and National Division]. Seoul: Han'guk chŏngsin munhwa yŏn'guwŏn, 2001.

Han'guk kŏl sŭk'aut'ŭ yŏnmaeng. *Han'guk kŏl sŭk'aut'ŭ osimnyŏnsa* [A Fifty-Year History of the Korean Girl Scouts]. Seoul: Han'guk kŏl sŭk'aut'ŭ yŏnmaeng, 1977.

Han'guk kyŏngjesa hakhŏe. *Han'guksa sidae kubullon* [The Chronological Division of Korean History]. Seoul: Ŭlsŏ munhwasa, 1970.

Han'guk poi sŭk'aut'ŭ yŏnmaeng. *Han'guk poi sŭk'aut'ŭ yuksimnyŏnsa* [A Sixty-Year History of the Korean Boy Scout]. Seoul: Han'guk poi sŭk'aut'ŭ yŏnmaeng, 1982.

Han Man'gil. "1950 nyŏndae minjujuŭi kyoyuk ŭi sŏnggyŏk [The Character of Democratic Education during the 1950s]." In Kyoyuk ch'ulp'an kihoeksil, *Pundan sidae ŭi hakkyo kyoyuk.*

Hausman, James, and Chŏng Irhwa. *Han'guk taet'ongnyong ul umjigin migun taewi: Hausuman chŭngŏn* [The American Commander Who Influenced Korean Presidents: Hausman's Testimony]. Seoul: Han'guk munwŏn, 1995.

Hŭimang ch'ulp'ansa, ed. *Sasil ŭi chŏnbu rŭl kisul handa: Yŏktae chuyŏktŭl ŭi silt'ohan migonggae chŏngch'i imyŏn pilsa* [An Account of the Full Facts: The Secret History

of the Inside Story of Politics as Told by a Generation of Leading Figures].
Seoul: Hŭimang ch'ulp'ansa, 1966.

Im Panghyŏn. *Kŭndaehwa wa chisigin: Han'gukchŏk minjujŭi ŭi inyŏm kwa silch'on*
[Modernization and the Intellectual: The Concept and Practice of Korean-Style
Democracy]. Seoul, 1974.

Im Taesik. "1950 nyŏndae miguk ŭi kyoyuk wŏnjo wa ch'inmi ellit'ŭ ŭi hyŏngsŏng
[American Educational Assistance and the Formation of a Pro-American Elite]."
In Yŏksa munje yŏn'guso, *1950 nyŏndae nambukhan ŭi sŏnt'aek kwa kulchŏl*.

Kang Man'gil. *Pundan sidae ŭi yŏksa insik* [The Historical Consciousness of the Era of
Division]. Seoul: Ch'angjak kwa pip'yŏngsa, 1978.

Kang Man'gil et al., eds. *Han'guksa*. 32 vols. Seoul: Han'gilsa, 1993–2002.

Kim Chongsin. *Pak Chŏng Hŭi taet'ongnyŏng kwa chubyŏn saram dŭl* [President Park
Chung Hee and His Inner Circle]. Seoul: Han'guk nondan, 1997.

Kim Chunyŏp. *Changjŏng: Na ŭi taehak ch'ongjang sijŏl* [Long March: My Years as
University President]. Seoul: Nanam, 1990.

Kim Hŭnggi. *Pisa kyŏngje kihŏekwŏn 33nyŏn: Yŏngyok ŭi han'guk kyŏngje* [The Thirty-
Three-Year Secret History of the Economic Planning Board: The Glory and
Shame of the Korean Economy]. Seoul: Maeil kyŏngje sinmunsa, 1999.

Koryŏ taehakkyo asea munje yŏn'guso. *Koryŏ taehakkyo asea munje yŏn'guso isimnyŏnji*
[A Twenty-Year History of the Asiatic Research Center]. Seoul: Asea munje
yŏn'guso, 1977.

Koryŏ taehakkyo kiŏp kyŏngyŏng yŏnguwŏn. *Kodae kiyŏn sasimnyŏnsa* [A Forty-Year
History of the Business Management Research Center, 1958–1998]. Seoul: Koryŏ
taehakkyo kiŏp kyŏngyŏng yŏnguwŏn, 1998.

Kwanhun k'ŭllŏp. *Kwanhun k'ŭllŏp sasimnyŏnsa* [A Forty-Year History of the
Kwanhun Club]. Seoul: Kwanhun k'ŭllŏp, 1997.

Kyoyuk ch'ulp'an kihoeksil, ed. *Pundan sidae ŭi hakkyo kyoyuk* [Education in the Era of
National Division]. Seoul: P'urŭn namu, 1984.

Maeil kyŏngje sinmun, ed. *Na ŭi yuhak sijŏl: Myŏngsatŭlŭi p'yŏlch'inŭn chŏlmŭnnal ŭi
kkum kwa yamang* [My Experiences as an Exchange Student: Well-Known
Individuals' Youthful Dreams and Desires]. Vols. 1–3. Seoul: Maeil kyŏngje
sinmunsa, 1986.

Mun Tonghwan and Im Chaegyŏng, eds. *Han'guk kwa miguk* [Korea and America].
Seoul: Silch'on munhaksa, 1983.

O Myŏngho. *Han'guk hyŏndae chŏngch'isa ŭi ihae* [Understanding Modern Korean
Political History]. Seoul: Orŭm, 1999.

O Wŏnch'ŏl. *Han'guk hyŏng kyŏngje kŏnsŏl: Enjiniŏring ŏp'ŭroch'i* [Korean-Style Economic
Development: Engineering Approach] I. Seoul: Kia kyŏngje yŏnguso, 1995.

Pak Chŏngin. *P'ungun ŭi pyŏl: Pak Chŏngin hoegorok* [Star of Fortune: The Memoir of
Pak Chŏngin]. Seoul: Hongik ch'ulpansa, 1990.

Pak Myŏngnim. *Han'guk 1950: Chŏnjaeng kwa p'yŏnghwa* [Korea, 1950: War and
Peace]. Seoul: Nanam, 2002.

———. *Han'guk chŏnjaeng ŭi palbal kwa kiwŏn, 2: Kiwŏn kwa wŏnin* [The Korean War's Outbreak and Origin, vol. 2: Origins and Causes]. Seoul: Nanam, 1996.

Pak Taegyun. "1956–1964 Han'guk kyŏngje kaebal kyehoek ŭi sŏngnip kwajŏng [The Process of Creating Korea's Economic Plans, 1956–1964]." Ph.D. diss., Seoul National University, 2000.

Son Insu. *Han'guk kyoyuk undongsa, 1: 1950 nyŏndae kyoyuk ŭi yŏksa insik* [A History of Korean Education, vol. 1: Historical Consciousness of the 1950s]. Seoul: Minŭmsa, 1994.

Song Insang. *Hoenam Song Insang hoegorok buhŭng kwa sŏngjang* [The Memoir of Song Insang: Recovery and Growth]. Seoul: 21 Segi puksu, 1994.

Sŏng Naeun. "Pundan sidae ŭi hanmi kyoyuk kyoryu" [Educational Exchange in the Period of Division]." In Mun and Im, *Han'guk kwa miguk*.

Tongguk taehakkyo. *Han'guk kŭndaehwa ŭi inyŏm kwa panghyang: Tongguk taehakkyo kaegyo yuksip chunnyŏn kinyŏm haksul simp'ojiŏm nonmunjip* [Modernization of Korea—The Ideas and the Orientation: Symposium in Commemoration of the Sixtieth Anniversary of the Founding of Tongguk University]. Seoul: Tongguk taehakkyo, 1967.

Yi Hallim. *Segye ŭi kyŏngnang* [The Century's Raging Waves]. Seoul: P'albokwŏn, 1994.

Yi Hanbin. *Ilhamyŏ saenggakhamyŏ: Yi Hanbin hoegorok* [Working and Thinking: The Memoir of Yi Hanbin]. Seoul: Chosŏn ilbosa, 1996.

Yi Hyŏnggŭn. *Kunbŏn ilbŏn ŭi oegil insaeng: Yi Hyŏng-gŭn hoegorok* [The Single Path Life of Soldier Number One: The Memoir of Hyŏng-gŭn Yi]. Seoul: Chungang ilbosa, 1994.

Yi Kihong. *Kyŏngje kŭndaehwa ŭi sumŭn iyagi* [The Hidden History of Economic Modernization]. Seoul: Poisŭsa, 1999.

Yi Man'gap. *Han'guk nongch'on sahŏe ŭi kujowa pyŏnhwa* [Structure and Change in Korean Villages]. Seoul: Sŏul taehakkyo ch'ulp'anbu, 1973.

Yi Tongwŏn. *Taet'ongnyŏng ŭl kŭrimyŏ* [Missing the President]. Seoul: Koryŏwŏn, 1992.

Yŏksa munje yŏn'guso, ed. *1950 nyŏndae Nambukhan ŭi sŏntaek kwa kulchŏl* [North and South Korea's Choices and Reflections in the 1950s]. Seoul: Yoksa pip'yŏngsa, 1998.

Yukkun sagwan hakkyo. *Taehan min'guk yukkun sagwan hakkyo osimnyŏnsa 1946–1996* [A Fifty-Year History of the Korean Military Academy]. Seoul: Yukkun sagwan hakkyo, 1997.

Yukkun sagwan hakkyo che p'algisaeng hoe. *Nobyŏngdul ui chŭngŏn: Yuksa p'algisa* [The Testimony of the Old Soldiers: The Eighth Class of the Korean Military Academy]. Seoul: Yukkun sagwan hakkyo che p'algisaeng hoe, 1992.

Index

Frei, Winifred, 217
Fulbright Program, 157

Galbraith, John Kenneth, 167
Girl Scouts, 189; American support for, 217–18
Gleysteen, William, 226, 228–29, 233, 234, 235, 236, 238, 241
Government Aid and Relief in Occupied Areas (GARIOA), 33
Green, Marshall, 118–19, 121
Green Berets, 121
Grubb, William, 206

Habib, Philip, 226
Haig, Alexander, 241, 242
Ham Pyŏngjun, 182–83
Hanahoe (One Association), 232
Han'guk Ilbo (Korea Daily), 55
Han Kisik, 169
Han Muhyŏp, 92
Han Ugŭn, 172
Han Wansang, 244
Harvard University, 180, 181; Harvard-Yenching Institute and, 51, 165; Visiting Scholars Association, 173
Hausman, James, 74–75
Herter, Christian, 111
Hodge, John Reed, 72
Hodges, Luther, 130
Hŏ Hyŏn, 46
Homestead Act, 20
Human rights, 227–28, 229, 242–43
Humphrey, Hubert, 140
Hwasin Group, 147
Hyundai, 146, 224

Illiberal democracy, 253
Im Panghyŏn, 55, 180–82
Im Songbon, 61
Inflation, 25, 36, 132, 143, 146
Intellectuals, South Korean, 133, 223,

257; American efforts to engage, 163–88; relationship with Park government, 164–65, 178–88; resistance to Yusin, 224
Interest rate reforms, 143–44, 153, 176, 254
International Farm Youth Exchange (IFYE), 211, 215
International Monetary Fund (IMF), 231
Iran, 237, 258

Japan, 1, 14, 130, 155, 169, 185, 191, 198, 199–201, 219, 245, 254; economic relations with South Korea, 140; normalization of relations with South Korea, 36, 133–36, 186, 254
Japanese imperialism, 1, 7, 18–19, 204, 210, 216, 252, 255, 258; influence on Korean education system, 42, 44–45; influence on Korean legal system, 157; influence on Korean media, 50; influence on Korean military officers, 84; influence on Park Chung Hee's economic policies, 146–47, 149, 161; influence on South Korean tax system, 143; influence on South Korean views of United States, 7–8; student resentment toward, 199–200
Japanese Kwantung Army, 75
Japanese Military Academy, 76
Johnson, Lyndon B., 124, 136; administration of, 136–37, 159, 254
Journalists, South Korean, 53–59, 139, 163; American efforts to influence, 53–55; commitment to freedom of press, 56–57; criticisms of Syngman Rhee, 56–58

Kal Ponggŭn, 179
Kang, David, 67
Kang Man'gil, 184, 244

The New Cold War History

Gregg Brazinsky, *Nation Building in South Korea: Koreans, Americans, and the Making of a Democracy* (2007).

Vladislav M. Zubok, *A Failed Empire: The Soviet Union in the Cold War from Stalin to Gorbachev* (2007).

Stephen G. Rabe, *U.S. Intervention in British Guiana: A Cold War Story* (2005).

Christopher Endy, *Cold War Holidays: American Tourism in France* (2004).

Salim Yaqub, *Containing Arab Nationalism: The Eisenhower Doctrine and the Middle East* (2003).

Francis J. Gavin, *Gold, Dollars, and Power: The Politics of International Monetary Relations, 1958–1971* (2003).

William Glenn Gray, *Germany's Cold War: The Global Campaign to Isolate East Germany, 1949–1969* (2003).

Matthew J. Ouimet, *The Rise and Fall of the Brezhnev Doctrine in Soviet Foreign Policy* (2003).

Pierre Asselin, *A Bitter Peace: Washington, Hanoi, and the Making of the Paris Agreement* (2002).

Jeffrey Glen Giauque, *Grand Designs and Visions of Unity: The Atlantic Powers and the Reorganization of Western Europe, 1955–1963* (2002).

Chen Jian, *Mao's China and the Cold War* (2001).

M. E. Sarotte, *Dealing with the Devil: East Germany, Détente, and Ostpolitik, 1969–1973* (2001).

Mark Philip Bradley, *Imagining Vietnam and America: The Making of Postcolonial Vietnam, 1919–1950* (2000).

Michael E. Latham, *Modernization as Ideology: American Social Science and "Nation Building" in the Kennedy Era* (2000).

Qiang Zhai, *China and the Vietnam Wars, 1950–1975* (2000).

William I. Hitchcock, *France Restored: Cold War Diplomacy and the Quest for Leadership in Europe, 1944–1954* (1998).